Inside Cultures

MW01195675

This concise, contemporary option for instructors of cultural anthropology breaks away from the traditional structure of introductory textbooks. Emphasising the interaction between humans and their environment, the tension between human universals and cultural variation and the impacts of colonialism on traditional cultures, *Inside Cultures* shows students how cultural anthropology can help us understand the complex, globalised world around us. This third edition:

- contains brand new material on many subjects, including anthropological approaches to anti-racism social movements in the Global North during 2020;
- includes findings in anthropological research regarding the COVID-19 pandemic and its relation to other recent global events and conditions;
- updates the organisation and presentation of cultural universals and cultural variations;
- presents updated and enhanced discussions of anthropological studies of humankind and the environment, with expanded analysis of industrial agriculture in the age of globalisation;
- includes more illustrations and updates to existing illustrations, sidebars and guideposts throughout the volume;
- is written in clear, supple prose that delights readers while informing on the content of one of the important courses in a liberal arts education, one that effectively bridges humanities and the sciences.

William Balée is Professor of Anthropology at Tulane University, where he has taught since 1991. He received a PhD in Anthropology from Columbia University in 1984. He spent many years in fieldwork among the indigenous Ka'apor people of the eastern Brazilian Amazon. He has field experience with other peoples, cultures and societies in Brazil, Bolivia, Argentina, Ecuador and Malaysia. He is the author of *Footprints of the Forest: Ka'apor Ethnobotany—The Historical Ecology of Plant Utilization by an Amazonian People* (1994) and *Cultural Forests of the Amazon: Historical Ecology of People and their Landscapes* (2013), which both won the Mary W. Klinger Award from the Society for Economic Botany. He was named Fellow of the John Simon Guggenheim Memorial Foundation in 2019.

Inside Cultures

An Introduction to Cultural Anthropology

Third edition

William Balée

Routledge
Taylor & Francis Group

NEW YORK AND LONDON

Third edition published 2022
by Routledge
2 Park Square, Milton Park, Abingdon, Oxon OX14 4RN

and by Routledge
605 Third Avenue, New York, NY 10158

Routledge is an imprint of the Taylor & Francis Group, an informa business

© 2022 William Balée

First edition published by Left Coast Press 2012
Second edition published by Routledge 2016

British Library Cataloguing-in-Publication Data
A catalogue record for this book is available from the British Library

Library of Congress Cataloging-in-Publication Data
A catalog record has been requested for this book

ISBN: 978-0-367-53380-9 (hbk)
ISBN: 978-0-367-53378-6 (pbk)
ISBN: 978-1-003-08168-5 (ebk)

Typeset in Bembo
by Deanta Global Publishing Services, Chennai, India

Contents

3   Cultural Variation   54

6 Social Organisation in Kin-Based Societies

7 Politics and Power

10 Collapse and Change   203

11 Applications of Cultural Anthropology   218

Preface to the Third Edition

This new edition of *Inside Cultures* goes to press after almost two years in which more than three million people have been killed in the greatest pandemic since the Spanish flu of 1918, in the form of a highly infectious, single-stranded RNA colloquially called COVID-19. This new pandemic and the associated lockdowns, travel restrictions, social distancing protocols, virtual meetings, and other preventive measures faced by billions worldwide have led to fundamental modifications in how institutions function and communicate, including educational institutions like colleges and universities. Some of these institutions have had to close their doors, sadly perhaps forever, and all of them have been affected in how course content is delivered to students and the ways by which in-person, hybrid, remote and HyFlex teaching methodologies are built upon digital learning platforms that all present students and teachers alike with costs and benefits in terms of what are attainable learning outcomes and what are not. This book is a textbook introduction to cultural anthropology. The pandemic, the response of colleges and universities to it and the virtual teaching and learning technologies now available have required instructors who use a textbook to teach in new ways and even to rethink the design of courses that they knew cold and taught with perhaps little preparation for many years. The need for new technology compels course content to be modified and structured in ways that better fit the demands of a partly in-person, partly (and sometimes mostly or completely) virtual world, the new normal. Society is changing, however, not only in terms of fundamental technological advances through 2021/2022. In the Global North, protests and demonstrations on scales not seen since the counter-revolution of the 1960s, focused primarily on issues of racial injustice and inequality, have taken place. A chasm between politics of the right and politics of the left in the United States saw a deeply conflicted presidential contest in 2020 that questioned the validity of democratic elections and the nature of constitutional government, with threats to that not seen, perhaps, since the American Civil War, such as the populist, violent, right-wing attack on the US capitol on January 6, 2021. In light of 2020-21 alone—together with the dramatic cultural and epidemiological changes that have led to the new normal both inside and outside the classroom—a new edition of my introductory textbook *Inside Cultures* seems aptly timed, apart from the usual imperative one has in updating material from the last edition, now five years of age. A lot has happened in five years.

Culture is dynamic, as I noted in Chapter 1 of this book's first and second editions; it is sometimes contested, especially in stratified societies, which is an observation I had not explicitly made before in the text, but which is now incorporated into the underlying structure and rationale of edits of, additions to and subtractions from the second edition in refining and updating this third edition. Anthropology and cultural anthropology, in particular, have also changed somewhat dramatically since the second edition, and in part the innovations noted are in synchrony, especially with transformations of culture in the United States and Europe in light of police (state) violence and injustices that can be traced back to the modern world system, chattel slavery, colonialism and stigma historically attached to people of colour, indigenous people and LGBTQ persons. These modifications to contemporary society have impacted anthropology and its approaches to human cultural similarity and diversity and are in my mind justifiably explored more fully in this new edition by way of interlinked chapters.

The late Morton Fried (1923–1986), an anthropology professor at Columbia University, noted that knowledge in cultural anthropology, as with knowledge in all fields, changes with time, but, he pointed out, in his kindly and sagacious way, anthropological knowledge tends to change more slowly than knowledge in other fields, such as physics, chemistry and medicine. The interpretation of anthropological facts—even new ones with every aspect of the current global crisis—draws on a mooring for the most part that for more than 100 years best explicates behaviours that are learned and shared by the human species living together in society with all its schisms, disaccords, collisions, and in certain cases, collapses. Every structural change entails cultural change that follows certain patterns—if not rules—and those rules and the institutions that get associated with them are the subject matter of this book. My reasons for this third edition of *Inside Cultures*, then, are not to reject the known patterns and rules of culture, or of the research methods used in their study, but rather to acknowledge the new contingencies in facts between the last edition and the present moment, especially considering that those facts have changed due to watershed events like the COVID-19 pandemic and demonstrations by many millions across the globe for more equity, diversity and inclusion in today's world.

New Orleans, Louisiana
May 2021

Preface to the Second Edition

A textbook writer's reasons for a subsequent edition usually are related to keeping the work up to date by featuring new findings in the field, correcting any typos and other mistakes in an earlier edition and continuing to be relevant to the educational needs of readers. My reasons are not much different from these, but I have some additional ones, too. In the time interval between the first edition and this edition of *Inside Cultures*, I have had occasion to mull over questions about how anthropological knowledge is transmitted. How does it get from me, the textbook writer in this case, to you, the student? Or to you, the instructor of an introductory course on cultural anthropology? I can say this much now: the knowledge embedded in these pages is not amorphous, did not spring from any stream of consciousness and can indeed be traced to reliable sources. Sometimes I am the source, when, for instance, the item discussed is something I have researched personally, especially something I have studied first-hand in the field (the main place where cultural anthropologists get their data first-hand). I have much more to say about the field, and what it means to cultural anthropologists, in the pages that follow.

In many cases, the source of some fragment of knowledge is other anthropologists, both in the present and the past. In others, it derives from writers about a past before there was an anthropology, or other nonanthropological authors dealing with current events having had some resonance in the world we inhabit now. One thing is certain: cultural anthropological knowledge is always changing, as is the central focus of the discipline, namely *culture*, upon which that knowledge rests inevitably, even if the rate of change in the field of cultural anthropology is not necessarily spectacularly fast. That is because the underlying principles remain the same, and they are worth repeating. The field has its own identity. It is a bona fide domain of knowledge. And it continues to grow.

The main question remaining for the textbook writer—me—is what to include, and what to exclude, in terms of *new data*, since one can obviously never capture everything in a field that is part of a discipline as vastly developed as anthropology in an introductory text. It suffices for my purpose today, therefore, to render to you, student and instructor alike in cultural anthropology, what I deem to be important findings, and illustrate them with examples and the occasional figure or photo or snapshot, in this second edition.

In particular, I have added substantial material to sections on the anthropology of race and racism, terrorism, epidemic disease and globalisation. All these matters increasingly have become arenas of anthropological discourse since the appearance of the first edition of *Inside Cultures*, and I think it's important to highlight them here. Judgement calls had to be made, of course, about what is important, and what is not so important, and I made those. My hope is that you will benefit in terms of your educational and pedagogical aims from the changes—additions, emendations, subtractions—made to the original text, as a whole package.

Acknowledgements from the Second Edition

No second edition of a textbook comes to fruition without support from people and organisations. I would like to first of all acknowledge cultural anthropology instructors João Felipe Gonçalves, Joseph Powell and James Andrew Whitaker, who all assigned the first edition to their students and who, on the basis of that experience, supplied me with helpful suggestions for this edition, as did several other instructors who sent in anonymous, constructive comments. I also thank Melinda Nelson-Hurst for sharing insights into ancient Egyptian kinship; Melissa Beske, Nicole Katin and Denise Schaan for redonating photos; Erin Patterson and Mark Zender for help in selecting and interpreting photos from Maya pre-Columbian sites; Michelle Treviño for careful manuscript editing; Ryan Harris and Jack Meinhardt of Left Coast Press, Inc. for encouragement; and Lisa Devenish for prompt and effective oversight of production matters. I thank my wife Conce Balée for her good taste and indispensable help on sundry other matters.

River Ridge, Louisiana 1 November 2015

Preface to the First Edition

In writing this textbook, I have made a few assumptions about you. One is that you're probably reading this book because it was assigned as part of an introductory course on cultural anthropology. There's a good chance that you have to read this book in order to get a good grade in the course. I'm also assuming that you don't know a lot about cultural anthropology yet, so I've taken care with the way I phrase things. Certain words that might mean one thing to you mean something else when used by cultural anthropologists. For that reason, I've endeavoured to define technical terms and avoid springing new concepts and vocabulary on you without some preparation.

In the following pages, you'll get a sense of where cultural anthropology has come from and where it's going in the twenty-first century. This book is subtitled '*A New Introduction to Cultural Anthropology*' because it discusses some of the most recent and exciting developments in the discipline, such as the role of ethnotourism, emerging forms of indigeneity and new methods to study cosmopolitan, transnational communities around the world. *Inside Cultures* also presents both the science and humanism of anthropology, highlighting how the discipline can be enriched by uniting these two perspectives on the human condition. While remaining concise, this account provides the examples and detail necessary to understand key anthropology principles. The first and foremost principle is that everyone alive today is as human as everyone else. Even when cultural anthropologists research groups of people different from their own group (such people are sometimes called the 'other' in anthropological jargon), they are still studying members of the human species. There is and has been only one species of humanity, *Homo sapiens*, for tens of thousands of years. That means anthropologists study the ways that humans have lived and changed over long periods of time and across great distances. They work wherever the globe is inhabited. Anthropology has the broadest definition of any discipline of what it means to be human. Because of its great scope, the study of humans is divided into four fields, one of which is cultural anthropology (Chapter 1).

Basic findings from cultural anthropology that I will discuss in this book are:

- Humans share distinctive traits, called *universals*, that make us who we are (Chapter 2);
- Culture is more variable than the biology of the species, and this variability can be explained (Chapter 3);
- Cultural anthropology, its theories and methods, developed into modern form during the twentieth century (Chapters 4 and 5);
- Humans are social beings with distinctive forms of organisation (Chapter 6);
- Socially complex societies are not necessarily better or more evolved than simpler societies (Chapter 7);

- All societies depend on and affect their environments (Chapter 8);
- The expansion of European society through colonisation led to major changes and new cultural forms in the last 500 years (Chapter 9);
- Culture can become less complex or even collapse due to various factors and contingencies, and loss of technology and societal collapses can lead to innovation (Chapter 10);
- Applied cultural anthropology can contribute solutions to the problems of modern life (Chapter 11);
- Globalisation is changing the ways we understand time and space, but the concept of culture endures and remains applicable to understanding our species (Chapter 12).

I've tried to present this formidable array of material in a way that you'll appreciate enough to not only do the assigned reading, but to develop an interest in the discipline of anthropology. It is my hope that this will be a textbook that you'll refer to again after you've completed the course. Develop your own opinions as you read. I trust that by the end of the book, you'll understand the principles that guide research and debate in the field of cultural anthropology.

Acknowledgements from the First Edition

I have meant to write this book for a long time. In getting it into print, I accumulated debts to specific individuals for various services rendered. For assistance, with formatting figures and text, I am grateful to Tulane graduate student research assistants Melissa Beske, Nicole Katin, Bryan Lenz and James Whitaker. I thank Nicole Katin also for advice on illustrations. I am indebted to all my colleagues in the Department of Anthropology at Tulane University for providing a genuinely collegial, engaged teaching and research environment in cultural anthropology. In particular, I would like to acknowledge Marcello Canuto, Shanshan Du, Robert Hill, Trenton Holliday, Judith Maxwell and Allison Truitt for commenting on sections of the text, for suggesting pertinent references or for simply sharing their insights and ideas on matters covered herein. I am also grateful to H. Russell Bernard, Loretta Cormier, Jeffrey Ehrenreich and Jane Mt. Pleasant for sundry useful remarks and suggestions and to Denise Schaan for providing a photo.

I don't think I could have written the book in its current formulation without having had the experience of teaching cultural anthropology to Tulane undergraduate students for 20 years and counting. In that regard and in many others, I am thankful to the hundreds of students who populated those classes, for they have, wittingly or not, prodded me to think long and hard about what people taking cultural anthropology ought to learn from a textbook like this one.

First, I am grateful to my friend David Campbell for reminding me, soon after I initiated the first draft, to back things up. After the writing began, I was fortunate to get very helpful editorial counsel from the staff of Left Coast Press, Inc. I am grateful to Mitch Allen, who contributed numerous insights along the way. And I thank both him and Jennifer Collier, in addition, for their continuing editorial support and encouragement since the inception of the project. I would like to acknowledge also the diligence of the three anonymous reviewers of the original manuscript: their constructive comments helped me refine topical foci and elements of presentation herein. Erica Hill performed a splendid job in editing the final preparation of this textbook. She did so with aplomb, perspicacity and sensitivity to the subject matter, and for all that I express my sincere appreciation. I am indebted to Conce Balée and our children, Nicholas and Isabel, for their considerable patience and understanding over the chunks of time it took me to work exclusively on this project, instead of doing things with them.

A final debt remains to be paid to the memory of the late S. Brian Burkhalter who, like me, was a student of cultural anthropology both at the University of Florida and Columbia University in the 1970s and 1980s. Brian was also a dedicated teacher of cultural anthropology. He asserted at one point that he liked cultural anthropology as a subject exactly because it provided an inner view of people, their societies and their shared traditions. It is a genuine study of us, he said, not just a dimly sketched, exoticised and mystified other. In so many words, he was saying that cultural anthropology could help you get inside cultures, perhaps especially your own. I am fairly certain, therefore, that Brian would have approved of the principles and objectives that have guided me in writing this textbook.

Bangi, Malaysia December 2011

Note to the Instructor (for the Third Edition)

Some explanatory remarks could ease your decision-making in whether and how to use this textbook for your course. I wrote the book in part to make my own teaching of the course easier. I was disenchanted with assigning bulky, expensive, four-colour textbooks, and had long not assigned them. Before my own textbook was first published, I taught the course 'cultural anthropology' for many years based entirely on monographs and my own lectures. I now use *Inside Cultures* to cover a lot of that material, and more. The textbook allows me, as instructor of record, to cover more material without having to expound on every single detail of theory and method, and therefore lack time to cover it all orally in class discussion, which could be relevant to understanding any ethnography.

The two earlier editions for the most part left implicit the choices I had made in including or excluding material to be covered. I think it could be helpful for me to be explicit about all that now. The original rationale was to produce a textbook that forms a pedagogical bedrock for an instructor's lectures together with one or two or three ethnographies (depending on whether one is teaching in a quarter or a semester system).

I believe the ethnographic monograph to be the essential product of the field in more than 100 years of cultural anthropology, so introductory students in my opinion should have some exposure to writing in that vein. I have consistently referenced in this book writings concerning a few ethnographic groups, such as the Nuer, Americans (Native and not—including the Nacirema—i.e., white middle-class Americans), the Ju'/hoansi, the Tiwi and the Mardu of Australia, and a number of others for which suitable ethnographic writing could be assigned in addition to the textbook (see map on the next page: peoples, cultures, languages, places). That objective—of connecting the textbook to ethnography, and especially monographs—remains the case. If the student only takes one class in anthropology, and it's this one, the text here considers cultural anthropology as only one of four fields. That is how it is conceived in most colleges and universities in the United States and a few other countries. Therefore, brief, comprehensive coverage of the other three fields and how cultural anthropology relates to them—linguistic anthropology, biological anthropology and anthropological archaeology—is given in the beginning. I believe all four fields are linked not just for practical or gerrymandering purposes but in a philosophic, holistic sense, as together they constitute the foremost discipline of the human species. That view may be superseded someday—and in a few institutions the four fields have gone through divorces from each other—but I believe the holism of anthropology and cultural anthropology, in particular, situates it well at the centre of a liberal arts and sciences education.

In the early twenty-first century, it's important to be up to date with the non-offensive terminology used to refer to oneself and others. That will not always be the case with

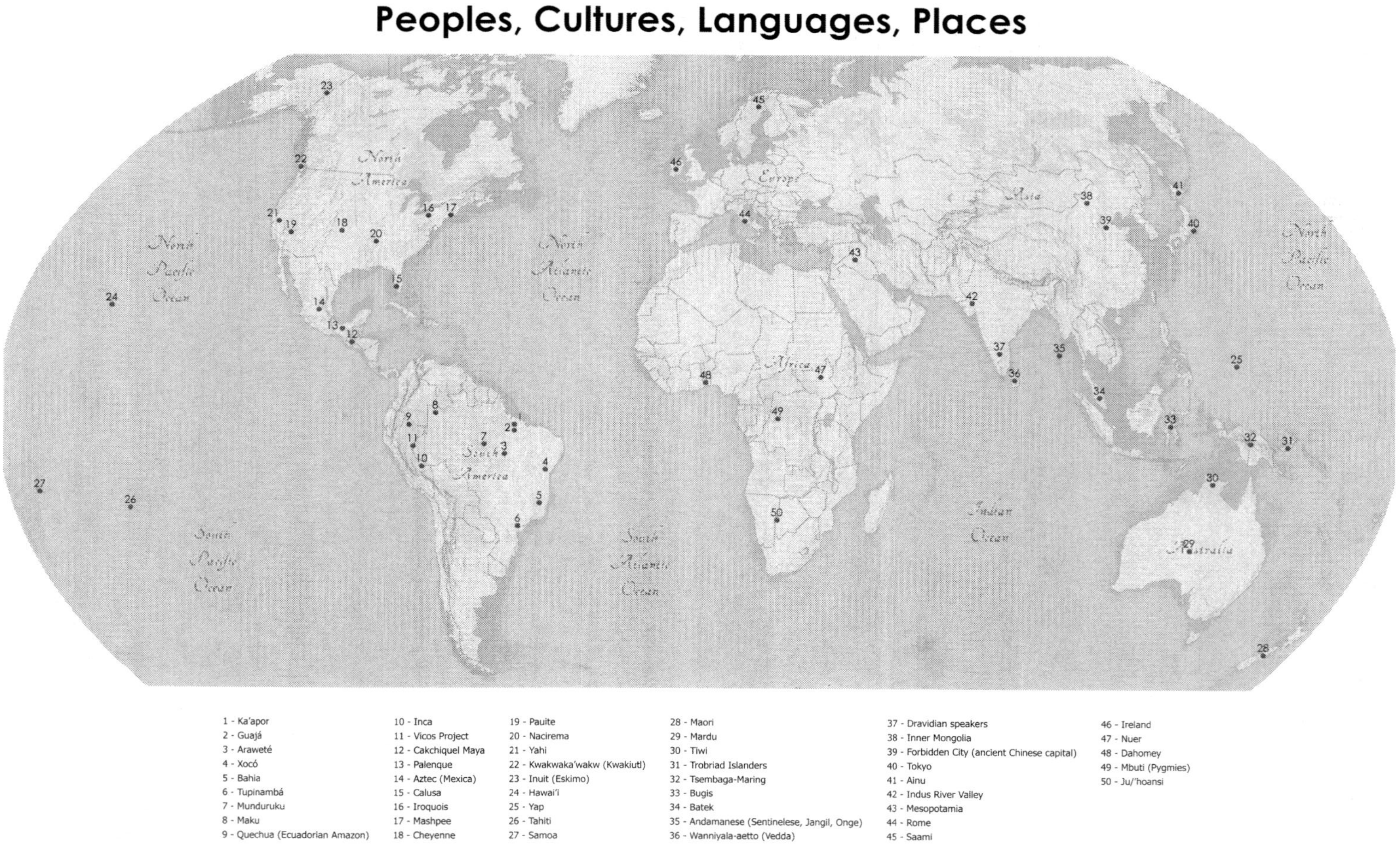
Peoples, Cultures, Languages, Places
North America
South America
Europe
Asia
Africa
Australia
North Pacific Ocean
South Pacific Ocean
North Atlantic Ocean
South Atlantic Ocean
Indian Ocean
North Pacific Ocean
1 - Ka'apor
2 - Guajá
3 - Araweté
4 - Xocó
5 - Bahia
6 - Tupinambá
7 - Munduruku
8 - Maku
9 - Quechua (Ecuadorian Amazon)
10 - Inca
11 - Vicos Project
12 - Cakchiquel Maya
13 - Palenque
14 - Aztec (Mexica)
15 - Calusa
16 - Iroquois
17 - Mashpee
18 - Cheyenne
19 - Pauite
20 - Nacirema
21 - Yahi
22 - Kwakwaka'wakw (Kwakiutl)
23 - Inuit (Eskimo)
24 - Hawai'i
25 - Yap
26 - Tahiti
27 - Samoa
28 - Maori
29 - Mardu
30 - Tiwi
31 - Trobriad Islanders
32 - Tsembaga-Maring
33 - Bugis
34 - Batek
35 - Andamanese (Sentinelese, Jangil, Onge)
36 - Wanniyala-aetto (Vedda)
37 - Dravidian speakers
38 - Inner Mongolia
39 - Forbidden City (ancient Chinese capital)
40 - Tokyo
41 - Ainu
42 - Indus River Valley
43 - Mesopotamia
44 - Rome
45 - Saami
46 - Ireland
47 - Nuer
48 - Dahomey
49 - Mbuti (Pygmies)
50 - Ju/'hoansi

Map 1 Peoples, cultures, languages, places.

ethnographies the instructor chooses to use or quotations from them. On gender, older ethnographies sometimes use 'he' and its inflections as the unmarked or gender-neutral third-person singular pronoun. In this book, I try to use 'they' and its inflections as the acceptable non-binary third-person pronoun, instead of s/he, which I used in the two earlier editions. The exception is where I knew the gender identity of the past to have been binary. Charles Darwin herein is 'he, him, his' and Margaret Mead is 'she, her, hers'. Binary gender pronouns also come up in employing a quotation from another source that indicates either the outdated gender-neutral pronoun and its inflections ('he, him, his') or assumes without other evidence binary gender status of some person(s) specifically mentioned.

Similar care is required with ethnonyms (names of ethnographic societies and groupings of these). You should also be aware that a few students might find some of the terms used in reference to ethnographic societies discussed in this book to be offensive or even to be microaggressions, committed either by me or by you or both of us. I would simply apologise to students and readers in advance now and indicate that the terms in use here have been chosen for the sake of clarity and minimal offensiveness to the members of the designated groups themselves at the same time. My choice is normally to employ the ethnonym or self-identifying term that people today use for themselves (such as Kwakwaka'wakw instead of Kwakiutl, Ka'apor instead of Urubu, Ju'/hoansi instead of Bushmen or !Kung). Some of the terms I use can be contested: American Indian and Native American as pan-indigenous terms for aboriginal peoples and their descendants in what is now the United States can be acceptable or unacceptable from aboriginal Western Hemisphere points of view—there seems to be no pan-indigenous agreement on the use of these terms right now. I would merely offer apologies now to the people of today and of the future who might be offended, for only singularity of reference is intended here, not a denigration of anyone or any group. Both sets of terms are owned, so to speak, by indigenous peoples of the Americas, just as Traditional Owners for Aboriginal Australia, First Nations for Canada, Nacionalidades for Ecuador—all refer to self-identifications *owned* by members of these particular, pluralistic ethnic and indigenous groupings. On more specific levels of the lexicon, words such as Munduruku Indians, Guajá and Gypsies could be called into question. In all cases, no offence is intended, only clarity, because other possible terms could be misleading even if self-identifying for one possible group (such as Awá for the Guajá, which is the name for themselves, but it is also cognate with numerous other Tupí-Guaraní speaking groups and means, simply, 'people'; Guajá was also preferable to the hyphenated Awá-Guajá, not in everyday use among any Amazonian groups themselves). Munduruku Indians is Anglophone terminology for an indigenous society in the Brazilian Amazon and is merely used as an exonym: the cognate terms in Portuguese are not currently offensive in that country. They are not known by other terms outside that range of reference. Gypsy is a cover term for several ethnic groups with diverse origins and languages, including Roma and Sinti, and is used in that sense, not as a racist term of offence but rather as a reference to a non-ethnically defined analytical grouping of ethnicities (being defined as what they do, rather than who they are genealogically, which incidentally is the official case with Saami of Sweden, though I am using that term instead of outdated Lapps because Saami is what the people themselves have called for, and some Saami find Lapps offensive). For anyone taking offence at any of these terms—whether autonyms or exonyms—I offer apologies now and hope that one day universally non-offensive terms can be used scientifically (anthropologically) in the ongoing attempt to describe and discuss the origins of cultural and linguistic similarities and differences.

xxii   *Note to the Instructor (for the Third Edition)*

Throughout the volume, I also include reference to ethnographic groups not covered in the monographs—a necessity in a general textbook obviously—including the Ka'apor people of Brazilian Amazonia, among whom I have done ethnographic and ethnobotanical fieldwork over the last 40 years, with some consistency across the chapters, and these can be found on the map on page xx. I refer to many specific groups both in the text and in cultural snapshots regardless of whether I have assigned monographs or ethnographic writings about them in my own class, as thematic threads linking chapters to real people and places in the lens of anthropological fieldwork over the twentieth and twenty-first centuries, and in a couple of cases the nineteenth century (such as the Iroquois)—I think that approach helps students to remember the concepts better than if ethnographic groups are constantly changed from chapter to chapter, in terms of evidence gathered from participant observation.

The illustrations are in black-and-white, and the reasoning here is to keep costs down. I have meant from the beginning to keep the cost to students accessible enough so they might also afford one or two ethnographies in the course you are teaching. The original text was designed to be taught in-person. This current edition can also be taught along with a relevant ethnography or two remotely, or in hybrid or HyFlex formats. I have done this myself using a learning management system (LMS) and students often purchase the *e-book* of the second edition (the first does not have an *e-book*). This third edition is also available as an *e-book*. There are also *e-books* available for some (though not all) the ethnographies one might want to use if teaching in a hybrid or similar format. Because remote teaching requires certain asynchronous activities in order to be effective, and these are not always simply reading assignments or homework or quizzes, but rather activities like student-to-student discussion boards and uploading of low-stakes audio or video files, I have usually reduced the pages of required reading from given ethnographies in the traditional in-person teaching format by about one-fourth, but I have still required students to read the entire textbook. I haven't listed in the textbook the numerous resources one can find on YouTube, Spotify and possible links that can be embedded for teaching purposes without issues concerning copyright and the like, since I assume instructors can find these links in any LMS for themselves. This plan works for me using an LMS like Canvas, which is the one my university currently subscribes to. I am confident other such platforms could also be used to good effect to introduce cultural anthropology to beginning students. The principal learning objective behind my writing of the textbook was and continues to be in this edition to put as much useful information about the field into as concise a manner as possible, and still be accessible in price as well as clarity, so that the textbook can serve as a guide for students to decode, assimilate and retain knowledge about the purpose and practice of ethnography, with a holistic comprehension of the discipline itself. I hope that objective will materialise as the main learning outcome for your course.

Acknowledgements

I am grateful to the four anonymous referees Routledge chose to review the text and for their suggestions, most of which I have addressed herein. Edith Wolfe kindly recommended references regarding the major in anthropology (Chapter 13). Sarah Mellman recommended figures and bibliographic references. Marcello Canuto helped design and generate the map on page xx. Jeffrey Ehrenreich provided the cover photo. I thank also Tod Swanson and Janis Nuckholls for supplying photos. Connie Balée drew my attention to the cooperative, social behaviour of strand-feeding by Bottlenose dolphins (Chapter 2). At Routledge, I am grateful to my editor Katherine Ong and her assistants Amy Doffegnies and Stewart Beale, who have been helpful and encouraging throughout.

1 The Study of Us

Culture: learned, shared,
change over time.

Overview

The most important concept in cultural anthropology is *culture*. Another important and related term in cultural anthropology is *society*. Culture is in daily use; we see or hear it on the internet, radio, television, newspapers, movies, magazines and in conversations that occur in homes, offices, restaurants, coffeehouses and schools as well as on the telephone or in text messages. The term is used in diverse languages worldwide, every day. It doesn't, however, always mean the same thing. I have a lot to say about culture in this book. But to make sure you read and understand this most important term as intended, let me give a succinct definition now: *Culture is learned, shared human behaviour and ideas, which can and do change with time.*

Cultural anthropology is the study of human cultures, those shared behaviours and ideas that help people organise themselves; acquire food, clothing and shelter; and think about the world and their places within it. Cultural anthropology is also sometimes called *social anthropology*. Cultural and social anthropology, and sometimes sociocultural anthropology, mean the same thing and reflect the fact that culture and society are always linked in the real world. *Society* is a basic concept in the field. It refers to a group of people who establish boundaries that distinguish them from other groups of people. These boundaries are often defined by a common language or dialect, a shared sense of being one people with a common origin and past, a common belief system and a common culture. Members of societies sometimes, but not always, share a common government, economic system and homeland or territory. To the members of a society, culture is a set of shared ways of behaving and thinking that people learn from those around them.

Culture and society thus go together as elementary concepts in cultural anthropology, which is itself a branch of the discipline of anthropology. *Anthropology* is the scientific study of human beings and their closest relatives, both living and extinct, in the broadest sense possible. It focuses on what it means to be human, both as a member of the animal kingdom and as a species distinct from all others. Anthropology tracks humans in their diversity through time, across space and all the way to the very borders of the notion of a species. It takes into account every facet of human culture known and analyses each one in relation to all the others. It investigates our closest relatives in the animal world—apes and monkeys—to see what we share with them and how we differ. Anthropology describes and compares the languages of the world to understand their origins and development. It assesses the physical, technological and artistic things people make; when, where and how they live; and why they behave in certain ways. Anthropology looks at early members of the human lineage, including the nonhuman ancestors of everyone who is alive today.

Anthropology, it has often been said, is 'the most scientific of the humanities, the most humanist of the sciences' (Wolf 1964, p. 88).

In this chapter, we address the relationship of cultural anthropology to general anthropology; enumerate basic principles of both; examine what makes the human species distinctive; introduce the four fields of anthropology and what their practitioners do; show the relevance of the other three fields to cultural anthropology; and discuss the dynamic aspect of culture. The chapter concludes with a discussion of other disciplines that study humanity and how they are similar or dissimilar to cultural anthropology.

Cultural Anthropology and General Anthropology

Anthropology and its subdiscipline of cultural anthropology can be understood in terms of shared principles, which are:

- Humans of today are a single species that have a lot in common.
- Humans can be understood in terms of shared biology, distinctive origins, a penchant for language and both cultural differentiation and similarity.
- Humans living in distinct groups, or societies, differ mainly in terms of culture and language, not biology.
- Culture develops faster than humans evolve in nature.

The Species Known as 'Us'

Humans are a single species. A species is any group of organisms with a distinctive, shared genetic heritage, called a genotype, which is transmitted via DNA (deoxyribonucleic acid), molecules containing the material of heredity. DNA stores information. For that information to be transmitted from one generation to the next, reproduction needs to occur. Humans transmit their DNA by sexual reproduction. Not all species do that.

On the other hand, every species, including humans, is unique. Most anthropologists would agree that humanity's distinctiveness lies at least partly in its mental ability when compared with other life forms. This mental ability has enabled us to change the planet, sometimes for the better, sometimes for the worse. On the negative side, we are associated with climate change deriving from the unprecedented increase in greenhouse gases in the atmosphere since the early nineteenth century when production of goods like textiles, machines, vessels driven by steam power and iron founding became mechanised and dependent upon the combustion of fossil fuels such as coal, gasoline and oil. Humans alone cause massive oil spills and other forms of water pollution. Humans are also the only species to categorise members according to racial, ethnic and gender *stereotypes.* Stereotypes are simplified, usually pejorative, ideas about other groups that are believed to differ in fundamental ways from one's own group. Stereotypes can affect people's performance and self-esteem. For example, the stereotype that men are better than women at mathematics has been self-reinforcing, so that even women who are good maths students often quit taking classes because of the stereotype, not because of their lack of ability. This may be related to dominant cultural attitudes. For example, the gap between the sexes on maths tests in the United States is greater among whites than among Asian, Hispanic and African Americans. This suggests that the gap is not based on biology; it also highlights the dangers of stereotyping.

Another distinctive human characteristic is warfare on a large scale. Humans commit atrocities that have often been associated with racial and ethnic stereotypes that characterise the victims as less than human. These have been employed by political and military forces to justify wholesale slaughter, such as occurred in the death camps of World War II (1939–1945), where millions of Jews, Gypsies (sometimes called Roma or Sinti) and Slavs were gassed, starved or shot. Another example is the Srebrenica massacre (1995) during the Bosnian War, in which 8,000 Muslim men and boys were killed. Before that was the massacre by Ottoman Turks of more than a million Armenians in World War I. To their persecutors, the victims had the wrong ethnicity, race or religion: they were believed to be less than fully human because of negative racial and ethnic stereotypes.

The good news is that stereotypes and the stigmas associated with ethnic and racial minorities and gender bias can change. It was virtually unthinkable for an African American to be elected President of the United States before the Civil Rights Movement in the second half of the twentieth century because of widespread prejudice against people of colour. With the election of Barack Obama in 2008 (who was re-elected in 2012), such a milestone was finally reached. Along similar lines, Kamala Harris became the first woman of colour to be nominated for Vice-President by a major American political party in 2020, and the first woman of colour to be elected Vice-President of the United States. Cultural anthropology has provided substantial evidence that racial, ethnic and gender stereotypes lack scientific validity and cross-cultural comparability. They nevertheless persist, for example, in segments of North American society as well as in other parts of the world and are often at the root of international misunderstandings today. In 2020, around 20,000,000 people participated across the United States in protests against racial violence and injustice against people of colour, especially by the police, in the wake of a video-taped killing in Minneapolis of an unarmed black man, George Floyd by a police officer, who was arrested, charged, and in 2021 convicted of Floyd's murder. Similar demonstrations occurred in the United States and in several countries of the Global North (Figure 3.3) in 2020. Three-fourths of the US counties that had protests had white majorities, and more than 75% of those were 95% white. Those protests and the political ambience that resulted from them may lead to further positive changes with regard to equity, diversity and inclusion of racialised minorities in pluralistic societies of the Global North.

On the positive side, only human cleverness could have designed the great pyramid of Giza, written the Harry Potter books, developed the internet and cloned a sheep. Humans now permanently inhabit most of Earth's landscapes.

More than 40,000 years ago, humans made seaworthy vessels that took them, for the first time ever, from Asia to Australia. From about 35,000 to 15,000 years ago, only humans knew about and could sew garments warm enough to endure the long, freezing-cold winters of the ice ages in Europe and Asia. About 15,000 years ago, humans were able to travel from Asia into North America via the landmass called Beringia.

Rapid human spread across and successful occupation of the various environments of Earth can be understood in terms of *institutions*. These are social organisations that mobilise people for specific purposes. Society consists of these. Simply stated, society is a group of persons organised for a purpose, and institutions effect or accomplish that purpose. Culture is the collective ways those same persons think and behave. These ways of thinking and behaving vary even inside a society. That is, culture is variable and shared unequally. This sort of intrasocietal variation can sometimes result in conflict, such that culture, in addition to being learned, shared and dynamic, is—in some instances—conflicted, or contested. Institutions allow people in society to live together according to rules, to accomplish the production and sharing of food and other forms of wealth, to minimise conflicts and to teach and learn socially approved ways to behave and think. Cultural anthropologists routinely study the institutions of society, for example, by looking at how and why people work, paint, gamble, marry, raise children, vote, pray, define proper behaviour and classify themselves and others. The study of people, in terms of their culture, societies and institutions, is encompassed by anthropology, an immensely broad field of study.

The Four Fields

The study of anthropology is divided into *four fields*. Each one focuses on a distinctive aspect of humankind. The four fields are *cultural anthropology, biological anthropology, archaeology* and *linguistic anthropology*. There is some variation in the names of these fields. All of them have synonyms, such as social or sociocultural anthropology for cultural anthropology, physical anthropology for biological anthropology, anthropological archaeology for archaeology and anthropological linguistics for linguistic anthropology.

Cultural Anthropology

This book is about the first of these four fields, cultural anthropology. In later sections of this chapter, we briefly deal with the other three fields, and why and how they are important to the study of cultural anthropology. In a nutshell, cultural anthropologists assess the causes and consequences of people living in society. Their understanding of these causes and consequences comes from systematic study and comparison of particular societies and cultures of the past and present. Cultural anthropology has several subfields. This is because cultural anthropologists study not only the customs and beliefs of living people; they also compare diverse cultures for clues as to why some customs and beliefs are similar, yet others different. They look at the present as well as the past to understand cultures and their origins. The study of a specific culture and the written account of that research are called *ethnography*. Students reading this textbook might also be assigned one or more ethnographies for class. *Ethnology*, in contrast to ethnography, is the comparative study of cultures. It is sometimes called *cross-cultural comparison*. Both ethnography and ethnology are subfields of cultural anthropology. A third subfield of cultural anthropology, shared with archaeologists, is *ethnohistory*. Ethnohistory focuses on the study of specific cultures of the past through documents of the time period in question. Let's examine each subfield separately.

Ethnography and Participant Observation

Doing ethnography, which is also called *ethnographic fieldwork* or just *fieldwork*, involves living with members of the society you are studying, often for months or years at a time. An ethnographer might live in a village in the Amazon, as I did, to observe and participate in daily activities. Good ethnographic research requires the ethnographer to experience life within the society he or she is studying. This means eating the same foods, learning to do the same tasks and observing men and women of that society while they hunt, make pottery, sew clothing, care for children, tend to the dead, build houses and harvest crops. The purpose of spending weeks, months and sometimes years in the field is to help the ethnographer understand a society from the perspective of its own members. Anthropologists call this an *emic perspective*, and it usually requires learning the language people speak, the etiquette they observe and the beliefs and values they share. In contrast, the *etic* perspective involves ethnographers trying to explain a culture in objective terms from the outside. Both perspectives are needed in ethnographic research.

From 1985 to 1990, I carried out a study of five different South American Indian groups living in the Amazon region, including a society called the Ka'apor. I was comparing how people used, managed and named the plants in the tropical forests they occupied. Each group spoke a different language. Because I spoke the Ka'apor language, I felt fairly comfortable in learning how to communicate in the others, especially the Guajá (pronounced gwa-ZHA) language, which was closest to Ka'apor (kaah-POUR). On one sweltering afternoon in 1990, I had collected plants and learned their Guajá names and uses. Several Guajá men were acting as *informants*: people who share information, opinions and knowledge of their culture. As we were returning to the Guajá camp through the forest, I spotted some rotting, hard-shelled fruits of a massive palm tree called *wa'ĩ'y* in the Guajá language. I was getting a little hungry after the long day, and though we had all eaten lunch together earlier, I wanted to share a snack with my Guajá friends. It seemed strange that no one else had noticed the rotting fruits, which contained a delicacy.

I had learned earlier, from the Araweté Indians (are-uh-way-TAY), that these palm fruits could be gathered and broken open with rocks to extract the palm beetle larvae inside. The Araweté then flick these plump, juicy insects into their mouths live as a tasty treat. The larvae are fatty, white grubs about an inch long and half an inch wide. They have a mild, almost sweet odour and taste like coconut milk soaked in melted butter. Other Amazonianist ethnographers, including French anthropologist Claude Lévi-Strauss and American anthropologist Michael Fobes Brown (2014, p. 58) have also noted this rather peculiar but not altogether unpleasant taste. The palm fruits that I spotted along the trail were actually the perfect snack on a hot day with my Guajá friends. I was certain they would appreciate the live, squirming grubs inside, called *wanokia*.

I stopped and gathered some of the palm fruits and put them in my backpack. When we arrived at camp, I daintily extracted a grub, tossed it back and bit down on the juicy morsel. Then I realised that my Guajá friends were groaning and looking uncomfortable. One man was bent over, as if about to vomit. The others frowned and looked away. What had I done? All the other groups that I knew, especially the Araweté, customarily ate and enjoyed these grubs. It turns out the Guajá, according to my informants, do not eat insects of any kind. To them, it is unthinkable.

At that moment, it dawned on me that I was witnessing the visual—and visceral—manifestation of cultural difference. According to the rules of Guajá culture, people do not eat insects, including raw palm grubs. To do so violates etiquette, and it is disgusting. Even though the Guajá lived close to the Araweté and spoke a related language, their culture differed profoundly in something as basic as what they considered to be acceptable food. My experience with the palm grub, and the scandalised reaction to it, highlighted the diversity among human societies, even those that I naively thought to be similar.

Anthropologists from every field in the discipline do fieldwork. An archaeologist may travel to an excavation site in Mexico. A biological anthropologist may go to central

Africa to observe primate behaviour in the wild. A linguistic anthropologist may go to a small village in Alaska to record people speaking their native language. All of these are examples of fieldwork.

Ethnographic fieldwork with living human groups differentiates cultural anthropology from other academic disciplines. Ethnographic fieldwork involves usually at least one year of research, on site, with a society that is often, but not always, far from one's home, workplace or campus. What originally made cultural anthropology distinct from every other discipline in the human sciences, such as sociology, political science and economics, is that it engaged the anthropologist in fieldwork using the method of *participant observation* (Cultural Snapshot 1.1). Some sociologists and political scientists have adopted the anthropological use of participant observation to gather information.

The term *participant observation* was coined and personified by an anthropologist named Bronislaw Malinowski (1884–1942) (Figure 4.5). Although born in Poland, Malinowski worked within the tradition of British social anthropology. While recovering from typhoid fever as a young man, he chanced upon *The Golden Bough* by James Frazer (1854–1941), an encyclopaedic catalogue of mythology from around the world. Frazer's work was an epiphany for Malinowski, who became charmed by the notion that humankind and its beliefs could be analysed scientifically.

CULTURAL SNAPSHOT 1.1

Poking and Prying with a Purpose

Participant observation requires a research agenda. This means an anthropologist needs to have a formal proposal with a strategic goal behind it before embarking on fieldwork. Zora Neale Hurston was an African American woman (Figure 1.1) born in Alabama in 1891. She became one of the most important literary figures in African American fiction of the early twentieth century. She also studied anthropology at Columbia University. During the 1930s, she carried out an ethnographic study of the descendants of African American slaves using participant observation. She had learned participant observation while taking a course from a professor named Franz Boas. We will discuss Boas and some of his major contributions to cultural anthropology in Chapter 4. To Hurston, participant observation is 'formalized curiosity. It is poking and prying with a purpose. It is a seeking that [one] who wishes may know the cosmic secrets of the world and they that dwell therein'. 'Poking and prying with a purpose' is a useful description of participant observation, which involves the ethnographer living on site with the people whose culture is the object of study. When living in a community of people whose culture differs from that familiar to the ethnographer, she or he may be obliged to learn a new language, ask questions about people's thoughts and behaviours and seek to understand the cultural significance of events, activities and beliefs. This requires close attention, careful notetaking and faithful, detailed recording of all observed behaviour, both verbal and nonverbal. 'Poking and prying with a purpose' takes place on a daily basis, normally for a year or longer. It typically results in deep insights into the learned, shared ideas and behaviour of the people who are the focus of the ethnography.

Figure 1.1 Zora Neale Hurston, American participant observer, 1930s. Courtesy State Archives and Library of Florida.

After a brief foray into Australia, Malinowski went to the Trobriand Islands, a small group of atolls in the South Pacific, off the coast of New Guinea, from 1914 to 1918. Malinowski learned the Trobriand language, witnessed rituals and exchanges and developed an unequalled, first-hand knowledge of a 'primitive' culture. In his Trobriand ethnography, *Argonauts of the Western Pacific* (1922), Malinowski argued that it was the ethnographer's duty, and indeed the objective of cultural anthropology, to see the world as the native sees it. He noted that '[t]he goal is, briefly, to grasp the native's point of view, his relation to life, to realise *his* vision of *his* world'. That lofty mission required more than library research: it necessitated long-term interaction with living people on their home turf and on their own terms.

Participant observation is the quintessential method of cultural anthropology; it is an anthropological quest for understanding an exotic culture in a field situation—that is, *in situ*—on a face-to-face basis with members of that society for a period of time that encompasses all locally significant seasons and annual events. Participant observation involves both watching and recording human behaviour while being part of an interaction—linguistic and interpersonal—with the human subjects being studied. It means asking questions and exchanging ideas with a few key individual members of society, called informants. These are people one gets to know well and who may even become friends. Participant observation might involve eating the same food as your hosts, as I did when I ate the beetle larvae among the Araweté. By collecting palm fruits myself, learning from an Araweté woman how to crack them open with a stone tool and developing a taste for them, I was participating in a cultural activity, while at the same time, carefully observing, asking questions and making mistakes.

Participant observation often involves eating new foods, but it can also include digging potatoes in the Andes Mountains, dancing in a street festival in the Bahamas or listening, recording and taking notes on a story told by an elder in central Australia or former slave in the American South, as Zora Neale Hurston did (Cultural Snapshot 1.1; Figure 1.1). Doing it right requires establishing good relationships. It might involve talking to businesspeople in Kuala Lumpur, the booming capital of Malaysia, and asking them why they became entrepreneurs, and what they might like to accomplish in life, as did entrepreneur-turned-cultural anthropologist Patricia Sloane. She found that Malaysian entrepreneurs had different approaches to business than the Wall Street entrepreneurs with whom she was familiar. Malay entrepreneurs were partly influenced by a belief in fate and by Islam, the dominant religion of Malaysia. Sloane was able to do participant observation in part because, as she noted:

> I was, first and foremost, interested in the subject that interested them most. With my own background in business, I was not only good to talk to and a good resource; my appearance in their lives was also a validating sign of how far they had come in entrepreneurial development: *they saw themselves as good for me to talk to.*
>
> (Sloane 1999, p. 15)

The objective of participant observation is to watch and learn by living in the same way as members of the society you're studying. This opens a door into the lives, thoughts and feelings of people who live, think and feel in ways that are often very different from those of the anthropologist.

Ethnographers jot down everything they see and hear as part of this work, but they also ask specific questions connected to all aspects of culture, including birth practices, education, marriage, politics, economics, ecology, religion and art. They record verbatim accounts from native informants to understand why they do what they do. As an example, let's take the practice of *plural marriage,* which is being married to more than one person at the same time. Knowing that a society practices this sort of marriage doesn't tell us how people conceive of and feel about it. But participant observation can help an anthropologist to understand these things. The Ju/'hoansi (or !Kung) people of southern Africa traditionally hunted wild game and gathered plants to feed themselves and lived in small social groups called *bands* of about 30 people. Although most Ju/'hoansi (zhu-TSWAHN-see) are monogamous—they get married to only one person at a time—a few occasionally practice a form of plural marriage. Ju/'hoansi culture allows for a form of plural marriage called *polygyny*, which means that a man could have more than one wife.

As ethnographic research, cultural anthropologist Marjorie Shostak interviewed a 50-year-old Ju/'hoansi woman named Nisa about her life. Nisa gave Shostak information on a range of topics, including marriage. According to Nisa:

> When a man marries one woman, then marries another and sets her down beside the first so there are three of them together, at night, the husband changes from one wife to another. First he has sex with the older wife, then with the younger. But when he

goes to the younger wife, the older one is jealous and grabs him and bites him. The two women start to fight and bite each other... A co-wife is truly a terrible thing.

(Shostak 2000, p. 154)

We have a better understanding of how polygyny works in Ju/'hoansi society because Nisa explained it to Shostak and offered her opinions about it.

How to behave in a polygynous marriage, as Nisa did, or in a monogamous one, together with things such as proper meal etiquette, how to comport oneself on a first date or at a church service and when to speak out during an auction or keep quiet while attending a lecture are examples of rules people learn that govern their cultural practices. Such rules and practices vary across cultures. Cultural practices, in other words, including marriage forms, are not innate. Culture is not genetic. No one is born with it; it can only be learned. Culture is also not just an idea or a behaviour: it is a mixture of both the mental and the physical. Cultural anthropologist Clifford Geertz (1973, p. 6) noted that a wink is cultural, but a blink is not. Both are body motions, but a blink is an automatic behaviour while a wink involves a behaviour *and* an idea: a flirtation, jest or secret. A wink only makes sense within a certain cultural context.

Ethnology

The study and comparison of several cultures is *ethnology*, sometimes called cross-cultural research. Ethnological studies can be large scale, involving many disparate societies, or they can be focused on just a few. One might be interested, for example, in *polyandry*, another form of plural marriage. In polyandry, one woman is married to more than one husband at the same time. Polyandry is a rare practice, less common than polygyny. It is most common in Tibet and other parts of the Himalayas. In most Western societies, plural marriage of any sort, including polyandry and polygyny, is illegal and is sometimes seen as immoral. An anthropologist might conduct ethnological research to determine why different cultures accept or reject plural marriage. Why do some cultural groups in Tibet practice polyandry, when most people who live across the border in India do not? Polyandry is occasionally also found in the Amazon region, as with the Guajá people, according to ethnographer Loretta Cormier (2003, p. 42). The ethnological question that arises here is: why do the Guajá permit it while other groups in the same region do not? (Cultural Snapshot 1.2). Ethnologists, as cultural anthropologists, routinely compare different cultures that have the same marriage form to understand what else they might have in common.

Ethnological comparisons may involve societies that are widely separated geographically. For example, an ethnologist might study how people on two different continents with similar environments obtain their food. Why do the Saami of Scandinavia herd reindeer, while people living thousands of kilometres away in northern Canada hunt caribou? They both live in cold northern environments, but one group herds while the other hunts. Ethnologists sometimes need data on cultures that have been documented in the past, and they get this information from the subfield of cultural anthropology called *ethnohistory*.

Ethnohistory

Ethnohistorians use documents to study and understand past cultures. Sometimes these documents were written by ethnographers decades or even centuries earlier. James

Figure 1.2 Arapaho Ghost Dance, 1890s. National Archives photo #111-SC-87767.

Mooney (1861–1921) was a self-taught ethnographer of American Indians who worked for the Smithsonian Institution in Washington, DC, which has vast collections of information and artefacts about Native Americans. In 1892, he was sent to Nevada to meet a Paiute Indian prophet named Wovoka (1856–1932), who had just founded a new religion called the Ghost Dance. Those who followed Wovoka believed in his message of American Indian cultural renewal. Wovoka attracted followers from his own Paiute tribe as well as from the Arapaho, Navajo, Cheyenne and Sioux (Figure 1.2). Mooney interviewed Wovoka and reported that Wovoka believed he had been instructed by God to

> go back and tell his people they must be good and love one another, have no quarreling, and live in peace with the Whites; that they must work, and not lie or steal; that they must put away all the old practices that savored of war; that if they faithfully obeyed his instructions they would at last be re- united with their friends in this other world, where there would be no more death or sickness or old age.
>
> (Kehoe 2006, p. 6)

CULTURAL SNAPSHOT 1.2

Ethnology of Polyandry

Cross-cultural or ethnological comparison may involve any cultural trait and its distribution. Let's take, for example, polyandry—from the Greek roots *poly* ('many') and *andros* ('male')—which is plural marriage in which a woman is married to more than one man simultaneously. Polyandry is concentrated in Tibet and northern India today, and historically it also occurred in southwest India. Polyandry is also present in a few other places outside those regions, such as the Amazon Basin. Why does polyandry occur at all in the Amazon, where monogamy—marriage between one man and one woman—is the usual marriage form? In the Amazon, *polygyny*, or plural marriage in which one man is married to more than one woman at the same time, is fairly common. Polygyny comes from the Greek roots *poly* and *gyne*, meaning 'female'.

The Mucajai Yanomama of southern Venezuela is one society that practices polyandry. An ethnography of the Mucajai explains that they have 'partible paternity'. Partible paternity is the belief that a child is born to one mother and potentially many 'fathers': her mother's 'husbands', all of whom the child grows up calling 'father'. The Mucajai believe that the child is made up of semen deposited in the mother's vagina by one or more of these fathers. Other Amazonian societies, such as the Guajá and the Suruí, also practice polyandry. Both groups speak Tupí-Guaraní languages, but they are separated by about 400 miles of forest. Ethnographic studies of these groups reveal that both have: 1) small populations of less than 200 people; 2) adult sex ratios of about three or four males to one female; and 3) a belief in partible paternity. Polyandry in Amazonia may therefore be a practical arrangement. Ethnology of polyandry and partible paternity suggests that these practices allow all eligible adults to participate in culturally approved practices of marriage and parenthood.

In 1935, some 40 years after the Ghost Dance began, ethnographer and ethnohistorian Leslie Spier (1893–1961) went to study unpublished material about the phenomenon in archives and libraries. He found that the Ghost Dance had precursors in earlier Native North American religious movements such as the Round Dance, which existed even before the arrival of Europeans in North America. According to Alice Kehoe, a modern ethnohistorian who analysed Spier's study and Mooney's earlier report, Wovoka had envisioned a new religion. In it, through the two-day, nonstop dance of the Ghosts, people could experience an altered state of consciousness, known as *trance*, and gain a sense of peace and consolation. Kehoe interpreted Wovoka's story based on the study of primary sources: first-hand accounts such as military and missionary reports, diaries and recorded testimonies of native people who witnessed the Ghost Dance.

Ethnohistorical research such as Spier's and Kehoe's yields a more comprehensive and sophisticated understanding of the origins of social institutions, including religious ones such as the Ghost Dance. Early ethnographies, like Mooney's, are similar to primary sources in that they describe behaviour that is now vanished and provide detail on beliefs, customs and attitudes that cannot be directly observed. One major difference between ethnohistory and ethnography is that the ethnohistorian cannot question first-hand observers like Mooney and the followers of the Ghost Dance, whereas an ethnographer can return to the field, ask more questions and make additional observations.

Ethnohistory is also used by archaeologists to understand past cultures. For example, an archaeologist might study a description written by an architect of how a house was constructed in the 1800s in New England to interpret the remains of a nineteenth-century structure. Or an archaeologist working on an Aztec site in Mexico might consult administrative reports, explorers' diaries, maps and codices and accounts by native people or missionaries that were written down shortly after the conquest of Mexico in 1519. The archaeologist may use these primary sources to interpret the artefacts and features he or she excavates at a site inhabited prior to the arrival of Europeans.

Another source of information about the past is texts written by the people themselves, such as the Maya, who had their own writing system (Figure 1.3). *Epigraphy* involves deciphering such texts. Cultural anthropologists, linguists and archaeologists can all be epigraphers. The search in ethnohistory and epigraphy, as with ethnography and ethnology, is for clues to how people lived and thought, past and present. The overarching aim of cultural anthropology is to investigate and comprehend the totality of human experience, both mental and behavioural. To do that, anthropologists may specialise or gain skills and knowledge that overlap with other disciplines. For example, the study of how people interact with living things, which cultural anthropology shares with the life sciences, is called *ethnobiology*. *Ethnozoology* involves the study of humans and their use

Figure 1.3 Stela at the ancient Mayan city of Palenque, Mexico, featuring hieroglyphs, a form of writing studied and decoded by epigraphers. The text here includes a dedication to a patron deity of Palenque, dated 11 January AD 692. Courtesy Middle American Research Institute, Tulane University.

and classification of animals. The study of native perceptions of the cosmos is called *ethnoastronomy*. The study of non–Western religions is comparative religion, which is shared with theologians and philosophers. Other interdisciplinary areas of cultural anthropology include environmental anthropology, economic anthropology, political anthropology, urban anthropology, ethnomusicology and ethnomedicine.

Cultural anthropologists are sometimes called upon to put their knowledge of different societies into practice, not just in the study of human subjects, but in a way that will affect people's lives in a direct and positive way; this is called *applied anthropology* (Chapter 11).

Enculturation and Cultural Relativism

Ethnographers study social organisation as well as culture. Social organisation is like a blueprint that lays out rules connecting people, allowing them to live together and reproducing society in the next generation. Ethnographers uncover these rules by 'poking and prying' (Cultural Snapshot 1.1), that is, by participant observation, among other methods. Ethnographers try to minimise any preexisting *ethnocentrism* they might have. Ethnocentrism is the false belief that one's own culture is better than everyone else's. Instead, ethnographers attempt to see the people of the culture they are studying as behaving in the ways they were raised and taught. These ways of raising and teaching young people the rules of culture are part of the process of *enculturation*. The Guajá and Araweté have different attitudes to eating raw palm beetle larvae because they were enculturated differently. When a person realises that the people whose behaviour he or she found strange or repulsive were enculturated to act that way, that person begins to lose his or her ethnocentrism and begins to think like an ethnographer. Only then can one appreciate why Guajá culture is not necessarily better than Araweté and vice versa; the two cultures are just different. This important and basic principle of cultural anthropology—that cultural traits of different people in different societies are not necessarily superior or inferior to each other—is *cultural relativism*. The principle of cultural relativism also applies to the other three fields of anthropology. Let's begin with the one that studies human origins, human biology, and our closest nonhuman relatives.

Biological Anthropology

Biological anthropology—sometimes called physical anthropology—is the study of humans as organisms who live and evolve. Biological anthropology is especially relevant to cultural anthropology because of its window into where the human species came from and the similarities and differences it has with other species, in particular, other primates. Biological anthropologists investigate the evolution of humans and the comparative anatomy and behaviour of our closest relatives, living and extinct, in the animal kingdom, the primates. Primates include monkeys, apes, humans and some other mammals known as prosimians. All primates share certain features, not any one of which is necessarily unique to them among mammals, the most important of which are:

- prehensile hands and feet;
- stereoscopic ('3-D') and colour vision;
- long period of infant dependence;
- small litter sizes; and
- large brain size relative to body mass.

Humans/great APeS!

These features taken together are associated with high intelligence and dependence on learning, as well as heredity for the knowledge needed to survive and good vision and acrobatic skills, which were required for what was originally a life in trees. Biological anthropology also assesses special relationships within the family of humans, Hominidae (hominids), which includes us, our fossil ancestors, the African great apes (chimpanzees, bonobos, gorillas), and orangutans. Of these, humans are most closely related to chimpanzees and bonobos.

Biological anthropology is divided into several subfields, including *palaeoanthropology*, which is the study of fossil *hominins*—the tribe of humans, including fossils ancestral to modern humans—and *primatology*, the study of nonhuman primates, their anatomy and their behaviour. Physical anthropologists may also specialise in the causes and distribution of contemporary human diseases, which is sometimes called medical anthropology. They may examine human remains and associated artefacts within the context of the archaeological record, called *bioarchaeology*. They may also analyse human biological variation, those genetic, phenotypic or observable physical differences between human populations.

Biological anthropologists may concentrate on prehistoric diseases and their incidence in a population, known as *palaeopathology*, and the study of ancient patterns of reproduction and population growth, called *palaeodemography*. Forensic anthropologists study causes of death and identify human remains in crime contexts, as seen in the television program *Bones*. Forensic anthropology has fewer full-time practitioners than the fields of palaeoanthropology, palaeopathology and palaeodemography. These subfields, in part, depend on analysis of *fossils*: mineralised organic remains, especially bones and teeth, and sometimes indirect evidence of an organism's anatomy or behaviour, such as imprints of a skeleton or footprints. Another subfield, called *palaeoprimatology*, deals with the origins of *anthropoid primates*: monkeys, apes and humans. We now examine some of the findings of palaeoanthropology, the subfield that is most relevant to cultural anthropology, because one of its principal aims is to distinguish the anatomy and behaviour of fully modern humans—the ones cultural anthropology studies—from all other ones.

Studying Human Origins and Evolution

Evidence of human antiquity comes from various types of fossils. Palaeoanthropologists have celebrated a 50-meter-long trail of fossil hominin footprints in volcanic ash at a site called Laetoli in Tanzania, Africa, which is 3.6 million years old. These fossil footprints prove these ancient creatures, ancestral to modern humans, were walking around on two legs rather than on all fours. That method of locomotion—*bipedalism*—is one of the features that makes them hominins, or members of the human tribe. Bipedalism enabled hominins to explore the far reaches of their territories and beyond. In contrast, knuckle-walking, which is how the African great apes amble on the ground, does not help a creature get too far from home. On average, an adult human can walk a little more than ten miles a day, whereas a knuckle-walking adult chimpanzee can only cover about half that distance in the same amount of time. Chimpanzees are better tree climbers than humans, though. Standing on the savanna, early hominins were just tall enough to peer over the high grass still found on the sub-Saharan plains and see the horizon, spot ungulate carcasses from lion kills and perceive possible threats, such as hungry leopards.

Of course, leopards could see bipedal hominins more easily, too, so there was a downside to bipedalism; it is also the case that humans injure their backs and get things like hernias much more than other primates on average because they carry loads, sometimes heavy ones, on two legs only. Palaeoanthropologists debate the origins of bipedalism, whether it emerged in the forest or savanna first, and whether it could have evolved more than once or not. One of the earliest hominins, *Ardipithecus ramidus*, or 'Ardi', which dates from 4.4 million years ago and has very long arms and ape-like toes, seems to have been able to get around bipedally; bipedalism seems suited to a life on the savanna, but Ardi was also adept at living in trees, which is more appropriate for a forest animal; indeed, the fossil record comes from an area believed to have been tropical forest at the time Ardi lived. Bipedalism is one of the most important adaptations of hominins, yet the exact evolutionary reasons for it remain unresolved and elusive.

Bipedalism freed the hands for purposes other than locomotion, such as making tools, though bipedalism preceded toolmaking by about one million years. The earliest tools, such as choppers, could be used to crack open bones of prey animals and extract the high-protein marrow to eat. Hominins gradually developed other skills such as hunting, rather than scavenging. They increasingly needed more sophisticated social organisation for hunters to cooperate and communicate effectively and share their kills with each other's families. They also needed better tools, including projectile points and spears. These necessities required greater intelligence and greater social skills, which came about through natural selection (Chapter 4), resulting in hominins with much larger brains than those before. Large and intricately organised brains may be due to the need to use one's social skills in increasingly large groups: humans have the largest group sizes of all primates. These group sizes can reach tens of millions of people, most spectacularly in megacities (metropolitan areas exceeding 10,000,000 people), of which there are about 37 in the world today: of these, 14 exceed 20,000,000 inhabitants, with Tokyo at the top of the list with around 38,000,000 people.

Fossil hominins began with much smaller populations, and it was only in the twentieth century that megacities came into existence, about 150,000 years after the first

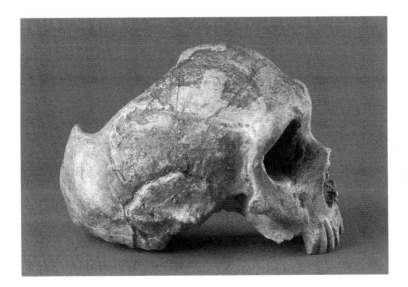

Figure 1.4 Neanderthal skull from Gibraltar, one of the last places where Neanderthals lived. Getty Images.

anatomically modern humans evolved in Africa. One of our early human relatives, called *Homo erectus,* migrated out of Africa into Asia and Europe about 1.8 million years ago. These hominins lived on the planet for well over a million years, from about 1.9 million years ago to about 400,000 years ago. After that, there were transitional species that ultimately evolved into us: modern humans. These earlier species all went extinct, with few exceptions, by about 25,000 years ago. Palaeoanthropologists have studied the morphology of the skeletons of other hominins, such as brawny, large-brained Neanderthals (Figure 1.4) and their ancestors in Europe and Western Asia, which date from about 350,000 to 25,000 years ago. Modern humans evolved in Africa about 150,000 years ago, then spread into Europe, Asia and points beyond. Throughout the process of evolution, human brain sizes were increasing, a critical adaptation. But how is it that modern humans are the only hominin species left on Earth (Cultural Snapshot 1.3)?

CULTURAL SNAPSHOT 1.3

How We Ended Up Alone

In Europe, a hominin related to *H. erectus* lived and reproduced between 500,000 and 450,000 years ago. That hominin may have been the ancestor of the Neanderthals, muscular, large-brained hominins similar to modern humans. Neanderthals may have had language, but their technology was simpler than that of *Homo sapiens.* In the Middle East, Neanderthals and modern humans coexisted. We now know that Neanderthals and modern humans mated occasionally, and that some modern humans are descended from their progeny (Cultural Snapshot 1.4). Anatomically modern humans frequently used small, sharp *blade tools,* whereas, with a few exceptions, Neanderthals hunted and scavenged using simpler *flake tools.* Neanderthals were stronger than modern humans; they probably hunted at close quarters using spears as thrusting devices. That could account in part for the typical injuries sustained on many Neanderthal skeletal remains recovered thus far. In contrast, modern humans used projectile devices such as *spear throwers,* which gave them great range and velocity in dispatching large game animals. Spear throwers enabled them to kill animals from a distance and probably saved many early modern humans from being gored to death prematurely by powerful Pleistocene megafauna. Modern humans also appear to be more flexible in their range of diet than Neanderthals were, who seem to be exclusively meat eaters. If their source of meat were to suffer a decline for whatever reason, they could suffer from hunger. Climate change seems to have affected the range and distribution of large game animals late in the Pleistocene in Europe. There was a major cold snap about 50,000 years ago, which evidently contributed to a rapid depopulation of the remaining Neanderthals, who by 45,000 years ago were living only in small, isolated groups. As the climate cooled and glaciers advanced ever southward, the last Neanderthal populations, which were smaller and genetically less diverse to begin with than those of modern humans, died out. That left only us.

New finds of fossils, skeletons and tools of ancient hominins tend to inspire debate among palaeoanthropologists. In 2003, a cache of parts of eight hominin skeletons associated with stone tools was found in a limestone cave on the Indonesian island of Flores. The material was found in an archaeological context dating from 94,000 years to perha[ps] recently as 13,000 years ago. The only skeleton found with an intact skull was tha[t of] an adult female who stood about 3.5 feet tall and whose braincase would have been [the] size of a chimpanzee's at around 400 cm3 of volume. That is less than half the ave[r]age brain size of *Homo erectus*, of which the first known fossil was discovered nearby on Java by Dutch anthropologist Eugene Dubois in 1893 and given its scientific name at that time. The Flores hominins belonged to our genus *Homo* but were not modern *H. sapiens*. The debate about exactly who were the Flores hominins, sometimes called the 'little people of Flores' or 'hobbits' because of their diminutive stature, continues: several palaeoanthropologists believe the female skull is not representative of a hominin population, but instead is from an anatomically anomalous individual, such as a person afflicted with Down syndrome. The hominins from Flores had fire and relatively sophisticated stone tools, like anatomically modern humans. The discoverers of the Flores hominins in the limestone cave argue that they had discovered a new species, *Homo floresiensis*. The diminutive size of *H. floresiensis* is correlated with the small sizes of other ancient fauna of the island, such as miniature elephants. Evolution may select for small-size fauna because of the space limitations on islands. Future fossil finds will enrich anthropological understanding of the human past, so our knowledge and reconstructions of the past are always changing.

One of the problems in classifying *H. floresiensis* is that no DNA has been recovered yet; the tropical conditions where these fossils are found are not conducive to the preservation of genetic material over lengthy time spans. Biological anthropologists are of course interested in what defines humans as a species different from others. So they look at genes—the information of heredity carried by DNA—that direct the synthesis of proteins essential to the composition and development of living bodies, like ours, and to brain functions involved in learning language and culture. The human *genome* (the entire sequence of genetic material of our species) differs from that of our closest relatives, chimpanzees and bonobos, only by about 1 per cent. Somewhere in that fractional difference is the code for habitual bipedalism, larger brains and a penchant for advanced culture and genuine language (Chapter 2). The discovery that humans and apes are so closely related has caused biological anthropologists to reclassify chimpanzees, bonobos, gorillas and orangutans as hominids, members of the same family as humans. Don't confuse *hominids*—humans, the great apes and all of their ancestors—with *hominins*, which is a more restrictive category that just includes humans and their most closely related bipedal relatives, living and extinct.

An important finding reported in 2010 shows that modern humans thousands of years ago did interbreed with Neanderthals, who lived from 350,000 to 25,000 years ago in Europe and Western Asia (Cultural Snapshot 1.4). Neanderthals and modern humans first coexisted in the Middle East 80,000 years ago, but palaeoanthropologists debated whether they mated with each other, avoided each other or killed each other. Research on the human genome from different continents shows that some of us share genes related to cognition and skeletal development with European Neanderthals. Europeans and Asians in the study sample showed inheritance of about 4 per cent of their genes from Neanderthals, whereas Africans in the study sample had no signs of genes contributed by Neanderthals. This suggests that modern humans interbred with Neanderthals after some of them left Africa. When modern humans then expanded farther into Asia and Europe, they carried Neanderthal genes with them. This subfield is sometimes called *molecular anthropology* (Cultural Snapshot 1.4); it complements the findings of human palaeontology, which focuses on fossils other than ancient DNA, especially the skeletal and dental morphology—the shape and structure of bones and teeth—of early hominins.

CULTURAL SNAPSHOT 1.4

Out of Africa vs. Multiregional Hypotheses

Genomic research since the early 2000s suggests we may find the reason we are alone by looking at the *nuclear genome* of extinct hominins. In 1989, the human *mitochondrial genome* was found to differ so little in modern humans from across the planet that it was possible to postulate a single ancestor of all of us, called 'mitochondrial Eve' (a female, because mitochondrial DNA is inherited in the cytoplasm of the mother only, following a rule of *maternal inheritance*), who lived in Africa. This led to an interesting debate in the 1990s and early 2000s about where all of us came from: some people, especially genome biologists, argued that everyone came from Africa and all earlier hominin cousins—such as Neanderthals in Europe and West Asia—simply went extinct when they were replaced by modern humans, about 50,000 to 25,000 years ago. That was called the 'Out of Africa Hypothesis' of human origins. Others, especially some palaeoanthropologists who were focused on body shape and size (i.e., *morphology*) of fossil hominins, thought there had been some independent development of modern humans on different continents thanks to previously existing DNA of older hominins. It came to be called the 'Multiregional Hypothesis'. Both hypotheses were based on the same data: fossils and mitochondrial DNA. Additional data that showed neither hypothesis was exactly correct came from advances in technology that allowed for the sequencing of ancient nuclear DNA. Nuclear DNA is found inside the cell nucleus; most of the DNA that codes for amino acids, polypeptides and proteins, which are the building blocks of human bodies, is found in the nuclear DNA. Mitochondrial DNA is found in the organelles called mitochondria (the singular is mitochondrion), which are responsible for producing the energy in animal cells. In the late 1990s, the mitochondrial DNA of a Neanderthal skeleton found in Neander Valley, Germany, in 1856, the so-called 'type' specimen, was proven to be significantly different from that of modern humans, which suggested that the two hominins did not mate, or if they did, their offspring went extinct with the Neanderthals about 30,000 years ago. Although the existence of Eve in Africa is well supported, later research on the nuclear genome (which is much harder to sequence) of Neanderthals, by the same research group led by Svante Pääbo at the Max Planck Institute for Evolutionary Anthropology in Germany, showed that a number of nucleotides (single units of the DNA molecule that consist of a nitrogenous base, a pentose sugar and phosphate group; the building blocks of DNA, so to speak, of which humans have about 36,000,000,000) of modern humans outside Africa were the same as those of Neanderthals, but different from apes. These suggest derived features, or shared mutations, in Neanderthals and modern humans that came about through sexual intercourse and fertile offspring between them. Moreover, it is interesting to note that Africa has the most diverse nuclear genomes of our species today, which is itself indirect evidence that we evolved there first; modern Africans also don't show the same mutations shared between Neanderthals and modern humans outside Africa, suggesting that intergroup mating took place, as expected, where Neanderthals evolved: Western Asia, if not also Europe. Molecular anthropology gives us a viewing platform into a very deep time of human history. In addition, knowledge of this history moves forward thanks to advances by human palaeontologists, who study fossils such as mineralised bones and teeth of extinct hominins, and by archaeologists, who study artefacts such as early hominin stone tools and living sites.

Major questions of concern to biological anthropologists include: what makes *Homo sapiens* different from the other members of our genus, all of which went extinct (including *H. erectus*, *H. floresiensis* and the Neanderthals)? What distinguishes the genus *Homo* from other genera of hominins? Which aspects of our biological heritage do we share with our primate cousins, especially monkeys and apes, and why? Which behaviours found in all human societies are biologically determined, or inherited, and which are not? Apart from these questions, biological anthropologists are engaged in separating cultural from natural effects as they try to understand human diversity over time and space. In other words, like cultural anthropologists, they make use of the concept of culture and cultural relativism in their work. Their findings help other anthropologists interpret the development of culture both past and present.

Anthropological Archaeology

All human cultures have changed through time. Archaeology is the science of these past changes. Anthropological archaeology, or just archaeology, intersects with cultural anthropology because it shows how, why and where certain cultural traits of modern human societies originated and developed over time. Anthropological archaeologists tend to focus on cultures whose long-term heritage cannot be understood apart from artefacts. The study of the remote past of some ancient societies, especially in Europe, Africa and Asia, has been divided into fields that may be found in university departments other than anthropology. For example, the archaeological study of the ancient Egypt of the pharaohs and pyramids is often referred to as Egyptology; the study of early civilisations in China is sometimes called Sinology; and that of India, Indology. Researchers working on Mediterranean (Greek and Roman) antiquity are often found in classics departments. All these fields historically have contributed to archaeological knowledge.

Archaeology is an empirical science of the remote past. That means it is based on data, or facts, that specialists can examine, evaluate and interpret. Archaeologists seek to unearth and bring to light past cultures, just as ethnography does for living cultures and ethnohistory does for people of the relatively recent past. Archaeology is also problem oriented, zeroing in on technological changes accompanying human evolution, as well as developments that have occurred in one or more cultures since the appearance of behaviourally modern humans around 70,000 years ago in Africa.

Archaeologists study *artefacts, or things made by people*. An artefact could be a projectile point, stone axe, bone needle, a broken piece of a ceramic bowl or anything else—including smartphones and notebook computers—resulting from human ingenuity, creativity and dexterity. Artefacts are found in archaeological sites, where past people worked, ate, slept, partied, made love, raised children and told stories at night. An archaeological site could be a rock shelter where people cooked their meals and slept, a quarry where they got the raw material for tools and weapons, an earthen mound where a political or religious leader lived, an abandoned fort on what was once a frontier or the centre of an ancient city, now covered by freeways and parking lots.

Given their concern with past people and events, archaeologists are interested in the passage of time itself and how to measure it. Time is measured in archaeology not with calendars, for most ancient cultures did not have these, but by known rates of decay of carbon-14, a radioactive isotope, and other geological and organic phenomena. The physical sciences allow for the dating of organic remains, such as charcoal in a hearth from an abandoned house, and inorganic remains, such as a pot that was fired thousands of years ago.

Archaeologists also study fundamental events of the human past, such as the origins of agriculture, urban life, the state and the world system. Like ethnohistorians, archaeologists generally do not have living informants. Instead, they rely on the material remains left by earlier peoples and in some cases documents by or about earlier peoples. Today, some archaeologists, in a subfield called ethnoarchaeology, observe how living people make and discard artefacts to get clues as to how these behaviours occurred in the past, in times before writing existed. Archaeologists often seek to understand site formation, the processes that account for the way archaeological sites appear today, such as erosion, volcanic activity, silt deposition or deliberate destruction. Archaeologists distinguish short-lived fashions or styles of art, technology, ideas and practices involved in social and political organisation from long-term developments. For example, some form of visible body ornamentation, with the purpose of enhancing one's attractiveness, is known in all modern

human societies. Yet all of it—clothing, jewellery, featherwork, body piercing and painting, makeup and hairstyle—varies due to changing standards of beauty, cultural concepts of modesty and available resources. Archaeologists study both the general fact of body ornamentation as well as fashions over time and across space by comparing the practices of different cultures. Fashions usually have an identifiable centre from which they spread to distant areas by *diffusion*, which is the transmission of cultural material in the form of shared ideas, words and artefacts from one society to another (Chapter 2). Cultural anthropologists draw on archaeology because it gives their research greater time-depth compared with that of other social sciences, such as history, political science, sociology and psychology.

Linguistic Anthropology

In ethnology, or the comparative study of cultures, the peoples who are under the analytical gaze of the cultural anthropologist are frequently in some sense related by language or dialect. Language is a complex, formal and integrated array of symbols and rules for their combination that permits the expression and comprehension of complete thoughts. Most linguistic anthropologists see language as the quintessential attribute of the human species. In Chapter 2, we discuss language in greater detail. For now, it's important to recognise that the *capacity* for language is heritable, or hardwired into the brain. Linguistic anthropologists examine evidence in living languages for such inborn tendencies. That evidence consists of phenomena shared by all spoken languages, such as the fact that all have noises called consonants or vowels, words classified as nouns and verbs and rules for composing sentences.

Linguistic anthropologists also study and systematically describe variation in sound patterns among spoken languages and the grammars of little-known languages. They examine relationships that exist between a language and the culture of the people who speak it. For example, linguistic anthropologist Janis Nuckolls carried out years of field-work among people in the rainforest of the Ecuadorian Amazon who speak Quechua (Figure 1.5). She found that in everyday speech they use many *ideophones*. Ideophones are sounds and phrases that imitate life, such as *arf arf* in English or words such as *crash, dash, bash, gash, smash, splash* and *stash*, all of which convey and sound like some type of rapid action. Quechua uses more ideophones than English. According to Luisa, one of Nuckolls' informants, Quechua speakers can talk about the sounds of a person cutting down a tree in the forest using only ideophones. People cut down trees to make room for an agricultural field. Describing that involves three ideophones: *Gyauuuuuuuuuŋŋŋ* (creaking), *blhuuuuuu* (falling) and *puthuŋŋŋ* (hitting the ground). Nuckolls points out that the 'creaking' sound is considered sad, as if the tree being cut down is crying:

> The more the tree 'cries' the greater will be the productivity of the agricultural field... Although it took me twenty years to realise this, the description of the tree's falling with all of the dramatic sound imitation that accompanied it, was not simply a vivid aesthetic description. It communicated something about that tree's reaction to being acted upon by humans.
>
> (Nuckolls 2010, pp. 355–356)

Figure 1.5 Linguistic anthropologist Janis Nuckolls, specialist on ideophones, takes notes in the field with a Quechua informant. Photo by Jaren Wilkey.

As this example demonstrates, culture is intertwined with meaning and language: one needs to be familiar with the culture to understand the linguistic meaning of a phrase. For that reason, the subject areas of linguistic and cultural anthropology often overlap. In spite of linguistic variation based on cultural differences, human language represents a feature found in all known societies.

Linguistic anthropologists study languages for six major reasons:

- To document and record speech, meaning and sound patterns in unwritten, undescribed languages still found in places such as the Amazon, Papua New Guinea and Australia.
- To examine the difference between rules of grammar in a language and how people actually speak.
- To assess how speakers of a native language acquire competence in the language and use it to become successful in life.
- To evaluate how languages are influenced by other languages in contact situations involving face-to-face communication as well as various kinds of media, including radio, TV and the internet.
- To examine the relation of language to culture, such as how a language reflects prevailing attitudes and customs.
- To understand how and why ways of speaking change with time.

The concept that language is a code that underlies consciousness is a forerunner to the idea that language has a basis in the biology of the brain, a point we address in Chapter 2. This notion is based on the fact that we, as speakers of a language, use it instinctively—biologically—without thinking about it. The twentieth-century philosopher Ludwig Wittgenstein recognised this when he wrote that humankind

> possesses the capacity of constructing languages, in which every sense can be expressed, without having an idea how and what each word means—just as one speaks without knowing how the single sounds are produced. Colloquial language is a part of the human organism and is not less complicated than it.
>
> (Wittgenstein (1922) 1996, p. 6)

This approach differs from the blank-slate approach taken by philosophers of the 1700s when anthropology was in its infancy (Chapter 4). For eighteenth-century philosophers, the brain was a *tabula rasa* for imprinting cultural information through the learning experience, or what we now call *enculturation*. Enculturation, as we will see in Chapter 2, is a learning process common to all cultures, whereby shared ideas and behaviour are passed from one generation of society to the next. Enculturation helps account for cultural differences.

The blank-slate idea—that the mind has no preexisting knowledge at birth—is probably too simple. Enculturation acts on human brains that already have a common capacity for culture and language. Linguistic anthropologists acknowledge that language capacity is an innate biological trait shared by all humans.

Holism and the Four Fields

Anthropology is a holistic discipline. Holism (from Greek *holon*, 'the one') is the integrated approach to the study of humans, where all factors are taken into account and seen as interdependent. Holism is different from reductionism, which is a focus on just one or two factors of humanity as determinants of the rest. Taken together, the four fields of anthropology provide the student with a solid, comprehensive and authentic account of humankind and its closest relatives across time and space.

All human societies display elaborate traditions of learned and shared behaviours (Cultural Snapshot 1.5). Cultures vary from one group to the next and from one time period to another within the same society. Culture—any culture—changes, for better or worse. These cultural changes can occur as a result of diffusion. They may also result from *contingency*: unforeseen historical and environmental events that can have lasting impacts on culture and society.

The European conquest of indigenous societies in the Americas, including the Spanish defeat of the Aztecs in 1519, was a contingent, historical event that profoundly changed the lives of the people of Mexico. Their descendants developed new cultures as a result of that conquest. Likewise, the nineteenth-century potato famine of Ireland led to political changes and altered how people grew food. Incidentally, the introduction to Ireland of the potato, which originated in the Peruvian Andes, was itself contingent. So are events such as biological invasions, volcanic eruptions, tsunamis, catastrophic hurricanes and climate change. Julius Caesar's crossing of a stream called the Rubicon with his army in 49 BC, which foreshadowed the end of the Roman Republic and the coming of the Roman Empire, was a contingent event. The impact of contingent events is not predictable based on the previous history of a given society. Such impacts have led to the decline and collapse of entire societies and to social reorganisation and innovation. We examine contingency more closely in Chapter 10.

CULTURAL SNAPSHOT 1.5

What Is Learned and Shared

The word *culture* has multiple meanings in English and related languages. In 1952, anthropologists A. L. Kroeber and Clyde Kluckhohn found more than a hundred different definitions of culture in print up to that time. Apart from the definition given in this text, culture sometimes means 'civilisation'. This usage generally refers to the intellectual side of civilisation, or to an appreciation of the arts. One might say, 'Our hosts are such *cultured* people', meaning that they have good taste in decorative art, classical music and home furnishings. *Culture* has also been used to mean the growing of certain plants or animals, as in the terms 'agriculture', 'aquaculture' or 'apiculture' (raising bees). These usages are far from the anthropological meaning of culture.

Marvin Harris, a cultural anthropologist, suggested that you could comprehend an anthropologist's views on human life in society by understanding his or her definition of culture. Yet, anthropologists of different theoretical persuasions tend to agree on two crucial features of culture: that it is 1) *learned*, not inherited biologically from one's parents; and 2) *shared*, not the idiosyncratic product of a single mind. These two assumptions have linked cultural anthropology to the other three fields of anthropology. The notion that culture is learned and shared has entered common usage with terms such as 'corporate culture', 'university culture' and 'military culture'. These terms derive their current meanings from the findings of cultural anthropology, which have seeped into the popular and global consciousness since the 1990s.

Culture and Change

Apart from being learned and shared, culture is dynamic. Culture changes in a person's lifetime, whereas an individual's DNA does not, except in extreme conditions. The rate of cultural change is faster, in principle than the rate of human biological evolution. Ancient Greek philosophers knew that geometry, for example, is 'knowledge of that which always is'. Unlike geometry, culture changes due to alterations of the physical environment or to shifts in social and political organisation. It is difficult to predict how a given culture will change in the future, in part due to contingent, or historical, events. Cultural anthropology is based on observation but not experimentation, which means that it is easier to retrodict—to say what did happen—than it is to predict social and cultural change.

Global warming is a contingency of climate change in our own time, and it is difficult to determine with exactitude what will happen because of it. We can retrodict that early modern humans in Europe and Asia survived glacial winters because they developed warm clothing and knew how to make fire for warmth on icy nights. We also know that greenhouse gases have increased in the atmosphere since the Industrial Revolution and that ice melts faster at higher temperatures. One can then infer that temperature increases will eventually melt polar ice caps, melting ice will cause sea levels to rise and higher sea levels will flood islands, low-lying areas and coastal cities worldwide. Those are general outlines of a contingent future. What is impossible to predict is the specific events and their sequence. The future is therefore contingent on whether people organise themselves politically, refocus their institutions and implement policies to reduce greenhouse gas emissions on such a scale that the impacts of global warming can be minimised.

Like global warming, culture change is not wholly predictable, which is why archaeology and ethnohistory are relevant to understanding humans both past and present. When an anthropologist studies culture, they may be looking at a phenomenon that has been around for thousands of years, such as Hinduism, or something that is new, such as twentieth-century hip hop. The study of culture, and hence cultural anthropology, involves the examination of both the human past and present to describe what *has* happened, to better understand what *is* happening and to assist in future policy- and decision-making.

Anthropology and Related Disciplines

Like cultural anthropology, other social sciences—sociology, political science and economics—take the human species as their subject matter. One of the chief differences between cultural anthropology and these disciplines, however, is that only anthropology has systematically described non-Western, nonindustrial and politically leaderless or noncentralised societies and cultures. Some have considered sociology, the science of Western society, to be the science of the obvious, and anthropology to be the study of the exotic 'other'.

Because of that, some scholars have felt that academic anthropology, when it began in the late nineteenth century, was only necessary because it picked up the leftovers, the 'primitive' societies that other social sciences had no interest in. While that observation is partly accurate, the attention anthropology has paid to non-Western cultures does not mean that it has a narrow subject matter. In principle, the discipline as a whole is dedicated to the exhaustive documentation and explanation of human cultures, and humanity itself, at all times and in all places. Culture is central to understanding all human societies both past and present. Only the field of cultural anthropology has as its express mission the explanation of cultural differences.

The other three fields of anthropology complement and intersect with cultural anthropology but cannot replace it. To appreciate cultural diversity, one needs to be able to recognise in humans all the behaviours that distinguish them from other living organisms. Biological anthropology contributes an understanding of the intersection between biology and culture; it documents the evolution of the human body, describes the range of human diversity and explores the capacity for toolmaking and language. Linguistic anthropology studies the relationship between language and culture; it has shown that all languages ultimately come from a preexisting template in the brain but develop along distinct historical and cultural trajectories. Archaeology documents those trajectories through the study of material culture, illustrating the similarities and differences among human adaptations in the past. It tracks the development of increasingly advanced technologies, from the earliest stone tools to the most modern supercomputers. These capacities—to design tools, to walk upright and to communicate using language—are part of what makes us human and are all linked through culture. Culture is dynamic: it has changed with time, and it is changing right now. In the following chapters, we will examine a few principles of cultural anthropology. First, all humans belong to a single human species: biologically and genetically, people are the same everywhere. Second, unique attributes of the species include advanced capacities for language and culture. Third, culture varies due to contingent historical events and the diffusion of ideas, artefacts and behaviour. Finally, the intricate links among biology, culture and language and the time–depth represented by the human species require anthropology to be divided up into fields. As the only field that studies living human culture through participant observation, cultural anthropology is of pivotal importance. It defines the central problem of the field: determining what accounts for the similarities and differences through the study of us.

Summary

Anthropology is the study of humankind and consists of four fields. These are cultural anthropology, biological anthropology, archaeology and linguistic anthropology. Cultural anthropology focuses on the description and analysis of cultural similarities and differences. It has three subfields: ethnography, ethnology and ethnohistory. Ethnography involves fieldwork with a distinct group of people using a method called participant observation. Ethnology is the comparative study of societies. Biological anthropology is the study of human biology and evolution. Archaeology is the study of the human past through material culture. Linguistic anthropology is the study of human language, how it defines our species and how languages vary in different social contexts. Anthropology in its four fields is a holistic science; its objective is the understanding of humans in all times and places.

Further Reading

Adams 1998; Balée 2009; Beard 2004; Berdan 2005; Brown 2014; Buchanan et al. 2020; Chomsky 1965; Cormier 2003; Dunbar 2003; Duranti 2001; Geertz 1973; George 2011; Gibbon 2011, 2013; Green et al. 2010; Henshilwood and Marean 2003; Kehoe 2006; Larsen 2011; Lévi-Strauss (1955) 2012; Lips 2008; Livingston 1958; Morwood et al. 2005; Murphy 1971; Nuckolls 2010; Pääbo 2014; Pickering et al. 2011; Pinker 1999; Plato 1999; Rice 2014; Rogers 1983; Said 2003; Saussure (1916) 1959; Shostak 2000; Sloane 1999; Wade 2006; White et al. 2009; Wilford 2013; Wittgenstein (1922) 1996; Wolf 1964; Zeitzen 2008

Cultural Snapshots

1.1   Hurston 1969 (p. 182); Rony 1996
1.2   Beckerman and Valentine 2002; Cormier 2003; Early and Peters 1990; Zeitzen 2008
1.3   Bar-Yosef 1998; Finlayson 2004; Gibbon 2011; Morwood et al. 2005; Pickering et al. 2011; Rice 2015; Wade 2006
1.4   Pääbo 2014; Larsen 2011
1.5   Harris 1976; Kroeber and Kluckhohn 1952

2   What Makes Us Human

Overview

The essential givens of our species are often called *sociocultural universals*. Sociocultural universals, or just universals, are the core of behaviour and belief that makes us human. As descendants of anatomically modern humans who originated in Africa, we are the only remaining bipedal primates on the planet. We have an innate predisposition to sophisticated forms of language and depend on highly complex, group-living arrangements based on shared, learned behaviour and ideas that change with time.

We know early modern humans did not become *behaviourally modern* until about 70,000 years ago, meaning they didn't start acting and thinking like us until long after they were already physically able to do so. But when they did, we see an explosion of tools such as needles, blades and burins, which are instruments for boring holes. Cave art, personal ornaments and new ways of making and using clothing appear. New developments in art and religion, reflecting modern ways of thinking, show up first in Africa about 70,000 years ago, and modern humans have been on the move ever since. They were in temperate Europe and Asia at least 45,000 years ago, Australia about 40,000 years ago, New Guinea about 33,000 years ago, the high Arctic about 27,000 years ago, the New World about 15,000 years ago and Polynesia about 2,000 years ago. They first set foot on Antarctica in the nineteenth century and travelled into outer space in the twentieth.

In addition to technology, ancient behaviourally modern humans had certain things that other hominins lacked. They had a belief system and distinct ideas about an afterlife. Evidence for this includes burials—and sometimes reburials—of the dead and ancient rock art portraying spirits in Australia, South Africa, western North America, Amazonia and Southeast Asia. Ideas about the supernatural are still part of every culture and society since that time. Modern human burials from tens of thousands of years ago contain beads, teeth, shell ornaments for necklaces and bracelets and red ochre, a naturally occurring pigment that they probably painted on their bodies. Certain activities carried out by behaviourally modern humans are still found everywhere today: that is why they are called sociocultural universals. What underlies all these developments in modern humans are the capacities for culture and language.

Why We're All the Same

We—the species called us—are all the same in the sense that everyone is as modern as everyone else, in an anatomic way—none of the so-called races, such as white, black, Asian, Amerindian and any and all possible mixes of these—are any more advanced or modern than any of the others, whether singly or in combination. We are also all what anthropologists call *behaviourally modern*. We know early modern humans did not become behaviourally modern until about 70,000 years ago, meaning they didn't start acting and thinking like us until long after they were already anatomically (and genetically) able to do so. But when they did, an explosion of tools such as needles, blades and burins, which are instruments for boring holes, made from stone, bone and wood, all occur everywhere about the same time. Cave art, personal ornaments and new ways of making and using clothing appear in the archaeological record. New developments in art and religion, reflecting modern ways of thinking, show up first in Africa about 70,000 years ago, and modern humans have been on the move ever since. That was a time when there was one language and one culture, and no races or classes or oppressed and marginalised minorities. There was a bottleneck of modern humans around 100,000 years ago, as they began to migrate out of Africa and into the rest of the Eurasian land mass. Modern humans came to temperate Europe and Asia at least 45,000 years ago, Australia about 40,000 years ago, New Guinea about 33,000 years ago, the high Arctic about 27,000 years ago, the Americas about 15,000 years ago and Polynesia some 2,000 years ago. They set foot on Antarctica in the nineteenth century and travelled into outer space for the first time in the twentieth.

In addition to technology, ancient behaviourally modern humans had certain things that other hominins lacked. They had a belief system and distinct ideas about an afterlife. Evidence for this includes burials—and sometimes reburials—of the dead and ancient rock art portraying spirits in Australia, South Africa, western North America, Amazonia and Southeast Asia. Ideas about the supernatural are still part of every culture and society since that time. Modern human burials from tens of thousands of years ago contain beads, teeth, shell ornaments for necklaces and bracelets and red ochre, a naturally occurring pigment that they probably painted on their bodies.

The Capacity for Culture

Humans are born with a capacity to acquire the appropriate ways of thinking, feeling and acting in a given society. In the book *Primitive Culture* (1871), British anthropologist Sir Edward Burnett Tylor defined culture as

> that complex whole which includes knowledge, belief, art, morals, law, custom, and any other capabilities and habits acquired by [humankind] as a member of society.
>
> (Tylor 1924 [1871], vol 1, p. 1)

The key parts of Tylor's famous definition are 'complex whole', 'acquired' and 'member of society'. Culture involves complex behaviour and ideas and, indeed, nearly the totality of conscious and unconscious human existence. It is 'acquired', which is another way of saying that it is *learned*, not inherited. We are not born with American or Chinese or Nigerian culture, any more than we are born speaking English or Chinese or Yoruba, though we do come into the world with a capacity to learn a human culture and to acquire native fluency in a human language. 'Humankind as a member of society' points to the fact that culture is *shared* by people who identify with one another while partaking in the same culture. My definition of culture as *learned and shared human behaviour and ideas, which can and do change with time*, strips Tylor's definition down to its essentials and adds a dynamic historical dimension to it.

The *capacity* for culture is a distinctive human attribute. It means that people are born already prepared to live in society, not to survive as solitary organisms. The capacity for culture is stored in our DNA, but any given culture—American culture, cowboy culture, Afghan culture, the culture of European court life—is a product of historical factors and events, called *contingencies*, that accumulate over time. These contingencies are unrelated to biological evolution. Contingency and change, including increased elaboration of society and its institutions or its opposite, collapse of society, which interact with history and the environment, are basic principles of anthropological understanding and explanation (Chapter 10).

Cumulative Culture

Human culture is cumulative—or additive—because it is based on knowledge, discoveries and inventions that occurred over many generations and are retained from one generation to the next, setting the stage for new ones. Other animals such as bottlenose dolphins and chimpanzees, also have culture, but theirs is not as complex as human culture, which is based both on digital and gestural phenomena, like full-blown natural language.

In different parts of Africa, discrete chimpanzee populations groom each other differently. These differences are cultural because grooming behaviours are learned. In one area, chimps scratch each other daintily, whereas in another they use a long, raking style of scratch. Even though the chimps have not yet discovered or invented the back scratcher, change in cultural traditions of chimpanzees occurs, but much more slowly than human cultural change. Ape culture does not seem to be cumulative over time, as with humans: new discoveries do not seem to build on earlier ones. Nevertheless, chimpanzees and bonobos have formidable skills in tool use, as do many other animals (Cultural Snapshot 2.1).

Chimpanzee culture has not become more complex, despite the six to eight million years of evolutionary history since the ancestors of modern humans and chimpanzees diverged. In contrast, human culture has built—year by year and person by person—upon earlier discoveries, ideas and material culture. Knowledge is transmitted with each succeeding generation expanding, modifying, and rejecting the ideas that came before. This is *cumulative culture*, a prodigious set of cultural beliefs and practices that is the product of thousands of years of teaching, learning, and communicating, using language. Like human culture, language is extraordinarily diverse, though it is based on a limited number of sounds and a finite set of rules for combining those sounds in meaningful ways.

CULTURAL SNAPSHOT 2.1

More Than One Species Makes Tools

Making tools, once believed by scholars to be a definitive characteristic of our species, is now known to be an ability we share with other animals. Some 30 species of birds use tools. For example, in 1848, Australian Aborigines described to an English zoologist how black-breasted buzzards scared emus away from their nests. The buzzards then dropped stones from their large beaks to break open the emu eggs. Primatologist Jane Goodall found chimpanzees in Gombe National Park, Tanzania,

Figure 2.1 Kanzi at 31 years of age in 2011. Like most nonhuman primates, Kanzi has a dark outer covering (called sclera) of his eyeballs. Some anthropologists suggest that the white sclera of human eyeballs allows one to see where the pupil and iris are focused, which means you can see what other people are looking at and they, in turn, can see what you are looking at. The dark sclera of other primates doesn't allow for that. The white sclera of human eyes indicates the importance of gesturing and cooperation, necessary steps in human sociality and human evolution. Getty Images.

'fishing' for termites using special twigs that they stripped of their bark. Not just any twig will do; the chimps select those that secrete a substance that sticks to the termites. In West Africa, chimpanzees use stones as anvils and hammers to smash open palm nuts. They also use sticks to scoop honey out of beehives and to pick brains from the skulls of small animals they have hunted and killed. Some animals even make sophisticated tools. The New Caledonian crow makes three-dimensional barbs from two-dimensional pandanus leaves, which are then used to catch prey. A crow in captivity learned to make a hook from a straight piece of wire, which it then used to lift a bucket containing food. Kanzi (Figure 2.1), a captive ape, has been able to percussion-flake stone tools after he learned the technique from archaeologists. Percussion flaking is an ability that was once believed to be restricted to hominins. Although humans have profound dexterity in the use of hands and fingers, we are not the only tool users. Nor, for that matter, are we the only tool *makers*.

The Capacity for Language

All societies share the human universal of language, a system of communication associated with specific functions of the human brain. The development of language may have occurred because humans needed to communicate in detail with one another as they learned to live in increasingly large and complex social groups. All humans have an underlying capacity for language, *any* human language. All languages, whether spoken in a tropical forest village in Borneo, an adobe structure in rural Mexico or a stockbroker's office on Wall Street, share attributes that distinguish them from other forms of communication, including animal communication.

Animal Communication

Species other than humans communicate with one another, sometimes in sophisticated ways. For example, distinct populations of humpback whales produce songs that can be heard over long distances. These songs consist of sequences of notes that seem to follow rules, like words in a sentence. The songs differ from one group of humpback whales to another, just as chimpanzee grooming styles vary from group to group. The songs, like grooming styles, are probably partly learned. Learning is also involved in birdcalls. A mockingbird in the wild can learn the calls of other birds, the sounds of mammals and even the metallic sounds of a piano. Learning, a sure sign of intelligence, is also involved in the mimicry of human speech by parrots.

The most impressive animal communication systems yet studied are those of captive apes. Research in the late 1980s on an eight-year-old captive bonobo named Kanzi (Figure 2.1) showed that he rapidly acquired knowledge of hundreds of words from his human trainers. Bonobos are African apes very similar to chimpanzees that differ from humans in about one percent of their DNA. Kanzi did not use words and phrases, since his vocal apparatus, like that of all other apes, cannot mimic the range of human speech sounds.

Kanzi pressed a button on a keyboard of symbols when he wished to communicate a word or idea. To play 'keep-away' with his trainers, he pressed buttons meaning 'water balloon' and then gestured to a nearby water hose used to fill the balloon. Kanzi showed knowledge of more than just individual words. Most impressively, he understood several kinds of sentences in which word order is important. For example, he knew the difference between 'put the ball on the rock' and 'put the rock on the ball'. To date, Kanzi, now an elderly bonobo much esteemed by his human handlers, is the most impressive animal in history in terms of communicative skills, some of which were previously thought to be unique to humans. Yet Kanzi's impressive linguistic abilities, in terms of comprehension and performance, are still not on a level that would compete with a three-year-old human child. Apes do not teach each other language in the wild, though they have intricate systems of gestures and calls that can communicate moods, emotions and needs (Cultural Snapshot 2.2).

CULTURAL SNAPSHOT 2.2

Gestures, Calls and Language

In animal communication, gestures and calls express current states of feeling and cannot refer to past or future conditions. In humans, gestures include smiling, frowning, staring, nodding one's head from side to side or up and down and putting one's arms on one's hips or folding them across one's chest. Calls include laughing, sobbing, shouting and screaming. Gestures and calls are sometimes combined, as when someone laughs uncontrollably and at the same time claps her hands together. Both gestures and calls are part of language. They can intensify a sentence and sometimes negate it, as when a person says at the end of a trying day at the office, or after a three-hour zoom conference, 'No, really, I'm fine', yet numerous subtle gestures suggest the opposite. They—or rather we-- can understand a lot by eye contact also, knowing exactly what the other person is looking at, or not looking at, in part because our sclera—the covering over the eyeballs—is white. It helps expose the location of the pupil and iris, and therefore what another individual is focusing on. In contrast, chimpanzees and bonobos have dark covering (*sclera*) over their eyeballs and are limited in how they can gesture with their eyes (Figure 2.1). In *The Silent Language*, anthropologist Edward T. Hall wrote, 'Sentences can be meaningless by themselves. Other signs may be much more eloquent' (1990, p. 96). There are few meaningful signs, or gestures, when compared with the number of possible words and sentences in a language. Unlike language, gestures do not involve phonemes, morphemes, syntax and productivity. Even though gestures are not grammatical, they enhance spoken communication of emotions, needs and moods, adding nuance and emphasis to what we say. Many of us shake hands upon greeting. In contrast, a visiting Ka'apor may greet another by putting the palm of the right hand on his right cheek, holding the elbow of his right arm with the palm of the left hand. He may say 'Good to see you' or, literally, 'I come here' (*Ko hẽ ajur*), to which the appropriate verbal response, accompanied by the same cheek and hand gesture, is '*Ko nde rejur*' or 'Here you come'. Gestures are important to the Ka'apor apart from social niceties: they have developed their own sign language because historically many of them are deaf.

Their capacity to communicate may be due to a gene called *FOXP2* that is shared with several mammal and songbird species as well as with humans and Neanderthals. The capacity for complex language, however, may be due to the fact that *FOXP2* codes for a different protein in humans than in all other animals.

Attributes of Language

As with the capacity for culture, the capacity for language is inborn. Human language consists of certain attributes that distinguish it from most systems of animal communication:

- finite inventories of minimal units of perceived sound called *phonemes*;
- minimal units of meaning called *morphemes*;
- arbitrary connection between a word and what it stands for;
- rules for making complete sentences;
- ability to refer to other times and other places; and
- ability to produce new utterances that make sense.

Let's look at each attribute of language separately.

Human language has a limited number of *phonemes*, which are representations of sounds in a language. Changing one phoneme for another in a word alters the meaning of the word or renders it unpronounceable or meaningless. In English, *p* and *b* are similar because both are bilabial stops: the lips close and interrupt the flow of air from the lungs when these sounds are pronounced. They differ because the *b* is voiced (the vocal cords vibrate) and the *p* is unvoiced (the vocal cords do not vibrate). You can hum a *b*, but you can't hum a *p*. That humming is called voicing. Voicing is *phonemic* in English. That's why the words *bit* and *pit* and the words *cup* and *cub* sound different to native English speakers. They hear a sound difference that matters. Incidentally, the word *emic* (Chapter 1), which denotes an emphasis on the perspective of the people who are the object of ethnographic research, is derived from the term *phonemic*. Linguistic anthropologists begin the description of new languages on the basis of their sound systems (Cultural Snapshot 2.3). The relationship between *phonemic* and *emic* suggests how important language is to understanding the informant's perspective in ethnographic research.

Language contains a set of rules for stringing together phonemes to make words and minimal units of meaning called *morphemes*. The word *cat* is a single morpheme. *Cats*, however, consists of two morphemes: *cat* plus the suffix -*s*, which in this case is a morpheme meaning more than one. Morphemes do not have to be words; they only need to have a meaning of some kind. The suffix -*ed* is an example of a morpheme that is not a word. When the suffix -*ed* is added to a verbal morpheme, such as *learn*, English speakers understand that the action occurred in the past.

With few but notable exceptions, language is *arbitrary*: no natural link exists between the strings of phonemes that make up words and the things those words refer to. There is no reason why *cat* should not have been called *tack* or *act*, each of which contains the same phonemes in different combinations. One exception to the rule that language is arbitrary is *ideophones* (Chapter 1), which include onomatopoeic words such as *meow*, *tweet* and *arf arf* that imitate the sounds of creatures they're associated with.

Language has rules for generating grammatical sentences. These rules are collectively known as *syntax*. Syntax governs word order in a sentence. English syntax forbids 'Pauline to about spoke Jill Jack'. The same words when strung together as 'Jill spoke to Pauline about Jack' are permissible. The latter sentence is grammatically correct because it follows the rules of English syntax.

CULTURAL SNAPSHOT 2.3

An Experiment in Phonology

Let's conduct an experiment. Hold a sheet of paper close to your face, with the bottom of the sheet in front of your mouth. Say the word *spit*. Now, say *pit*. Did you notice the sheet of paper ripple when you said *pit* but remain motionless when you said *spit*? If so, you have just observed the distinction between the two different *p*s in English. The *p* in *pit* is *aspirated*: a jet of air is ejected when the sound is pronounced. The *p* in *spit* is *unaspirated*: it lacks that jet of air.

In ordinary speech, English speakers are unaware of the sound difference between the two *p*s: they 'hear' aspiration, but they don't register it. It is unrelated to meaning in English. Aspiration is therefore not a *phonemic* property of English. On the other hand, voicing—the vibration of the vocal folds when they are close together and air from the lungs passes over them— is phonemic. We hear and *register* a difference in the pronunciation of *bit* and *pit* because the *b* in *bit* is voiced, while the *p* in *pit* is unvoiced. Other aspirated and nonaspirated pairs in English are the consonants *t* and *k*, and the words *top* and *stop*, *cool* and *school*. In each case, the aspirated consonant ripples the sheet of paper, even though it's unvoiced: it's not phonemic and it isn't registered, but it is physically and acoustically real. There is only one phoneme *p* in English. In languages where aspiration is phonemic, there are at least two *p* phonemes.

Language involves *displacement*: it is possible to refer to other times and places and to people and objects that are not present. Displacement allows speakers of a language to refer to events in the past, present and future whether visible or not to the speaker and his or her listeners. A cat arching its back and hissing at a dog means that it is upset in the presence of the dog. What the cat can't communicate is how it got similarly aggravated because of another dog's audacity yesterday. Nor can a cat indicate whether it will purr contentedly in its owner's lap tonight after its meal. Humans, in contrast, can talk about the future and the past. They can discuss places other than right here, right now. Here's an example with instances of displacement shown in italics:

> In *a phone conversation*, Jill tells her *childhood* friend Pauline *in Kansas* the following: '*Earlier today* as I was sitting in my university library *in New York*, restless and bored, I wondered about my boyfriend *Jack, who has been on a tour of Europe. Earlier today* he emailed telling me about what a great time he had *last night in Dublin*'.

On the surface, the distress calls made by vervet monkeys in Africa appear to be functioning like displacement. One call refers to an approaching predator on the ground, such as a leopard; another call denotes an imminent danger in a tree, such as a pit viper. A third call references a predator flying down from above, such as an eagle. These calls communicate potential danger, but they are not truly displacement because they are confined to the here and now. They are vocalised in the immediacy of the moment, as responses to perceived threats.

Language has infinite *productivity*: surprisingly, from a few sounds and a limited set of syntactic rules, an infinite number of new sentences can be generated. Productivity is a profoundly important feature of all human languages. An excerpt from the poem 'In Cabin'd Ships at Sea' by poet Walt Whitman illustrates the concept:

> Here are our thoughts, voyagers' thoughts,
> Here not the land, firm land, alone appears, may then by them be said,
> The sky o'erarches here, we feel the undulating deck beneath our feet,
> We feel the long pulsation, ebb and flow of endless motion,
> The tones of unseen mystery, the vague and vast suggestions of the briny world, the liquid-flowing syllables,
> The perfume, the faint creaking of the cordage, the melancholy rhythm,
> The boundless vista and the horizon far and dim are all here,
> And this is ocean's poem.

No one before Whitman in his vivid, expressive poem ever said, thought or wrote the same thing, in the same words. But even though the combination of words is unique, all fluent

English speakers can understand what Whitman means. Productivity exists even whether people understand the meaning of an utterance or not. In other words, a sentence can be grammatically correct but meaningless, a point famously made by linguist Noam Chomsky when he pointed out that although the sentence 'Colorless green ideas sleep furiously' likely has never before been uttered and is perfectly grammatical, it is completely meaningless (in contrast, another arrangement of exactly the same words is equally meaningless and yet ungrammatical: 'Furiously sleep ideas green colorless'). The point is to show that syntax (rules of sentence construction and word order in any language) and meaning are independent of each other. Stand-up comedian Dana Carvey grasped the point of productivity in his monologue about a made-up religion, the 'Cult of the Golden Orb':

> We put on our sandpaper pants and we get in the Plastic Punishment Room; we ask each other the holy question, Are you the lemon? ...
>
> [T]his can go on for weeks or months...[Lemons are] fitted with a sacred diaper made of pudding skins and duct tape...they wear wax lips and hum the theme to *Hawaii Five-O* 47 times; then they straddle a chicken, a small chimpanzee is attached to their back, they are fitted in a harness, and hoisted a hundred feet in the air; they are lowered slowly into a giant vat of lukewarm chocolate pudding as the other church members grab hands and repeat the sacred prayer, 'Squatting monkeys tell no lies'.

Ordinary speakers of any language, not just poets, dramatists, novelists and stand-up comedians, continually come up with new, grammatical sentences and other utterances that can be appreciated by others who speak the same language. Language productivity has emergent properties in the sense of the potential to generate infinitely complex, yet coherent, sentences (Cultural Snapshot 2.4). Productivity is only one part of what makes for great prose, poetry or comedy, but it is an indispensable part. Productivity, along with the other attributes of language and the ability to acquire a human culture, is fundamental to understanding sociocultural universals.

CULTURAL SNAPSHOT 2.4

Productivity and Emergence

Infinite productivity is a feature of human language that distinguishes it from other systems of communication, both human and nonhuman. The infinite productivity of language, what some call 'creativity', is an instance of emergence in the sense used in the physical and computer sciences. According to computer expert John Holland, emergence theory seeks to explain how life originates from simple physical and chemical components; for example, how a magnificent redwood arises from a small seed or how an ant colony functions without a central authority or complex intelligence. Chess is an example of emergence. Based on a limited number of playing pieces, a board and fewer than 25 rules, an infinite number of games can be played. In contrast, a game of tic-tac-toe has a limited number of predictable outcomes. The game is neither emergent nor especially productive.

According to Steven Pinker (1999, pp. 5–7), language involves combinatorial rules that give it infinite productivity. There are about 100,000 grammatically correct sentences in English that one can come up with that are five words long. 'A rose is a rose' is the kind of sentence structure for which there are tens of thousands of possibilities. For example, *a*, the first article or determiner in that sentence, could be replaced with *any*, *the*, *that* or *this*. Similarly, thousands of words in everyday English could be substituted for the noun *rose*. In fact, each word in the sentence could be replaced by others and still be grammatical. *On average*, for each word in a grammatical sentence like this one, there are about ten choices. For a five-word sentence, there are therefore 100,000 possibilities. For a six-word sentence, there are a million possibilities, and for a 20-word sentence, there are 100 million trillion possibilities.

Human language is like chess due to its inherent creative and emergent properties. Animal communication systems, in contrast, are more like tic-tac-toe. Only language is combinatorial and almost infinitely productive.

Selected Universals

Sociocultural universals, or just universals, are relatively easy to list, yet harder to define and explain. We talk about nine of them here, though there are in fact many more. Simply stated, universals are customs, behaviours or characteristics that are shared by all humans living in societies. Universals, though shared, are rarely identical. People everywhere construct shelters for themselves.

However, these refuges or homes vary from one place and society to another. Some people live in masonry houses, others in adobe structures built into cliffs; some have slept beneath rock overhangs, others inside skin-covered tipis or igloos built of snow or sod or thatched structures more than a hundred feet long called longhouses. While the specific form varies, every society makes use of a shelter of some kind. The universals covered in this chapter, all of which are significant to understanding human social life and the learned and shared traditions on which it depends, are:

- sociality (living in social groups);
- transmission of culture (enculturation and diffusion);
- religion and art;
- rules governing behaviour;
- ethnocentrism (bias against others);
- sex, gender and age categories;
- economy and exchange;
- classification of the environment.

Sociality

Perhaps the most obvious human universal is society itself. One can only understand the rest of the human story by grasping the rule of *sociality*, which is living in social groups. Social life and cooperation are key aspects of humanity, though not unique to us. Bottlenose dolphins in only a few places have learned to cooperate in strand feeding (Figure 2.2), indicative of sociality and culture in other mammals.

Figure 2.2 Bottlenose dolphins strand feeding at Kiawah Island, South Carolina, a learned and shared behaviour. Together facing the shoreline, these dolphins cooperate in producing a pressure wave that forces fish onto a mudbank, upon which the dolphins then leap to catch and devour them. Alamy.

Exceptions to this rule among humans are only temporary or illusory. Certain individuals have survived alone for extended periods of time, but no man or woman is truly an island. Ishi, the last known Yahi Indian (Chapter 4), had lived alone for years in the chaparral country of central California before coming to the attention of anthropologists in 1911 (Figure 2.3). Ishi had survived due to skills he had learned from his elders as a youth, such as fishing for salmon with a harpoon, hunting deer with a bow and arrows and making fire from scratch. Have you ever tried to make a functional harpoon or bow by yourself? Have you ever successfully rubbed two sticks together to ignite some kindling to start a fire? If you succeeded at either of these endeavours without any instruction, blog it or tweet it, then get pictures and put them on Facebook, for it would be worth announcing to your friends. Believe it or not, I know a few small societies in the Amazon that have *lost* the ability to make fire and an aerodynamically efficient arrow. These two activities are very difficult to complete successfully without assistance or instruction. All societies have mechanisms for conveying information, such as how to start a fire, to younger generations; the process of teaching and learning these cultural characteristics is *enculturation*.

Even eccentric recluses or medieval hermits grew up in a human society of some kind. They learned how to speak, behave, think and understand in ways that allowed them to survive the particular conditions in which they lived. Parents, siblings, friends, elders and other members of society all contributed in some way to their enculturation. Even if they were temporarily isolated from contact with fellow humans who shared their culture, as Ishi was, these individuals were socially dependent organisms, just like the rest of us.

Sociality involves communicating and learning ideas and behaviour. Cultural anthropology examines not only cultures found among groups of people and how these vary, but also investigates the underlying plans that people have for living and cooperating together. These underlying plans are blueprints of rules and regulations that render each

Figure 2.3 Ishi demonstrates binding the points of a harpoon, Deer Creek, California, 1914. © Phoebe A. Hearst Museum of Anthropology and the Regents of the University of California. Photograph by Alfred Kroeber. Catalogue no. 13030.

society distinctive. At the same time, these rules contain principles that are shared by all humankind, such as the importance of finding or constructing some form of shelter.

All societies consist of at least two generations: young and old. Humans experience a period of long infant dependency and child development. Because infants cannot walk, find food on their own, feed themselves or communicate their needs and desires in speech, they require care from older, enculturated humans.

This care typically lasts well into adolescence. In many societies, parents support their children, financially at least, well into biological adulthood. Care and financial support, regardless of where they are found, are typically, but not always, based on descent and kinship, or human relatedness.

The universality of a concept of human relatedness based on blood or any other shared substance was questioned by cultural anthropologist David Schneider (1918–1995), who studied people living on the island of Yap in the West Caroline Islands of the Pacific. To Schneider, that idea that 'blood is thicker than water' is a Euro–American belief, not a universal. The Yapese recognise that a person always has a living 'father' and 'mother' even if the parents are dead, because upon death, parents are replaced by persons from a 'reservoir' of other potential 'fathers' and 'mothers'. The Yapese do not reckon relatedness on the basis of biology. What in English is called a father–son relationship, for example, may not really exist in Yap, because while *citamangen* refers to a person classified as 'father' and *yak* refers to someone classified as 'son', a *citamangen* might simply be someone who gives food to a *yak*, not someone related to him biologically. According to Schneider, the Yapese concept of relatedness involves nurturing and giving, rather than genealogical, shared substance and descent from a common ancestor. Although there are terms for 'father', 'son' and other relatives, such as 'mother', 'aunt' and 'uncle', these terms describe relationships in the abstract, rather than those based on biology. 'Father' terms in many languages of Australia and Melanesia often mean simply 'husband of the mother': one's father is whoever one's mother happens to be married to at the moment and need not have anything to do with what Westerners call paternity. In contrast, if a Nuer widow cohabits with a man who is not in her dead husband's kin group and she bears children, they are considered to be the children of her deceased first husband, not their biological father. Relatives of the deceased husband can even take the children away from such a man legally. While all human societies have kinship systems and ways of classifying relationships, the structure of these systems, and the ways in which relationships are defined, vary from culture to culture. Still, most societies group people into a descent group based on a notion of relatedness through males, females or both. All societies use certain words, known as *kinship terms*, to classify relatives, such as 'aunt' or 'brother'. Every society has a method for determining how people are connected to one another

Ascribed and Achieved Status

All societies have a descent rule, which defines who one's parents are. It may not always be keyed to a biological relationship, as with adopted children and adoptive parents, though it often is. A descent rule is a notion of pedigree; it is an example of an *ascribed* status, or a position or social attribute that is given at birth. In many ancient societies, leaders were born, not made, as with the divine right of rulers who were believed to have descended from heaven, a belief found throughout ancient complex societies of Europe, Asia and the Americas. Being born into a role, such as that of ruler, exemplifies what is meant by ascribed status. In contrast, people may relate to others in terms of things they have accomplished in life, such as winning friends, gaining business associates or getting married. It is even possible to acquire kinship status through adoption or by participating in the same activities and sharing goods and services with everyone else. These roles represent *achieved* status, or a position or social attribute that someone attains through his or her own actions.

One's friends are part of an achieved status. One's family members, except in cases of adoption or kin gained through some activity, are given at birth. In all societies, the number of one's family members can be increased through adoption. Kin relations that are not ascribed include *affines*—in-laws—and *fictive kin*, which is the technical term for adopted persons, godparents, godchildren and sometimes friends whom one might call by terms such as 'brother' or 'sister'. Ethnographer Janet Carsten studied people living in a Malay fishing village on the island of Langkawi. She found that kinship was not simply given but developed from what people believed about shared substance. The people of Langkawi consider the substance of kinship to be blood (*darah*); they hold that mother's milk comes from blood. Infants who nurse from the same woman are therefore considered to be blood-related, whether they have common biological ancestry or not. Sex relations between those who nursed at the same breast are prohibited as incestuous, a common belief among Muslims, such as the people of Langkawi. Blood itself is made from food; thus, people who reside together around the same hearth in the same household and who consume the same foods are believed to share blood. Carsten (1997, p. 108) concludes that 'The hearth, and who one eats with, are as important in the formation of blood through life as the blood that one is born with, and which connects a child at birth to its siblings and other kin'. The people of Langkawi are not alone in the belief that kinship can be achieved. All known societies allow for adoption including *fictive kinship*.

Transmission of Culture

Learning how to live in the society of which one is a member is called *enculturation*. *Diffusion* is the adoption of cultural traits and behaviours by a recipient society from a donor society. Therefore, enculturation and diffusion involve one action common to both: transmission of culture. Enculturation is the transmission of culture across

time, from one generation to the next. It has sometimes been described as the vertical transmission of culture to distinguish it from diffusion, which is the horizontal transmission of culture across geographic space. Enculturation can also occur in a single generation, at school playgrounds, over the radio and on the internet.

Enculturation involves teaching and learning through use of a shared language. Although similar in sound, *acculturation* is a different notion. It refers to a society changing its identity due to contact with another society, which happens, for example, in colonisation (Chapter 9). Not all societies end up being acculturated, but all have ways of passing on shared behaviours and ideas to the next generation. Acknowledging the importance of enculturation permits anthropologists to appreciate cultural differences. For example, as we saw in Chapter 1, the Guajá consider insect larvae to be inedible. On the other hand, the Araweté people of the Amazon regard juicy beetle larvae found inside rotting palm fruits to be delicious. Ancient Roman aristocrats also considered beetle larvae to be a delicacy. The Romans and Araweté were enculturated to eat beetle larvae; the Guajá and most North Americans were enculturated differently.

Upon greeting a friend of the opposite sex, Parisians and Brazilians typically place air kisses on both cheeks or just lightly touch each other cheek-to-cheek. Japanese and Koreans, in contrast, bow to one another and typically find kissing in public rather rude. The French and Brazilians on the one hand and the Japanese and Koreans on the other have been enculturated differently regarding the use of gesture in greeting one another. Direct eye contact between acquaintances may also be interpreted differently: some cultures view it as positive and honest; others see it as potentially offensive or sexually suggestive. Variable views on eye contact, greeting methods and edibility of foods, when seen cross-culturally, are due to differences of enculturation.

While enculturation can explain many cultural differences, diffusion, in contrast, accounts for many similarities. Cultural anthropologists were pioneers in understanding the importance of diffusion of innovations. Ideas and objects diffuse from one society to another because they are useful. For example, the use of horses as mounts diffused from the Spanish explorers of the 1500s to the Plains Indians of North America. Most of the things we eat and drink today diffused from somewhere else: coffee, okra and cantaloupe come from Africa; potatoes from Peru; corn and tomatoes from Mexico; wheat, cattle, goats and sheep from the Near East; and rice from China. Inventions diffuse also, such as rugs (Persia), toilets (ancient Rome), hammocks (South America), gunpowder (China) and space technology (Russia and the United States).

Religion and Art

Religion is the organised belief in phenomena that cannot be demonstrated scientifically or empirically. Religion involves shared concepts of the supernatural, things that are imagined or are not evident to the senses. Supernatural concepts entail things people cannot see, touch or hear, though they may imagine themselves to do so. Religion typically brings with it a code of proper human conduct; that code, as with spirituality, which denotes the emotional intensity of religion, is learned and shared. For that reason, cultural anthropologists are very interested in religion and how people are influenced by it. Beliefs in the supernatural and ritual practices in general are markers of group identity that others may disdain, reject or find intolerable. Such attitudes may be the product of enculturation.

In the earliest human societies, art was probably fused to religion insofar as it could enhance spirituality, an emotional connection to unseen powers. Art is a fundamental aspect of behavioural modernity and it is found in every culture studied by anthropologists, though most societies, with the exception of Western ones, do not have a word for 'art' as a distinct domain. Art is notoriously difficult to define, but one way of describing it is as the aesthetic depiction of thoughts by a person, or artist, usually using materials outside the human body for the purpose of affecting or influencing the perceptions of others. Art, like religion, is universal. Visual art includes sculpture, painting, photography and architecture.

Many archaeologists are interested in the earliest known examples of art, such as the cave paintings of Pleistocene megafauna in France created about 35,000 years ago and of a red disk in Spain around 40,800 years ago (Figure 2.4). Thus far, the oldest known stencilled outlines of hands—which are typically found in most cave art—have been dated to 39,900 years ago on the Indonesian island of Sulawesi. All this artwork in diverse parts of the world suggests a flowering of behaviourally modern humankind in the late Pleistocene. Archaeologist David Lewis-Williams interprets these cave paintings, especially those of animals and human forms, as the work of individuals who underwent trance (an altered state of consciousness) to depict visions they may have had through contact with the supernatural world. Lewis-Williams argues that these paintings reflect altered states of consciousness to which humans are innately inclined due to neural circuitry in the brain unique to modern humans. In this sense, the human brain paradoxically accounts both for irrationality and rationality. Other archaeologists, such as David Whitley, think that only special persons with biologically determined mental problems, such as major clinical depression, would have had such visions and created images of large Pleistocene mammals paired with stick-figure humans or figures that are part human, part animal. Such people would have been society's specialists in the supernatural realm. Arguably, Palaeolithic cave painters were at one and the same time religious and artistic (Figure 2.4).

Symbolic sounds apart from speech can arguably be based on spirituality and emotion. John Blacking, an anthropologist and ethnomusicologist—a person who studies music cross-culturally—defines music as 'humanly organized sound' (Blacking 1973, p. 10).

Though cross-culturally people may not agree about what constitutes 'music', music itself is a universal form of art. According to ethnomusicologist Bonnie Wade:

> Every known group of people in the world exercises their creative imaginations to organize sound in *some way* that is different from the way they organize sound for speech.

> (Wade 2004, p. 3)

It probably has its origins in a fusion of symbols of spirituality and sound. And while the rules of organisation are different, music and speech are similar in interesting ways.

Figure 2.4 Famous rendering of the 'Sorcerer', a 13,000-year-old wall engraving inside the cave of
Trois-Frères in the Occitanie region of southern France. The ancient artist seems to depict
a human figure disguised in animal skins of several species, including a bear's forelegs and
a horse's tail, which suggests a belief in the changeability of humans into animals, real or
imaginary or vice-versa. Alamy.

Ethnographer and ethnomusicologist Anthony Seeger, who studied the relationship between the social organisation of the Suyá Indians of Central Brazil and their music and music-making, noted:

> With a limited number of phonetic possibilities, people around the world say many different things; with acoustical resources limited by the physics of sound production and perception, people around the world make many kinds of music for many different reasons.
>
> (Seeger 2004, pp. xiv–xv)

Ethnomusicologists tend to be cultural relativists. Ethnomusicologist Patrick Burke (2015, p. 24) says, 'We don't argue that one kind of music is better than another, because there isn't an objective position from which to make such a claim'. And whether one can appreciate it cross-culturally or not, music is clearly a universal art. So is dance (Figure 2.5). Both music and dance can be organised in a religious or spiritual context, and not only for aesthetic or entertainment purposes.

Figure 2.5 Waorani women of the Rio Napo basin, Amazonian Ecuador, participate in a ceremonial dance in 2019. Dance according to anthropologist Donald H. Brown (1991) is a human universal. Photo by Tod D. Swanson.

Rules Governing Behaviour

All known societies have rules that prohibit certain behaviours. The sum total of prohibitions is a code of morality. Although not all societies have 'law' in the sense of a written text with rules on how to proceed in the punishment of crimes and misdemeanours, they all have measures for dealing with disruptive, antisocial behaviours such as theft, verbal and physical abuse of others and homicide. Many traditional, kin-based societies used capital punishment to deal with the most serious offences, such as random violence and homicide. Other unacceptable behaviours may be seen as violations of moral codes and are punished by both civil and religious or supernatural penalties. These reprehensible behaviours are therefore considered to be *taboo*.

The Notion of Taboo

A taboo, from the ancient Polynesian word *tapu*, refers to a cultural prohibition on some behaviour or thought, the transgression of which is punishable by spiritual or civil penalties. It can also refer to people in special states who should be avoided, such as those mourning the loss of a loved one, mothers who have recently given birth or people who are endowed with special powers, such as chiefs or shamans or mothers-in-law. We discuss these categories of persons who should be avoided, or given special deference, in more detail in Chapter 3. In all societies, a taboo against incest defines persons who cannot be sexual partners.

The *incest taboo* is a rule specifying those kin, especially close kin, with whom sexual intercourse is expressly forbidden. Kin are people who share blood or DNA or whatever substance is considered to be the basis for a relationship determined by birth. A widely held biological explanation for the incest taboo is that the mating of close relatives will result in a large proportion of offspring with genetic disorders. This evolutionary explanation assumes that people are aware of such grave results. In most cultures, however, the emic explanation given for why most people do not engage in sexual activity with close relatives is related to revulsion at the thought of it, perception of immorality and the threat of supernatural punishments, such as being struck by lightning, rather than a fear of birth defects.

Tylor, who originally defined 'culture', as noted above, believed early humans would have gone extinct early on if men took their own sisters and daughters as wives. Tylor believed the incest taboo existed to force *exogamy*, which is the practice of marrying someone outside of one's own group. This idea is summed up in Tylor's famous dictum: 'Marry out or die out' (Tylor 1889, p. 267). Exogamy and the incest taboo, however, are not synonymous. One could logically commit incest and still marry out of one's nuclear family, reprehensible as that sounds. Finnish sociologist Edvard Westermarck proposed in 1891 that the incest taboo existed because people, when reared together as children, typically did not wish to have sex with one another. He believed that 'familiarity breeds contempt'. This concept is the familiarity or association theory of the incest taboo. Cultural anthropologists found support for Westermarck's theory in Taiwan and Israel. In Taiwan, wealthy families tended to pay *bridewealth* to other families to acquire a wife for their unmarried sons. Bridewealth refers to cash, goods in kind or both; it is a required payment made by the groom's family to the bride's family. Marriages that involved bridewealth tended to last a long time. Poor families could not always afford bridewealth, though.

Poor parents wishing to acquire a bride for their son had the option of adopting a girl from an even poorer family, without paying bridewealth. When she and their unmarried son were of the proper age, though raised together, they would marry. These marriages had high rates of instability and divorce. Similarly, people reared and enculturated together in Israeli communes did not tend to desire each other as sex partners or spouses; their marriages were often brittle, unhappy and infertile.

Two questions about Westermarck's theory as an explanatory tool remain: if people truly abhor the thought of sexual relations with close relatives, why is there a need for the taboo? What if a brother and sister are not reared together? Some, like Oedipus in Sophocles' play, might be separated from their nuclear families at birth. Incest could occur without the contempt formula because by definition such individuals were not reared together. An incest taboo, to be truly effective, would require that people recognise their close relatives. In *Oedipus Rex*, Sophocles tells us this might not always happen: Oedipus failed to recognise Jocasta as his mother. That failure of recognition is, of course, the central irony of the play. Westermarck's theory was not intended to explain the taboo's effectiveness; rather, he sought to explain the universality of the incest taboo and the fact that it covered most potential cases of incest in which close relatives know and recognise each other.

Some cultural anthropologists have questioned whether the incest taboo is really universal because apparent exceptions exist. Brother and sister marriage was required in the ruling dynasties of a few societies. The Inca emperor of the Andes, in the last 30 or so years of that empire, was required to take his full-blooded sister in wedlock; the Ptolemaic dynasty of Egypt required that each pharaoh be the product of brother–sister marriage. Both the Inca emperor and the Egyptian pharaohs were considered to be deities on earth, not human beings, so the incest taboo that applied to ordinary mortals did not apply to them. In the early sixteenth century, the leader of the Calusa Indians of southwest Florida took his sister as one of his many wives. Powerful chiefs in Hawai'i likewise married their sisters. Such chiefs were believed to have awesome power. A commoner who—even by mistake—touched the chief could be put to death. These high-ranking chiefs were the offspring of brothers and sisters who themselves had brothers and sisters as parents. While incest was accepted among chiefs, commoners who committed brother–sister incest were put to death.

These deviations from the universality of the incest taboo are isolated, though they have something in common. The incest of royalty is an extreme condensation of the descent rule that protects the perceived purity of the ruling line and its material possessions. In other words, all the wealth, power and property stay in the family when the offspring of an incestuous union inherit.

Ethnocentrism

Cultural relativism considers all cultures to be, in principle, equal in moral and intellectual terms to one another. In contrast, *ethnocentrism* is associated with the notion that one's own group is more ethical and worthy of one's love, respect and allegiance than any other group. Ethnocentrism is the prejudice that members of another culture, cultural 'others', are leading lives unsuited to proper human beings. Ethnocentrism is not necessarily outrageously bigoted and ludicrous; it can be subtle. Edward Said (1935–2003) was a literary critic who influenced many cultural anthropologists. He wrote:

It is perfectly natural for the human mind to resist the assault on it of untreated strangeness; therefore cultures have always been inclined to impose complete trans- formations on other cultures, receiving these other cultures not as they are but as, for the benefit of the receiver, they ought to be.

(Said 2003, p. 67)

Ethnocentrism usually involves stereotypes characterising those other cultures as disgust- ing, shameful, inferior, ill-bred, disreputable and moronic. In its extreme form, it may question their status as humans (Chapter 1). Ethnocentrism is a generalised xenophobia, or fear of outsiders, that varies cross-culturally, but is nonetheless found in all societies.

Any society that consists of several different *ethnic groups* may have ethnocentric beliefs. An ethnic group, or ethnicity, is a subset of society whose members are self-identified by certain habitual behaviours or characteristics they exhibit. Ethnic groups differ from kin groups, which are defined in terms of human relatedness via some shared substance. Practices or characteristics that define an ethnic group may include clothing, architec- ture, distinctive shared religious activities and beliefs, naming practices and language dia- lects. Some of these may conflict with standards of another culture; in 2010, the French Parliament banned the use of any clothing concealing the face in public venues. It's called the 'Burqa Bill' and prohibits specifically the use of masks, balaclavas and niqabs. The *niqab* is the traditional Hanbali Muslim female veil that covers the face entirely except for the eyes. The reason for the ban is twofold. France is a secular state, and therefore does not accept the use of religious paraphernalia being publicly displayed. In addition, in some government circles, there are security concerns specifically focused on the veil or other kinds of body covering that could be used to conceal a weapon, such as a bomb by a would-be suicide bomber. In contrast, there is a group in France called the Collective Against Islamophobia that is trying to cultivate tolerance for certain Islamic religious prac- tices, including women's obligations to use the full veil in certain sects, such as Hanbali Islam, of the religion.

Dress styles are among a few of the criteria that set an ethnic group apart from the rest of society; other factors may be historical or economic, such as specialisation in certain crafts or professions that members of other ethnic groups avoid. In some cases, a society restricts members of an ethnic group to a few selected occupations and allows them no other way to make a living. Or ethnic groups can be assigned to special kinds of housing distinctive from everyone else; in some Islamic countries, the size of Christian churches is restricted so that they do not appear larger than mosques. Ethnic groups usually develop a chronology of their past that includes migration from a place of origin and share an experience of discrimination in that place.

Cultural anthropologists have helped reduce the incidence of ethnocentrism by chal- lenging the validity of xenophobia and racial and ethnic stereotypes. For more than a century, they have done so by advancing the concept of culture, including the reasons it stays the same through enculturation and the reasons it changes through historical contin- gency. In place of ethnocentrism, anthropologists have promoted cultural relativism as a superior basis on which to begin t o understand different cultures.

Sex, Gender and Age Categories

Cultural anthropologists have also worked to distinguish between sex differences and gender. One's sex—man or woman if assigned male or female at birth—is a biological fact; gender, in contrast, is socially constructed, based on how people conceptualise sex differences and what they consider proper behaviour for each sex. Therein lies the variability cross-culturally. Sex differences in humans and other mammals are rather straightforward: they result from the presence or absence of a Y chromosome. A male inherits his Y chromosome from his biological father; a female inherits an X chromosome from her father. These chromosomal characteristics result in differences in male and female endocrine systems and genitalia. External, physical differences between the sexes are known as *sexual dimorphism*. Societies construct

gender in part upon sexual dimorphism. Gendered differences cross-culturally are seen in dress and hairstyle differences. In the Amazon, Araweté men cover their genital area by tying the foreskin around the glans penis with cotton cordage; Araweté women use cotton fabric they make themselves to fashion knee-length skirts, always worn in public, which they dye dark red. Ka'apor men wear trousers today, though they formerly wore a string to tie up the foreskin of the penis, as with the Araweté; the women wear homemade dresses cut from a single piece of fabric, though they used to wear cotton skirts, like the Araweté. The raw material in bodily ornamentation may be the same, such as cotton fabric for clothing in these cases, but the way it is worn differs. For example, in peninsular Malaysia, Batek males can wear flowers as armbands; only women can wear flowers in their hair for decorative purposes.

Beliefs about sexual dimorphism and human physiology may also be gendered. Societies often assign emotional states and certain abilities or inabilities to the people who behave, dress and speak according to a specific gender norm. For example, among North Americans, people—often women—who behave in ways we consider feminine may be considered poor drivers, but such people may also be thought to be more considerate or sensitive, in general, than people—usually men—who behave in masculine ways.

Fragrances are commonly gendered. Although there are many brands of deodorant, Western society has two main categories: one for men, one for women. The same is true of cologne and perfume. One fragrance is not necessarily more pleasing than another, but we categorise one as feminine, and the other as masculine. Among the Ka'apor, only women use the perfumed roots of a cultivated sedge, tied to their waists, to enhance their body fragrance. Ka'apor men, in contrast, may use the sweet-smelling resin of a tree in the frankincense family to rub in their armpits as deodorant.

Where the sexual division of labour is sharply delineated, there is a political hierarchy of genders in which males dominate females in public space and political discourse, though perhaps not in domestic settings. Reversals of gendered political authority, if seen at all, occur in myth and literature. The Munduruku of the Central Amazon live in circular villages with a clubhouse or men's house in the middle. Adult men spend most of their leisure time in the men's house; their wives and children of both sexes live in family dwellings arranged along the edge of the village circle. The division of labour is fairly strict: only men hunt and clear gardens; only women make manioc bread, gather firewood and fetch water.

The men's house has a darkened chamber attached to it that contains three long, wooden, cylindrical trumpets called *karoko*. These are phallic symbols—representations of the penis—that call to mind male domination of society, according to ethnographers Yolanda and Robert Murphy. They are similar in sound and construction to the *didgeridoo* used by Aboriginal Australians. Among the Munduruku, only men can play *karoko*; women are not allowed to touch or even look at the trumpets. They are considered the source of male power, and their sound is believed to be pleasing to totemic ancestors of Munduruku clans, which are patrilineal. But according to Munduruku cosmogony, women once owned the trumpets; when they did, men were subordinated to them. At that time, men lived in the dwellings along the village perimeter, and women occupied the clubhouse; men gathered firewood, prepared manioc bread and cared for children. The one thing women could not do, however, was hunt; men could hunt, and game meat was used as a sacrifice to the trumpets. Men won the trumpets from the women because only men could please the trumpets with this kind of sacrifice. In this way, the men wrested control of the trumpets from the women, expelled women from the men's house and took over the public space, according to the myth.

Politics, public discourse and occupation of public space were also male dominated in ancient Athens, Greece. Yet there are reversals of male power in literature, especially Greek tragedies. In Sophocles' play *Antigone* (ca. 441 BC), the king forbids his niece, Antigone, to bury her brother, alleging him to be a traitor. But the moral code of the family in ancient Greece required a sister to bury her brother, so Antigone defies her uncle. The king then sentences her to death, but in doing so incurs the wrath of the gods, who destroy him and his family. Women's rights are vindicated over a male-dominated political system by an appeal to morality in the play. In fact, most Greek tragedies of this period, though written by men, feature powerful, pivotal women characters. It is a literary reversal of male-dominated political society, not so different in concept from the mythical matriarchy of the Munduruku.

Gender differences permeate most activities regardless of culture or language. In other words, gender has a powerful influence on individual ideas and how they are perceived and expressed, as well as on a person's behaviour, including speech behaviour. On average, men have the lowest pitches because of the size of the vocal cords. They typically exploit a lower end of pitch range of human speech than women. But most speech by both sexes in all languages occurs in the same range. The highest and lowest ends tend to be female and male voices, respectively; on the other hand, men speaking in falsetto can duplicate high pitches normally only in women's range. The potential pitch range of women's speech nevertheless is double that of men's. In many cases, women's higher pitch is used to express a wider range of emotions. For example, Japanese has a variety called 'women's speech' (*onna kotoba*) that is ideally polite, soft and indirect. Yet gendered speech is not always directly related to sexual dimorphism: in Malagasy (spoken in Madagascar), feminine speech is direct and blunt, whereas masculine speech is indirect and low-key.

I found differences in the ways plant names (and other nouns) are pronounced among the Sirionó indigenous people of the eastern Bolivian Amazon region depending on the speaker's sex. Women often stress syllables in plant names differently than men. In men's speech, many tree names, such as the name of a tree with fibrous bark very useful for making rope, are stressed (or accented) on the last or next-to-last syllable: for this tree, men say *imbei* and women say *ímbei*. Another tree, called the 'grasshopper tree', men call *turukushin*, whereas women say *turukushín*. Different accent patterns therefore sound either feminine or masculine to the Sirionó ear, even though they refer to the same kind of tree.

In these ways, tasks, behaviours, clothing and other forms of material culture and even language come to be associated with one category of people rather than another. The categories are only partly derived from the biology of sex. One's sex is either male or female. Gender is universally recognised socially as consisting of at least two categories: masculine and feminine. In Chapter 3, we consider how gender varies cross-culturally.

In addition to distinguishing between the sexes using gender roles, all societies divide people into age categories. The process of enculturation begins in the earliest of these age categories. In my dialect of English, these categories can be labelled as infant or baby, very young child or toddler, older child or juvenile, adolescent or teenager, young adult, middle-aged or mature woman or man, elderly or old woman or man and very old or very elderly woman or man. These labels refer to *age grades*. Although they do not calculate years of a person's lifetime with a calendar, Mardu Aborigines of western Australia are much more specific than I am in their socially acceptable, nonnumeric age-grade terms. For example, for 'infant' or 'baby', they use myriad terms with distinct meanings, including 'newborn', 'unable to sit up', 'able to crawl' and 'walking but only just' (Tonkinson 1991, p. 82). There are at least four terms for the toddler category in Mardu, suggesting that they recognise and name younger age grades on the basis of behaviour. Finally, all human societies are organised into some form of age hierarchy. Older people generally have some power over younger people. The universality of this rule is at least partly based on the success of enculturation.

Economy and Exchange

All human societies have some kind of economy, which is the patterned production, distribution and consumption of goods and services, the most basic of which is food. All human societies develop ways to acquire and produce food, but these methods are often quite different cross-culturally. Likewise, all societies have ways to distribute food and appropriate ways to consume it.

Reciprocity

Reciprocity, which is the near-equal exchange of goods and services among individuals over time, is found in all societies in some form. Anthropologist Marcel Mauss (1872–1950) considered gifts to be fundamental to the organisation of society itself, not just to the economy. Mauss discovered that in virtually all cultures, gifts were not simply material items passed from one person to another. Gifts were actually obligate bonds of continuing interpersonal relationships. That is, when someone has vouchsafed a gift by another, they often feel honour-bound to give something back in return. Then the original donor makes another contribution to the original recipient and the cycle of giving and receiving continues. In other words, reciprocity *obligates* people to be in continuous, face-to-face relationships.

There are three kinds of reciprocity, according to the late cultural anthropologist Marshall Sahlins (1930–2021). *Generalised reciprocity* is the principal mechanism of exchange of food and many other goods and services in small-scale, relatively self-contained societies, though it is found in some form in all societies, especially within networks of families and friends. The other forms of reciprocity are *balanced reciprocity*, which involves the tendering of gifts of relatively equal value between two trading partners at the same time, and *negative reciprocity*, which assumes haggling and the attempt by each party to get the better of the other. All three forms occur typically in face-to-face situations.

Reciprocity, especially generalised reciprocity, is part of the survival and success of hunting-and-gathering societies worldwide, including the Ju/'hoansi, who, according to ethnographer Richard Lee (2013, p. 198), 'reproduce themselves as a society while limiting the accumulation of wealth and power'. Everyone is expected to share goods and services with others, all of the time. This means that individuals are discouraged from hoarding wealth at the expense of the group, which could lead to local shortages, famines and disruptions of society in the Kalahari Desert where they live. Unfortunately, with the recent infusion of alcohol and AIDS into Ju/'hoansi society, this pattern of life is breaking down.

Food sharing is at the root of generalised reciprocity. Ethnographer Loretta Cormier (2003, p. 43) described the Guajá, who until recently lived exclusively as hunter–gatherers in the eastern Brazilian Amazon (Chapter 1), as a people with a code of *demand sharing*:

> If someone asks for food, it is always given; not only from the cooking pot, but even from the bowl out of which one is eating… An individual may stop in a hut, eat a little or a lot from another's bowl, bring in additional foods to be shared, and then move on to another hut.

Reciprocity in egalitarian societies, as with the earliest of human societies, constituted an essential element of survival. For that reason, reciprocity was very likely part of the moral system of the earliest human cultures. The end result of exchanges in a system of generalised reciprocity is roughly equal, the time to repay a gift is not specified and the value of a gift is not explicitly calculated. Such reciprocity is not unique to egalitarian societies such as the Ju/'hoansi and the Guajá.

Generalised reciprocity in complex Western societies is seen in acts of seemingly selfless food sharing within and between friends and families: people try to invite friends to dinner to reciprocate an earlier invitation. They usually do so without saying something like, 'The real reason we've invited you over tonight is because we have to pay you back for the dinner you served us at your house'. People tend to remove the price tags of purchased gifts for others in modern, complex societies, another example of reciprocity in capitalist society. In Japan, when people give each other money, they put it in an envelope both to conceal it and to emphasise its nonfinancial importance to the giver; in addition, the person receiving the gift should not open it with the donor being present, perhaps because the value of the item might exceed what the recipient might be able to reciprocate in the future. These are also ways to dequantify the gift, as gifts are supposed to be personal, and money is by definition impersonal (Chapter 9). In terms of societal rules and institutions, reciprocity through food sharing is a positive rule; it is a basic required activity. *Taboos*, in contrast, are negative rules.

Classification of the Environment

All societies name and classify important aspects of their environment, including the plants and animals that make it up: the climate, weather and astronomical phenomena they observe; the landscapes, waterscapes and geographic features that occur locally such as hills, mountains and ravines; the colours of things, animate or not, in one's surroundings; and the effects people have on their environs, for example, through the construction of roads, buildings, irrigation canals, dams and so on—what is sometimes called the built environment. For the purpose of illustration, we examine the classificatory systems for colour and living things.

Basic Colour Terms

At first glance, colour would seem to be a category of equal importance to people no matter what language they speak. But anthropologists Brent Berlin and Paul Kay suggest that it isn't. They analysed 11 basic colour terms such as *black, white, red* and *green* in 98 languages from six continents. They found that all languages had colour terms and that a society's level of technology was associated with the number of terms. Of the 11 basic terms identified, the Dani of New Guinea had only two: black and white. English and languages associated with industrial technology had at least 11: black, white, red, green, yellow, blue, orange, pink, grey, brown and purple. Other languages had between two and 11 colour terms. Berlin and Kay also found that colour terms are encoded in a given sequence cross-linguistically. No language had fewer than two terms, black and white. If a language had three terms, the third was red; if four, the term was green or yellow and so on. If a language had a term for blue, then it would also have the terms yellow, green, red, white and black. This sequence is called an *implicational universal.*

The definition of basic colour terms and their evolutionary sequence has been critiqued. Berlin and Kay suggested the colour spectrum be defined by hue, or tonality of a colour (the redness of red, for example); saturation, or the degree of blackness or whiteness of a colour; and brilliance, which makes some colours dazzling, like fuchsia pink, whereas others are dull, like muddy brown. Cultural and linguistic anthropologist Victoria Bricker noted that in some languages, colours are discriminated not so much by hue, saturation and brilliance, but by texture, moisture, shape and size, as in Yucatec, a Maya language spoken in Mexico. According to Berlin and Kay, Maya languages had five colour terms. Using the criteria suggested by Bricker, Yucatec had more than 20. These findings and other studies by linguistic anthropologists suggest that colour is an important feature of classifying and describing aspects of the environment cross-culturally, regardless of how the category is defined.

Names for Flora and Fauna

Ethnobiology is the study of how humans categorise and interact with plants, or flora, and animals, or fauna. Brent Berlin proposed that most languages categorise living things by one criterion: gross morphological discontinuities in nature. Everywhere, people distinguish between a tall, erect tree and a flattened, squiggly vine. They are recognising gross morphological differences: a large, straight-growing stem versus a twisted, curving one. In my dialect of English, terms such as *tree* and *vine* are used to distinguish these types of plants on the basis of shape and size. Such terms, found in all languages, are referred to as *life form* terms. The capacity to distinguish between and classify life forms is believed to be universal. Discontinuities recognised by speakers of a language can be identified through the study of the terms and the system of ranking them that a society uses, such as the Linnaean system of plant and animal classification, which begins with *kingdom* and ends with *species* or *subspecies* at the least inclusive level.

If a language has only one plant life form term, according to cultural anthropologist Cecil Brown, it is *tree*; if two, they are *tree* and *grerb*, a category for grasses and herbs. English discriminates between types of trees and types of vines. One might identify several one-word terms for a tree, such as *oak, maple* or *pine*. These terms are *folk generics*. Found in all languages, folk generics are the first thing people think of when you ask them to list all the members of a life form, such as *tree* or *bird*, that they know. In most cultures, folk generics are the most readily available concepts that come to mind when people think about flora and fauna.

Another way of saying this is that, of the different ranks in ethnobiological classification, folk generics have the most *salience* to society. One might also know two-word expressions, such as *white oak*, *black oak* or *live oak*. These are *folk specifics*: kinds of the folk generic *oak*. Another example of a folk generic is *bear*, which in English is part of the larger class, or life form, *mammal*. *Black bear* and *polar bear* are folk specifics of the folk generic *bear*, in the emic classification of animals in English. A *koala bear* is not a folk specific of *bear*. It's not a bear at all; it's a marsupial, which most people would distinguish from real bears. For that reason, Berlin has pointed out that naming practices, or nomenclature, used to identify plants and animals are not perfect guides to emic classification. In other words, a linguistic anthropologist cannot be certain that every animal named *bear* actually belongs to the conceptual category of *bear*. This holds cross-culturally.

Life forms, folk generics and folk specifics are three different, universal ranks of ethnobiological classification recognised cross-culturally. Another rank is *unique beginner*, which refers to the name of an entire *semantic domain* or set of objects or ideas that speakers of a language associate together. *Plant* is a unique beginner in English; it refers to the semantic domain of vascular photosynthetic organisms. Similarly, *animal* is a unique beginner that refers to a domain including all vertebrate and invertebrate fauna. Many languages do not have a word for plant or animal; in other words, they don't have a label for these unique beginners, throwing into question whether any ethnobiological semantic domains are universal. Berlin argued that even without a label, the notions *flora* and *fauna* exist universally because terms that refer only to things and parts of things we would call *plant* or plant material and *animal* or animal parts are found in the domain. This suggests that some conceptual domains, such as *plant* or *animal*, are universal, and therefore have some biological basis. When there is no term for a domain recognised by the speakers of a language, linguistic anthropologists call it a *covert category*.

According to cultural anthropologist Scott Atran, there is a primordial human proclivity to name and classify living things and the natural environs, which suggests that even the Linnaean classification system is part of an enculturated Western folk system. Anthropologists interested in ethnobiology study the similarities and differences in how people categorise and name living things. Classification and nomenclature systems, as with the rest of culture, are learned and shared. Their study reveals how people recognise, understand and behave towards their environments over the long term.

Summary

Learned and shared concepts and behaviours that are found in all cultures are called *sociocultural universals*. These are derived from capacities we have inherited for acquiring language and culture. Human culture, which always involves learning and sharing, is also cumulative: innovations from past cultures are retained and elaborated through time. Human language consists of several definitive attributes including syntax, phonology, arbitrariness, displacement and productivity. Capacities for language and culture are evident in universals. Nine universals are discussed here: sociality, transmission of culture (through enculturation and diffusion), religion and art, rules governing behaviour, ethnocentrism, sex and gender distinctions, age categories, economic and exchange patterns and thinking about and classifying the environment.

Further Reading

Abe 1995; Ames and Maschner 1999; Atran 1993; Balée 1997; Befu 1963; Bellwood 2005; Berlin 1992; Berlin and Kay 1969; Besnier 1990; Bilefsky 2014; Blacking 1973; Bricker 1999; Brooker 2009;

C.H. Brown 1984; D.E. Brown, 1991; Burke 2015; Burling 2005; Burton 1985 (pp. 129–131); Campagno 2009; Carsten 1997; Chomsky 1957; Coe 2003; Cormier 2003; Ember 1996; Endicott 1999; Endicott and Endicott 2008; Evans-Pritchard (1940) 1969 (pp. 192–193), (1951) 1990 (p. 116); Fagan 2010; Galvin 2001; Gates 2004; Goggin and Sturtevant 1964; Goodale 1994; Gray and Jordan 2000; Guynup and Ruggia 2004; Henshilwood and Marean 2003; Henton 1995; Hewlett 1991; Hewlett and Cavalli-Sforza 1986; Itakura and Tsui 2004; Kelly 2000; Keyes 1997; Kobayashi and Kahshima 1997; Kroeber 2004; Lai et al. 2001; Lee 2013, 2007; Lee and Daly 1999; Lévi-Strauss 1969; Lewis-Williams 2010; Martin 1996 (pp. 132–133); Meggitt 1965; Moffitt 2008; Murphy and Murphy 2004 (pp. 111–117); *New York Times* 2008; Pitulko et al. 2004; Polanyi 1957; Read 2001; Rogers 1983; Rupp 2003; Sahlins 1972, 1976b; Savage-Rumbaugh et al. 1998; Schneider 1984; Seeger 2004; Senders and Truitt 2007; Stringer 2012; Tomasello 1999, 2003; Tonkinson 1991; Tylor (1888, p. 267) 1924 (vol. 1), 1889; Wade 2004; Wen-Hsiung and Saunders 2005; Westermarck 1891; Whitley 2009; Wilford 2014; Wolf 2004; Wolf and Durham 2004

Cultural Snapshots

2.1   Brown 1991; Burling 2005; Burton 1985; Goodall 1986; Hunt and Gray 2004; Mithen 1996; Simmel (1900) 1978; Weir et al. 2002

2.2   Burling 2005; Hall 1990

2.4   Burling 2005; Harrison and Raimy 2007; Holland 1998; Pinker 1999

3   Cultural Variation

Overview

Cultural anthropology focuses on the study of similarities and differences in culture. Chapter 2 covered certain key sociocultural universals. This chapter examines more of the ethnological variation anthropologists have concerning those same universals. That is, this chapter is about the differences, focusing on the specific institutions of humankind that exhibit cultural variation. Cultural variation comes about through historical contingencies. Societies have their own unique histories of political developments, population growth or decline and technological change. They have experienced different patterns of immigration and emigration, acculturation, assimilation and environmental change. These contingencies have made societies different from each other since the first modern humans left Africa some 100,000 years ago.

Variation in Key Cultural Institutions

Cultural institutions are fundamental building blocks in society, practices or beliefs that people identify as central or fundamental to who they are culturally. Ethnologists explore the reasons for and expressions of cross-cultural variation in institutions. In terms of specific variations on each of them, we examine the same sociocultural universals discussed in Chapter 2:

- Sociality
- Transmission of culture
- Religion and art
- Rules governing behaviour
- Ethnocentrism
- Sex, gender and age
- Economy and exchange
- Classification of the environment

Naming Practices

The universal of sociality means all human societies include social institutions that formally connect some people to others. One way to do this is to identify individual members through personal names. Naming practices like these connect people to their children while both are living. They also connect married couples to each other, since both parents are named for the child they have in common. In the case of the fishing and hunting people of the mangrove forests of western Malaysia, the Ma' Betisék (also known as the Mah Meri), when a married couple (called a *kelamin*) sets up a household of their own, they acquire a household name (*gelah odo'*) that they use instead of their given names. Ma' Betisék naming therefore identifies an individual with other individuals, or a group larger than his or her immediate family. The same is true of last names in North American society, which identify children with their father, his brothers, his unmarried sisters, his father, his father's brothers and unmarried sisters, his father's father and so on. This naming system relies upon the use of *patronyms* (literally, 'father's name').

In rare cases, as with the Matsigenka Indians of Peru, people may not receive a given name at all; instead, they get nicknames referring to something unusual they did or that happened to them that may be used by only one or two other people. Most Matsigenka refer to each other by kin terms, making personal names unnecessary. Some cultures produce many given names, others few, or, in the Matsigenka case, none.

Kinds of Names

In many societies, people only get one name at birth or shortly thereafter. Mongolians have a stock of 15,000 names. These names are sometimes borrowed from Russian or Tibetan, but most names are derived from things in the environment. The idea is for each individual to be named separately. Thus, Mongolian names do not identify people with specific ethnic or kin groups, even though the stock of names is, in proportion to population, quite large. Elders are rarely called by their names; rather, they are addressed with kinship terms or other terms of respect.

As among Mongolians, naming practices elsewhere often reflect social status. Unless given permission to do so, one would not normally address the President of the United States by his or her first name, but rather as Mr or Madame President. The Queen of England is similarly referred to as 'Her Majesty'. Use of a nickname by anyone other than a close friend or family member would be inappropriate and disrespectful. As in these examples, names can reflect the ways in which a society ranks or organises its members. They can also indicate activities or occupations, as do surnames (last names) in English and many European languages. Such names originated in the medieval period when people lived in small communities with a limited number of craftspeople and only a few occupations. Some examples include Baker, Brewer, Butcher, Carpenter, Mason, Merchant, Miller, Shepherd, Smith, Taylor and Weaver. These names initially would be passed down to the next generation only if a man's son went into the same occupation, which was common in medieval times. Acquiring the father's surname was also important for passing on property in medieval Europe; inheritance rules tended to follow a patrilineal rule. Surnames were inherited as patronyms (names from one's father) in civilisations as disconnected historically as Western Europe and East Asia. Ethnographer James C. Scott suggests the reason surnames became standard in many societies has to do with the consolidation of state power; with everyone having both a first name and a surname, the state's centralised taxing and political authority could now 'identify, unambiguously, the majority of its citizens'. In some cultures, there are rules for name sharing, as is the case of the Ju/'hoansi hunter-gatherers of Africa. The Ju/'hoansi do not have surnames, and they have a limited number of personal names: there are only 35 possible men's names and 32 possible women's names. For Ju/'hoansi, name sharing connotes common identity and substance in a literal way. They live in a society with thousands of persons divided into many small, mobile groups called *bands*. Therefore, many people have the same name, something that Mongolians try to avoid. The Ju/'hoansi culture requires that a person's namesake call his or her relatives by the same terms the name source would call them. The Netsilik people of the central Canadian Arctic likewise have such name sharing. Like the Ju/'hoansi, the Netsilik are mobile and depend on personal ties across a network of kin on both sides of their families that are spread out over thousands of square miles. Name sharing in both cultures means that if a man named Adam arrived in the house of someone also called Adam, the new arrival would call his host's father 'father', his mother, 'mother', his sister, 'sister' and so on. Name sharing results in ready-made families of sorts, and if family members owe one support in the form of services and favours, the more the better in an environment where survival skills alone are not enough to keep one alive and well for long.

Personal names, though, can be potentially dangerous, depending on the cultural context. In criminal subcultures of the United States and elsewhere, it is common practice for an individual to go by numerous different names—or aliases—during her/his lifetime to avoid detection and arrest. Killers of enemies and sorcerers—real or perceived—among the Awajún people of the Peruvian Amazon sometimes changed their name up to three times in the course of their adult lives to evade being singled out for revenge. The Ka'apor and Munduruku Indians of the Brazilian Amazon have strict rules against speaking the names of the dead, which they assert might attract the unwanted attention of malevolent spirits. Similar beliefs are found in Inner Mongolia, where parents do not name infants in honour of deceased ancestors. In fact, children's names should not even be spoken. Instead, parents sometimes use names such as 'Bad Dog', 'Smelly' and even 'Shitty', according to ethnographer Caroline Humphrey. This way, the spirits will not become jealous of healthy, robust children and attack them. Given names are only used once a child has survived the dangers of infancy. The Awajún (formerly Aguaruna) people once known for shrinking trophy heads of enemies do not believe death comes naturally but from sorcery. Men who have killed others accused of sorcery were allowed to change their names up to three times in their lifetimes to evade being singled out for revenge.

Personal names in modern complex societies can also become glorified or vilified as cultural attitudes change towards the individuals who carried those names. In the United States, in the wake of racial injustices in the 2010s, including rogue police violence, projects of renaming buildings and streets that had been originally named to honour white supporters of slavery or segregation in the Jim Crow (segregationist) past have been underway. Statues and monuments dedicated to such figures have been taken down in many cities (Figure 3.1). These activities increased considerably after the death of George Floyd, an unarmed African American man killed by police in May 2020 in Minneapolis. Labels of professional sports teams that reference Native Americans, and whose fans sometimes paint themselves in redface (which is deemed as racist as whites painting themselves in blackface), are under review and being changed. These include the Washington Redskins (currently Washington Football Team), Cleveland Indians, Chicago Blackhawks and Kansas City Chiefs.

Cultural anthropologists care about personal names because the rules governing their bestowal, acquisition and use convey information about social organisation and the relationship of the individual to the group. As with all cultural phenomena, naming practices are learned. They are part of the process of enculturation. Just as beliefs about names vary cross-culturally, so too do rituals related to the life cycle. Societies recognise and celebrate different stages of life in a number of diverse ways.

Figure 3.1 Confederate General Robert E. Lee's brass statue is removed on 19 May 2017, in New Orleans. The mayor and city council determined that it represented white supremacy at the time it was erected (late nineteenth century). The statue's removal preceded the removal or destruction of several other monuments honouring figures associated with racism and slavery, in cities across the United States, after the police killing of unarmed African American George Floyd in May 2020. Photo by Margaux Fisher.

Diverse Concepts of Human Relatedness

The shared substance of kinship, however, tends to vary cross-culturally. For the Mae Enga of New Guinea, it is semen, not blood, that links men (fathers, brothers and sons) as relatives; for ancient Koreans, it was bone. Sometimes, it is a concept or action, such as dreaming, which is necessary for reproduction and relatedness to others to occur. For example, at birth, a Tiwi Aborigine of Australia is believed to belong to his or her mother's descent group. The Tiwi believe an infant is conceived by a spirit that enters a mother's womb. Sexual intercourse is also necessary for pregnancy to occur, but it was believed to be insufficient for reproduction. The spiritual element was essential.

No matter how people determine relatedness—by blood, semen or bone—they reckon kinship to those both living and dead, often reaching back several generations. In the pastoral Nuer society of sub-Saharan East Africa, which has several clans or descent groups, everyone belongs to the clan of his or her father. Nuer clans may have begun 12 generations ago, but people's genealogical memory lapses after about five or six generations. As a person's ancestors become increasingly distant through time, memories of them begin to fade. Compared with many other societies, however, Nuer genealogical memory is relatively long. This may be related to complex rules concerning the inheritance of a deceased person's property, foremost of which are cattle. In the case of the Kwakwaka'wakw of the Northwest Coast, it was a point of honour to know one's genealogy and to be acquainted with the history surrounding the family crest (or *totem*). These are societies in which genealogies are important.

Royal houses can typically trace ancestral lines far into the past: both Queen Elizabeth II of the United Kingdom and Queen Margrethe II of Denmark are linked by Conrad I of Oldenburg, a common ancestor 19 generations ago who reigned from 1344 to 1368. Whereas before the internet most people in Western societies probably did not have a firm grip on their genealogies beyond three or four generations, new genealogy businesses and organisations have enabled the extension of many persons' genealogical memories back multiple generations because so many records and databases are now available electronically. In contrast, many Ka'apor and Munduruku people of Amazonia, along with the Mardu Aborigines of Australia, may not be able to 'remember' their ancestors even two or three generations back. These groups have a taboo, or rule, against speaking the names of the dead. Such a taboo results in a loss of knowledge of one's recent ancestry, known as genealogical amnesia. Among these groups, taking pride in specific ancestors and descent lines borders on bad manners. According to ethnographer Robert Tonkinson, genealogical amnesia among the Mardu exists in part

> because wealth and status are not acquired through inheritance, and there are no human ancestor cults of any kind (spirits of the dead are not enjoined to assist their living kin in worldly affairs), so it is pointless to trace family trees into the distant past.
>
> (Tonkinson 1991, p. 69)

Whether genealogical memory and specific biographical knowledge of past ancestors extends deep into the past or not depends on the cultural importance of descent groups, inheritance of goods, notions of an afterlife and the reckoning of relationships based on kinship. No matter how hazy genealogical memory is, all human societies share a concept of relatedness to people both past and present. In other words, kinship is fundamental to modern humans.

Transmission of Culture

The examples above give you some idea of how cultures vary in such common practices as naming individuals and calculating relatedness. *Enculturation* produces the observed differences. Because of enculturation, religious Hindus believe that people are born and reborn as members of a certain *caste*, which is an in-marrying social group. In contrast, fundamentalist Protestants believe that to be saved and go to heaven, the congregant must change his or her beliefs and become Christian. Both sets of beliefs are products of enculturation, which is the formal and informal transmission of norms of belief and behaviour. Formal enculturation encompasses schooling and initiation rites; informal methods include mass media such as broadcasting, the internet, film and popular music. It can also occur in the context of informal playgroups with children of different ages and athletic teams in societies with organised sports. French ethnographer André-Georges Haudricourt long ago observed that people learn to walk in distinctive styles depending on their culture of origin; bipedalism is universal, of course, but gait is not. Societies vary in what ideas and practices they choose to assign value to and transmit to the next generation. This variation produces cultural differences.

All cultures ceremonially mark events in the life cycle through *rites of passage*, which consist of three steps: *separation, transition* and *reincorporation*. These involve enculturation into adult society. Usually, the first rite of passage that an individual goes through is a birth rite. Such rites are embedded within beliefs about conception, which vary cross-culturally. Some South American indigenous groups, for example, believe that several men can be considered simultaneously fathers of a single infant, due to their concept of partible paternity (see Cultural Snapshot 1.2). In contrast, Trobriand Islanders traditionally had no notion of paternity. To them, conception occurred not through sexual intercourse but by the entry into a woman's womb of a spirit child who mixes with the woman's blood to create a foetus. Similar notions of conception are found in Aboriginal Australia among the Tiwi and Mardu.

Birth Rites

In many societies, the first rite of passage concerns careful observance of taboos and injunctions surrounding the birth of an infant. Many Melanesian societies seclude mothers and infants and observe certain restrictions for days or weeks. Among the Trobriand Islanders, the young nursing mother must sit on a high bed at the rear of a room and avoid interaction with others; she also must abstain from eating pork and yams, which otherwise are highly desired foods. These bans are in force for two months. Only her husband can bring her what little food she can eat. Were she to violate these taboos, it is thought her infant would be harmed.

Among the Ka'apor, both the father and the mother of the infant must seclude themselves in a darkened room for about a month after birth. The parents must avoid the most desirable of meats, such as peccary, and content themselves only with fish and tortoise meat to avoid harming their child. They must remain in darkness and not bathe in the village stream for several days until the infant is 'strong'. As with other South American native societies, the Ka'apor have a custom called the *couvade*, which is a simulation of pregnancy and motherhood by the father; it is a not-so-subtle recognition of some material substance linking a father to an infant.

Rites of Initiation

Rites of passage involving the transition from youth to adulthood are called *rites of initiation*. These sometimes involve painful body modification and deprivations that youths must pass through to become part of adult society. During initiation rites, the Tiwi Aborigines of northern Australia divide a camp into two groups: *activists* and *mourners*. Mourners are the kinsfolk (*consanguines*) of boys who will be taken away from the camp into the bush to be initiated into manhood. Activists are *affines*: older males who are potential in-laws of the boys. These activists are responsible for teaching traditional knowledge about plants and animals (Cultural Snapshot 3.1). They are also responsible for plucking out the pubic hair of the novices and later for *circumcision*, the surgical removal of the foreskin. Among the Mardu of the Western Desert of Australia (Figure 3.2), males undergo circumcision at adolescence. Later, when they are about 20 years old, they are subjected to subincision, which involves cutting the underside of the penis to the depth of the urethra, leaving a permanent opening. Normally the wound does not become infected. It is a mark of manhood; without it, one is not fully initiated into adult male Mardu society.

Figure 3.2 Mardu man, Western Desert of Australia, 1971. In the Western Desert as well as across much of Aboriginal Australia, only males underwent rites of initiation. National Archives of Australia, A6180/1, 3/11/71/5.

Ethnographer Michael F. Brown found the Awajún people, who were long ago known as warriors, hunters and shrinkers of enemy trophy heads, required male adolescents undertake a vision quest involving purification and sacrifice that could last up to several months, in which they lived alone in a forest shelter; could only eat plantains; had to sleep on elevated bunks to be protected from pollution by things that occur below them, such as sex, excrement and pets; and had to ingest hallucinogenic plant decoctions that yielded visions of fearsome spirits. The end result would be visitation by a long-deceased spirit of a warrior who would appear to promote each youth to manhood, which meant being able to detect alien enemies and sorcerers from their own group. Plains Indians societies of the nineteenth century were well known for requiring adolescent males to undergo a vision quest involving fasting, self-mutilation and altered consciousness to acquire the protection of a guardian spirit that would in principle help sustain them later in life on the battlefield.

CULTURAL SNAPSHOT 3.1

Initiation of Young Aranda Men

Central Australian initiation rites were usually spread over about ten years. Aranda adolescent boys had to undergo a four-stage initiation ceremony to reach manhood. When a boy was about 11 years old, male affines—the men who were his potential future brothers-in-law—would toss him up in the air several times, catching him each time as he fell. The boy's consanguines—his biological or 'blood' relatives, especially his female kin—cried and danced around the ritual group. Then one of the affines painted the boy's body in the design of the affine's own totem. The totem is an animal or plant that represents a person's clan. Afterwards, the Aranda novice would be taken into seclusion in the bush. On the fourth night, the boy was taught what would be expected of him as a man, as well as about society's traditions and secrets. The next morning, his male affines circumcised him by removing the foreskin of his glans penis. After five to six weeks, the subincision ceremony occurred. The man who performed this operation had two helpers. With the boy in a prone position, a man grabbed the boy's penis and stretched it out. Using a razor-sharp stone knife, another man sliced open the underside of the penis, slitting through the urethra lengthwise. The boy then squatted and allowed his wound to bleed over a wooden shield. That blood would later be poured over a special fire. From that moment on, the initiate was no longer a boy, but a young man. After subincision, he still had to learn about his society's totems, including the frog, kangaroo, bandicoot and emu. Once that stage was completed, he could marry a woman in the proper category of potential spouses.

The Ka'apor people have a rite of initiation for girls that occurs shortly after a girl's first menstruation. She is called *yay-ramo* ('one who has had recently had first menses'). She is secluded in a special darkened hut. The only animal food that is not forbidden to her is meat from the tortoise, *yaši*. Menstruation (*yay*) is believed to be connected to the lunar cycle. The moon is called *yahy*.

These Ka'apor words—*yaši*, *yay* and *yahy*—are closely related, reinforcing their ritual connection. The initiate's feet cannot touch the ground, so a palm mat is put on the floor of the hut so the girl can get up and out of her hammock when she needs to. The seclusion of girls and preventing their feet from touching the ground seem to be common practices found in girls' initiation rites worldwide. After 10 to 12 days, the Ka'apor girl emerges from seclusion and her senior male and female relatives shave off her hair. Once the girl's hair regrows long enough to reach her shoulders, she may marry. Immediately after her hair is shaven, strings of living ants are attached to her forehead and chest. These ants sting her repeatedly, but she must not cry out in pain. Ant ordeals are commonly found in the northern Amazon Basin among many different indigenous societies.

Cultural anthropologists have sought explanations for why painful rites of passage are necessary. They have explored both emic and etic explanations (Chapter 1). The Ka'apor say that girls are initiated through the ant ordeal so they will not fear the forest. Ka'apor culture does not expect boys to have such fears, and hence there is no corresponding ceremony for boys. In contrast, adolescent Wogeo male initiates in New Guinea, who have fasted and had their tongues and penises cut, weep and scream in pain. Their elders allow this and comfort them by explaining the necessity of the ritual, which prevents something worse from happening. Anthropologists have written more about adolescent rites of initiation, including those involving painful ordeals, than any other rite of passage. These rites appear to be related to the establishment of adult roles for men and women. Painful rites seem to be associated with learning what is considered to be appropriate adult behaviour. All rituals involve some notion of repetition.

In his famous parody of the Nacirema (America read backwards—see map on page xx), Horace Miner objectively studied the uses of the American medicine cabinet as if he were describing an alien society's daily rituals regarding healthcare. In the bathroom, what he calls a 'shrine', because secret rites take place in there, one finds 'a box or chest which is built into the wall. In this chest are kept the many charms and magical potions without which no native believes he could live'. The strongest of these charms and potions are received from 'specialized practitioners' [that is, doctors], 'whose assistance must be rewarded with substantial gifts'.

Sodalities

In complex societies, rites of initiation are no longer universal. In certain circumstances, they may only be found in association with religious institutions, such as synagogues, temples, mosques or churches. Voluntary societies, or *sodalities,* recruit and sometimes initiate individuals independently of kinship and religion. Sodalities in Western society include the Rotary Club or a softball team. The military Bowstring Society of the Cheyenne Indians of the nineteenth century was a sodality. Each sodality has its own emblems, etiquette for proper attire and aesthetic features such as distinctive songs and dances, which initiates must learn. Fraternities and sororities are also sodalities with their own rites of initiation, called 'hell weeks' on many university campuses.

The cover of this book shows Black Mardi Gras Indians in the Tremé neighbourhood of New Orleans. They are African Americans who 'mask Indian', in a sense paying homage to Native Americans, who they believe gave shelter and succor to their runaway, enslaved ancestors. Their performances—which originated in the Jim Crow era in the US South— are subtly anti-racist, and anti-white-supremacist. There are about 35 Mardi Gras Indian groups in the New Orleans area, and while they call themselves 'tribes' or 'gangs', they represent, anthropologically, sodalities that according to Jeffrey Ehrenreich (2013, p. 106) display 'social, economic, psychological, political, religious, and spiritual dimensions that together are part of a complex tradition rooted in African cultures and the history of slavery'.

Rules Governing Behaviour

Taboos, which are negative rules specifying behaviours and activities in which individual members of society should *not* engage, are universal. Yet the objects or activities tabooed vary. We will look at two widespread sets of taboos, those on food and those on contact and verbal behaviours.

Food Taboos

The rules among the Trobriand Islanders and the Ka'apor people about what foods to avoid while undergoing rites of passage are food taboos. Likewise, Orthodox Jews taboo the eating of pork and shellfish; such foods are on a list of 'abominations' in the Biblical book of Leviticus. Many Hindus and Buddhists must not eat beef; Muslims cannot eat pork because of taboos found in the Koran. Cultural anthropologists have explained such taboos using both emic and etic explanations.

Mary Douglas (1921–2007) offered an emic explanation of the Jewish taboo on pork and shellfish by showing these organisms to be anomalous in ancient Jewish classification of the environment. Shellfish and pork are taboo because they don't fit in with the way the Jewish world classified animals. Unlike edible ungulates, such as cattle, sheep and goats, the pig produces no hide, cheese, wool or milk. Although pigs have cloven hooves, like cattle, they do not 'chew the cud' as ruminants such as cattle, sheep and goats do. Pigs therefore do not conform to the edible category of ungulate or ruminant. They are out of the general order of things, hence tabooed as unclean and impure. Similarly, shellfish (oysters, shrimp, clams) are taboo because they are not shaped like other marine organisms: they lack fins and scales. Nor do they swim like fish. These peculiarities of shellfish, in the domain of water, set them apart as different and strange, and hence impure and taboo. Douglas notes that things that are out of place from an emic perspective are often considered to be unclean. In Western culture, for example:

> Shoes are not dirty in themselves, but it is dirty to place them on the dining table; food is not dirty in itself, but it is dirty to leave cooking utensils in the bedroom, or food bespattered on clothing; similarly bathroom equipment in the drawing room; clothing lying on chairs; out-door things in-doors…and so on. In short, our pollution behaviour is the reaction which condemns any object or idea likely to confuse or contradict cherished classifications.
>
> emic : ethography , etic : ethology.   (Douglas 1966, pp. 35–36)

Marvin Harris (1927–2001) disagreed with Douglas's emic explanation of food taboos and took an etic approach. He argued that the taboo on pork in Orthodox Judaism and Islam originated as a result of problems of ecological adaptation in a desert environment, not because of how people classified their environment. Unlike sheep and goats, pigs required shade and mud puddles for cooling off, which were uncommon in the desert environment of the Near East. In addition to only having one use—as pork and bacon— pigs also competed with people for the same plant foods. Not being ruminants like sheep, cattle and goats, pigs cannot eat grass. From an etic perspective, pigs were too costly to maintain and were therefore tabooed. Harris (1974, p. 40) concluded: 'The Bible and the Koran condemned the pig because pig farming was a threat to the integrity of the basic cultural and natural ecosystems of the Middle East'.

Neither Douglas's nor Harris's single-factor explanations, however interesting, explain all food taboos. Biological anthropologist Katharine Milton proposed that different food taboos among four groups of Amazonian societies, the Arara, Parakanã, Araweté and Mayoruna, could be explained by the need to differentiate among themselves in exploiting the same environment where they are potentially 'dietary rivals'. The groups would be less of a threat to each other if their foods were different. Milton found this to be a form of 'cultural character displacement', or a way of maintaining distinct ethnic identities in the tropical forest.

Contact and Verbal Taboos

In Polynesia, where the term originated, taboos applied to touching corpses and touching or even looking at chiefs. Those who have done such things usually must undergo rites of purification to be restored to an earlier state of normality. In some cultures, the handling of certain living things, including dogs and pigs, can render a person dangerously unclean. Many Americans love their dogs, but to some conservative Muslim groups in Southeast Asia, touching or petting any canine is taboo; even if one accidentally comes into contact with one, s/he must be ritually bathed to be restored to cleanliness and purity. Among the Tiwi, anything that was sacred and untouchable was *pukimani* ('taboo'). *Pukimani* included people in mourning, boys undergoing initiation rites, corpses before burial, grave posts and the names of the dead. Among the Crow Indians of Montana and Wyoming, a man was not allowed to speak with his wife's mother or grandmother, and a woman was forbidden to speak or look at her son-in-law. The rule in the United States of not interrupting the president when he is addressing a joint session of Congress is a taboo. It is also a taboo to utter profanities in many places of worship. Because of their variability, taboos can serve as ethnic boundary markers. Indeed, one of the cultural differences between the Guajá and Araweté, as I noted in Chapter 1, became markedly clear because of the Guajá aversion to eating palm grubs. Taboos are important to cultural anthropologists because, by emphasising what is forbidden, they highlight ideas and principles that organise social relationships and preferred behaviours.

Ethnocentrism

Ethnocentrism—intolerance of and disdain for ethnic divergences from one's own culture or subculture—is learned when children are enculturated to believe that groups other than their own are inferior. Even children's rhymes, fairy tales and games can contain ethnocentric and even racist language and wordplay, the negativity of which is unbeknownst to the children learning to hold ethnocentric views. If ethnocentrism can be learned, it can be unlearned too. *Cultural relativism*, the opposite of ethnocentrism, is learned, often at home or in school. It holds that, in principle, different cultures are morally and intellectually equivalent. It's a good starting place in any case for the comprehension of another culture. Cultural relativism is the most basic and pervasive axiom of cultural anthropology (Chapter 1). The attitudes of some groups are more relativistic than others, depending on the trait in question. A common cultural prejudice involves accusations of cannibalism (Cultural Snapshot 3.2) or incest against another group. I believe ritual cannibalism and any kind of incest or child abuse are immoral and unethical acts. It is the accusations, however, that one group might make against another group involving such acts that may be false, misleading or misguided. Such accusations are often a way of communicating the idea that group members aren't human and therefore shouldn't be tolerated. A cultural relativist can understand cannibalism as an expression of culture, in contrast to an ethnocentric view of the practice as sick or primitive.

Ethnocentrism is founded in fear of the unknown and a belief that groups of people vary as much among themselves as do dissimilar species of animals and plants. In other words, ethnocentrism derives from a conviction that not all persons are 'real' people and that the only people who are 'real' are members of one's group, kinfolk first of all. This is seen again and again in *ethnonyms*—group self-designations—that mean 'the people'. Such ethnonyms are found among egalitarian societies throughout the nonindustrial world.

The ethnonym *Ka'apor* means 'forest footprints', though the usual term for 'we the people' in related Tupi languages, *awa*, is used in the Ka'apor language in the phrase *u'u ym awa*, or 'one does not eat such things', meaning that 'real people', namely the Ka'apor, do not eat certain foods. The Ka'apor refer to the Canela people, another indigenous Amazonian society, as 'snake eaters'. The Ka'apor taboo eating snakes and distinguish themselves from the Canela by highlighting this distinction between the two societies. The Ka'apor refer to the neighbouring Guajá people as 'forest dwellers', or '*Ka'apehar*', which is a derogatory reference to the fact that the Guajá did not practice agriculture, which many Ka'apor deem to be an essential adult human activity. The Guajá take a dissenting view on this matter. The Guajá word for themselves is *awa*, 'people', or 'real people'. They traditionally took pride in being hunters and gatherers and told me that 'real people don't plant crops' (*nuh toom awá*), with the implication that those who toil away in fields cannot possibly be human.

CULTURAL SNAPSHOT 3.2

Cannibalism

Two forms of cannibalism are known to occur: *exocannibalism*, which is the consumption of people outside of one's group, often enemies; and *endocannibalism*, the consumption of group members, often as part of a funerary ritual. The Aztecs waged 'wars of flowers' to capture enemies for sacrifice to the god Huitzilopochtli, who required blood to keep the world functioning smoothly. Some archaeologists have suggested that the Aztecs also consumed the bodies of the sacrificial victims. The Tupinambá of sixteenth-century Brazil also took captives from the battlefield to later sacrifice and eat them. Several societies in New Guinea and South America practised *mortuary cannibalism*, usually in the form of ash-and-bone soup following cremation. However, among the Wari' of Brazil, the *affines*, or in-laws, of the bereaved helped the survivors dispose of the deceased by consuming his or her flesh. Only through this form of endocannibalism could a fitting funeral occur. Ethnohistorians and ethnographers suggest that societies practising cannibalism did not do so for nutritional or subsistence purposes, but rather for religious and social purposes.

Cannibalism has also occurred for medicinal purposes or as an expression of fury or disgust. The Saint Bartholomew's Day Massacre in France in 1572 involved some people taking bites out of the corpses of dead Huguenots. The Huguenots were members of a Protestant religious group; thousands were killed by Catholics. Cannibalism has also occurred in Europe, China, and Japan for medicinal purposes between the sixteenth and eighteenth centuries. Such practices represent the commodification of the body: the conversion of human body parts into saleable items with market value. Most parts of the human body had some utility according to the *Bencao Gangmu*, a sixteenth-century Chinese book of medicine. And an early modern European tradition recommended consumption of the blood and fat of executed criminals to cure a number of maladies.

A fairly common though not universal ethnocentric attitude concerns the distinction between right- and left-handedness. In many but not all cultures, left-handedness, which accounts for only about 2 per cent of people, is seen as impure, wrong or inappropriate. In much of Asia, the left hand is used for wiping the anus after defecation. In South India, the left hand is sometimes called the 'hand of filth', and the lowest castes are sometimes called 'left hand castes'. Such customs from afar can help us understand historically why we are enculturated to shake with the right, not the left hand.

(Handshaking might be eclipsed by some other greeting in the future due to the COVID pandemic of 2020–2021). In South India, jobs of left-hand castes include handling hides (believed to be ritually impure, coming as they do from cattle, which are surrounded with taboos), sweeping streets and cleaning up dung, handling corpses and other things considered to be untouchable or dangerous to people in all the higher castes. The label 'left hand' elsewhere is simply a shorthand way of identifying a minority group even if the members of such a group are not all or mostly left-handed, because in nature, left-handedness is uncommon, just as are the people who are most discriminated against in society because the majority frowns upon their cultural traits. The most extreme form of ethnocentrism is racism: the belief that other ethnic groups are inferior because of biological inheritance, about which they can do nothing.

Race and Racism

Racism is a special form of ethnocentrism, and it is certainly not universal. It is learned and often directed towards minorities; the reasons for it are often economic. Racism is rooted in a pernicious folk biology that classifies some groups of people as superior—in intelligence, moral worthiness, physical beauty, cleanliness or some other quality deemed to be desirable—and others inferior, based on what are perceived to be innate and immutable traits. What is remarkable is that race is a relatively recent idea, becoming formalised only in the eighteenth century after about 200 years of European colonialism and the institution of *chattel slavery* of Africans during that period. Chattel slavery means buying and selling people as if they were things or livestock, like heads of cattle or herds of sheep, because of their perceived race. Race is usually used in common parlance to denote minor phenotypic differences identified with specific geographic regions. These differences include skin colour, height, blood group, texture of hair, hair colour and shapes of nose and lips. Any of these features can be found in any supposed race. Johann Blumenbach (1752–1840) originally defined five races: Caucasian, Mongolian, American Indian, African and Australoid. None of these so-called races is, in fact, a genuinely biological category. It is not only blackness that constitutes a social construct; it is also the case that a white or Caucasian category did not exist in Western discourse before about 1800. If white were to be eliminated from society's classificatory scheme of race, the other so-called races would also disappear. That may be happening in the United States, which since 2000 has allowed for people to indicate membership in more than one race. In the 2000 Census, 68,000,000 people chose to check off more than one race; in 2010, 32 per cent more persons considered themselves multiracial. Multiracial people are one of the most rapidly increasing categories in the United States Census, and this is actually a positive, more scientific sign of recent years in American self-identification.

Race as a singular category is simply not scientifically valid. In recognising this and related findings as a principle, society in the twenty-first century could eventually become free of bias, bigotry and hatred based on faulty and anti-scientific perspectives on what constitutes personhood and what does not, defined in terms no more important than the hue of one's epidermis, the texture of one's hair, the shape of one's lips, nose, eyes, buttocks and so on. Anthropology will receive its due eventually as having been the field that made these pathbreaking findings about our species.

In biology, race denotes a population of a species that breeds only with its own members. No human groups qualify as 'races' by this definition. In fact, all humans belong to one species with minimal genetic variation. Chimpanzees in Africa actually have a more diverse genome than *all* living humans today. Certainly, differences exist among human groups. But the variation is not based on reproductive isolation. It comes from evolutionary adaptations to local conditions, especially climate, disease and topography. Sickle-cell anaemia, a genetic disorder, is actually an adaptation to malaria, which is endemic in parts of West Africa. People from West Africa may carry a version of a gene that causes sickle-cell; they may also have dark skin. Yet skin colour is not directly related to the sickle-cell disease. Rather, sickle-cell anaemia remains common in Africa where malaria is endemic. Darker skin is also common in Africa, where it developed as a way of protecting the body from high levels of ultraviolet radiation.

Where race is recognised culturally and linguistically, social and economic consequences can ensue. Racial classifications in the United States are partly based on the long-lasting legacy of slavery of African Americans. People were classified according to whether they had any black 'blood' at all, not whether they had any white ancestry. This refusal to recognise white ancestry in people classified as 'black' was a way of preventing the offspring of white masters and the slave women they had intercourse with—whether consensual or not--from being counted as members of the white aristocracy, and instead to add them to the slave population in the next generation.

Cultural anthropologists call the rule that was operating during slavery and Jim Crow (segregationist) days *hypodescent*: the belief that the 'race' of any one ancestor overpowers the influence of all other ancestors of a different race. In other words, if someone has any black relatives, even if the rest of the family is white, that person would be classified as black. In many southern states, marriage between blacks and whites was illegal until after the civil rights movement of the 1960s. Such laws treated blacks and whites in the South like members of different castes, separating them into two separate *endogamous*, or in-marrying, groups distinguished by color. In 1982, a light-skinned, blue-eyed blonde Louisianan named Susie Phipps went to apply for a passport and only then found out she was listed as black on her birth certificate. She petitioned the state to be reclassified as white. An existing statute required one to have no more than 1/32 black ancestry to qualify as white, called the 'one thirty-second law.' The state argued that the woman had a great- great-great-great grandmother who was black and other ancestors of mixed racial backgrounds. Cultural anthropologist Munro Edmonson (1924–2002) gave expert testimony in the case, pointing out that there is no such thing as a pure 'race' in the sense of an isolated breeding population. By this logic, the calculation of the percentage of blackness of Ms. Phipps was a farce, and the law that defined her race as either black or white was 'nonsense' (Dominguez 1994, p. 2). The law was repealed the next year. Although hypodescent makes no sense biologically, laws like the one in Louisiana had increased the number of people who could be enslaved in an economic system heavily dependent on chattel slavery, from the eighteenth century to 1865, with the defeat of the US South and the outlawing of slavery.

One of the problems with the term 'race' is that it is defined culturally; that means that it is learned. In Brazil, more than a hundred racial terms are used. The Brazilian terms *branco* (white) and *preto* (black) do not match the North American categories of white and black. Many people who are identified as *branco* have dark skin, and many of those called *preto* have light skin. Skin colour is only one—and certainly not the most important— criterion in Brazilian emic classification of human phenotypes. In fact, anthropologists found that ancestry was less important in Brazil than phenotype in determining a racial identity--children with the same parents could be classified into different racial groups. Nevertheless, people of dark skin colour in the Americas in general, including the United States and Brazil, are disproportionately represented among the underclass.

Social inequalities on the basis of perceived differences begin early in life, as do racial distinctions. Anthropologists have noted that in elementary schools, students make friends with students belonging to different emically defined races, but by the time these students get to sixth or seventh grade, they are segregating into groups in cafeterias and at parties. Ethnographer Beverly Tatum has pointed out that though white teenagers tend to be assigned to age categories, black adolescents are not seen as 'aged beings' but as 'racial beings'. Other ethnographers found in a study of an elementary school in the southeastern United States that while Asian, Latinx and white students tended to avoid talk of 'race', black students often spoke of it. Many white students classified black students as 'trouble-makers', and students accused each other of racism. They formed racially homogeneous cliques, even though the school encouraged a 'politically correct' understanding of race relations and racial equality. I am convinced that the perception of racial hierarchy, and the actual discrimination against African Americans for centuries on United States soil, are tied to the historical accident of colonialism and enslavement in the past; racism and its consequences can be rectified through education and the findings of modern anthropology. In 2020, about 20,000,000 people in the United States protested racial injustice and police violence against people of colour after the police killing of George Floyd in May (for which the officer responsible was convicted of murder in 2021); Black Lives Matter, a grassroots anti-racist movement that began in the United States after the police-related death of African American Michael Brown in 2014, then motivated protests throughout the Global North against racial bigotry and injustice (Figure 3.3). It is actually a hopeful sign that in the culture where racism began (i.e., colonialist Europe and the United States), and in spite of being contested, culture can change and become anti-racist. The American Anthropological Association, the largest professional organisation of anthropologists launched a 5,000 square foot travelling exhibit called 'Race: Are We So Different?'

Figure 3.3 Rome, Italy, June 2020. Protests against racial injustice, especially after the police killing of George Floyd in 2020, spread throughout the world, especially in Europe and the United States. Note the use of masks—because of the COVID-19 pandemic—by many demonstrators. Riccardo de Luca, Alamy Images.

Figure 3.4 The 'Race: Are We So Different?' exhibit at the Carnegie Museum of Natural History, Pittsburgh, Pennsylvania, August 2014. Photo by author.

(Figure 3.4) to educate the public about the unity of the human species, the arbitrariness and contingency (historical nature) of the social construct of 'race' and the implications for a democratic society of continuing to classify and systemically discriminate against people based on race-based categories and stereotypes. One million people had seen it before the COVID-19 pandemic of 2020–21. Current information about this initiative is at www.UnderstandingRace.org.

Sex, Gender and Age

Gender and its associated activities, those that a society associates with one sex or another, vary cross-culturally. From the outset, sex and gender are different, yet related things. The border between the two sometimes is difficult to specify, especially in cultures that recognise only two genders. Sex or genetic sex is fundamentally a binary thing and depends on what sex chromosome the person got from their father. If one got a Y chromosome with the *SRY* region that determines sex, they are genetically male; if the sex chromosome they inherited from their father is an X, they're female. In 1976, Renée Richards, who had been born with a Y chromosome, but who had self-identified in all other possible ways as female, including having undergone sex reassignment surgery, was denied permission to play in the US Open in tennis because of a rule stipulating that women players had to have been born as females; otherwise, they were ineligible to compete in the tournament. The rule later changed, and a person who had been successfully reassigned from one gender to the other could then be counted as a member of the sex corresponding to that gender. Renée Richards's sex might biologically be male because of their chromosomes, but the gender corresponding to the female sex—the female gender—is what the US Tennis Association finally accepted, in part due to a court order. In June 2015, the US Supreme Court in *Obergefell v. Hodges* officially barred states from blocking same-sex marriages in civil courts; in some cases, same-sex marriages could logically consist of different genders. For example, a transgender person born as a biological male (i.e., a person whose diploid cells contain a Y chromosome) who self-identifies with the female gender and is therefore a 'she' (sometimes referenced as *hir*, though increasingly as *they/their*), such as Caitlyn (formerly Bruce) Jenner, could in theory marry another biological male who self-identifies with the male gender. That would perhaps be a same-sex union from a biological standpoint, but definitely a two-gendered matrimony from the legally accepted status of transgender individuals. In most Western societies thus far, only two genders have been distinguished for legal purposes. The two-gender dichotomy in these societies is not universal; it is part of human cultural variation in fact, and it too is changing globally (see below). Although no cultures recognise fewer than two genders, some acknowledge more than two.

In most societies, tasks—the specifics of work and other activities, including sport—are divided up more or less according to gender. For example, among the Ka'apor, women tend to be responsible for planting, harvesting and preparing bitter manioc, while men tend to do most of the hunting. However, among the Mardu, women do a significant amount of hunting, especially of lizards and small game, both of which contribute significantly to the diet. Mardu men hunt larger game animals such as kangaroos and wallabies, but with lower success rates. Despite these cross-cultural differences, some patterns emerge in which activities are assigned to whom. Women tend to collect shellfish among the cultures of the Northwest Coast, whereas men engage in whaling and sealing among the Inuit of Alaska and Canada. In some societies, genders are derived from sex as it is emically interpreted. In many modern complex societies and traditionally among the Plains Indians of North America and the Chukchi of Siberia, the two can be distinct.

These societies recognise third genders. Prejudice against LGBTQ people, therefore, is not a sociocultural universal. People in the Western world who self-identify as trans or genderqueer or bigender would be accommodated in certain societies as nonbinaries. If a society has only two genders, these are invariably male and female. The Chukchi and the Crow (as well as other Plains Indians) had a third gender, who was neither male nor female, but in some ways both. The Crow refer to these individuals as *two-spirits* (formerly called *berdache*, a term now considered pejorative). The two-spirits were revered for their spiritual quality. Two-spirits dressed like females and did some but not all the same tasks as females yet had distinctive access to the spiritual realm unlike either the male or female genders. Third genders are often seen to have shamanic or divinatory power, or the capacity to bless others and their relationships, in particular that of marriage.

One of the most remarkable examples of traditional societies with multiple genders is the Bugis of Indonesia, who, according to ethnographer Sharyn Graham Davies, acknowledge five emically valid genders, which can be understood in terms of a continuum from masculine to feminine at the two extremes. In the middle are the androgynous shamans known as *bissu*. The *bissu* have special responsibilities in local society, including granting blessings for good health and good harvests, protection from catastrophes and organising the spirituality of the royal court. They also assume leadership positions during rites of passage (especially birth, marriage and mortuary rituals). Islamic law does not recognise more than two genders, and Indonesia is an officially Islamic country, but the

Bugis's multiple genders are nevertheless tolerated at the local scale on the large island of Sulawesi; indeed, they seem to predate Islam there. The case is similar to the *hijra* of India. Hinduism, like Islam, does not endorse multiple genders in society, even though in ancient iconic art and religious belief, androgynous deities are sometimes portrayed. Hijra are biological males who exist in a third-gender state; their role in blessing weddings of devout, high-caste Hindus of northern India has been well-noted by ethnographer Serena Nanda.

Interestingly, some institutions in the Western world are beginning to agree with the Bugis in recognising multiple genders. As part of equity, diversity and inclusion initiatives, many institutions encourage their members to indicate their preferred pronouns, like she/her/hers and they/them/theirs. The University of Southern California's Engeman Student Health Center's required form 'consent for treatment' has a section that students fill in called 'gender identity'. One checks one of five boxes: female, male, transfemale (MTF), transmale (FTM) or gender non-conforming. A separate field inside square block lines to the right of the gender field is 'sex assigned at birth', having one of two boxes, female or male, to check. Instructions here are 'Fill in only if gender identity and sex assigned at birth differ'. The document is an accurate reflection of the gender continuum and how it is distinguishable from the binary category of sex. The University of Southern California is reflective of numerous institutions in the United States that are adopting multigender possibilities along with multiracial categories also explicit in the US Census Bureau from 2010 on. In other words, the findings of ethnography on distinctions of sex and gender are becoming institutionalised, just as the findings of anthropology that race is a social construct and not a biologically distinct breeding population within a species, have been taking root in officialdom. These are reasons to be positive, not negative, about a future free from bigotry and prejudice rooted in racialist, gender-biased, LGBTQ-biased preconceptions and stereotypes. That is progressive.

Genders vary in terms of their access to power and authority. It was once thought that there was no society with only two genders in which both were equally esteemed. Many anthropologists in the twentieth century believed all societies were masculinist to one degree or another. More recent research has shown, however, that some societies exhibit gender egalitarianism. This means there is significant overlap in activities assigned to one gender or the other, and that the two genders are complementary in their work and family relationships. One does not subjugate the other in domestic and public politics. Gender egalitarianism has not been widely reported. It is found in certain hunting-and-gathering societies, such as the Batek of Malaysia, and among a highland agricultural people in southern China, the Lahu. In both cases, women's and men's tasks are seen as complementary, not as divisive. Batek women may perform almost any tasks usually done by males, including hunting. Although there are restrictions on women handling male tools and weapons, such as blowguns and poison darts, in many horticultural societies of South America and Melanesia, there are no such taboos among the Batek.

Beyond distinguishing gender and sex, societies differ in how the human body, particularly the female body, is interpreted and understood. These contrasts begin with a recognition that the body itself can represent an emic map of a culture's attitudes towards femininity and masculinity. These gendered concepts are important in how a society defines religious versus secular situations. For example, female virginity is held in high esteem in some cultures, such as the Nuer, who trace descent through the male line, whereas in societies with matrilineal descent, such as the Trobriand Islanders and the Iroquois, virginity is less of a concern. In societies with patrilineal descent, paternity is critical. In contrast, in matrilineal Trobriand society, the father is merely 'husband of the mother' and one's membership in a kin group is determined by one's mother.

Age grades are found in all societies. However, only some societies have *age sets*, which are formal groups recruited for certain tasks on the basis of a common range of ages. These are frequently found in central Brazilian and East African indigenous cultures. They are usually but not always specific to each sex. The series of *age grades* in a person's life span, from infancy to old age, is called the *life cycle*. Important events in the life cycles of both sexes are marked by rites of passage, which are ceremonies such as naming, initiation and marriage. When several people go through the process together because they are of the same age, they are said to belong to an *age set*. The pastoral Nuer people of eastern Africa have seven age sets for men. Every four years or so, a group of boys, called a *ric*, is initiated together through a rite of passage. At initiation, an older man cuts their foreheads in six lines from ear to ear (Figure 6.1), a symbol of Nuer manhood. As soon as the boys in the *ric* have been initiated, they take on new behaviours as young men. For example, milking cows becomes taboo. They are on their way to Nuer-defined manhood, which can only occur after they have married and fathered children. Age sets are also found in Central Brazil. In Central Brazil, ethnographer James Welch points out that these age sets are recruited across different groups, as sodalities, except people have no choice in joining. Age sets are superficially similar to groups that graduate together from high school or college. If you're in the class of 2025, you will also be in that class, as will your classmates, long after 2025. The same is true for classes of 2026, 2027 and so on. The difference with age sets is they are limited in number, and they are recycled. Among the A'uwē-Xavante, Welch (2021) reports eight age sets: 'the cycle repeats every eight age sets, with the newest age set adopting the name that was used eight age sets previously'. Each age set shares secret knowledge, and 'a deep sense of identity' along with 'interest in one another's affairs'.

Religion and Art

Religion is organised belief in the scientifically improbable or unprovable and includes belief in spirits, demons, witches, deities and unseen, impersonal, supernatural things, such as *mana*, luck and the mystical force of taboos.

Animism and Totemism

Where does religion come from? Tylor, who bequeathed to cultural anthropology his enduring definition of culture, proposed that *animism*—belief in souls or spirits—was the most basic form of spirituality and religious behaviour. To Tylor, it was obvious that everyone had a religion, if religion was defined by what he called the 'doctrine of souls', involving the need to explain life and death, health and desire, sleep and dreams, trance and vision. Tylor suggested that the belief in the immortality of souls, which is found to some degree in all cultures, was evidence of a preexisting fear of death and a means of repressing that fear, at least temporarily. The fear of death and knowledge of its inevitability do seem unique to the psychology of humans.

Animism was the basis of religion to Tylor, not belief in a supreme deity, the practice of sacrifice, written liturgy or elaborate rituals. Émile Durkheim, in contrast, saw *totemism*—worship of plants or animals or other phenomena in nature such as celestial bodies—to be the most basic form of religion. Totems represented human clans—kin groups defined by a descent rule. In totemism, the members of a clan were considered to form a kind of congregation or a community of believers who practice their religion together by worshipping the emblematic natural thing that is their totem. Stated simply, animism involves conceiving of animals or plants as people, as though they had souls; totemism, in contrast, involves thinking of people as animals or plants.

CULTURAL SNAPSHOT 3.3

Veneration of Ancestors

Herbert Spencer (1820–1903) and Sigmund Freud (1856–1939) believed the veneration of ancestors was the source of all religion, partly because people 'see' their ancestors in dreams. Ancestor worship often involves placing offerings at gravesites or shrines believed to harbour ancestral spirits. The ancient Inca ayllu was a group of people who believed they were descended from a common ancestor, who was often preserved as a mummy or associated with a special stone. Ayllu members shared labour and owned agricultural land as a corporate group; ayllus still exist today in parts of the Andes. Similarly, Chinese descent groups are men and women linked by fathers, brothers and sons with a collective interest in agricultural lands. They share a shrine devoted to a male ancestor in the patriline, the male line of descent. Traditional Chinese religion was based on a set of beliefs and principles called Confucianism. Confucianism promoted family life, filial duty and piety towards ancestors. Some modern Chinese continue to honour the dead, sometimes with great tombs. They may even have electric lights installed so they may feast in comfort with their ancestors.

Clans are usually represented by animal or plant emblems, or totems. According to Durkheim, Australian Aborigines had totemism. Durkheim thought of Aranda totemism, which involved worship of the Emu, Kangaroo and various other animal totems of clans, as the workshop of society itself, insofar as the emblem of each totemic plant or animal represented an identifiable social group. The Nuer also had totemism, even though they exhibited genealogical reckoning up to five generations back through real people, not plants or animals. Beyond those four or five generations of genealogical memory, Nuer kinship merged with totemism.

Both animism and totemism often involve some concept of an afterlife as well as the veneration of deceased ancestors. Some anthropologists have suggested that ancestor veneration is essential to any religion (Cultural Snapshot 3.3). The Nuer, for example, believed that ancestral ghosts, like people themselves, are mobile, accompanying herders and cattle during their annual migrations in search of pasture. These ghostly ancestors supposedly watch over and protect their living descendants. Although ancestor veneration is widespread, it is not universal. Societies with widespread genealogical amnesia, such as the Ka'apor and Mardu (Chapter 1), rarely venerate ancestors.

Art—with music as an example—and religion sometimes go together in Western societies but not always: rock concerts and choirs are attended for dissimilar reasons. Spirituality is no doubt enhanced by musically organised sound, but how this sound is perceived is variable. Not all languages have a word that translates into English as 'music'.

The word *sangita* in Hindi, spoken in India, refers to both dance and music. What is considered music in one culture is not necessarily music in another. The recitation of the Muslim sacred text, the Koran, has often been called 'music' by non-Muslims; yet in Arabic, the word *musiqa* does not include recitation of the Koran, since it refers only to nonreligious, secular music. The same is true with the Muslim call to prayer; it's not music from an emic point of view, though the sound is organised independently of words and exhibits to many an aesthetic, emotional appeal apart from speech. The Suyá people of the Central Brazilian Amazon have a distinctive concept of aesthetics concerning music. Some Suyá music might sound harsh, dissonant and improvised to Western ears attuned to a 12-tone scale (a relatively recent invention, incidentally, in human history) and used to rock, hip-hop, classical, blues or jazz harmonies and rhythms. Suyá music might even sound out of tune because they have microtonal rising, meaning they can sing between the typical notes (tones) of the Western 12-tone system, and to Suyá ears it is beautiful. Yet also to the Suyá people the sounds of Western music can sound befuddled, pointless, uninspiring and irreligious. All Suyá music is endowed with social meaning, including the ceremonial songs that are sung at the times boys are initiated into name sets (a group of names assigned individually to men who perform complementary activities, ceremonies and competitions with men from other name sets) and later age sets.

Organising Behaviour and Belief

Cultural anthropologist A.F.C. Wallace united the approaches of Tylor, who focused on religious *belief*, and Durkheim, who stressed religious *organisation*. For Wallace, religion involves both institutionalised behaviours and beliefs in supernatural phenomena. Wallace proposed four types of religious behaviour: 1) the individualistic, in which the locus of action is a single person; 2) the communal, associated with rites of initiation and intensification, usually consisting of activists and mourners, two ritually dissimilar but complementary groups; 3) the shamanic, involving a central figure who mediates between the spirit world and the real world and who undergoes altered states of consciousness, called trances, for divination, healing or sorcerous purposes; and 4) the ecclesiastical, sets of religious institutions unique to state societies. State societies have centralised political authority and stratification, which divide people into groups with unequal access to wealth and power. Ecclesiastical institutions in states feature religious personnel who have special knowledge of scripture, doctrine and calendrical rites, or liturgy. All societies seem to have the first three types of religious behaviour and organisation; only fully centralised state societies have ecclesiastical institutions.

Individualistic Religious Behaviour. Individualistic practices follow a societal belief system, but they are carried out at the level of a single person, not a group. The Mardu Aborigines believe individuals can control problematic weather conditions, such as drought. An individual may be able to divine evil spirits holding back the rain, and may converse with, scream or frighten them through dance or invocations. Individual love magic is also known among the Mardu. A man desiring a woman might whirl a bullroarer above a secret place in the desert, with the belief that the deep howling sound made by the bullroarer will reach his love object's ears and fill her with passionate desire for him. Another form of love magic, performed by both men and women, is to sing special songs. Individualistic behaviours include the Plains Indian vision quest, crossing oneself with holy water, avoiding thirteenth floors in buildings and rituals related to numerology and astrology.

Communal Religious Behaviour. Communal religious behaviour involves a specific group of people and occurs during transitional periods of the human life cycle. Communal groups perform *rites of passage*, such as the bar or bat mitzvah of Judaism; ant ordeals among some Carib and Tupian societies of South America; male and female circumcision in Africa and the Middle East; and subincision, hair plucking and tooth removal in Aboriginal Australia (Cultural Snapshot 3.1). Rites of passage are enculturation in action: they involve formal learning and passing on of traditional knowledge and behaviour believed to be appropriate to one's gender and age.

Shamanic Religious Behaviour. All societies, even our own, have individuals who are believed to have special relationships with supernatural forces and entities. Such individuals include palm readers, fortune-tellers and mediums who perform at séances. In other societies, such individuals may call upon unseen supernatural beings and forces to heal others. These kinds of activities are shamanic. Shamanism may be part-time or full-time; it usually is based on oral transmission of knowledge rather than written doctrine (scripture). Shamans are believed to have the ability to contact supernatural beings for the purpose of healing and improving the material conditions of society, such as weather, rainfall, game availability and crop growth. Shamans are often called upon in moments of crisis or contingency.

In southern Africa, according to ethnographer Richard Lee, Ju/'hoansi shamans are any adults, women or men, who have access to a mystical spiritual power called *n/um*, which is believed to reside in their stomachs. Those who have *n/um* are called 'medicine owners'. They heal sick people with magical sweat they exude after having gone into trance, which is caused by many hours of constant dancing. During trances, they believe they see spirits of the dead. They can put the healing power of *n/um* into sick people and into their own apprentices via their sweat. Lee noted that 90 per cent of the conditions they treat would have become better on their own regardless of any medical procedure, so the odds are on the shamans' side. Like the Ju/'hoansi, Wari' shamans of the Brazilian Amazon, who are usually male, can make their apprentices into shamans by magically transferring material from their own bodies into that of the apprentice. Shamans are often diviners, people who are believed to be able to predict the future, find lost objects and the like. Clerics in ecclesiastical institutions may also be diviners.

Ecclesiastical Religious Behaviour. Ecclesiasticism refers to religion with full-time, educated, professional practitioners and a laity comprising people who aren't specialists in supernatural esoterica. Ecclesiastical religions are always associated with states and stratification. They include world religions such as Christianity, Judaism, Islam, Buddhism, Hinduism and Baha'i with internal hierarchies that reflect the structure of the rest of society. Professional ecclesiastics include Catholic and Anglican priests, Buddhist and Hindu priestesses and priests, Jewish rabbis, Muslim imams and Protestant reverends, pastors and preachers. Ancient Roman religion included priestesses called Vestal Virgins; similarly, the Inca Empire had a class of 'chosen women' who lived in a convent-like structure and were required to remain chaste.

The ecclesiastical type of religious belief and practice, in contrast to shamanic and individualistic types, has calendrical rituals and usually some sort of writing or other methods of record keeping and planning. Roman Catholics have a liturgy, based on a lunar calendar, which determines the dates each year of Lent, Easter and other feast days. The Aztecs of Mexico had a liturgical calendar in addition to a solar calendar. Both calendars had good days, bad days and neutral days, all of which were associated with supernatural forces (Cultural Snapshot 3.4). Calendrical rites associated with ecclesiastical organisations contrast with the crisis rites of shamanism and the unprogrammed rites of communal and individualistic religious practices.

CULTURAL SNAPSHOT 3.4

Numbers, Magic and Fate

Days of the week and numbers can acquire mystical features in ecclesiastical religions. There can be lucky days and unlucky days, lucky numbers and unlucky numbers. Luck is seen in many behaviours related to belief in the supernatural; the practice of baseball players touching their caps or uniform letters is an example. In some religions, the names of deities, saints and even certain days have sacred properties and should either not be spoken or, if mentioned, only with great care. Examples of ecclesiastical concern with numbers include the three persons of the Holy Trinity in Catholicism, the six points on the Star of David in Judaism and the number 108 in Hinduism, Buddhism and Sikhism. The Aztec liturgical calendar had 260 days. The days of each month were numbered one through 13 and each month had a name, such as 'Rabbit II'. Days had names that combined numbers with terms for natural phenomena or animals, such as rabbit, alligator, lizard, dog or monkey. There were good days, bad days and neutral days, all determined by the calendar and associated with supernatural forces. The goddess Mayahuel was patron of all the rabbit days. She was also the goddess of the maguey plant, used in *pulque*, a fermented alcoholic beverage and the precursor to tequila. People born on rabbit days were thought to become alcoholics later in life. Such fascination with numbers is not the same as literacy and numeracy, which are found only in states.

Cosmologies and Explanations of the Unknown

A *cosmology* is a society's system of beliefs that renders intelligible the passage of time and the events that unfold within it. In some cases, cosmology explains society's origins, as with the biblical story of Genesis. In others, it foretells inevitable conclusions, as in Mesoamerican concepts of fate and destiny. Accounts of origins, like Genesis or the Big Bang Theory, are called *cosmogonies*; they are often embedded in myth. Origin myths are oral or written texts that illustrate a concept or interpretation of occurrences at the time of society's, or the world's, presumed beginnings. The Dreaming Beings in the cosmology of many Australian Aborigines are seen as the entities who gave life to humans and who created landscape features, celestial bodies and known plants and animals. They also bequeathed to society a moral code of conduct known as the Law. The Law prohibits incest, child abuse and random violence; it lays out the rules for initiation rites, marriage and parenting, and sharing and reciprocity.

All societies have cosmologies, though not all have cosmogonies. Ethnographer Aparecida Vilaça found that the Wari' of the Brazilian Amazon 'possess no genesis myth or cosmogony. For them, everything that exists in the world always existed'. In contrast, Kenelm Burridge finds the Dreaming Beings of Australia to be ever-present:

These beings or powers are always present, sensibly manifesting themselves from time to time much in the way they did when they were engaged in creating the world... Creation is both a continuing fact as well as a unique historical...event. Created once and for all time, the world and everything in it dies and yet renews itself or is recreated.

(Burridge 1973, p. 73)

Cosmological notions may be scientific; the Big Bang Theory in astronomy and physics, which explains the origins of the universe, is both science and cosmology. More often, cosmologies represent alternative, nonscientific ways of understanding the world. Science explains observable phenomena through testable hypotheses and replicable methods. In contrast to science, religion defines and explains good and evil, morality and immorality, sickness and death, and the existence of souls, spirits, demons, deities and an afterlife. Religion also offers nontestable explanations of how people fit into society and the world at large.

Economic Organisation

All societies have economies that involve making, giving, receiving and consuming essential goods and services. How those activities are organised and accomplished is a society's mode of production: how a society sustains itself economically. Mode of production varies across cultures. Members of some societies traditionally hunted and collected wild foods, such as the Ju/'hoansi hunter-gatherers, the Inuit of the Canadian Arctic, the Shoshone people of the North American Great Basin and the Mardu and Tiwi peoples of Australia. Others collect wild foods but supplement their diet through trade with agriculturalists. This mode of production is known among several tropical forest hunter-gatherer societies, including the Mbuti, Aka and Efe peoples of equatorial Africa, the Maku of the northwest Amazon and the Agta of the Philippines. Some societies rely on extensive agriculture (Chapter 8), which involves long fallow periods; among them are the Ka'apor, the Kabre of West Africa, the Dayak of Borneo and the Trobriand Islanders of Melanesia. Archaic state societies, such as the Inca of Peru, the Aztec of Mexico, the Chinese who built the Great Wall and the ancient Romans, depended on intensive agriculture. This mode requires more labour and energy than either hunting-and-gathering or extensive agriculture and often involves fertilisation, irrigation and terracing of permanently cultivated plots of land. Pastoral societies in the Near East and Africa obtain most of their food from livestock such as camels, sheep, goats and cattle. Examples of pastoralists include the Bedouin of North Africa and the Maasai of East Africa. Most food produced today comes from industrial agriculture involving the use of fossil fuels, highly selected strains of hybrid cultivars and a significantly reduced labour force. The amount of energy that goes into industrial food production, ironically, is actually more, in terms of kilocalories, than what comes out, because of the highly concentrated energy values in petroleum and related fuels.

Like mode of production, forms of economic exchange vary cross-culturally. Some exchanges are based on reciprocity—give and take on a long-term basis—rather than on making a profit or accumulating wealth. While all societies have reciprocity (chapter 2), some involve other methods of exchange found in *redistribution* and *market* economies. In societies with reciprocal economies, the exchange of goods and services generally occurs between people who are roughly equal in status. In contrast, redistributive economies funnel wealth to an authoritarian individual, such as a powerful chief, or into a bureaucratic centre. Goods are then reallocated by the chief or by bureaucrats. Market economies are based on the exchange of goods and services with more or less standardised values and involve money or some other widely recognised currency, including credit and now anonymous, intangible but emically valuable cryptocurrencies like bitcoin and Ethereum.

Redistribution

Reciprocal economies involve face-to-face relationships between people. Redistributive economies, which are based on feasting—giving and receiving invitations to lavish parties where wealth is given away—likewise entail a social element. The redistributive feast of the Northwest Coast, known as the *potlatch*, traditionally involved lavish and abundant gift giving. Gifts included blankets, shields called 'coppers', smoked salmon, silver bracelets, canoes and even slaves. These gifts required even more extravagant reciprocation by the guests; otherwise, they would lose prestige and social status. The potlatch has been described as 'fighting with property'.

Redistribution as an economic exchange principle was also characteristic of much of Oceania. On the Polynesian island of Tahiti, the paramount chief had a maximum amount of an impersonal supernatural force called *mana*, which made him dangerous to commoners, who could be harmed by this power. These beliefs in an impersonal, supernatural force were *animatist*. Indeed, any object the chief touched became tabooed to others, and any food he touched was believed to become lethal poison for those beneath him in rank. These chiefs were owed tribute or offerings from their subjects, including the first fruits of harvest. According to Elman Service (1915–1996), there was

> no market exchange among the people of Tahiti. The gifts to the chief, and from lower chiefs to higher chiefs, can be seen as a means by which an exchange of goods is accomplished. The chiefs accumulate the surplus of products given them and then redistribute it at great feasts.
>
> (Service 1963, p. 260)

Taxation

The Inca of Peru also had redistribution as a principal method of exchange of goods and services. In contrast to Polynesia and the Northwest Coast, the Inca system involved a complex, state-level sociopolitical organisation. Expanding out of Cuzco, the Inca established an empire, taking over other societies throughout the Andes by military conquest and extending their rule from Ecuador in the north to northern Chile and Argentina in the south. The Inca were ruled by an emperor believed to be a living divinity on Earth. The Inca redistribution system was coercive, taxing conquered peoples by demanding labour, textiles and agricultural produce. The tax on labour is called *corvée*.

All farming communities in the Inca domain had their lands divided up into three equal parts: some land was owned by the community itself, some by state religious institutions and some by the emperor and his royal house. Maize, potatoes and other crops were produced on land owned by ecclesiastical authorities and supported priests and priestesses. Crops from the emperor's lands were stored in granaries and storehouses built along the Inca road system. Produce from community lands filled local storehouses. The local chief would divide up the harvest to feed the families in his community based on need, according to archaeologist Michael Moseley. The food produced for the emperor fed him, his family and other elites; it also fed warriors and was redistributed to those suffering famine elsewhere in the empire. The Mongol Empire of China also had redistribution with a *corvée* labour tax. Italian explorer Marco Polo wrote around AD 1300 that the emperor (the Great Khan) of the Forbidden City (Beijing):

> bestows charity on the poor people…this provision includes clothing inasmuch as the Great Khan receives a tithe of all the wool, silk, and hemp used for cloth-making… since all the crafts are under obligation to devote one day a week to working on his behalf, he has this cloth made up into garments, which he gives to the poor families.
>
> (Latham 1958, p. 157)

Classification of the Environment

Many of the world's more than 6,000 languages have rich vocabularies referring to plants, animals and the natural world, whereas others, such as mainstream English, do not. Many linguists have suggested that comparative richness of vocabulary in a certain area of meaning, known as a *semantic domain*, reflects what is most economically or culturally important to the people who speak the language in question. For example, Americans have many words for types of breakfast cereal; Australian Aborigines have numerous terms for sand iguanas; and the agricultural Hanunóo people of the Philippines have about 90 words just for rice. The Sapir–Whorf hypothesis, named after linguistic anthropologist Edward Sapir and his associate Benjamin Whorf, holds that language affects cognition and therefore culture. In other words, language influences the culture of its speakers. Although languages are, like cultures, equally valuable expressions of unique varieties of human experience, linguistic theory of the second half of the twentieth century stressed the commonality of all human languages, beginning with the essential attributes of language and ending with the proposition that human language is a biological construct in the mind. In contrast, linguistic relativists have argued that some semantic domains, such as 'plants' and 'kinfolk', are not truly translatable. This debate led to important research during the twentieth century, especially with regard to the domains of colour, plants and animals. The ways that people name and classify plants, for example, vary cross-culturally and reflect culture-specific beliefs and preferences as well as local ecological conditions. By studying semantic domains and classification systems, cultural anthropologists can learn about what people think is important and how they conceptualise the world around them.

Summary

Cultural anthropology is concerned with cross-cultural similarities and differences. The study of universals focuses on what institutions all cultures share; variation deals with the differences. Institutions that vary cross-culturally include personal names and their uses, life cycle rites, taboos, enculturation, manifestations of ethnocentrism, gender roles, spirituality and religious behaviour, economy and emic classification schemas.

Further Reading

Balée 1994; Balikci 1970 (p. 138); Barry 1996; Becker 1973; Berdan 2005; Brooker 2009; Brown 2014; Burridge 1973; Conklin 2001; Covey 2008; Crocker and Crocker 2004; Damon 1990; Davies 2007;

Dominguez 1994; Douglas 1966; Dumont 1970; Durkheim (1912) 1995; Edmonson 1971; Ehrenreich 2013; Ember 1996; Endicott and Endicott 2008; Evans-Pritchard (1940); 1969; Fagan 2010; Fuller 2014; Funderburg 2013; Graves 2001; Harris 1974; Harris and Kottak 1963; Harris et al. 1993; Hart et al. 2001; Haudricourt 2010; Hertz 1973; Hoebel 1988; Hogbin 1996; Humphrey 2006; Isbell 1997; Johnson 2003; Jones 2009; Karim 1981; Knight 1991; Latham 1958; Lee 2013; Lewis-Williams 2002; Lucy 1992; Meggitt 1965; Milton 1991; Miner 1956 (p. 504); Moseley 1992; Murphy and Murphy 2004; Nanda 1999; Nuwer 1999; Polanyi 1957; Radcliffe-Brown 1929; Rosman and Rubel 1986; Roughgarden 2004; Schaffer and Skinner 2009; Schniedewind 2004; Scott 199; Service 1963; Shostak 2000; Smedley 1993; Spencer and Gillen (1899) 1938; Tatum 1997; Tonkinson 1991; Tylor (1871) 1924 (vol. 2); van Gennep (1909) 1960; Vilaça 2010; Wallace 1966; Weiner 1988; Welch n.d.; Wierzbicka 1997; Wikipedia (https://en.wikipedia.org/wiki/Renée_Richards)

Cultural Snapshots

3.1   Spencer and Gillen (1899) 1938); Tonkinson 1991, 2007; Whitley 2005
3.2   Awaya 1999; Berdan 2005; Clastres 1995; Conklin 2001
3.3   Freud 1938; Spencer 1870; Isbell 1997
3.4   Aveni 1995; Berdan 2005; Gmelch 1992

4   Where Anthropology Comes From

Overview

Anthropology, like all disciplines of knowledge, is an outcome of centuries of discourse, thought and debate among different minds. The history of ideas in anthropology is not just a linear transmission of knowledge on the subject, passed on dutifully from ageing teacher to eager young student, generation after generation, even though enculturation is partly how the field has been passed on to the present day. Knowledge in anthropology has also advanced with new discoveries of fossils, artefacts, sites, villages and cultures. Theories have changed, too, with influences from society itself, such as world wars, international treaties, human migrations and the internet. In this chapter, we trace the development of thinking in anthropology in North America and Europe from the Enlightenment in the 1700s to the end of World War II in 1945.

The Eighteenth Century

North American anthropology, like European anthropology, originates in the philosophical time period called the Enlightenment (Timeline 4.1). Although some of the questions asked by ancient philosophers are similar to anthropological questions today, the research generated by those ancient questions at the time did not lead to a specific science devoted to the explanation of cultural similarities and differences. The fifth-century BC Greek historian Herodotus wrote descriptions of other cultures; for example, he described the cultures of the Ligurians in what is now France and of the Sigynnae in what is now Romania with a focus on their subsistence patterns, marriage customs, circumcision and attitudes to shame, nakedness and privacy. On the other hand, whereas the Enlightenment of the eighteenth century would lead ultimately to the profession of anthropology, ancient Greek philosophy about cultural similarities and differences did not. Cultural anthropologist Clyde Kluckhohn (see Cultural Snapshot 1.5) noted that in ancient Greece, a person called '*anthropologos* [anthropologist] was…nothing more than a gossip or busybody' (Kluckhohn 1961, p. 27). The Enlightenment, in contrast, undertook a deliberate project of objectification of the other, and though its initial results are debatable, it did lead to a genuine science of humankind. Perhaps another difference was the conception of the development of humanity and culture; thinkers in ancient Greece and several other ancient civilisations as diverse as Vedic India and Aztec Mexico believed human history began in a Golden Age and that society had increasingly deteriorated since then. The Enlightenment philosophers of the North Atlantic in the eighteenth century believed that utopian society would be in the future, not the past. Perhaps that is because ancient Greece, India and Mexico were replete with monumental architecture mostly fallen into ruins made by even earlier societies, whereas Western Europe and eastern North America were not apparently the seats of ancient states and empires. For those more recent philosophers, the future held the key to human advancement and the benefits of civilisation.

The Enlightenment in North America is exemplified in the book *Notes on the State of Virginia* ([1785] 1999) by Thomas Jefferson, who became the third president of the United States in 1801. In many ways, Jefferson is also the first ethnographer, linguist and archaeologist of the United States. *Notes* accounted for the distribution of 40 indigenous cultures and languages in Virginia and along the Atlantic coast. In addition, Jefferson excavated an Indian mound using archaeological methods that are essentially modern.

Jefferson was interested in the origins of the American Indians. Many Anglo-Americans living in the 13 colonies thought the Indians were descendants of the Ten Lost Tribes of Israel, an idea that laid the groundwork for the religion of Mormonism. Many colonials of Jefferson's day thought that Indian mounds had been built by people who had preceded the current indigenous societies, a supposedly superior 'moundbuilder race'. These moundbuilders were believed to have either disappeared or *degenerated* from a technologically sophisticated culture into the simpler Indian societies familiar to the colonials. Another contemporary opinion was that the Indians had defeated the moundbuilders and forced them to disappear; ethnocentrism directed towards the American Indian resulted in the belief that their cultures and traditional knowledge were incapable of producing earthworks and other aspects of complex landscape transformation. Jefferson's excavations of a mound using stratigraphic excavation, the careful removal and analysis of a site layer by layer, showed that Indian mounds had accumulated by successive burials and deposits over multiple generations. He realised that the prehistoric mounds could have been constructed gradually over hundreds of years and that an advanced 'moundbuilder race' was not necessary to account for the landscapes he observed. Jefferson and others would later develop the idea that American Indians originated in Asia, which recent genetic and dental evidence has shown to be true.

The Enlightenment in Europe and North America

Jefferson's thinking about American Indians as objects of inquiry, as people who could be studied to understand humanity, was influenced by the European Enlightenment, a period of rapid intellectual change that set the stage for the development of modern anthropology. Enlightenment philosophers were interested in the progress of humanity and the possibility that a science of people could be as rigorous as any natural science (Timeline 4.1; Cultural Snapshot 4.1). Enlightenment developments also influenced physical anthropology and linguistic anthropology. During this period, people began to recognise that humans, like other animals, were a part of nature. In 1735, Carl Linnaeus, the Swede who created the modern system of classification of living things, placed humans in the animal kingdom and gave them a species name, *Homo sapiens*.

The field of linguistics (then called philology) expanded as scholars began to compare languages from East and West. In 1786, Sir William Jones proved that Greek, Latin and Sanskrit, an ancient written language of India, had 'sprung from some common source' (Timeline 4.1). The 'common source' that Jones identified is proto–Indo-European, the ancestral language of a diverse family that includes French, English, Russian, Persian and Hindi. That discovery was the precursor of linguistic anthropology as we know it.

Timeline 4.1 The age of Enlightenment.

Ideas in Europe	Ideas in the United States	Events in early anthropology	Events in world history
• human progress • science of humanity • natural law • human universals KEY PUBLICATION *Sketch of the Progress of the Human Mind* (1795) by the Marquis de Condorcet	• Native Americans as objects of study • investigation of origins of Native Americans • degeneration theory KEY PUBLICATION *Notes on the State of Virginia* (1785) by Thomas Jefferson	• humans as the species *Homo sapiens* (1735) • stratigraphic excavation (1785) • discovery of Indo-European language family (1786) • establishment of learned societies KEY PUBLICATION *Third Discourse to the Asiatic Society of Bengal* (1786) by Sir William Jones	• American Revolution (1775–1781) • Industrial Revolution begins • French Revolution (1789–1799) • formation of European empires

In the fledgling United States, right after the American Revolution, Jefferson had begun to recognise the importance of linguistic patterns in determining relationships between groups of people. He wrote that the comparison of American Indian languages 'would be the most certain evidence of their derivation which could be produced...[and] the best proof of the affinity of nations'. Enlightenment scholars such as Jefferson and Jones considered human societies and cultures as appropriate objects of study. They, along with Enlightenment thinkers elsewhere (Cultural Snapshot 4.1), were particularly interested in the idea of preordained human progress. They believed that civilisation, as they understood it—the cities of Europe and the ancient ruins of Greece and Rome—was destined to become increasingly more refined in art, science, technology and government.

CULTURAL SNAPSHOT 4.1

Turgot and Condorcet on Progress

Many cultural anthropologists have shown certain small-scale societies to be resistant to developing into complex ones because they have ways of keeping people more or less equal, such as demand sharing (Chapter 2), and a preference for leisure time over material assets such as money and property. Others have argued that even egalitarian, kin-based societies, if they survive the acculturative forces of complex society, will eventually develop into stratified, class-based societies. In the eighteenth century, such developments were called progress. In 1750, A. R. J. Turgot (1727–1781) first defined progress as the increasing 'perfectibility' of humankind. He wrote, 'The whole human race, through alternate periods of rest and unrest, of weal and woe, goes on advancing, although at a slow pace, towards greater perfection' (Meek 1973, p. 41).

He suggested that small-scale foraging and pastoralist societies could serve as analogies for the human past:

> The current state of the world…spreads out before us at one and the same time all the gradations from barbarism to refinement, thereby revealing to us at a single glance, as it were, the records and remains of all the steps taken by the human mind, a reflection of all the stages through which it has passed, and the history of all the ages.
>
> (Meek 1973, p. 42)

Thomas Jefferson so admired Turgot that he kept a bust of him in the foyer of Monticello. Turgot also influenced his friend Nicholas de Condorcet (1743–1794), an acquaintance and correspondent of Jefferson's, who had a theory of progress based on ten stages, beginning with hunter-gatherers—what he called 'tribal society'— and culminating in French civilisation at the time of the Revolution (1789–1799). Jefferson's role in the American Revolution inspired Condorcet. Condorcet was progressive: he saw the end of absolute monarchy and the development of republican government as inevitably bound to improve the human condition, including arts, sciences, technology and even happiness. For both Turgot and Condorcet, progress proceeded according to laws of human development that were as deducible as laws of physics. A central point linked Turgot and Condorcet's frameworks of progress: simple societies are destined to become complex ones. Whether that is true or not, Enlightenment confidence in the supposed laws of human development influenced nineteenth- and twentieth-century anthropology via theories of positivism and cultural evolution.

The Nineteenth Century

The Enlightenment influenced nineteenth-century philosopher Auguste Comte (1798–1857), who believed in a universal law of progress that 'necessarily results from the instinctive tendency of the human race to perfect itself'. Comte founded a school of thought called *positivism*. Positivism held that society could be studied scientifically in the same manner as one studied chemistry or physics. In the nineteenth century, many thought the road to the perfectibility that Comte envisioned could be seen through the study of other societies. The comparative method used other cultures to represent earlier presumed stages of human progress. The comparative method certainly had its predecessors in the Enlightenment, and even as far back as classical Greece. Scottish Enlightenment philosopher Adam Ferguson (1723–1816) held that Greek historian Thucydides (460–400 BC) initiated the study of the other—called barbarians by the ancient Greeks—to understand their own past: 'Thucydides…understood that it was in the customs of barbarous nations he was to study the more ancient manners of Greece' (Ferguson [1767] 1995, p. 80). Several important nineteenth-century thinkers believed humans had started off their careers in a simple state of nature and that they gradually became more complex. In the history of cultural anthropology, the most important of these thinkers were Darwin, Morgan and Marx.

Charles Darwin (1809–1882)

Before Darwin, most naturalists thought that species of plants and animals, including humans, had been created by God, and that God's plan involved human progress. But in the mid-1850s, the British scientist Charles Darwin proposed a theory that differed radically from Enlightenment and positivist concepts of progress or ideas about the development of society and technology.

Darwin was interested in why plants and animals changed over time. New research in geology and the study of the fossil record were making it clear that some plants and animals had existed in the past but had gone extinct. Other species, some of which Darwin observed himself, seemed to be new. Darwin proposed that species had changed over long stretches of time, what he called 'descent with modification' (Darwin (1859) 1998, p. 132). Darwin showed that the Earth was much more ancient than generally believed. Historian Sidney Pollard remarked:

> Darwin had vastly lengthened the time span within which social evolution could be presumed to have taken place…and made the opposite, a static view of the world, impossible to hold by anyone aspiring to a scientific outlook.
>
> (1968, p. 134)

Naturalists had made such observations before, as early as the Greek philosopher Aristotle; however, they did not know *how* species changed. Jean Lamarck, who believed species had changed over time and that life was related, as did Darwin, proposed that an animal could change its form spontaneously due to some stimulus in the environment. Darwin (1859, p. 13) admitted to not knowing the 'laws governing inheritance' (what today is called genetics), but he realised that some natural force acted upon species and caused them to change. He called this force *natural selection*, a basic principle of biology today. It is a mechanistic theory for change in species. Natural selection is the idea that those creatures with a trait that gives them the best chance of surviving will reproduce and pass on that trait. Darwin pointed out (1859, p.139) that tails of different species of squirrels ranged on a continuum from minimally flattened to very wide and to the flying squirrel's tail that is connected by tissue to a 'broad expanse of skin, which serves as a parachute and allows them to glide through the air to an astonishing distance from tree to tree'. From that, he argued that each environment selected for squirrels' differences of tails: 'each structure is of use to each kind of squirrel in its own country, by enabling it to escape birds or beasts of prey, or to collect food more quickly, or…by lessening the danger from occasional falls' (1859, p. 139). There is still variation in each species, and if the environment were to change, Darwin predicted that 'some at least of the squirrels would decrease in numbers or become exterminated, unless they also became modified and improved in structure in a corresponding manner' (1859, p. 139).

One of Darwin's most important findings for cultural anthropology is that biological evolution is not the same as cultural change. The evolution of organisms is driven by a mechanism that has no ultimate objective of 'progress'. Evolution by natural selection is largely contingent on environmental conditions and the survival of those individuals best adapted to them. Cultural change in contrast depends on many factors, including both evolutionary forces and historical contingencies--history itself, in fact.

Lewis Henry Morgan (1818–1881)

American lawyer Lewis Henry Morgan (Figure 4.1) was also interested in change through time, but not the biological kind that Darwin studied. Morgan wanted to understand social and cultural changes and how they related to human progress. Like Darwin, he did not confuse biology with culture. He believed that human cultural evolution began with a stage he called 'Lower Savagery', in which language begins, and people subsist on fruits and roots; the period ends with the acquisition of fire and the know-how to subsist on fish.

According to Morgan, cultures in the Lower Savagery stage lacked rules governing sexual access: people mated with whomever they chose in what Morgan called 'promiscuous intercourse'. In these early, savage societies, it was impossible to know who one's father was since a woman could have had sexual relations with a number of men. For Morgan, these earliest societies had no idea of paternity, as he understood it. Therefore, societies were organised according to a rule of descent through females, what anthropologists call *matrilineal descent*. Morgan had learned about matrilineality first-hand among the Iroquois. He wrote, 'Not the least remarkable among their institutions, was that which

Figure 4.1 Lewis Henry Morgan, who developed a scheme of cultural evolution. Alamy.

confined the transmission of all titles, rights and property in the female line to the exclusion of the male' (Morgan (1851) 1995, pp. 79–80).

Morgan mistakenly equated matrilineal descent with *matriarchy*, or political rule by women. Iroquois women had more influence and power than women in many other societies that were not matrilineal—they owned the houses in which people lived, they could nominate leaders and they controlled how food and other goods were distributed—but they did not have sole political power.

Morgan considered recognition of *paternity*, or biological fatherhood, to be the first step towards *patriarchy*, rule by men, which in his evolutionary scheme was more advanced than matriarchy. Once people could recognise paternity, momentous changes in society started taking place. Men would then own property, so inheritance from one's father became something of value. Once men were in charge of wealth and could determine who got it, a woman's virginity and her sexual loyalty to her husband after marriage became highly valued. According to Morgan, 'far back in barbarism [men] began to exact fidelity from the wife' (Morgan 1877, p. 389) for the sake of property and inheritance in a patriarchal system. Morgan believed that this occurred sometime after the fall of matriarchy. In his scheme, patriarchal families with land and other property would eventually become nuclear families, or what Morgan called 'monogamian families', with individual property ownership. Morgan conceived of such property and family organisation as the pinnacle of human achievement and an important step towards capitalism.

Morgan's basic evolutionary scheme for the human species was divided into three sequential stages:

Savagery → Barbarism → Civilisation

To Morgan and others, the Savagery stage was a time of scouring the earth for food and the invention of fire and ended with the invention of the bow and arrow. During Barbarism, pottery, agriculture and iron smelting were invented. Civilisation involved the emergence of writing and literacy. In addition to these inventions, Morgan envisioned changes in social organisation, morality and property ownership. In essence, society and the family went from being group oriented with shared concerns to individualistic, monogamous and propertied. Morgan's ideas are important to cultural anthropology because in his research on human origins and development, he discovered differences in the way people classify one another, specifically in terms of kinship. He invented the study of human kinship systems (Chapter 6), which would occupy more pages in the literature of cultural anthropology in the twentieth century than any other topic. Although his evolutionary scheme of human advancement has been abandoned, many late-twentieth-century cultural anthropologists valued his idea that the increasing complexity of social forms is based on whether property was communal (as in 'Savagery' and 'Barbarism') or individually owned (as in 'Civilisation'). In that way, Morgan influenced the way twentieth-century materialists understood cultural evolution.

Karl Marx (1818–1883)

Morgan influenced Marx, who proposed a materialist theory of human society. Materialists believe institutions are ultimately derived from environmental and economic conditions that are empirically observable. Depending on their relationship to raw materials, the organisation of labour and the structure of property ownership, societies may be stratified—organised into groups that have differential access to power and wealth—or classless and egalitarian, without such distinctions. Marx wrote about mid-nineteenth-century factory workers, their poverty and their inability to own the products they made: he called workers like this the *proletariat*. Marx studied textile factories, equipped with steam engines and power looms and managed by overseers, in which the workers were exploited by the factory owners, or capitalists. Marx argued in his book *Capital* that the proletariat worked for half of what they really earned. The value produced by the factory worker was double what the factory owner paid for the labour; this excess value was profit. The workers were therefore alienated from their products because they did not own the means of production: the machines and the natural resources used to make goods for sale. Capitalists, who were the elite, owned the means of production and had control of most of the money, which was used as the basis of exchange. They paid workers money in the form of wages in exchange for their labour. The workers used their money to purchase necessities. Such capitalist societies are stratified, with elites and commoners, rich and poor. The society's economy was organised in terms of how the capitalists, those who owned the means of production, interacted with the workers in a class system: this was called the relations of production. Together, the means and relations of production were a society's mode of production. The mode of production of nineteenth-century factory workers and most people today is *capitalism*.

Poor working conditions and long hours along with the unrestricted use of child labour led to an inherent class conflict, Marx argued, between factory workers and capitalists. He thought such conflict would only be resolved by the overthrow of capitalism and its replacement by a classless, communist mode of production. That prediction has led to debate and controversy on Marx's contribution to the development of anthropology as a science of humankind. His prediction of a classless, state society never materialised, in spite of efforts in the twentieth century by political leaders in countries such as the Soviet Union, China, Cuba and Vietnam. That is because all states are stratified, divided into economically and politically unequal groups.

Marx's work opened the door to the ethnographic study of class, a segment of society, such as industrial workers or elites and entrepreneurs, which occupies a particular economic position in society. Cultural anthropologists today study not only small-scale egalitarian societies but also individual classes. They evaluate how stratification and elite ownership of property, such as the factories and resources that are the means of production, affect the ways that people produce food, exchange goods and services and relate to each other as groups. Marx's ideas about capitalism and social classes have been important influences in cultural anthropology and have structured the ways that anthropologists understand modern social and economic systems.

Museums

In 1796, President George Washington stated that government should 'promote as an object of primary importance…institutions for the increase and diffusion of knowledge'. He thought that it was 'essential that public opinion should be enlightened'. Part of the enlightenment that early American positivists sought for the wider public concerned the American Indian. Early ethnographers had an interest in indigenous material culture, such as weaponry, basketry, ceramics, clothing and dwellings, as well as in languages and folklore. Documentation of artefacts was increasingly left to museum curation and interpretation. Indigenous artefacts were displayed in ways that reflected the contemporary view of cultural progress from supposedly less civilised to more civilised, as in the Smithsonian Institution, which was founded in 1846 by Englishman James Smithson 'for the increase and diffusion of knowledge'.

An important undertaking in American museum anthropology was the study of Native American societies, especially after the Civil War (1861–1865), which was often conducted by former soldiers especially of the US, or Union side of that conflict. The most important figure in this period of American anthropology was John Wesley Powell (1834–1902), a Union army veteran who became director of the Bureau of American Ethnology in 1879 (Figure 4.2), located in Washington, D.C. Powell was influenced

Figure 4.2 John Wesley Powell, a dominant force in American anthropology and military ethnography, in his Washington, DC, office, c. 1896. Smithsonian Institution and the United States Geological Survey Photo Library.

by Morgan's cultural evolutionary scheme. His goal was to found a 'science of man' on the basis of research on North American Indians. He hired many former soldiers to do 'military ethnography' by documenting Native life and collecting artefacts for museums.

The Early Twentieth Century

Franz Boas (1858–1942) and the Boasian Research Program

Franz Boas, a geographer and physicist by training, may be called the first professional anthropologist in the United States. He trained Zora Neale Hurston (see Figure 1.1; Cultural Snapshot 1.1) and many of the leading figures of anthropology in the twentieth century. As a young scholar from Germany, Boas had studied Inuit migration patterns on Baffin Island in the Canadian Arctic between 1883 and 1884. His interest was in the relationship of the physical world to mental phenomena.

Boas noted that the Inuit way of classifying reality was different from his own. In fact, his six months of fieldwork on Baffin Island changed his outlook on reality forever. He appreciated the Inuit way of making a living in the harsh environment of sea ice in winter and tundra in summer and admired the technology that allowed the Inuit to survive. He was interested in their classification of frozen landscapes, their understanding of living things, their folklore and mythology and the language they used to convey this knowledge. Boas learned to understand the Inuit people, their ways, mores, customs, language—in short, their culture—on their own terms. Boas would extend that appreciation, in principle, to all cultures different from his own, in a new way of thinking called *cultural relativism* (Cultural Snapshot 4.2). Cultural relativism means tolerance of other people who have been enculturated differently from oneself. It is the opposite of ethnocentrism (Chapter 3). Boas felt that an ethnographer could not really grasp the customs of another people without first adopting an attitude of tolerance, or at least one of objectivity, as much as possible. To do this required suppressing, if necessary, any pre-existing ethnocentric bias against other cultures and their customs. He also argued that all languages were equally sophisticated. Boas was one of the first to propose that there are no savage, barbarous or primitive languages. No language known in the world is simple, rudimentary or easy, something that linguistic anthropologists have demonstrated numerous times since Boas' observation.

CULTURAL SNAPSHOT 4.2

Boas' Relativism

Boas believed all cultures and languages were equally virtuous and sophisticated in principle. He argued that biological variation in human populations, which he called race, was of no importance for understanding differences of language and culture between different societies. There were neither barbaric nor advanced cultures and languages, just different ones. To fully understand the human condition, it would be necessary to carry out research on all known societies, because each one had a different history. Thus, Boas' view of cultural similarity and variation is sometimes called historical particularism. With this view, change in culture was explained in terms of environmental and social contingencies and through diffusion. Boas pointed out that 'as soon as two groups come into close contact their cultural traits will be disseminated from the one to the other'. He also pointed out that:

> Unless we know how the culture of each group of [people] came to be what it is, we cannot expect to reach any conclusions in regard to the conditions controlling the general history of culture.
>
> (Boas 1948, p. 258)

To Boas, language, culture, and human biological diversity were not necessarily linked: all had independent histories. This insight was essential to the new science of anthropology as Boas envisaged it.

Boas felt that his mission was to educate his students—and ultimately, the American public—on the evils of racism and ethnocentrism, the value of all cultures and the need to document everything there was to know about Native cultures, which he believed were disappearing. Boas and his students sought to understand humanity in the holistic way. They understood that cultural, linguistic, biological and archaeological data were needed. The four fields of modern American anthropology emerged from their work. During the early twentieth century under Boas, anthropology became a profession with a distinct career path for its practitioners. The basic premise of the new discipline was that humankind was one species composed of diverse cultures and languages that were of scientific value despite their differences.

To Boas, every culture had a history and a timeline of its own. This belief challenged the evolutionist legacy of Morgan and blocked the adoption and teaching of the concept of unilinear cultural evolution in American anthropology for the next 50 years. Boas was not opposed to the idea of biological evolution by natural selection; his objection was to Morgan's concept of cultural evolution. He rejected attempts to classify aboriginal societies into stages of savagery or barbarism. Nor were native people living fossils, evidence for some earlier stage in human evolution, an idea that Boas found ethnocentric and racist. Boas also opposed the reduction of 'human nature' to single traits (Cultural Snapshot 4.3).

Despite physical differences in head shape, stature or skin colour, some of the usual indicators of folk 'race' in Western science of the time, Boas believed that there were no real cultural or mental differences between humans. He wrote: 'The psychological basis of cultural traits is identical among all races, and similar forms develop among all of them' (Boas 1938, p. 33). The same principle, Boas said, applied to language: 'Neither race nor language limits differences of ideas and inventions typical of civilization' (1938, p. 37). For Boas, the vocabulary and grammar of a language were specific to time and place. Language was part of the human adaptation to the environment, as were phenotypic differences he referred to as 'race' and 'culture'. Language and culture were also influenced by the diffusion of ideas and technology from without (Cultural Snapshot 4.2). Any child could learn any language or culture, which meant that the colour of a person's skin had no intrinsic link to either culture or the language an individual spoke. A child with dark skin born to an Australian Aboriginal family had the capacity to learn the language and culture of the United States just as an Anglo-American child born in

Timeline 4.2 Developments in sociocultural anthropology, 1893–1939.

Europe	United States	Developments in the other three fields
• Malinowski popularises method of participant observation • Durkheim proposes the *conscience collective* (1893) • Malinowski publishes *Argonauts of the Western Pacific* (1922)	• Four fields of anthropology are consolidated • Boasian emphasis on cultural and linguistic relativism • Boas publishes *The Mind of Primitive Man* (1911) • Kroeber publishes • *Anthropology* (1923)	• Sapir–Whorf hypothesis in linguistic anthropology • seriation in archaeology • fossil hominins in Africa first identified as human ancestors

Boston could learn to speak an Aboriginal language and survive in the Western Desert of Australia. Boas argued that phenotype did not determine language or culture; all humans were equally capable of speaking any language and learning any culture. This principle is part of Boas' relativism: the idea that all cultures are of equal value. Like languages, cultures are neither inferior nor superior. They are all human and modern to the same degree (Timeline 4.2). It does not mean that everything that pertains to the cultural rules of any given society is good or bad, moral or immoral, smart or stupid. It simply means that as a starting point of analysis, comparisons of cultures are best undertaken by researchers who have made a sincere, vigorous effort to remove any possible ethnocentrism or bias in their approach to such study.

CULTURAL SNAPSHOT 4.3

Homo **this, that and the other**

Boas, his students and modern cultural anthropologists have sought to 'poke and pry' into doctrines of human nature. These doctrines are inherently vulnerable because only one counterexample undermines the whole edifice. Boas stated that 'initial investigation…shows that forms of thought and action which we are inclined to consider as based on human nature are not generally valid, but characteristic of our specific culture' (Boas 1948, p. 258). Here are a few ways that the human species has been conceived in Western thought. Each one reduces human nature to a single trait:

* *Homo loquens* (humans as linguistic, or talkative). Some apes, like Kanzi (Cultural Snapshot 2.1), are uncanny in their communication skills too (Chapter 2).
* *Homo bellicosus* (humans as bellicose, or warlike). Cultural anthropologist Raymond Kelly notes that the only societies that do not practice warfare are some egalitarian foraging groups. If they did engage in killing, it was for self-defence. These groups include the indigenous Sirionó people of the Bolivian Amazon, the Batek hunter-gatherers of peninsular Malaysia and the Guajá hunter-gatherers of the Brazilian Amazon. As Enlightenment philosopher Rousseau wrote, 'individuals are enemies accidentally, not as *men*, nor even as citizens, but as *soldiers*; not as members of their country but as its defenders'.

- *Homo nobilis* or *Homo ecologicus* (humans as ecologically noble savages). Biologist Kent Redford coined the term 'ecologically noble savage' to refer to the mistaken belief that indigenous peoples live in harmony with nature and never destroy it. Humans, including native people, have caused countless animal extinctions. The giant moa, a flightless land bird of New Zealand, was driven to extinction by overly enthusiastic human hunters. It seems likely according to archaeologist Gaspar Morcote-Rios and his colleagues (2021) that humans contributed to the extinction thousands of years ago of the giant ground sloth and perhaps other megafauna like Ice Age mastodons and horses in Amazonia, for people had seen them, probably hunted them, and even rendered them in spectacular ancient rock paintings—recently discovered--that date from more than 12,000 years ago.
- *Homo devastans* (humans as destroyers). This doctrine holds that humans naturally annihilate the plants and animals in their environment. However, some egalitarian societies have created habitats that foster biodiversity. Ancient societies of Amazonia built giant earthworks and causeways in flooded savannas. Few plants could grow on the savannas naturally, but atop the earthworks today are tropical forests rich in flora and fauna not otherwise found in the savanna. Other examples from Africa and Oceania also show that humans can *contribute* to biodiversity, rather than destroy it.

Human nature is neither completely destructive and warlike nor ecologically noble; human societies exist at various points between these two extremes.

Salvage Ethnography

Boas' students commonly recruited elderly persons as informants to understand the time before colonialism destroyed Native ways of life. They were engaged in *salvage ethnography*, the attempt to find out all they could before indigenous cultures vanished—they believed—forever. In the United States, anthropologists doing salvage ethnography recorded verbatim the reminiscences of the oldest people on Indian reservations. Included in the scope of salvage ethnography was asking elders to describe Native culture, including dances, songs, basketry designs, masks and myths, before their meanings were lost to the world.

Salvage ethnography had been going on since the work of John Wesley Powell in the late nineteenth century, before Boas and his students took up the study of American Indian cultures. They refined it with new theories and approaches. Like almost every other cultural anthropologist of his generation, Alfred Kroeber, a student of Boas and a specialist on American Indians, was a salvage ethnographer. He studied California Indians and founded one of the first anthropology departments in the United States at the University of California, Berkeley. He was well known for his association with Ishi, the last surviving Yahi Indian (Figure 2.1).

Ishi appeared in Oroville, California, in 1911, hungry, exhausted and alone after escaping from white ranchers and miners who had killed many of his relatives, including his sister. Kroeber, together with another student of Boas, linguist Edward Sapir (1884–1939), recorded as much as they could about the precontact language and culture of the Yahi while Ishi resided at the Phoebe Hearst Museum of Anthropology as a sort of in-house informant and living exhibit until his death in 1916 from tuberculosis. Ishi's story is not unique; there are other cases of people who are the last surviving members of their societies (Cultural Snapshot 4.4).

Patterns and Configurations of Culture

Women's Dress Fashions. Kroeber's main theoretical contribution to cultural anthropology was to show that culture is a learned and shared thing outside the body and mind of any one individual, what he called the *superorganic.* The superorganic was another way of saying culture but in a special sense. Kroeber envisioned culture not just as a set of rules that people lived by, but as a distinctive, historically defined social medley—or configuration—of thoughts, morals, values and attitudes. Kroeber (1876–1960) saw fashion as an aspect of culture more prone to change than others. He studied women's dress catalogues from the late 1700s to the early 1900s looking for changes in fashion. He found that the fashions changed incrementally every year or so in terms of hem-, neck- and waistlines, sleeve length and overall silhouette. He determined that these changes were cyclical; they repeated over several decades. Fashion was a part of culture that could be revealed through analysis of its artefacts over time. It changed without conscious intent and was an instance of the superorganic in that it operated independently of any felt need, physical or otherwise.

CULTURAL SNAPSHOT 4.4

An Ishi Story from the Amazon

In October 1987, the Brazilian government enlisted my help in identifying newly found indigenous people living along a logging road in the eastern Amazon. The previous June, two men had arrived at a farmer's house and caused a stir because they were naked and appeared to be from an uncontacted society. Government agents later met the two men at the forest's edge and began the routine process of finding the other indigenes they thought lived nearby. But as time went by, no one else showed up. One day, one of the government workers and I walked into the forest and found the last two campsites of the men. We called them Auré and Aurá. Both had lived together in lean-tos with makeshift roofs tied to nearby trees using vines. They had slept on palm thatch and appeared to have been eating tortoises and Brazil nuts, food that can be gathered by hand on the ground. One had an old bow and arrows with points of deer bone and bamboo. Making bows and arrows is a skill that takes years to master. Most boys do not do so until late adolescence in most parts of Amazonia. The bow this man was using was twisted and lacked tensile strength. The arrows were all top-heavy, making it difficult to hunt successfully.

I suspected that Auré and Aurá had been orphaned many years ago and had not learned some of the basic skills of their society. I could put together rudimentary questions and understand their answers because I knew languages closely related to

Figure 4.3 Aurá, speaker of a Tupí-Guaraní language previously unknown to science, and the next-to-last living member of his tribe in 1995, shortly before his death. Photo by author.

the one they spoke. In fact, they spoke a language never before recorded, one new to science, and they were the only speakers known to be still alive.

I asked Auré about his father, and he answered, '*Manũ*' ('he's dead'). I then asked, 'What killed him?' The man's reply was instantaneous, '*Awa-yu yuka*' ('The yellow people killed him'). The 'yellow people' had apparently massacred everyone in their society when the two men were adolescents; only they had survived to adulthood in the forest, eating and making things by hand, with minimal technology and little skill. They had not been fully enculturated, unlike Ishi (Figure 2.1). I saw the two again in 1995, when they were living in a government agency camp in the forest. Aurá (Figure 4.3) died some years ago. The only survivor is Auré, who like Ishi, is the last of his tribe.

Forgotten Geniuses. Kroeber studied genius as a way to demonstrate the independence and superorganic essence of culture. For Kroeber, genius—defined as possession of prodigious mental gifts of discovery or creation—was not always confined to individual minds. Discoveries could occur in more than one mind in a culture simultaneously, indicating that the superorganic accumulation of ideas made the time ripe for the discovery in question. For example, sunspots were discovered independently by Fabricius, Galileo, Harriot and Scheiner in 1611. The telescope was independently invented by Janssen, Lippershey and Metius in 1608. Oxygen was discovered by Priestley and Scheele in 1774. The telephone was independently invented by Gray and Bell in 1876.

The important point is that inventions are inevitable, not just products of individual genius. Kroeber remarked, 'No one denies that there are great men…The fallacy is to infer from this that everything important in history must have had a great man as its specific cause' (1948, p. 365). Change in science and technology is not just driven by individual genius. Rather, it is a shared, superorganic *group* phenomenon that has historical, contingent causes, not biological ones. Kroeber's theories regarding the superorganic— that set of beliefs, values and attitudes that exist independently of individual minds and bodies—contributed to an interdisciplinary field called *culture and personality*.

Culture and Personality

Psychological anthropology emerged from the study of attitudes, values and norms in society, which began with the work of cultural anthropologists Ruth Benedict (1887– 1948) and Margaret Mead (1901–1978). Their work on culture and personality, together with national character studies of the World War II era, focused on the development of the individual during childhood and his or her relationship to culture. As students of Boas, Benedict and Mead were interested in the human psyche and the use of the concept of culture to understand observed psychological differences across societies. Benedict studied American Indian cultures and viewed culture as the expression of a distinctive shared group personality.

She classified cultures into the polar extremes of *Dionysian*, after the Greek god of wine, meaning intemperate and grandiose, and *Apollonian*, after the Greek god of beauty, meaning sensitive and measured. She viewed the Kwakwaka'wakw (Kwakiutl) Indians, studied by her mentor, Boas, as Dionysian. She emphasised what she believed to be the excessive and competitive nature of their culture evident in the potlatch (Chapter 3; Figure 4.4). Benedict suggested that potlatches caused people to work themselves into a frenzy, competing for status in displays of irrational liberality and destruction:

> In [Kwakwaka'wakw] institutions, such rivalry reaches a final absurdity in equating investment with wholesale destruction of goods. They contest for superiority chiefly in accumulation of goods, but often also, and without a consciousness of the contrast, in breaking into pieces their highest units of value, their coppers, and making bonfires of their house planks, their blankets and canoes.
>
> (Benedict 1946, p. 196)

Benedict contrasted the Kwakwaka'wakw with the Hopi of Arizona, whom she characterised as peace loving and given to moderation in all things. Her approach has been criticised for its *psychological reductionism*; that is, reducing cultural similarities and differences to the single variable of individual psychology.

Margaret Mead, a friend and contemporary of Benedict, did fieldwork in American Samoa in the early 1920s. She studied the sexual attitudes and behaviours of Samoan girls. Her data suggested that the girls had uncomplicated and guilt-free premarital sexual experiences, which she contrasted with the difficulties experienced by American girls during their teen years and the strict regulation of their sexual behaviour. Mead argued that although biological factors such as hormones influenced behaviour, culture was a more important variable. Like Boas, she believed that culture overrode biology in certain instances. Mead's work was criticised 50 years later by Derek Freeman, who suggested that she was misled by the Samoan girls who spoke to her about their experiences.

Figure 4.4 Kwakwaka'wakw potlatch ceremony on Vancouver Island, Canada, ca. 1914. Alamy.

In World War II, cultural anthropology was used to assist in the Allied war effort. American officials sought to understand their enemies by viewing them in terms of personality types. They wanted this information to defeat and successfully occupy nations such as Japan and, later, the Soviet Union, after the hostilities were over. This attempt to accumulate information on the personality types of people in other countries, called *national character studies*, was accomplished by a method known as 'ethnography at a distance'.

Benedict studied the art, lore and history of Japan, and though she never went there, published a national character study of the country called *The Chrysanthemum and the Sword* in 1946. The book portrayed Japanese culture as paradoxical: on the one hand, displaying pride in the aesthetics of bonsai and flower arrangements, and on the other hand, promoting the aggressive masculine culture of samurai warriors. Benedict saw contradictions in the Japanese national character in the samurai *chu* principle of fighting to the death and, conversely, in the change of heart after defeat in World War II, when the Japanese 'outdid themselves' by cooperating with the occupying US forces. Benedict explained these contradictions through the strictly stratified, hierarchical nature of Japanese society that required people to follow their emperor in admitting defeat and displaying humility.

The Problem of Reductionism

Cultural anthropologists also studied the Soviet Union at a distance after World War II. Anthropologists Geoffrey Gorer and Margaret Mead collaborated on this study and traced the basic Russian personality to child-rearing practices, suggesting that enculturation in infancy was a defining feature of psychological development. They believed that

Russians became paranoid and stingy as adults because they were swaddled as infants: tightly wrapped so that they could not move their arms and legs. Swaddling, they wrote, caused infant paranoia. When freed of the constriction, the infant had a perceived need to reach out and stretch its arms and legs. That dreadful infant experience was correlated in a deterministic way with the Soviet Union's apparent need to protect its own borders by stretching out and conquering surrounding lands, such as Eastern Europe. Cultural practices in childhood supposedly accounted for the expansionistic tendencies of the state itself. In the 1950s, this idea became known as the 'swaddling clothes hypothesis'.

The pervasive problem in culture and personality research, by anthropologists and psychologists alike, was psychological reductionism. Benedict, for example, based her characterisation of the Kwakwaka'wakw as Dionysian on the behaviour of men. Yet Kwakwaka'wakw society also had women and children, whose behaviours differed from that of men. And not all men in Kwakwaka'wakw society behaved in the same way. Reducing an entire society to a single personality trait was inappropriate. Personality is part of how an individual relates to others in a specific culture, not the mental structure of an entire population.

In the 1960s, refinements were made to culture and personality studies in response to the charge of psychological reductionism. The concept of basic personality was replaced by the notion of *modal personality*, or the statistically most common personality type, which could be determined using a list of psychological attributes. Yet, as more attributes were used, more personality types emerged. By refining personality definitions to fit real, living human beings, the modal personality became difficult to identify. As anthropologists sought to delineate the most common personality in a society, they gradually lost their focus on shared social values and attitudes. An alternative approach was to study diverse individuals and their relationships to local groups that could be bounded by geographic, cultural and linguistic criteria, such as communities.

Community Studies

To improve the study of other societies, cultural anthropologists in the 1930s used the town or municipality as their unit of analysis. They called this unit the *community*. *Community studies* were ethnographic projects based on the notion that the whole of a culture could be captured in a single representative settlement with definable borders. The fieldwork was carried out much as one would carry out participant observation in a camp of Australian Aborigines and involved asking the same kinds of questions: how are people related, where do they come from and what was the past like for them and their ancestors? But in small, self-sufficient societies, such as that of the Aborigines, the village or camp could well be the entire society, perhaps the whole of the hunting-and-gathering band. In complex societies, hundreds or even thousands of communities interact with or are affiliated with a state-level organisation.

Cultural anthropologist Conrad Arensberg (1910–1997) conducted participant observation in a rural Irish community in the 1930s. He considered the community to be both the object of research and a sample of the larger society. It was placed-based, unlike the notion of the 'imagined community' by political scientist Benedict Anderson, in which people who have not necessarily ever met in person and who have never corresponded consider themselves to be members of a group to which all members of the group belong. The groups can be defined by ethnicity, like the Asian-American community; a shared gender or nonbinary identity like the LGBTQ community; or a group with shared professional interests like the 'scientific community', whether they agree on basic principles or not. In contrast, the term community in the ethnography of the mid-twentieth century was always a place-based town or county or village with reasonably distinct geographic boundaries. In a specific rural Irish town, Arensberg studied how people chose their spouses, courted and married, raised children, farmed, chose their occupations, determined what they included in their wills and who inherited what. In Arensberg's study, the larger, more complex society was the nation of Ireland; the town and its surroundings were the community that represented it. Community studies tended to be normative accounts of day-to-day life and included descriptions of the seasonal changes in people's daily activities during the year as observed in the course of fieldwork. Researchers engaged in community studies were typically interested in stratified societies within states, as in the United States, Latin America, Asia and Europe.

Social Anthropology in Europe

American cultural anthropologists before World War II were mostly concerned with the ethnography of American Indians. Such salvage ethnography was not really about 'saving' the culture of American Indians, or that of other societies subjected to conquest and colonialism, which most anthropologists of the early twentieth century considered to be doomed. Rather, it was centred on documenting each culture anthropologically before it disappeared. This salvage work involved tracing the history of societies without written records and reconstructing patterns of diffusion and contact, defining the contours and limits of the superorganic and examining the relationships between individuals and culture. As we now know, not all the societies being studied were disappearing. Some have survived, although in altered forms.

While American ethnographers worked with North American Indians, their European counterparts studied the indigenous societies of European colonies in Australia, Oceania, India and Africa. Two of the most important anthropologists of European origin who conducted research within a colonial context were Bronislaw Malinowski (1884–1942) and A. R. Radcliffe-Brown (1881–1955). Both anthropologists initially focused on interpretations of rationality and the functions of institutions in other cultures.

An Exception to Economic Man

Like Boas, Malinowski objected to the idea that humans could be characterised in simple terms, such as tool user, political animal or savage warrior. He showed that not everyone behaved in a strictly rational way economically. *Economic rationality* is the belief that humans as a species seek to maximise benefits and minimise costs of goods and services. Some anthropologists believe that economic rationality is a behavioural characteristic of the species, that it is an evolved sociocultural universal. But Malinowski's data from participant observation refuted the universality of economic rationality, just as Mead's data had contradicted the psychologists' belief that adolescence was a biologically determined period of psychological stress.

Malinowski studied the Trobriand Islanders (Figure 4.5), who lived off the coast of New Guinea in the South Pacific. He observed that the Trobrianders placed inordinate, immeasurable worth on armbands and necklaces made from shells. These ornaments, known as *vaygu'a*, were not worn, used or permanently owned by anyone. The Trobrianders did not have a universal medium of exchange, such as money. Instead, they

Figure 4.5 Bronislaw Malinowski doing participant observation among Trobriand Islanders, ca. 1918. Alamy.

used shell ornaments, exchanging armbands for necklaces and vice versa. These exchanges of *vaygu'a* occurred over a period of years. The Trobriand Islanders and their neighbours, the Dobuans to the south, lived in a circle of small islands separated by open stretches of the Pacific. They conducted trading voyages, known as *kula*, between the islands and exchanged *vaygu'a*. The *kula* connected the islands economically in a system Malinowski called the *kula ring* (Figure 4.6).

In the *kula* system, necklaces moved clockwise and armbands moved counterclockwise. On a voyage to a neighbouring island, a man would present a necklace to his trading partner. The necklace brought with it a history of prior exchanges, since the *vaygu'a* could not be kept by a single owner indefinitely; it was imperative that one pass it on to one's trading partner on the nearest island. The recipient would express joy at the gift of the necklace and recount with the giver the history of its travels. At some point, the new owner would then stash the necklace in a special part of his house and leave it untouched until it was his turn to take the necklace to his trading partner on the next island in a clockwise direction. Every trader ideally had at least two overseas trade partners, one in each direction. Some men, such as chiefs, had hundreds of *kula* partners. Over time, necklaces and armbands passed through all the islands and ultimately back through their points of origin, often several times over the course of many years.

Malinowski argued that the *kula* ring ensured a peaceful coexistence, even between traders who might not see one another frequently due to distance and the dangers of ocean travel. As the trade in *vaygu'a* occurred, ideas, words and technology diffused, leading to cultural similarities in the region. The *kula* ring was part of the Trobriand economy, but it was not based on the principles of minimising costs and maximising

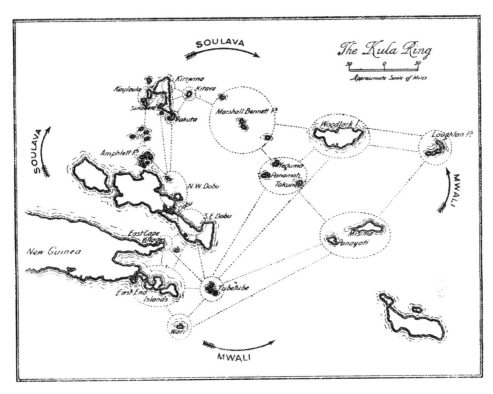

Figure 4.6 The *kula* ring in the South Pacific. The necklaces are exchanged clockwise, and the armbands move counterclockwise over time across the Trobriand Islands. Map by Malinowski (1922) [in public domain].

material benefits. Rather, it was an example of a *reciprocal economy*, which is a nonmarket economy in which the values of goods are determined not by supply and demand, but rather in social terms. Trobriand necklaces and armbands had *noninstrumental value*; their worth could not be calculated in monetary terms. Because of the time between the exchange of an armband for a necklace, the *kula* ring is an example of *delayed reciprocity*. Delayed reciprocity is a kind of generalised reciprocity, which is sharing of goods and services among people who know each other. This method of exchange occurs throughout the world, especially in economies like that of the early twentieth-century Trobrianders.

Some of Malinowski's findings were later criticised. For example, he did not address the influence of women in Trobriand politics or the fact that *kula* exchanges involved some competition for prestige among men. However, his insights into the *kula* ring and the idea that *kula* was an economy without a market or an anonymous currency, such as money, remain important to cultural anthropologists today (Chapter 11). Malinowski suggested that the notion of economic rationality current in the early twentieth century was inapplicable to the *kula* ring, which was something that could only be understood through participant observation. It required understanding the Trobrianders on *their* terms. So, what aspects of *vaygu'a* exchange conflict with the principles of economic rationality?

- Owners could not keep *vaygu'a*, nor could they be exchanged for other material things, except other *vaygu'a*.
- Owners could not use their *vaygu'a*, as ornamentation, for example.
- One could not receive payment or exchange of something else at the same time one gave *vaygu'a* to a trading partner; despite the delay in exchange, no interest accrued.

In his later years, Malinowski claimed that human behaviour was determined by visceral and psychological needs, which he called *basic needs*. Humans were animals, and culture served animal requirements: food, sex, reproduction, clothing and shelter, safety, relaxation, movement and growth. In meeting basic needs, humans experienced what Malinowski called *instrumental* and *symbolic needs*. An instrumental need, for example, was one that organised and controlled society. A symbolic need was the desire to understand and explain how the world worked, which humans satisfied through magic and religion. Institutions of society satisfied these deeply rooted individual needs, which were shared by all humans. Malinowski's approach to basic needs and human organisation was functionalist. *Functionalism* is the view that the institutions of a society carry out operations that serve the interests and needs of its members or help maintain and perpetuate society. Malinowski sought to understand social institutions in terms of the basic physical and psychological needs that he believed to be common to all societies.

The Organisation of Primitive Society

A. R. Radcliffe-Brown, an early British social anthropologist and Malinowski's contemporary, also developed a functionalist view of society. He sought to explain how different parts of society related to the whole social structure, regardless of individual needs. He used field data to support his theories about how societies functioned and came up with his own 'natural science' of human society. Radcliffe-Brown's thinking in anthropological theory was influenced by the work of French sociologist Émile Durkheim (1858–1917). For Durkheim, society had a life of its own, apart from its individual members' lives and bodies. Durkheim believed that people in small-scale societies had a division of labour based on age and sex differences only; every adult of each sex could do the same work as all the others. Members of such societies shared a similar *collective conscience*, a similar worldview and sense of what is right or wrong. The collective conscience of a small town can be seen in the event of, say, a sex scandal. According to Durkheim, the local people:

> stop each other on the street, they visit each other, they seek to come together to talk of the event and to wax indignant in common…There emerges a unique temper…which is everybody's without being anybody's in particular. That is the public temper.
>
> ([1893] 1933, p. 102)

Durkheim's 'public temper' was the collective conscience, and it was very similar to Kroeber's superorganic and Tylor's concept of culture. Individuals were mechanical duplicates of one another; they did the same jobs and they had the same views of things. Durkheim called the social organisation of such groups *mechanical solidarity*. The social organisation of complex societies, on the other hand, Durkheim called *organic solidarity*, because of the profusion of different professions and occupations. Rather than duplicating each other, people in complex societies complemented one another organically, working together to function in a way analogous to the organs of the human body. The collective conscience in such complex societies was much less unified than it was in simpler societies.

Radcliffe-Brown, influenced by Durkheim's writings, went to study the natives of a British colonial outpost, the Andaman Islands in the Bay of Bengal, off the east coast of India. He published *The Andaman Islanders* in 1922, the same year that Malinowski published *Argonauts of the Western Pacific* on the Trobrianders. Later, Radcliffe-Brown did fieldwork among Australian Aborigines, where he sought to apply Durkheim's concepts of organic and mechanical solidarity.

Structural-Functionalism

Radcliffe-Brown was especially interested in Aboriginal family organisation and kinship terminologies and how these related to social life. He saw the study of human society as a branch of natural science and viewed society as having its own structure and function, similar to the anatomy and physiology of an organism. The functionalist school of thought Radcliffe-Brown founded came to be called *structural-functionalism*. Structural-functionalists viewed society as a social body with parts integrated into an interdependent whole. Just as the function of the heart is to pump blood, the function of a taboo on contact between a man and his *affines*, or in-laws, was to prevent competition and conflict over his wife. Structural-functionalists viewed the organisation of society and the behaviour of its members as distinct from ideas, technology and other aspects of culture. This idea separated British social anthropology from American cultural anthropology.

Playwright George Bernard Shaw famously noted that 'England and America are two countries separated by a common language'. His observation also applies to the two Anglophone schools of anthropology in the early twentieth century. American anthropologists tended to be interested in culture: learned behaviour and the artefacts, or *material culture*, such behaviour produced. On the other hand, Radcliffe-Brown and his students were concerned with how the parts of society and human behaviours bolstered the integrity and solidarity of the whole.

Radcliffe-Brown disdained nineteenth-century cultural evolutionism: the idea that humans progressed along a unilinear cultural trajectory. But he was also ill at ease with the Boasian concept of culture and Kroeber's superorganic. He was more interested in how human behaviour reflected a social order that no one could escape. His emphasis was on the present, on society as a system of interrelated parts, and on how those parts functioned. Radcliffe-Brown argued that the rules governing kin relationships determined how one should act in public, for example, by avoiding some people and joking with others. These actions, once performed, reinforced people's belief in the rightness of the social structure and society's rules. In other words, when a person avoided a tabooed mother-in-law or joked with a cousin, as one was supposed to, that person was actually helping to maintain the structure of society. Structural-functionalism, however, tended to apply only to societies organised centrally around kinship principles. In other words, it was restricted to small-scale, kin-based societies.

Radcliffe-Brown's structural-functionalism, like Malinowski's functionalism, explained how human societies stayed the same, not how they changed. Nor did these theories explain how or why cultures differed. This is the weakness of all functionalist theory: it explains how a system of relationships works but cannot account for changes in that system unless they are cyclical, predictable and repetitive. Change in a functionalist system involves a return to an earlier, supposedly steady state of organisation, similar to the idea of equilibrium in other sciences.

Summary

Early anthropology was based on the notion that reason rather than religious revelation could lead to insights into human society and institutions. That notion and the concept of progress that went with it originated in the Enlightenment, along with the belief that the human species could be studied from a scientific perspective. In the nineteenth century, the idea of progress was expressed in positivism and in Morgan's cultural evolutionism, in which human culture developed in stages, from savagery to civilisation. Darwin's work showed how the evolution of species, including humans, was separate from divine guidance and had no particular goal. Marx proposed that societies could be best understood not in terms of their beliefs and attitudes, but in terms of people's material relations to one another and to their work. At the end of the nineteenth century, in the United States, Franz Boas reacted to the classification of societies as 'savage' or 'barbarian'. He argued that each society had a unique history and advocated cultural and linguistic relativism. His student, Alfred Kroeber, made important contributions to the concept of culture by formulating the idea of the superorganic. New theories and areas of study arose in the twentieth century, including culture and personality, community studies, functionalism and structural-functionalism.

Further Reading

Eighteenth Century

Adams 1998; Bidney 1954; Cannon 1990; Hallowell 1960; Jefferson (1785) 1999; Mitra 1933; Renfrew and Bahn 1996; Trautmann 2011

Nineteenth Century

Carneiro 2003 (pp. 43–48, 70); Comte 1975; Crehan 2002; Darnell 1977; Darwin (1859) 1998 (pp. 13, 139); Hallowell 1960 (pp. 101–102); Hinsley 1981; Leslie 1963; Marx (1867) 1977b; Meltzer 1985; Mitra 1933; Pels and Salemink 1999; Pietz 1999; Wolf 1997; Worster 2001

Early Twentieth Century

Arensberg 1988; Boas 1938, (1911) 1991; Brondizio 2008; Brown 1991; Eggan 1963; Goodale 2006; Hewl-ett and Cavalli-Sforza 1986; Hinsley 1981, 1999; Kroeber 1948; MacCabe and Yanacek 2018; Rosman and Rubel 1986; Stocking 1974; Worster 2001

Social Anthropology in Europe

Adams 1998; Malinowski (1922) 1984, 1944; McGrane 1989; Pandya 2007; Pels and Salemink 1999; Radcliffe-Brown 1952; Tomas 1991; Weiner 1988

Cultural Snapshots

4.1   Adams 1998 (p. 20 n58); de Condorcet (1795) 1955; Harvey 1989 (p. 13); Meek 1973 (pp. 7, 42–43); Pollard 1968 (pp. 78–80)

4.2   Bayliss-Smith et al. 2003; Erickson and Balée 2006; Fairhead and Leach 1996; Kelly 2000; Sahlins 1976b (p. 9)

4.3   Boas (1911) 1991, 1948 (pp. 250–251)

4.4   Balée 2013, pp. 12–18

5 Contemporary Theory and Method

Overview

Anthropology underwent major changes in the years around World War II (1939–1945). The discipline moved away from the particularistic emphasis on individual cultures, as pioneered by Boas and Malinowski, to concentrating on *explanations* of cultural differences and variation. These explanations originated in different research programmes. A *research programme* is a particular way of thinking about an object of study. It consists of several basic assumptions about the most likely reality and most accurate interpretation of the object of study. Research programmes also employ specific theories about given cultures, such as structural-functionalism, which assumes that the constituent parts of society are interdependent.

In contrast to structural-functionalism, materialist research programmes assume that cultures are best understood in terms of conflicts between social groups, such as classes or families, over access to resources such as clean water, arable land and raw materials for technology and construction. The dominant research programme in the United States in the 1920s and 1930s was the Boasian research programme (Chapter 4), sometimes called *historical particularism*.

By the 1940s, the Boasian research programme had been abandoned and was replaced by modernist programmes as American and European anthropologists began to do fieldwork in new locations. Anthropology since 1945 can be divided into two broad periods: modernity (1945–1980s) and postmodernity (1980s–early 2000s). Modernism is essentially the continuation of Enlightenment ideals of human progress and rationality. It represents a conceptual break with religion and explanations that rely upon divine intervention in human history. Modernism sought to understand the human condition through positivism and scientific data collection and analysis. In anthropology, broad research programmes emerged with the objective of comparing human social institutions to understand cultural differences and similarities. Modernist anthropologists were interested in understanding transformations of society—for example, from small-scale to stratified—or social stability and the maintenance of the current conditions, the status quo. They asked why some societies change while others stay the same.

Postmodernism, in contrast, questions the optimism of the Enlightenment belief in the clocklike progress of the human species and abandons the positivist endeavour to explain cultural similarities and differences scientifically. The principle of cultural relativism is the postmodern baseline for understanding difference. Postmodernists hold that ethnographic research is rooted in *observer bias*, the notion that ethnographic writings on other cultures cannot be impartial because the ethnographers themselves are biased. They, too, were enculturated in childhood and they bring their own preferences, attitudes and beliefs into the field.

Postmodernism holds that human culture is subjective and contingent. Unlike phenomena such as atoms, molecules or chromosomes, culture does not lend itself to study by scientific methods; people do not always behave in predictable ways, or according to universal laws, such as those that govern physical or chemical processes. Postmodern anthropologists have promoted not only cultural relativism but also *epistemological relativism*, the perspective that there is more than one way of knowing things in an anthropologically valid way and that objectivity in the study of human culture, past or present, is unattainable. For postmodernists, knowledge about society is based on interpretation, not scientific proof; therefore, it is subjective, not impartial.

Postmodernism is basically an extended critique of the Enlightenment and the nineteenth-century origins of modernism in positivism and evolutionism. Currently, cultural anthropology is characterised by elements of both modernism and postmodernism. In this chapter, we examine some debates in the evaluation of anthropological research and conclude with a discussion of current methods available in the toolkit of cultural anthropology and an assessment of participant observation.

Modernism

New Approaches to Cultural Evolution

The two major figures in reviving the concept of cultural evolution in the twentieth century were White and Steward. Leslie White (1900–1975) was an American anthropologist who admired Morgan and felt that his legacy had been misunderstood. And although he did not agree with unilinear evolution (the idea that all cultures are destined to follow one line of progress to civilisation), he did argue that culture as a whole evolved through time and that one could look at human culture on a global scale as if it had become more complex since the origins of human life itself. He had a relatively simple formula for assessing cultural evolution, and that involved the capture of energy per unit capita. Energy, or the ability to do work, was more concentrated the more organised a society, or human society in general, became. Technology enabled higher energy capture per unit capita. The formula was this: $E \times T \rightarrow P$, where E= energy (ability to do work), T= technological capacity to use the energy, or concentrate it, and P= product or 'human need-serving goods and services' like food, water, clothing, shelter. The key to understanding cultural similarities and differences was to know the amount of energy harnessed per capita in any given society according to White.

Julian Steward (1902–1972) was a student of Alfred Kroeber. He studied Numic speaking Indians called the Shoshone, who lived in the Great Basin of the western United States. His informants were on reservations by the time he conducted his fieldwork. Like other salvage ethnographers of his generation, Steward worked to reconstruct Native culture before colonialism and confinement to the reservation using oral accounts of elders. Unlike most of his cohort, Steward studied in the field what few ethnographers, except Boas, had yet encountered: foraging people with a nomadic lifestyle and a low population density. The Shoshone were hunter-gatherers, like Ishi, the last Yahi and many other North American Indians and Eskimo-Aleut peoples.

In contrast to Indians of the Great Plains, the Shoshone studied by Steward were 'foot Indians'. They did not make great use of horses. Steward's work with the Shoshone focused on the environment, especially factors such as rainfall, temperature, elevation, geology, flora (plant life) and fauna (animal life). Steward saw the desert environment of the Great Basin, which includes much of Nevada and Utah, as a constraint on population growth. Steward believed the Shoshone could not have developed high population densities, fixed settlements and complex political institutions because the environment in which they lived was too limiting. For Steward, Shoshone culture represented one of many possible ways that a society could adapt to its environment. This insight is now called *multilinear evolution*: the idea that many different cultural adaptations are possible, depending on the available resources and other environmental factors. Steward's cultural evolution focused on the question of how small-scale societies became more complex and stratified over time, an issue that had also occupied Enlightenment philosophers, positivists and nineteenth-century progressivists.

In the Shoshone, Steward found a society with one of the lowest recorded population densities on Earth: about one person every 30 square miles. This density is comparable with that of the Central Inuit of Canada and the Mardu Aborigines of the Western Desert of Australia. Steward believed that Shoshone society was structured by the available technology and environment of the Great Basin. Shoshone families in the desert were *nuclear*: they had a father, mother and unmarried children. Steward suggested this family structure was the product of an environment in which food and water resources were scattered, not concentrated. He called their social organisation the *family level of sociocultural integration*; two different social organisations were folk (or community) and state levels of sociocultural integration. Among the Shoshone, small, isolated patches of potable water also supported animals and the growth of wild plant foods, such as edible grasses, sedges and pine nuts. To feed themselves and survive on such scattered resources, the Shoshone broke down into small social units—nuclear families—and spread out across the desert. The research programme that assumes a causal relationship between the environment and social organisation in small-scale societies, like the Shoshone living in the Great Basin amid limited, scattered resources, Steward called *cultural ecology*.

Social and Cultural Anthropology

In the mid-twentieth century, the distinction between British *social* anthropology (French *anthropologie sociale*) and American *cultural* anthropology began to break down. British social anthropology before the 1950s had followed the Durkheimian emphasis on society as a congregation (Chapter 3) and on Radcliffe-Brown's structural-functionalist views (Chapter 4). Both Durkheim and Radcliffe-Brown saw society as an organism with interconnected parts, like the organs of the human body (structure), that functioned together as a whole. Boasian cultural anthropology had focused on salvage ethnography, studying Native culture of the protohistoric or precontact period, especially artefacts (material culture), beliefs, myths and ritual rather than social structure per se.

By the 1950s, the differences between social and cultural anthropology had largely dissolved, with both American and British anthropologists agreeing that society and culture were different phenomena: *society* is living people and *culture* is one of the things they share. American and British anthropologists developed a mutual respect for each other's research findings. Americans began to study social organisation and the British began to deal with the concept of culture more explicitly. Ethnographers considered society and culture equally important objects of study. There was one exception, however, to this apparent meeting of the minds: *structuralism*.

Social Structure and Totemism

French anthropologist Claude Lévi-Strauss (1908–2009) (Figure 5.1) conducted field-work during short forays into the Amazon rainforest in the 1930s. His reputation was secured with a monumental comparative study, *The Elementary Structures of Kinship*, first published in 1949. Lévi-Strauss suggested that kinship structure and terminology (terms used for relatives, such as 'mother', 'brother', 'uncle' and 'cousin') were rooted in the composition of the human family. He considered the mother–child bond to be instinctive both to humans and other animals. Humans, however, recognised links that went beyond motherhood (Chapter 6) and they had an incest taboo (Chapter 2). Lévi-Strauss defined elementary structures as rules that divide everyone into one of two groups: people you can marry and people you cannot because they are too closely related to you. This means *exogamy*—outmarriage—was key to understanding family structure; it was a basic marriage rule and an elementary structure.

Lévi-Strauss developed his ideas about kinship systems and the rules that underpinned social organisation after fieldwork in Brazil. He suggested that human behaviour, and therefore social structure, was determined by proclivities based in the human mind itself that were entirely unconscious. To Lévi-Strauss, the mind made binary distinctions: something either *is* or *is not*. For example, a person either is or is not prohibited as a sexual partner. Similarly, food is either raw or cooked. At its most basic level, human society is organised according to how the mind makes such binary distinctions: us as opposed to them; blood relatives as opposed to in-laws.

Lévi-Strauss was influenced by Durkheim in conceiving of society as a group of people organised according to rules and institutions. He disagreed with Durkheim, however, on whether these rules and institutions derived from totemism. Durkheim believed that totemism (Chapter 3) was the primordial basis of all religion and social organisation. Totemism is the belief that human groups are descended from specific plants and animals. These plants and animals are *totems*. Examples of totems include eagles and ravens, as among the Tlingit Indians (Figure 5.2), or yams and kangaroos, as among some Australian

Figure 5.1 French anthropologist Claude Lévi-Strauss in the field in Brazil, 1930s.

Figure 5.2 Tlingit totem pole, Hoonah, Alaska. Alaska State Library, Frank LaRoche Collection, ASL–P130-013.

Aborigines. Totems indicate lineage and descent, and sometimes they are even heraldic, as in the brightly coloured coats of arms featuring animals or plants that symbolise dynastic houses of Europe (e.g., lions for the English monarchy, fleur-de-lis for the French monarchy). Heraldry is seen as well in totem poles of the Northwest Coast, which can indicate, with animal imagery, notable feasts and ceremonies or other important events of the past sponsored by a chief and his retainers. Totemic images, like those seen carved and painted on totem poles (Figure 5.2), are treated with great respect and pride among many Northwest Coast Indians. Traditionally, personal identity is closely linked to totems and structures how an individual relates to members of other kin groups. Ranking and status hierarchies in Northwest Coast societies are reflected in the fact that people feel pride belonging to a specific, named kin group, and in their ability to recount their genealogy from memory.

From a structuralist perspective, as understood by Lévi-Strauss, totemism was a social institution—a structure—that reflected the organisation of the human mind. *Structures* in structuralism are those rules, institutions and relationships that make up a social group. The totemic associations between humans and animals or plants were part of the way that people categorised the world around them and organised themselves into groups. For example, some societies have a form of social organisation called a *clan*. Clans are kin groups that trace descent through either the father (patrilineal) or mother (matrilineal); they are identified by totems.

Let's say there are two descent groups in a society: a Fox clan and a Duck clan. Fox people cannot marry other Fox people and Duck people cannot marry other Ducks. To do so would be incestuous. Such societies are divided into two halves, or *moieties*. Each moiety practices exogamy. Therefore, Foxes can only marry Ducks. If the society is matrilineal, the child of a Fox woman and a Duck man will be a Fox. The matrilineal Iroquois had eight clans divided into two groups. Members of Bear, Beaver, Wolf and Turtle clans could only marry people in the Deer, Hawk, Heron and Snipe clans. In addition to Northwest Coast Indians and Aboriginal Australians, the patrilineal Tikuna people of the upper Amazon River are organised into moieties: tree people and bird people. Each moiety is composed of multiple clans. There are 15 tree clans and 21 bird clans. These groups practice both clan and moiety exogamy.

Contrary to Durkheim, Lévi-Strauss argued that totems were not part of indigenous religion at all. Using plant or animal names to identify human groups was simply a way to understand social relationships and to clearly identify prospective marriage partners. Lévi-Strauss believed that institutions—structures, such as marriage rules and kinship terminologies—were designed to promote exogamy and widen the network of persons upon whom one could count as affines, or 'in-laws', and potential allies in conflict.

These structures were understood and justified through myths and beliefs about totems. Another way of understanding this is to think of totemic plants and animals as heuristic devices: things that help people learn, remember, think and talk about important social principles. Returning to our example, Foxes and Ducks are completely different categories of animals: they are dissimilar in appearance, locomotion, food preferences and reproduction. One could never mistake a Fox for a Duck. By extending these differences to human groups—the Fox moiety and the Duck moiety—society ensures that a Fox will never mistake another Fox for a potential marriage partner, and therefore commit incest. Foxes must not marry other Foxes; they must be exogamous and marry Ducks. For Lévi-Strauss, totems ensured exogamy and prevented incest. They had nothing to do with religion, as Durkheim had suggested. Rather, totems reinforced critical social principles; such principles constitute the core of human society in structuralist thought.

Ecological and Materialist Theories

Roy Rappaport (1926–1997) founded a school of thought known as *ecological anthropology*, which was built upon Julian Steward's cultural ecology. The problem with cultural ecology, according to Rappaport, was culture. Because culture involved ideas, it could not be quantified, objectified and studied in a scientific way. Rappaport advocated looking at humans and their environment in terms of energy exchange within a closed and formal system of boundaries—within an *ecosystem*. Humans—like any other animal—needed to be studied as populations of the same species interacting with other populations of living things. These populations operated within ecosystems. Rappaport explained human behaviour as predictable responses to energetic changes in the ecosystem over time. These changes were cyclical: you could predict them in advance because they occurred on a regular basis and could be understood as nodes on feedback loops. These and other studies in ecological anthropology emphasised food supply in relation to diet and nutrition. Like cultural ecology, this approach placed small-scale societies in a steady state with the environment.

Rappaport studied the Tsembaga-Maring people of New Guinea, a population bounded by mountains in a river valley. He argued that this society kept its population in check through ritual, which he thought of as a regulatory thermostat. Culture, in other words, was the means to an ecological end: equilibrium with the environment (Figure 5.3). The Tsembaga grew sweet potato gardens and reared pigs. The sweet potatoes supplied most of the energy in their diet, and the pigs were a protein resource. Pigs

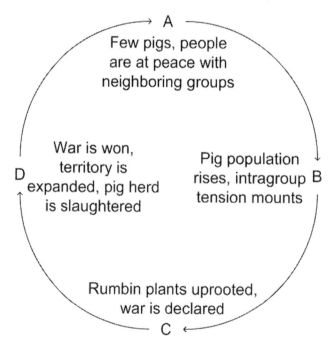

Figure 5.3 The *kaiko* cycle of the Tsembaga-Maring, Papua New Guinea (adapted from Rappaport 2000).

ate sweet potatoes, and so did humans. Women fed pigs and both men and women tended gardens; gardens were owned by families.

Let's say ten families each have ten pigs (point A in Figure 5.3). Over time, the pigs multiply since they can only be slaughtered on ritual occasions. The increase in the pig population requires more gardening by women for the same number of calories (point B). Women complain to their husbands about the extra work. Pigs begin to invade neighbouring sweet potato gardens and cause conflict between families. But the pigs cannot be ritually slaughtered and eaten until the Tsembaga fight with neighbouring clans. Tensions mount. At point C, the Tsembaga signify the start of a war by uprooting a fence on their frontier made from the *rumbim* plant. At point D, the group experiencing the undesirable pig population growth wins the war, a brief affair with few casualties. They replant the *rumbim* plants farther out to mark their expanded territory, which will allow for an increase in both human and pig populations. The victors then hold a festival (*kaiko*), invite their allies, slaughter most of the pigs and eat them. According to Rappaport, the cycle then starts anew: pig populations begin to increase, tensions rise and, once the thermostat clicks back on, warfare and ritual start all over again.

The work of Rappaport and others who advocated an ecological perspective on culture in the late twentieth century is *materialist*. A materialist perspective views culture as the product of how people make a living and interact with their environment. The material nature of their existence—their technology, available resources and living conditions—determines how they think, what they believe and how they organise socially. Modern materialist thought dates to Marx in the mid–nineteenth century (Chapter 4), but materialism was substantially revised during the 1970s by several cultural anthropologists who had encountered societies not divided by class conflict; indeed, societies that had no classes at all. These scholars were specifically interested in relations among people,

Superstructure

(ideology, magic and religion, art, music, science)

↑

Structure

(politics, economics, social control)

↑

Infrastructure

(technology and environment, demography)

Figure 5.4 The universal pattern of sociocultural systems (adapted from Harris 1979).

technology, work and the environment—that is, materialism—as a general perspective on the human condition.

Marvin Harris (1927–2001) was the principal twentieth-century theorist of materialism in cultural anthropology. He referred to his research programme as *cultural materialism*. From this perspective, culture is composed of three parts: infrastructure, structure and superstructure. *Infrastructure* is technology, environment and the rate of population growth in a society; the material constraints of a given time and place (Figure 5.4). The *structure* of society is its political, economic and social institutions. *Superstructure* is ideology, art and religion. For cultural materialists, the infrastructure is what most influences human thinking and behaviour.

Postmodernism

The modernist research programmes in cultural anthropology of the twentieth century—functionalism, structural-functionalism, structuralism, ecological anthropology and cultural materialism—began to yield to postmodern approaches in the 1990s. As a set of ideas about the human condition that questions the objectivity of earlier research programmes, postmodernism involves a critique of cultural anthropology as a science. Postmodernism posits that because humans, including anthropologists, are cultural, and because each culture is unique, an ethnographer cannot be completely impartial while doing fieldwork.

Postmodernist cultural anthropologists questioned the scientific basis of ethnography. Some conceived of ethnography as a form of autobiography, reflecting an individual anthropologist's background and experiences more than those of the society being studied. Postmodernists argued that each ethnographer in a field situation saw what they wanted to see, depending on previous life experiences. These individual differences accounted for variation in the way anthropologists described the same societies.

For example, American ethnographer Robert Redfield (1897–1958) first studied the Mexican village of Tepoztlán in 1926–1927. Redfield found Tepoztlán society relatively peaceful, harmonious with nature and stress-free. In 1943, another anthropologist from the United States, Oscar Lewis (1914–1970), restudied Tepoztlán and found the people to be envious, fearful and distrustful towards each other. Redfield admitted later that the differences observed by Lewis were true. However, he and Lewis had different personalities and so tended to focus on different behaviours. Redfield, as an optimist, emphasised what he found appealing about life in Tepoztlán, whereas Lewis, a sceptic regarding the possibility of harmony in society, stressed the negativism and conflict he found there.

Another example is the different findings of two anthropologists working in Samoa. Boas' student, Margaret Mead (1901–1978), conducted fieldwork in American Samoa in the mid-1920s. She found female Samoan adolescence to be stress-free and sexually easy-going, in contrast to widely held perceptions of American female adolescence as a time of stress and sexual conflict. Derek Freeman (1916–2001) studied Samoans over a longer time period in the 1940s and 1950s. He concluded that Mead's findings were deeply flawed. He found female Samoan adolescence to be a time of sexual violence, including rape, as well as pervasive fear and guilt over sexual matters in general.

Mead's defenders were quick to point out that Freeman's data were collected at a much later time, and that Samoan culture had changed since her fieldwork in the 1920s. In addition, Freeman's informants were elderly men, whereas Mead's informants were mainly young women. Freeman's description was also sexist in its portrayal of both Samoan women and Mead herself. This famous controversy highlighted the question of whether two professionally trained ethnographers could agree on basic aspects of a culture, given differences in life experience, age and sex. One line of postmodern thinking drew attention to the role of the anthropologist in the analysis of culture and suggested that, rather than objective accounts of human behaviour, ethnographies were literary interpretations of culture as text.

Culture as Text

Postmodernism in anthropology drew heavily upon the work of Clifford Geertz (1926–2006), who believed that reality lay beneath the fabric of society, embedded in individual experiences of religion and other symbolic behaviour. His ethnography was based on the psychological insights originating in one-on-one relationships between the ethnographer and a key informant, the 'Other'. Geertz did fieldwork in Indonesia and Morocco. He wrote that the human species is an 'animal suspended in webs of significance', the analysis of which should not be 'experimental science in search of law but an interpretation in search of meaning' (1973 p. 5). Although he did not completely discard a scientific approach, Geertz was more interested in understanding culture in a literary, interpretive way than in terms of its economy, ecology and structure. The role of the ethnographer should be to describe this meaning as close to the indigenous understanding as possible, as though the ethnographer were a translator, not of a language, but of a culture. To do that required not so much scientific study but rather the ability to think like a native, so to speak, and then render the ethnographic experience into an account that people in a different culture could understand.

From this perspective, ethnography was more similar to literature than to science. Postmodern cultural anthropologists suggested that ethnography had its own literary *tropes*, or devices, styles and genres. For example, many ethnographies of the twentieth century contained an 'arrival story', a common trope in anthropological literature that describes how the anthropologist first set foot in the community they studied. If anthropology was a literary endeavour, then ethnographers were not writing objective accounts of human behaviour. Instead, they were *writing culture*.

Anthropological Sciences versus Humanist Trends

By the end of the twentieth century, scientific theory in cultural anthropology was at odds with humanist and postmodernist approaches that argued against the possibility of an impartial science of human culture. Some anthropology departments even split up based on these theoretical differences. One particular focus of controversy concerned the reality of culture. Methods were developed in cultural anthropology to test the hypothesis of the reality of culture as a shared phenomenon. A *method* is any research procedure employed to evaluate a *hypothesis*, which is a statement about a given phenomenon that can be supported or disproved empirically, that is, with facts or data. Quantitative methods underlying the attempt to prove the reality of culture had been unavailable to ethnographers such as Boas and Malinowski. The result of research using these methods seemed to support Durkheim's original point that social facts, like facts about the material world around us, are *things* that can be studied empirically and analysed rationally: 'The first and most fundamental rule is: *Consider social facts as things*' (Durkheim [1895] 1964, p. 14; emphasis in original).

Cultural anthropologists influenced by a postmodernist, humanist viewpoint tended to interpret culture, rather than analyse it empirically and statistically, in the belief that objectivity was impossible. Long gone were the days of Boas, Malinowski, Kroeber and Radcliffe-Brown when informants were believed to present their cultures faithfully. Postmodernism led to a focus on the *individual*—as understood in terms of her or his body, psychology and behaviour—not on society, since natives were as biased as ethnographers in their own ways.

Part of the postmodern critique of twentieth-century anthropology is based on disputes like these. Postmodernist reflections on anthropology and highly divergent interpretations, like those of Redfield and Lewis at Tepotzlán or Mead and Freeman in Samoa, showed that fieldwork could not be defined by a scientific, empirical approach. Individual anthropologists, like cultures, vary. And their experiences reflect those personal differences. Even so, postmodern criticism of the anthropological enterprise uncovered some consistent patterns in what ethnographers focused on and how their fieldwork proceeded. Participant observation—the principal method employed in ethnographic research—unfolded in a series of identifiable stages. In the following sections, we consider the development and current state of participant observation, together with its toolkit of allied methods.

Methods in Cultural Anthropology

Participant Observation Revisited

The core method of anthropological fieldwork is participant observation, which may involve the ethnographer as participant observer—one who is actively engaged in local behaviour—as well as observer participant, in which the ethnographer spends time watching, listening and recording speech and behaviour of the objects of research, the 'other' or the 'native'. According to ethnographer John Van Maanen, participant observation has been a 'sprawling and primitive' way of getting data because, while there is no one way or single formula for how to do it, there is no substitute for it, either. Ethnographer Theodore Bestor studied the largest fish market in the world, Tsukiji, in Tokyo, Japan. On any given market day, 2,345 metric tonnes of saltwater fish are bought and sold in that place. Bestor studied auctions for more than a year and interviewed auctioneers of all kinds and quantities of fish that moved in and out of the market daily. He found that auctioneering of fish at Tsukiji involved 'a burst of abbreviated jargon; a blur of waving hands; quick, almost imperceptible gestures: all signify prices asked and offered, then a sale is over' (2004, p. 177). Bestor himself couldn't offer to buy and sell fish so, in a sense, to study the market he emphasised observation, not participation. He called his principal method 'inquisitive observation' rather than participant observation. Malinowski considered the goal of cultural anthropology to be grasping 'the native's point of view, his relation to life, to realise *his* vision of *his* world' (Chapter 1). Boas held a similar opinion: 'If it is our serious purpose to understand the thoughts of a people the whole analysis of experience must be based on their concepts, not ours' (Boas 1943, p. 314).

Some of the most interesting recent research on how to understand 'the native's point of view' or the 'thoughts of a people' comes from ethnography of the different places where they live their lives and carry out activities, and sometimes the ethnographer becomes part of that life. Ethnographer Mark S. Fleisher studied the lives of urban street criminals in Seattle. He also studied street people who were serving time in prisons in Washington (Walla Walla) and California (Lompoc). He received consent to do that research from the Federal Bureau of Prisons and the wardens. In addition, he took a full-time job as a corrections officer in the Federal Bureau of Prisons and was able to do life history interviews with convicted felons on the side. He studied street gangs including Bloods and Crips both in terms of street life and life in jail and prison. On the street, he conducted focused interviews with a few selected street informants who were hustlers and he also spot sampled (or did time allocation—see below) regarding the same individuals at different times—morning, afternoon, evening—over the course of his study. Another example of taking a job in order to understand people in the workplace as well as in their home environments is Steve Striffler's study of a Tyson Foods poultry processing plant in Arkansas, where he worked on a production line. He was one of the few whites working there; the most common languages were Spanish, Lao and a Micronesian language; three-fourths of the workers were Latin American. Striffler found that most of the line workers who dealt with live chickens hanging upside down on an overhead rail system were female; each person processed about 80 birds/minute. Striffler became a breading operator (a machine for turning out certain kinds of chicken products like nuggets) from which job he observed other people who worked with marinades, hangers of the chickens and moving bags of flour on the factory floor (see also Chapter 8 and Figure 8.4)

That emphasis on an emic perspective in the context of face-to-face fieldwork and interaction is what gives participant observation its validity as the ethnographic method that most increases knowledge about the subject matter under study. Validity is the overall believability of the information and conclusions that come from field research. Ethnographer H. Russell Bernard wrote that one is making progress as an ethnographer when one could decode people's sense of humour, and even deliver a joke that is actually understandable, and funny, to one's informants:

> If you are a successful participant observer you will know when to laugh at what your informants think is funny; and when informants laugh at what you say, it will be because you *meant* it to be a joke.
>
> (1994, p. 137)

One hundred years of modern fieldwork have revealed that participant observation involves several stages, or ethnographic 'occasions'. The first stage is sometimes called *fore-field*, which is the period when the ethnographer seeks funding, makes contacts with officials whose approval is needed to do the fieldwork and meets professional colleagues in a host country who can assist or give advice. The second stage is often called the *arrival scene*, which is a description of the ethnographer's first encounter with the community. Eventually, the ethnographer begins to observe and record information; they are *coproducing* knowledge about a society with informants. The informants give the anthropologist information about their society that the anthropologist later writes up in the form of an ethnography. The validity of the ethnographic account derives from the anthropologist's direct observation of people in the community and participation in activities that occur there.

Arrival Scenes

Most ethnographies contain what is known as an *arrival scene*, the moment the ethnographer steps into the public arena of the society they have chosen to research. Arrival scenes are sometimes abstracted and generalised from real events, independent of any specific moment, and portray how the place of study would appear to a visitor for the first time. I authored an arrival scene as follows:

> Upon arriving in a Ka'apor village after a long walk through the forest, a visitor is usually greeted with the squealing of young children, shouting of adolescents, barking of dogs, squawking of parrots, and more subdued, respectful welcomes extended by adults. Some adults are…away from the village temporarily, engaged in hunting, fishing, gardening, collecting fruits, gathering material for firewood, house construction, or other artifacts, bathing, and so on. Those who have remained in the village are likely processing manioc flour, repairing a leaky roof, carving a new bow, eating manioc meal, nursing an infant, or perhaps just relaxing in their hammocks.
>
> (Balée 1994, p. 49)

French ethnographer Philippe Descola described how before he arrived in the indigenous settlements of the Achuar people of the Ecuadorian Amazon, he first had to spend some time living in a town of colonists located along the edge of the rainforest. He needed to outfit his expedition and contract labour and transportation to get to his field site. The colonists Descola met, like those who surround indigenous societies throughout the world, cannot be ignored in doing participant observation. They are part of a contact zone, like a suture, that one must cross before one truly *arrives*. Descola wrote:

> It is in one of these gloomy observation posts that ethnographic research usually begins. I embarked upon mine in Puyo, a town of colonists immersed in the graceless present, situated at the foot of the eastern slopes of the Ecuadorian Andes…Puyo was indifferent not only to time but also to its immediate environment. I thought that I would be making no more than a short stop here at the end of the negotiable road that takes one in a few hours from the large towns of the central Sierra right down to the Amazonian forest, but I soon realized that I would have to find ways of diverting my impatience. The first thing I had to do was find out where the Achuar Jivaros, whom I hoped to visit, were to be found and by what means I could reach them…My earlier readings of a number of ethnological monographs on Ecuadorian Amazonia—which, incidentally, were impossible to find in the country to which their research related—had enabled me to know more about the Indians than the very people who lived within striking distance of them.
>
> (1996, pp. 2–3)

Evans-Pritchard had this to say about his arrival at Nuerland a little more than 80 years ago:

> I arrived in Nuerland early in 1930. Stormy weather prevented my luggage from joining me at Marseilles, and owing to errors, for which I was not responsible, my food stores were not forwarded from Malakal and my Zande servants were not instructed to meet me. I proceeded to Nuerland (Leek country) with my tent, some equipment, and a few stores bought at Malakal, and two servants, an Atwot and a Bellanda, picked up hastily at the same place.
>
> ([1940] 1969, p. 9)

Malinowski, who spent nearly two years of participant observation among the Trobriand Islanders, initially took an attitude of ownership towards the community he studied. Here is a diary entry from December 1917, as Malinowski's boat first approached the main Trobriand Island of Kiriwina:

> Early in the morning we sailed on past Dobu…I took the rudder now and again… Rapture over the beautiful forms. Marvelous steep mountain covered with shaded vegetation, dotted here and there with huts…Joy: I hear the word 'Kiriwina'…I get ready; little gray, pinkish huts. Photos. Feelings of ownership: It is I who will describe them or create them. Ashore; comical fences; miserable houses on pilings… The women ran away. Under each house implements for making pots. Yellow ocher pots lie under each house—I try to talk to them; they run away or tell lies.
>
> ([1967] 1989, p. 140)

The anthropologist's arrival is followed by a period of getting used to the people, climate, locale, landscape and language. Once the ethnographer has become more or less settled in the place of study, which may be a village, town or neighbourhood, much of what constitutes the background of the work takes place. This includes psychologically adjusting to the way people perceive the ethnographer. Conrad Arensberg wrote of his 1930s arrival, and of the native reaction, in an Irish town where he did fieldwork on the concept of the community:

> The arrival of a stranger in a west country Irish town is still an event. The age of machinery has not yet destroyed the leisure of curiosity. But when the stranger shows no intent of hurrying on, like an ordinary tourist, and sports none of the weapons of field and stream, the matter assumes no mean local importance. A new bank clerk or land commissioner is expectable; he soon sinks into the colour of his position and surroundings. Even a 'returned Yank', once his parentage and probable savings have been determined, and his clothes and manners scrutinized, soon drops out of mind… But there is no understanding a stranger whose only apparent business is to chat with people and to walk about with notebook in hand.
>
> (1988, p. 21)

It is the strangeness of the anthropologist that attracts attention. The fact that the anthropologist does not usually speak the local language well increases the likelihood that they will experience some psychological discomfort at first. This discomfort or despondency is *culture shock*. It normally abates before long, though never entirely, just as one is never likely to be as fluent as a native speaker in a second language unless one was raised speaking it.

Observations and Interviews

The course of participant observation normally entails language learning—usually from day one—to better understand the native point of view. Cultural anthropologist James Spradley pointed out that ethnographers draw knowledge about other cultures based on what people say, what they do and what things or artefacts they use. He noted that you need many observations to begin to see order, custom, and institutions in a society.

Recall that Malinowski's goal was an *emic* description. He wanted to record cultural knowledge as possessed by informants. In contrast, *etic* description is cultural knowledge as inferred from native behaviour by ethnographic observation. In fact, a complete description can only be accomplished by using both emic and etic approaches, and participant observation involves both. That is the essence of long-term fieldwork.

There is also the spatial and temporal context of fieldwork, which ideally constitutes part of the description. That context is the *ethnographic present* or the moment an anthropologist is researching and describing a culture in the field. One will often read in an ethnography the writer's disclaimer that she or he is writing about a culture in an ethnographic present of 30 or more years ago; in other words, things could be very different today, when you, the student, is reading about it. The ethnographic present is a descriptive snapshot of culture.

Arensberg's notion of the ethnographer with notebook in hand is very much part of fieldwork and how the ethnographer is perceived. It is necessary to record as much as possible of what one sees and hears in the field, either in a notebook, on a mobile phone or tablet, on tape, through photography or video or in some combination of these. The background work of the anthropologist often begins early in the research. This involves objective measurements of houses, public structures, gardens, rangeland, numbers and types of pets, quantities and types of food people consume and ways people spend their time since much of this work can be done without competence in the local language. It can be done by visual observation and etic description.

Emic description begins to emerge through interviews that are both structured and unstructured. Structured interviews take the form of survey questions on a particular topic prepared by the ethnographer in advance. The structured interview has an explicit purpose in mind, and it consists of a group of scripted questions; unstructured interviews are more exploratory and open-ended. Repetition is needed in a structured interview in order to explain the reasons for the questions. You could ask dog fanciers to tell you about the kinds of dog breeds they know; you might be interested in dog shows and what they know that, and that's why you're asking. After telling you a few names, say of hunting dogs, working dogs and lap dogs, you might then ask, 'can you think of any others?' In unstructured interviews, it's helpful to let informants know your ignorance—'I don't understand that—what is a dog breed? Can you elaborate?' The informant more or less leads that kind of interview. It's important in both kinds of interviews to be friendly, to develop mutual understanding and rapport and to elicit information that you then record, on paper or, if permitted, on a digital or tape recorder to be transcribed later. Interviews, in general, can range across any topic of research interest to the ethnographer, such as knowledge of plants (ethnobotany), knowledge of animals (ethnozoology), relations of people to the environment and what they think about it (ethnoecology), disease, technology, kin terms, social organisation, ethnomedicine, taboos, religious beliefs, economics and exchange, artwork and so on (Figure 5.5). Linguistic competence, which is necessary in emic description, ideally develops over time as part of normal interaction between the ethnographer and his or her informants. Because many languages have few speakers, sometimes less than a hundred, which is the case with many tiny societies of Amazonia, it is highly unlikely that one can learn the language without going to the field. It is partly for that reason that participant observation takes so much time, traditionally at least a year. If one cannot learn a language in the field, then an interpreter is necessary.

Informants are usually compensated in cash or in kind for their efforts. Their identities are normally kept anonymous and confidential, and ethnographers should abide by

Figure 5.5 Ethnographer and ethnoecologist Maria Gabriela Zurita Benavides conducts a free list of tree names in the Waorani language with a native Waorani respondent, near the Rio Nushiño, Ecuadorian Amazon, 2019. Photo by Author.

internationally accepted ethical guidelines that are intended to protect human research subjects. These rules are enforced by universities and research institutes through organisations called institutional review boards, or IRBs.

Ethnographic Writing

Writing is a continuous part of the fieldwork enterprise. It occurs as the ethnographer observes and records information about the community under study in the form of *field notes*. The ethnographer coproduces knowledge with his or her informant during the course of participant observation. The two collaborate, in a sense, in writing up observations and producing knowledge. Knowledge acquired in the field takes final form after the ethnographer returns home. Field notes are reviewed and the data are sorted as the ethnographer prepares the material for others to read and consume. Usually, but not always, ethnographers work alone when writing a book or article that describes the fieldwork and the research findings. According to Clifford Geertz, the ethnographer writes 'thick description', which he defines as the recording of human behaviour in the field and its attendant meanings. To do that accurately, one needs knowledge of culture and its meanings obtained by taking 'an elaborate venture in' a culture, a journey by way of participant observation. The story of getting inside culture, and relating it to the readers, is part of the 'thick description' of ethnographic writing. Understanding the meaning of a wink and finding humour in a joke require specific tools in addition to participant observation to elicit information about aspects of the culture in which they are most interested.

The Ethnographic Toolkit

Demographic Sampling

Often the first method employed by a cultural anthropologist when arriving at the field site is a systematic survey of the human subjects in the community. They could be a network of relatives and friends in a megalopolis such as New York or São Paulo, or the entire population of a small indigenous village in the rainforest. When the anthropologist is not fluent with the language spoken, which is often the case, they can survey the land and structures occupied by the inhabitants in the community. One can count the number of people living in a household, street or neighbourhood, and one can identify those individuals by sex and age. These results provide basic demographic information on the community and are the foundation for a more detailed data collection. As the ethnographer spends more time in the community and meets more people, it becomes possible to conduct meaningful, structured interviews.

Studying the Past: Documentary Analysis

Structured interviews, which ask specific questions about a domain of knowledge, usually focus on things that happened in the past. Such interviews can involve oral history, in which informants answer questions about the culture, society or landscape as they experienced it. This is the life history method, in which an informant's experience is used to understand cultural practices and past events (Cultural Snapshot 5.1). Knowledge of a society's past helps the ethnographer understand present conditions and interpret behaviours and cultural practices that may have developed as a result of earlier events. In some cases, very little is known of a community's past, and the only data available are the knowledge and memories of informants. Sometimes, historical documents exist that describe the community under study or record events that shaped the present form of a culture or group of people.

For this reason, many cultural anthropologists do *ethnohistory* (Chapter 1), which is documentary study and analysis that usually takes place in archives and libraries. Ethnohistorical research focuses on texts and images that describe or depict a culture or society of the past. Often, the writers were outsiders, such as Catholic or Protestant missionaries, military leaders or immigrant settlers who wrote about the cultures they encountered in colonial contexts (Chapter 9). These outsider views may be the only historical documents available since, in many cases, the cultures they describe did not have written traditions of their own. This is the case with most indigenous societies of Africa, Australia and the Americas.

In a few cases, local people were taught how to read and write in the language of conquest, and they wrote accounts of their own acculturating societies. Much of what we know about indigenous societies and cultures we owe to research in ethnohistory. Work with ethnohistoric documents may require special training in other languages, such as Latin, or in palaeography—old writing systems—to decipher colonial documents.

Studying the Past: Oral History

The past of a culture and society can also be accessed by talking to living informants. Salvage ethnography of American Indians (Chapter 4) was based on interviews by cultural anthropologists of elderly informants living on reservations. The objective was to understand indigenous culture and society *before* confinement on reservations, and it was seen as urgent because informants were often aged. In the 1930s, Boas' student Zora Neale Hurston (Cultural Snapshot 1.1) interviewed some of the last African Americans who had lived as slaves in the American South to record aspects of their cosmology and religion. Hurston's original informants are now long deceased, but contemporary ethnographer Antoinette Jackson interviewed descendants of enslaved African Americans to reconstruct plantation life prior to 1865. Such information from oral history can enrich the interpretation of historic sites and provide modern visitors with a richer understanding of what life was like more than a century ago.

CULTURAL SNAPSHOT 5.1

Life History of Leprosy

Ethnographer Cassandra White studied leprosy and its treatment in Rio de Janeiro, Brazil. With more than 38,000 reported cases, Brazil is second only to India in the incidence of leprosy. White wanted to know how people managed their disease, so she collected life history data in the form of 'illness narratives' from 43 patients. She had structured life history questions that permitted informants to give detailed information on the symptoms they had, the diagnosis, treatment and, in cases where they had been cured, post-treatment. As White conducted participant observation at the clinic, she modified her interview questions to make them more meaningful to her informants. Initially, she had used the Portuguese word *contratar* (to contract) in referring to 'contracting the disease' of leprosy with her informants. She soon found that while the verb had meaning to medical professionals, most of her patients did not use the term and did not understand the question when asked, 'How did you contract leprosy?' Through life history accounts, White learned that her informants spoke of leprosy transmission using the verb *pegar* (to get or catch the disease). So White changed the terms she used for these questions to be a more effective interviewer. White noted:

> I believe that establishing my status as an outsider, in terms of being an American anthropologist rather than a Brazilian physician, allowed patients to feel more comfortable speaking with me…I learned about some aspects of the medical encounter that were problematic for patients in their quest for diagnosis, for treatment, and for a cure for their illness.

Anthropologists can also be of assistance in conveying information in a nonthreatening way to vulnerable populations, as with some rural African Americans, who otherwise may doubt the efficacy or even safety of necessary vaccinations, as with the administration of vaccines against the COVID-19 virus.

Visual Anthropology

Visual anthropology refers to the documentation of culture in photographs or video. Since the early twentieth century, many cultural anthropologists have documented their subjects and the landscapes they inhabited in visual formats. Anthropologists have also collaborated with filmmakers or made their own ethnographic films. An especially noteworthy example is the classic *Nanook of the North* (1923), directed by explorer Robert Flaherty. *Nanook* records the lives of Inuit in the Canadian Arctic, documenting a walrus hunt and construction of an *iglu*.

Franz Boas and his student Margaret Mead were both interested in filming human behaviour. Mead considered film essential to good ethnography because certain culturally determined movements, such as dance or gait, were too fast for the unaided eye to record and study. Time-lapse photography and film technology could capture each movement individually. Mead believed it was important to understand how body movement in one culture differed from that in another. She considered film the best way to record these differences. Motions, as culturally determined behaviours, have even been considered 'moving artifacts', a term coined by an early pioneer of visual anthropology, Félix-Louis Regnault.

Although the technology used for rendering pictorial accounts of other cultures was once the almost exclusive domain of cinematographers, the relatively inexpensive and easy-to-use technology now available allows most cultural anthropologists to visually record activities and behaviours they consider important. This is especially useful because some behaviours cannot be conveyed adequately in words. For example, fully describing a dance accompanied by music and colourful costumes or the manufacture of a *tipiti*, a device woven from basketry materials used in the Amazon, would be quite inadequate in words alone. Many complex, rapid behaviours are involved in both activities, making them virtually impossible to describe without images.

Not all ethnographic film is objective or captures cultural reality as the subjects of the film perceive it. Along with critiques of written texts, postmodernism has questioned the objectivity of ethnographic film in terms of what is recorded and what is excluded, either during filming or editing. To lessen the bias of the ethnographer, collaboration between the filmmaker and the people being filmed is necessary. This is increasingly the case in anthropological film. In some instances, indigenous people have learned to make their own films, sometimes for political purposes, such as trying to garner government support for the protection of themselves and their lands.

Despite bias, ethnographic films about past cultures and societies made in the past hundred years often contain valid information. Culture is not just words or ideas: it is also shared and learned behaviours. Increasingly, old films are used for cultural renewal by societies where much of what people think of as traditional culture has disappeared, often due to globalisation (Chapter 12). For example, in the late twentieth century, *Nanook of the North* was being used in this way among Canadian Inuit. Visual anthropology in the form of photographs and video has an important place in current fieldwork in the documentation of culture.

Studying the Use of Time

Thomas Hobbes was a pre-Enlightenment philosopher who assumed that government was necessary for human well-being. Without it, he said, society faced 'continual fear…and the life of man [was] solitary, poor, nasty, brutish, and short' ([1651] 1985, p. 186). Ethnographers in the 1960s considered Hobbes mistaken about whether members of societies without government lived in fear and had rough, impoverished lives. Instead, they found that such people may be relatively well off and secure. Those living in egalitarian or *acephalous*, or 'headless', societies could lead comfortable lives, and they didn't work too hard since, based on research using new methods, they enjoyed significant free time. The time allocation method, pioneered by ethnographer Richard Lee among the foraging Ju/'hoansi, demonstrated this.

Lee wondered whether hunting and gathering was as hard a way to eke out a living as Hobbes and many others thought. To answer that question, he sought to find out exactly how many hours per day people actually spent hunting game, collecting plant foods, caring for children, cooking, cleaning the camp and their huts, making tools and eating, idling, visiting, singing or chatting. He began to observe what everyone was doing in the camp at sunrise and sunset and recorded these activities on a person-by-person basis. He also wrote down what each hunter brought home after each hunting expedition and what nuts, roots, tubers and berries women gathered. Lee weighed samples of these foods to determine their caloric value.

Based on research for a four-week period, Lee determined that the Ju/'hoansi spent a total of only two to three days per week looking for food, or about 20 hours per week total. Women worked slightly fewer hours than men, but their caloric contribution to the diet was greater. Plant foods collected by women, especially mongongo nuts, were more important in the diet than meat from wild game animals, which was acquired exclusively by men. The Ju/'hoansi diet averaged 2,360 calories of food energy and 96 grams of protein per person per day and provided sufficient vitamins and minerals to maintain health.

Lee showed that the Ju/'hoansi, who did not farm, had a standard of living equal to or superior in many ways to that of industrial societies. Their diet was adequate, yet they worked fewer hours and had more leisure time. Lee's groundbreaking study, together with similar data collected among Australian Aborigines in Arnhem Land, led Marshall Sahlins to conclude that 'The world's most primitive people have few possessions, *but they are not poor*' (1972, p. 37; emphasis in original). Sahlins identified hunter-gatherers as the 'original affluent society' and suggested that real wealth was measured in leisure time, stress level and quality of life, rather than in terms of dollars or possessions. The Ju/'hoansi, like other foragers, had few needs, and those needs were amply met. Refinement of the time allocation method included randomisation of observations, which confirmed Lee's finding that members of egalitarian societies generally have more leisure time than workers in industrial societies.

Free Listing

Free listing is a useful technique for defining shared, learned cultural categories, or semantic domains, by measuring the unconscious ranking of familiar items. Semantic domains in English include categories such as 'plants', 'animals', 'bad words', 'automobiles' and 'relatives'. Many different domains of meaning have been studied using this ethnographic tool, including disease, kinship terms, animals and trees. Free listing involves asking people to list every member of a specific domain, or category. You might be interested, for example, in what the people in an English-speaking culture consider to be vegetables instead of fruits. Some people think of tomatoes as vegetables; others think of them as fruits. Free listing allows you to figure out what most people think tomatoes are: fruits or vegetables. The technique is based on the principle that the more culturally important an item is, the higher on people's lists that item will rank. A statistic, Smith's *s*, can be used to determine relative cultural salience of different terms (Cultural Snapshot 5.2).

CULTURAL SNAPSHOT 5.2

Measuring Cultural Salience

Rank and frequency of appearance of a term on a free list are both factors that determine its cultural salience. Ethnographer Jerry Smith introduced a new method for weighting rank and frequency in order to come up with an index of salience, now called *Smith's s*. The individual salience of an item is:

$$S_j = 1 - (r_j/l_i)$$

where S_j is the psychological salience (its familiarity or importance) of item *j*; r_j is the rank of item *j* on an individual informant's list, and l_i is the length of the list. So, if a person listed 20 animal names and 'dog' was fourth on the list, the salience of dog would be:

$$1 - (4/20) = 1 - (.2) = .8$$

That is psychological, or individual, salience. Of course, in practice, because culture is shared, an item doesn't have an *s* value of 0.8 unless the average of a *group's s* values is 0.8, which would be cultural salience. No item can have a cultural salience higher than 1.0. Because Smith's *s* incorporates both the order and frequency of items on lists, an item listed second on everyone's *s* list would have a higher cultural salience than the first item people listed if that item was different in all cases but everyone had the same item listed in second place.

Table 5.1 Frequency (in parentheses) of the top ten fruits on free lists of 60 college students (from Weller and Romney 1988, p. 17).	*Table. 5.2* Frequency (in parentheses) of the bottom ten 'fruits' on the free lists of 60 college students (Weller and Romney 1988, p. 17).
1. apple (37)	47. currant (1)
2. orange (35)	48. elderberry (1)
3. pear (34)	49. huckleberry (1)
4. banana (33)	50. loganberry (1)
5. grape (32)	51. mandarin (1)
6. peach (30)	52. rhubarb (1)
7. tangerine (27)	53. salmonberry (1)
8. cherry (26)	54. squash (1)
9. grapefruit (26)	55. taro (1)
10. pineapple (26)	56. turnip (1)

One free listing exercise done with a sample of 60 students at an American university resulted in 56 items people considered to be fruits. The top ten, in terms of frequency, are listed in Table 5.1. Presumably, the most frequent fruits on the students' lists have a certain importance or familiarity to people, known as salience. Equally interesting are the items listed by only one or two people. These are presumably not very culturally salient.

The bottom ten 'fruits' on the list of 56 items are given in Table 5.2. As you can see, most people don't think of turnip, taro or squash as fruits. When the same sample of students was asked to list vegetables, squash appeared on 28 lists; turnips appeared on 23. Free listing helps the ethnographer sort through a domain of meaning in a culture to determine which items are salient and which are less so.

The idea of having informants free list the members of categories like these is to determine which of the examples are most important in a culture. In the 1960s, ethnographers A. Kimball Romney and Roy D'Andrade found that when Americans free list kin terms, the word 'mother' occurs about 97 per cent of the time as the first item. To inquire further into this semantic domain of words for relatives, they asked 105 high school students to list all the names for kinds of relatives and family members they could think of. They began this exercise with a couple of important suppositions about the data: 'We assumed that the nearer the beginning of a list that a kin term occurs, the more salient it is' and 'the more salient terms will be recalled more frequently'. In other words, the most salient terms will occur on a higher percentage of individual lists. They found that 93 per cent of the 105 students listed 'mother' and the average rank of 'mother' (the mean position in which it was listed on people's free lists) was first. That means 'mother' is the prototypical or most basic and culturally salient kin term in the English language. Of 15 terms for 'basic relatives', of which 'mother' was first, the term 'grandson' was listed last. I conducted a free list exercise on animal terms with my anthropology students. Cultural Snapshot 5.3 presents the results and illustrates the relative cultural salience of different terms.

CULTURAL SNAPSHOT 5.3

Free Listing

In 2009, I asked my students in cultural anthropology class to list all the animal terms they knew. The 28 students gave 372 valid terms. The average list length was 59 terms. The top ten terms by Smith's *s* (Cultural Snapshot 5.2) are listed below. Note that dog and cat are ranked 1 and 2, respectively. In fact, this is commonly found to be the case in animal free lists done by college freshmen across the United States. I got the same ranking of these top two terms on an earlier free list of animal terms by the cultural anthropology class of 2006. In addition, the earlier class shared seven animal names (dog, cat, lion, tiger, horse, mouse and zebra) in their top ten terms with the 2009 class, though the two groups of freshmen were separated by space and time, and both had listed hundreds of terms in total. That doesn't happen by chance alone—it suggests that an underlying shared cultural concept of 'animal' is at work.

Rank	Animal term	Frequency	Average Rank	Smith's s
1	dog	27 (96%)	7	0.863
2	cat	28 (100%)	11	0.837
3	lion	27 (96%)	17	0.685
4	giraffe	24 (86%)	15	0.685
5	elephant	25 (89%)	19	0.633
6	tiger	23 (82%)	18	0.605
7	horse	21 (75%)	23[*]	0.579
8	mouse	18 (64%)	20	0.456
9	alligator	22 (79%)	28	0.426
10	zebra	19 (68%)	23[*]	0.415

Number of respondents = 28; total number of terms = 372; average list length = 59.
[*]The average rank of 'horse' and 'zebra' is listed here as the same because of rounding.

Summary

Contemporary cultural anthropology emerged in the aftermath of World War II (1939–1945). Although classical unilinear evolutionism—the idea that states and other complex forms of social organisation, such as chiefdoms, emerged from simpler forms—had been discarded by this time, it became a focus of research in the multilinear evolutionism of Julian Steward. Steward also pioneered cultural ecology, the notion that technology and the environment played pivotal roles in the organisation of simple societies. Towards the end of the twentieth century, cultural materialism and ecological anthropology became important approaches in understanding relations between people and the environment. From the mid-1980s to the early 2000s, postmodernism, which rejected Enlightenment optimism about rationalism, human progress and the objectivity of science, took hold in cultural anthropology. In part, this was due to conflicts in the findings of different ethnographers who worked in the same communities, such as Margaret Mead and Derek Freeman in Samoa.

Some ethnographers in the late twentieth century developed new methods in an effort to combat bias and subjectivity in cultural anthropology. They began to question long-held views of lifestyles, such as foraging. Using new methods, such as time allocation and nutrition research, they found that assumptions about foraging as a difficult, impoverished way of life were mistaken. Other researchers developed new methods to support the concept of culture as shared, learned behaviour. These methods can be used by different researchers to obtain comparable results. If the methods are used properly and consistently, differences in the research results can be attributed to cultural differences rather than dismissed as biased observations or inappropriate use of methods. Free listing is one tool ethnographers can use to elicit information about specific domains of knowledge and meaning.

Further Reading

Adams 1998; Albach 2007; Berlin 1992; Bestor 2004 (pp. 177, 183); Borgatti 1992, 1999; Brown 1991; Carneiro 2003; Clifford and Marcus 1986; Codere 1950; di Leonardo 2001; Durkheim (1895) 1964 (p. 14); Firth 1989; Geertz 1973 (pp. 6, 19); Fleisher 1995; Harris 1979; Harvey 1989 (pp. 38, 45, 49);

Hinsley 1981 (pp. 83–84); A. T. Jackson 2011; J. Jackson 1990; Johnson 1975, 2003; Kelly 1995 (p. 224); Kroeber and Kluckhohn 1952; Lee 2013; Mackin 1997; Malinowski (1922) 1984 (p. 25), (1967) 1989 (pp. 69, 140); Marx (1844) 1977a, (1867) 1977b; Mauss 1990; Morgan (1851) 1995 (pp. 76–79); Murphy 1971 (p. 37); Nimuendaju 1948 (p. 717); Pels and Salemink 1999; Pelto and Pelto 1993; Pratt 1986 (pp. 39–40); Quinlan 2005; Rabinow 1977 (p. 5); Rappaport 2000; Romney and D'Andrade 1964; Rosman and Rubel 1986; Ruby 2000; Sanjek 1990 (p. 95); Shenk 2006; Smith 1993; Spradley 1979; Striffler 2005; Steward 1938, 1951, 1955; Strathern 1992; Tierney 2008; Tomas 1991; Tonkinson 1991; Weller and Romney 1988 (pp. 17–18); White 1959 (2007); Yanagisako and Segal 2006

Cultural Snapshots

5.1   White 2009
5.2   Borgatti 1992; Quinlan 2005; Smith 1993
5.3   Borgatti 1992; Smith 1993

6 Social Organisation in Kin-Based Societies

Overview

All societies, as we learned in Chapter 1, have notions of relatedness, including descent and kinship. Early anthropologists focused on studies of descent and kinship, but the topics declined in popularity in the United States in the late twentieth century when cultural anthropologist David Schneider (Chapter 2) suggested that the study of kinship was more about moulding societies into a Euro-American framework of 'blood is thicker than water' than objectively investigating human relatedness. Schneider pointed out that not all notions of relatedness were based on the concept of shared blood. His critique led to revisions in how kinship was studied and used to understand social organisation. In recent years, kinship has become increasingly important in cultural anthropology, due to its association with issues such as sex, gender and sociality (Chapter 2). Humans are a social species, as are all primates. In humans, however, this sociality is conducted not only by means of physical association but also by explicit rules governing group membership. These rules are expressed in marriage, which legitimates children, and in descent, which can take several forms. Because living arrangements are dictated by marriage customs, different kinds of families—different social structures—can be formed. In kin-based societies, people organise their activities and relationships on the basis of marriage and descent. These factors, taken together, produce diverse systems of classification of relatives and nonrelatives. In this chapter, we examine human relatedness in light of what we know about marriage and kinship in a cross-cultural perspective.

One Species, Two Sexes

Like other primates and early hominins, the human species has two sexes. Only one sex bears offspring, but it takes both sexes to mate and reproduce. Human sexuality and reproduction are partly regulated in many societies through marriage. Marriage is not, of course, always a monogamous union of two individuals for life. Although the *pair bond* (Cultural Snapshot 6.1), a lifelong, interdependent relationship between two individuals of opposite sexes, is found in other species, such as the osprey, grey wolf and French angelfish, it is not a universal in the human species.

Many marriage forms exist, and these unite the two sexes in different ways, usually for economic purposes as well as for sexual ones. Each sex is dependent on the other's work in small-scale societies, where essential tasks needed for survival and reproduction are assigned by sex. In societies where men and women routinely cooperate in the production of distinctive and indispensable goods and services, marriage and descent are crucial factors. Such societies are kin-based. In all societies, no matter how simple or complex, sex, marriage and kinship are intertwined.

CULTURAL SNAPSHOT 6.1

The Pair Bond

Marriage occurs in all societies, but we now know its cultural expression is highly variable. In the mid-twentieth century, most anthropologists assumed that a pair bond between husband and wife was universal, though few species are monogamous. While it is true that swans, geese, most hawks, eagles, falcons and many parrots mate for life, extra-pair copulations occur in many bird species. Mammals, as a class, tend to be promiscuous: only 3 per cent mate for life. None of our closest mammalian cousins—the great apes—mate for life. Aside from the gibbon, few primates are monogamous. Only about 17 per cent of known human societies are obligatorily monogamous. In other words, the practice of monogamy may be cultural, not biological.

A number of complex modern societies have a marriage form called *serial monogamy*. In serial monogamy, only one marriage at a time is allowed, but upon divorce or death of the spouse, an individual is free to remarry. A person may end up marrying several times in succession. Extreme examples of serial monogamy may be found among celebrities. Hollywood film star Zsa Zsa Gabor (1917–2016) was married to nine different husbands over her long marital and cinematic career. Academy Award-winning actress Elizabeth Taylor (1932–2011) was married eight times to seven different husbands. Although the traditional Tiwi Aborigines of northern Australia were polygynous, they also practised a form of serial marriage. A woman was traditionally betrothed while an infant still in the womb or at birth to a much older man. She was supposed to be married at all times until death. Because women's first husbands were much older, women were usually widowed as teenagers. At her dead husband's graveside, a woman had to marry another older man, one who was often already married. Older men sometimes had simultaneously ten or more younger wives by the time they died. Widowed again, and often elderly, a woman was required to marry still another man, this time usually much younger. She was often that new husband's first wife. Marriage practices such as these make establishing a lifelong pair bond unlikely, or perhaps unnecessary for fulfilment and happiness depending on the society.

The Sexual Division of Labour

In kin-based societies, women and men tend to have different yet complementary roles. This is the *sexual division of labour*, which varies cross-culturally but which is present in all kin-based societies to some degree. The sexual division of labour refers to economic and extractive activities performed exclusively or nearly so by one sex only.

In many hunting-and-gathering societies of tropical and semitropical deserts and steppes, women gather the bulk of the calories in the diet from roots, tubers, nuts, fruits and seeds. Men, in contrast, do most or all of the hunting of wild game. Traditionally among the Ju/'hoansi of the Kalahari Desert, according to Richard Lee, men hunted and women collected mongongo nuts, a mainstay of the diet, but also wild onions and various fruits. Likewise, the Mardu Aborigines of the Western Desert of Australia, according to Robert Tonkinson, get most of their food from the collective labour of women, while men hunt animals such as lizards and wallabies. Among both the Ju/'hoansi and Mardu, the sexes pool their food resources, often in the context of a pair bond, and give away portions of what they individually collected and hunted to various members of their band or camp. Usually, these camps are composed of *consanguines*, or blood relatives, and *affines*, or in-laws.

The sexual division of labour is less obvious in complex, nonkin-based societies, though not entirely absent. Apart from a few cases—only men (thus far) are popes or NFL football players—the sexual division of labour in modern society is relative, not absolute. In the United States, time allocation research shows that women on average spend significantly more of their time in caring for others, both within and beyond the household, in household activities and in purchasing goods and services; men on average spend significantly more time in paid work. Men outnumber women in some professions (engineering, medicine, roofing), whereas women outnumber men in professions such as the cultural anthropology professoriate, though these numbers change through time. The sexual division of labour is not a natural or biological rule, any more than descent rules are—both are arbitrary. The sexual division of labour is an arbitrary division of economic functions on the basis of one obvious binary difference between individuals: sex. For example, there is no biological reason that men make small musical instruments more frequently than women, but they do. Women in many Amazonian indigenous societies tend to make the pottery; men tend to make the basketry. There is no biological basis to that sort of division of labour.

The division of labour is otherwise connected to reproductive responsibilities, and these ultimately lead to what we call *kinship*. Women literally reproduce society through childbearing; in most kin-based societies, women perform most or nearly all the childcare, though there are exceptions. Childcare is done almost exclusively by women, not because of female biology or nature (that is, sex), but because of culture (that is, gender). This reproduction of society is accomplished through marriage and the division of labour tied to the pair bond.

Gender and Marriage

The sexual division of labour, which is variable across societies, is generally reflected in gender identities. These identities encapsulate culturally perceived differences between the sexes in a society: gender is merely the outwards construction and elaboration of sex. Women and men tend to decorate themselves differently cross-culturally, and where society is complex, there may be multiple gender ornamentation practices crosscut by class and status differences. In Western society, for example, heavier fabrics such as wool and denim tend to be associated with masculinity and lighter fabrics such as silk and cotton with femininity.

Ethnographer Kathleen Gough (1925–1990), who specialised in the cultures of Southwest India, defined marriage as a legal union between a woman and one or more persons, real or imagined, for the purpose of legitimating children and usually, but not always, for regulating access to sexual intercourse. That means that marriage is about classifying offspring and determining who can have sex with whom. As Gough's definition implies, marriage does not necessarily involve a man. Among the Nuer of East Africa and the Dahomey people of West Africa, a woman could marry another woman. The Chukchi of Siberia permitted marriages between men. These practices predate contemporary debate over same-sex marriages in Western societies. Same-sex marriages might be more appositely termed *same-gender* marriages, since in some cases, people of different sex (that is, one partner having a Y chromosome paired with partner exhibiting two Xs) though of the same gender might choose to marry (Chapter 3).

In the Chukchi case, certain male shamans, under the influence of spirits, were believed to become female. They were known as 'soft men', though they appear to have been anatomically normal men. They donned women's garb and practised women's customs; often they married another man. Third, fourth and fifth genders are recognised among the Bugis of Sulawesi, Indonesia; in northern India, the *hijra* are a third gender. Among the Plains Indians, two-spirits are third genders. Interesting in many cases, the gender(s) between the polar extremes of masculine and feminine often specialise in religious functions, such as blessings of people undergoing rites of passage, which are approved by society at large (see Chapter 3), and they may or may not be in marital relationships. Among the Dahomey of West Africa, marriage was primarily concerned with rights regarding children and property. Upon a man's death, his surviving spouse would become a social man, taking on the titles and property of the deceased husband. She could marry other women and she would have parental authority over the offspring of their sexual relationships with one or more men. The woman who inherited her wealthy husband's status in society became 'father' to these offspring. It was more economically advantageous to be a 'husband' to many women than to remarry a man, because if she did that she would become one of several cowives and could lose her ability to own and transmit property to her biological children. A comparable marriage practice occurred in pre-Communist China. When a young, married man of means predeceased his wife, his parents could bring a poor man into their household to marry her; children born of that union would carry on the dead man's name, not the name of the new husband. These examples demonstrate that there is no one marriage form universal to human societies.

How and Why People Get Married

Usual Marriage Forms

Despite cross-cultural diversity in marriage, two basic forms are nevertheless widely found: *monogamous* (one man and one woman at a time) and *plural.* Several plural forms are known from ethnographic research. Cultural rules specify a restricted range of marriage types, depending on the society, and different family forms are the product of these. A monogamous union with children results in a nuclear family (a married couple and their unmarried offspring residing together). Two kinds of nuclear family are recognised: the family that a person is born into (nuclear family of orientation) and the family in which a person reproduces as a spouse and parent (nuclear family of procreation). Monogamous couples with their nuclear families of procreation typically live in a dwelling of their own, separate from other kinfolk. Anthropologists are concerned with where couples live after marriage because residence, along with marriage type, determines household structure. In addition, how people organise their shared living space affects the enculturation of the young. Plural marriage usually creates opportunities for larger groups to live in close proximity.

Polygyny (from Greek *poly* 'many' and *gyne* 'woman') results in *extended family* households headed by one man and two or more wives and all their unmarried children. In societies that permit polygyny—the majority of the world's societies, in fact—women divide up labour among themselves and cooperate in various tasks for joint prosperity. In some polygynous households in Africa, each wife lives in her own house and rears her own children. The husband takes turns visiting and having intercourse with each wife. In parts of urban Africa today, a man might maintain one or more wives 'outside' his first marriage; these marriages are not fully recognised because the husband did not pay bridewealth, though the man supports such wives financially and their children are recognised as his. Usually in polygynous situations where all marriages are recognised, one wife—the first one—has seniority over the others. Sometimes, the cowives are sisters, a practice called *sororal polygyny*.

In Judaism of the ancient Hebrews, polygyny was permitted because a man was enjoined to take as a wife the widow of his deceased brother; if he had a wife already, his brother's widow became his second wife. Although plural marriage was abolished in Judaism, it continued to be practised among some European Jews into the Middle Ages. The rule that a man must marry his deceased brother's wife is called the *levirate* (named for Levi, son of Jacob from the Old Testament) and is widely found in polygynous societies worldwide, including the

Nuer. The idea behind the levirate is that a deceased man could continue to have children because he would be the 'social' father of the offspring sired by his living brother. The female complement to the levirate is the *sororate*, which is a rule requiring a single woman to marry the widower of her deceased sister. When a woman dies prematurely, she is replaced by another who is 'equal' to her: her sister. Radcliffe-Brown referred to this recognition of sameness as the *equivalence of same-sex siblings*, a principle of kin classification found in most of the world's languages.

Polyandry (from Greek *poly* 'many' and *andros* 'male') is the marriage of one woman to two or more men, as we saw earlier in Cultural Snapshot 1.2. Though relatively rare, polyandry among land-owning families was once common in Tibet. It also existed on the Malabar Coast of South India and in isolated pockets of South America, the Arctic and the Subarctic. In polyandrous Tibet, the husbands of a woman are brothers, and the eldest brother has the most authority in the marriage. This tends to eliminate quarrelling among the men that could erupt over sexual access to the same woman. This marriage practice is known as *fraternal polyandry*. Fraternal polyandry prevented family-held lands from being subdivided into smaller parcels over time, which would have been the case if each son married a different woman, and each got a share of his parents' land upon their deaths.

Contracting of Marriage

Bridewealth

In most societies, marriages are sealed by a contract, either implicitly by some kind of favour or overtly in the form of a gift. *Bridewealth* (sometimes called *bride-price*) consists of material goods given by the groom's family to the bride's to validate the transfer of the bride to the groom. The Nuer (Figure 6.1) do this; they pay with cattle. This is not like buying a bride, because not just anyone with the right number of cattle may make

Figure 6.1 Nuer man in South Sudan. In order to marry, he must have passed the rite of initiation into an age set (marked by six scars on the forehead) and his patrilineal kin (agnates) would have helped him accumulate enough cattle to pay bridewealth. Alamy Images.

the 'purchase'. Cattle are valuable, but they are not the same as money (Chapter 9), and money alone is not enough to 'buy' a bride among the Nuer. The groom and his clan must have the proper affinal relationship to the bride's clan; they must have an established pattern of exchanging marriage partners. Recall that a clan is a group defined by descent through one sex only. It has an emblem, or totem, such as a plant or animal, that represents the founder of the clan. Lineages are also unilineal kin groups, but trace descent from known human ancestors. Several related lineages make up a clan. The Nuer are patrilineal and patrilocal, meaning that upon marriage, the bride goes to live with the groom and his family, even though in terms of descent, she belongs to the clan and lineage of her father and his brothers. The bride's family will not give her up without the right amount of bridewealth.

At the time of Evans-Pritchard's original fieldwork with the Nuer, in the 1930s, the bridewealth payment, on average, was 40 head of cattle: 20 went to the bride's father's family and 20 to the bride's mother's family. This practice has changed with the advent of a cash economy. Traditionally, after these payments in cattle were made, the bride's parents could keep ten head of cattle each and divided the rest among their own kin in culturally prescribed ways. As this example shows, marriage was a contractual agreement between two families, not just between individuals. Divorces were uncommon, but if divorce occurred due, for instance, to an extramarital affair by the wife, the husband had the right to demand return of the bridewealth paid. Divorce was therefore the basis for dispute not only between the married couple, but also between entire lineages and clans. Marriage among the Nuer, as in most of the world, is an alliance between groups as well as a union between two people.

Brideservice

In many Amazonian societies, as with most tropical forest societies elsewhere, and in contrast to the Nuer, bridewealth is not exchanged at marriage. Rather, the groom performs tasks for his parents-in-law, and perhaps his brothers-in-law. These tasks are known as *brideservice*. For the Wari' of the western Brazilian Amazon, a newlywed young man is normally required to hunt for the family of his bride and help his father-in-law clear fields of trees and underbrush. Parents of a bride often welcome such assistance because an ageing father-in-law may not be as successful a hunter as his son-in-law. Game meat is highly prized, and the young man's brideservice ensures that his wife's family is well fed. This phase of a young couple's life together is only probationary, however. If they find they aren't suited to one another, they can separate. Once they have children, they tend to stay together and they may live near her parents or his.

The Ju/'hoansi hunter-gatherers of the Kalahari Desert also had brideservice. The preferred son-in-law was one who was a good hunter and willing to live *uxorilocally*—with his wife's family—for several years. He would ideally render brideservice by hunting for his parents-in-law for up to ten years after marriage. As with the Wari', brideservice among the Ju/'hoansi enabled younger men with their greater speed and strength to help feed the families of older men. Societies that do not store food or accumulate wealth tend to have brideservice rather than bridewealth. Ju/'hoansi brideservice patterns are breaking down with increasing sedentarisation as the Ju/'hoansi settle down permanently and abandon their mobile lifestyle. As some Ju/'hoansi begin to accumulate wealth, they are now using cattle and other forms of property as bridewealth payments in lieu of brideservice.

Dowry

Dowry should not be confused with bridewealth. Dowry was restricted originally to a small number of societies with very large populations in Europe, Africa and Asia. Dowry is a woman's inheritance from her parents before they die. It is not a payment to the groom's family, the way bridewealth is a payment to the bride's family. It is the passing of goods and property from one generation to the next. Dowry usually consists of movable wealth such as the trousseau (bride's wardrobe), cash, appliances, investments, tableware, livestock and bedroom furnishings.

Postmarital Residence

Residence patterns, or postmarital residence patterns, which are partially determined by marriage customs, help structure household organisation. Cultures vary in terms of norms regarding postmarital residence. The main difference is between groups in which the couple, upon contracting marriage, live on their own and those groups where the couple becomes part of a larger family group.

Monogamous couples with nuclear families in their own separate dwellings display *neolocal residence*: they live in a 'new place' of their own. *Uxorilocal residence* occurs when a couple lives in proximity to, or under the same roof as, the wife's family. A couple who lives near or under the same roof as the husband's kin have *virilocal residence*. Uxorilocality and virilocality are both forms of *unilocal residence*. Uxorilocal residence is often called *matrilocality*, and virilocal residence, *patrilocality*. Neolocal residence is found where nuclear families predominate; uxorilocal and virilocal residence, in contrast, invariably result in extended families. An extended family is a coresidential group of two or more nuclear families that often has material interests in common.

The Nuer people had virilocal residence. A hamlet consisted of fathers, brothers and sons coresiding with their wives and unmarried daughters. Wives married in; they came to live with the families of their husbands. The Iroquois had uxorilocal residence. A village consisted of mothers, sisters and daughters living with their husbands, who married in, and unmarried sons. Virilocal and uxorilocal residence patterns involve extended families (Figures 6.2a and 6.2b); neolocal residence does not.

Sometimes, extended families have interests in common, such as land, similar to the way a corporation might have stocks and bonds owned by its shareholders. For that reason, some societies with unilocal residence have *corporate groups* based on kinship. A corporate group is an organisation of persons that maintains a distinct identity through time, regardless of the changing identities of its members. A corporate group based on kinship—such as a clan or lineage—may be identified as a discrete unit of society even as old members die and new members are born. Membership in such groups is ascribed, a part of an individual's identity at birth.

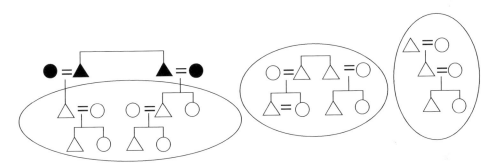

Figure 6.2a Three examples of extended families with virilocal residence. In each case, brides come to live with their husbands' families. Such extended families include men, their unmarried daughters and sisters and in-married wives. O = male; △ = female. An equals sign indicates marriage; a line indicates a blood relationship. Solid circles and triangles represent deceased family members.

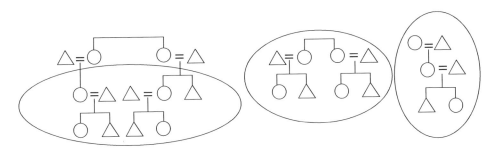

Figure 6.2b Three examples of extended families with uxorilocal residence. In each case, husbands come to live with the families of their wives. Such extended families include women, their unmarried sons and brothers and in-married husbands.

Descent Rules

Extended families, like all families, are organised by marriage rules and residence norms. Some extended families are organised by a principle of *unilineal descent*, which is a simple rule that one traces descent through one sex only. If male, the unilineal rule is called patrilineal; if female, it's matrilineal. Several societies in Africa, Oceania, Asia and the Americas have both rules operating at the same time: one is a member of both patrilineal and matrilineal descent groups. This is called *double descent*. The Tallensi of West Africa, for example, had a double descent system in which land, other assets and legal and ritual obligations were transmitted through the male line only; one got one's spirit, however, from one's mother.

Unilineal descent groups can be corporate groups that hold substantial wealth in common. In pre-Communist China, for example, a patrilineal descent rule combined with virilocal residence yielded local groups that held agricultural land in common. Each patrilineal group had a shrine within the household enclosure where offerings were made to male ancestors. When one spoke of 'my family' in public, it was in reference to the descent group that held land, movable assets, symbols and beliefs in common. Because descent groups with common material and spiritual interests outlive an individual, they can be considered patrilineal corporate groups.

Corporate groups can also be matrilineal. Among the Trobriand Islanders, land and heirlooms are held mostly by men, though women's wealth, which can translate into tons of yams and other crops, is also very important, according to Annette Weiner. Instead of passing from a man to his sons, land is passed from a man to his *sister's* sons, thus staying in the same descent group, since a man and his sister's sons are matrilineally related. The Iroquois of New York State had a similar inheritance pattern (Figure 6.3). A *sachem* (chief) of the Iroquois could not inherit his office from his father due to the matrilineal descent rule. Lewis H. Morgan noted that the son of a sachem:

> could neither succeed his father, nor inherit from him even his medal, or his toma-hawk. The inheritance…was thus directed from the lineal descendants of the sachem, to his brothers, or his sisters' children.
>
> ([1851] 1995, p. 80)

Postmarital residence is important in the continuity of kin-based corporate groups. Patrilineal societies are often but not always found with virilocal (patrilocal) residence; matrilineal societies are found with uxorilocal (matrilocal) residence, as with the Iroquois, or *avunculocal residence*. The term *avunculocal* is from Latin *avunculus,* or 'uncle', and *localis,* or 'place of'. Upon marriage, a man and his bride go to live with his mother's brother. Avunculocal residence in matrilineal societies is actually more common than uxorilo-cal. The Trobriand Islanders, for example, have matrilineal descent with avunculocal residence. This pattern fits the rules of inheritance and helps keep those who control the land—the corporate group—together in the same place.

While corporate groups usually hold material possessions such as land in common, in some cases, corporate groups exist for ritual purposes related to the life cycle. Ethnographer Miriam Kahn studied the Wamura people of Papua New Guinea, who have matrilineages or exogamous lineages based on matrilineal descent. Kahn noted that these 'matrilineages form corporate groups at important periods in the life cycle such as marriage, housebuild-ing, and death. They unite only for those feasts that celebrate the life cycle' (1994, p. 24).

Figure 6.3 Seneca-Iroquois wives and daughters, early twentieth century. Uxorilocal (matrilocal) residence kept mothers, sisters and daughters together. Descent and inheritance were also traced through females (that is, matrilineally). From the Albert R. Stone Negative Collection, Rochester Museum & Science Center, Rochester, NY.

A society has *cognatic* inheritance and descent when property can be conveyed through either or both the mother's and the father's lines. Each side of the family is potentially of equal importance. There are two types of *cognatic descent: bilateral* and *ambilineal*. Bilateral descent systems are relatively uncommon and found in industrial societies of the Americas, Europe and Asia and in small-scale, hunter–gatherer societies such as the Ju/'hoansi and the Inuit. Bilateral systems recognise kinship on both the mother's and the father's side. Ambilineal descent systems recognise kinship with some persons on one or the other side, though not with both. Frequently an individual can choose his or her ambilineal descent group. Ambilineal descent was recognised in European monarchies, among the nineteenth-century Kwakwaka'wakw and other Northwest Coast societies, and among the ancient Hawaiians, Maori and other Polynesians. Its purpose is to perpetuate distinctions of rank, prestige and material wealth.

An ambilineal kin group is known as a *cognatic clan*. A cognatic clan can be thought of as a pyramid, with a founding ancestor, called an *apical ancestor*, at the apex, and all his or her descendants through both sons and daughters forming the three outer triangular surfaces and base of the pyramid (Figure 6.4). In some societies, leaders of cognatic clans are almost always men. But gender can intersect with this bias, and cognatic clans may have genuinely equal status for women and men, despite rules that seem to favour masculine

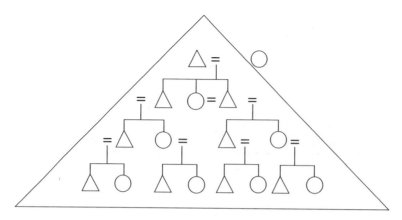

Figure 6.4 A Diagram of a cognatic clan illustrating ambilineal descent. Members of the clan may claim
descent through either father or mother.

authority. For example, in the eighteenth century, the Maori people of New Zealand had
a rule that first-born males should inherit the leadership of the cognatic clan.

  This kind of preference is called a rule of *primogeniture*. Maori cognatic clans owned
land and each was ranked higher or lower in terms of prestige within society. The
men who seemed to rule such cognatic clans and their first-born male descendants
were called *ure tu*, or 'upright penis'. Sometimes, a senior male had no male children.
Because of the ambilineal descent rule, if he had daughters, one of them could accede
to power in the cognatic clan. Despite beliefs about women as unclean and taboos on
their behaviour, a number of terms suggest that women were closely associated with
concepts related to land and origins among the Maori. A cognatic clan was *hapu*, which
also means 'pregnant': women were considered the mothers of cognatic clans. The land
of a cognatic clan was referred to as an 'umbilical cord', and people's umbilical cords
were buried on the land of the cognatic clan into which they were born. By giving
birth, Maori women were considered to be the founders of the cognatic clans. They
gave birth to the apical ancestor. This belief justified ambilineal descent and the fact that
women, in spite of cultural attitudes regarding female pollution, were potential power
players both politically and economically. Younger brothers, like women, could also
inherit power, depending on the situation. According to ethnographer Karen Sinclair,
cognatic descent among the Maori 'permits women to inherit land, to hold chiefly
office, and to participate in crucial decisions regarding their natal kin groups, as well as
to ensure their perpetuation' (2001, p. 170). Regardless of a seeming male bias in the
gender hierarchy of Maori society, ambilineal descent allows for corporate groups to be
led by men or women.

  Cognatic clans are different from unilineal (patrilineal or matrilineal) clans in that
descent is traced *either* through males or females (ambilineally). Such clans are also different from all the kin and nonkin organisations arising from bilateral descent. To some
extent, all societies are characterised by bilateral notions of descent since they recognise
relatedness on both sides of the family. What is distinctive is how this essential concept of
relatedness—through father and mother—applies to cultural practices related to marriage,
gender and inheritance.

Group economic interests in modern bilateral societies have replaced corporate groups such as cognatic clans, unilineal clans and lineages. Modern corporations, universities and governments are political and economic institutions that bring together unrelated individuals. These institutions perpetuate group interests over time regardless of individual membership. They are the basis of economic organisation in modern and postmodern complex societies. Extended family interests have given way to an emphasis on individual achievement, establishment of neolocal nuclear families and monogamous unions. Kin connections are deemphasised, though both the matri- and patrilines are, in principle, of equal significance.

The Atom of Kinship

Living in society, or *sociality*, is found among all human groups, as we saw in Chapter 2. Humans seem to be hardwired at birth with the capacity to live life in a group of their own kind. Beyond that, however, social groups vary tremendously in their structure, organisation and the rules that govern them. Cultural anthropologist Ralph Linton (1893–1953) thought the nuclear, or *conjugal family*, was the smallest indivisible social unit of our species. Recall that a nuclear family consists of a married couple living together with their unmarried offspring. It has also been called the 'biological family', though biological relationships may not match cultural ones. For example, 'father' in many societies may mean 'husband of the mother', not the actual biological father of her children. The nuclear family is mediated by marriages in each generation. Societies without nuclear families include those where most households are formed according to a rule of polygyny or polyandry. In polygynous households in West Africa, the husband of various wives may have legal authority over all their children. In polyandrous households in Tibet, several brothers sharing a wife are equally considered to be 'fathers' of all her children, without distinguishing a biological father.

Linton believed that the last man left alive on Earth would spend his 'last hours searching for his wife and child', but that would only be true if that last man were from a society that had intimate, independent nuclear families. Such families may have been a reality in the United States of the 1950s, when neolocal residence was widespread, but North American cultural norms regarding marriage, residence and the family have changed dramatically since then and continue to be in flux. In 1970, about 8 per cent of Americans ages 30 to 34 had never married; by 2003, that age group had more than tripled to 28 per cent. In 2000, according to the US Census Bureau American Community Survey, 50.3 per cent of all households were headed by an unmarried person. In 23 of the 50 states, such households have now become the majority. Census data compiled from 2010 confirm that nuclear families exist, but they are clearly no longer the statistical norm. Historically in the United States, nuclear family organisation is associated with land, movable wealth and ownership of other resources. In contrast, poor urban families in the United States, the Caribbean and Latin America often have *matrifocal* families: families centred on co-resident women who are related to each other as sisters, mothers and daughters. Matrifocal families help individuals cope with poverty because they make sharing essential services, such as childcare, easier.

Contrary to Linton's belief, there is little evidence that the nuclear family was the original, atomistic social unit of the human species. Nor is there evidence that the nuclear family is a sociocultural universal. Lévi-Strauss hypothesised that the defining moment of human kinship, after imposition of an incest taboo, was the extension of a person's

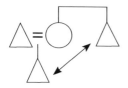

Figure 6.5 Atom of kinship.

notion of relatedness to the mother's opposite-sexed sibling; that is, to one's mother's brother. That recognition of an *atom of kinship* (Figure 6.5) takes the concept of relatedness beyond the maternal bond with the child and establishes a rule of *exogamy:* marriage with outsiders.

Lévi-Strauss claimed that the most elementary kinship structure—or arrangement of kin relationships—'can never be constructed from the biological family made up of a father, a mother, and their children, but that it always implies a marriage relationship' (1976, p. 83). He further noted that the atom of kinship is simply the 'the group consisting of a husband, a woman, a representative of the group which has given the woman to the man…and one offspring' (Lévi-Strauss 1976, p. 83) as rendered in Figure 6.3. To understand this concept, let's start with the individual as a point of reference; that individual is called *ego*. Ego belongs to the zero generation; ego's parents are the first ascending generation. In recognising a relationship of *affinity* to mother's brother, a man (ego) has linked two sexes, his mother (female) to her brother (male). That linkage, or crossing, is essential to ego's recognition of kin other than his mother and his siblings. This is the atom of kinship, as Lévi-Strauss termed it: a small social unit that contains a *consanguineal*, or 'blood' relationship, such as that between a mother and son, and an *affinal* one, such as that between ego and his mother's brother. Ego can be certain that the woman who bore his mother's brother's children was not ego's own mother or her sister, because of the incest taboo. Instead of seeing mother's brother as a relative in a matrilineal society, Lévi-Strauss pointed out how commonly ego married the daughter of mother's brother. Such a union is called a *cross-cousin marriage* and occurs on six continents.

A Minimal Society Constructed from Kinship

From this reductionist perspective—sometimes called an *egocentric* view—one can comprehend society by starting from an atom, or minimal unit, of kinship, to see how an individual relates to his or her immediate kin. Another way of thinking about kinship is to look at it from a synthetic vantage point, to see the entirety of it independently of the parts that make it up, known as a *sociocentric* perspective. The atom of kinship can be viewed in the larger context of a matrilineal society, as seen in Figure 6.6, which is a simplified diagram of society consisting of two lines of descent that are simultaneously two exogamous groups: A and B. Let's assume that ego's membership in group A or B is determined by his mother's group membership. If ego's mother is A, then ego and ego's siblings are As; if his mother is B, then ego and ego's siblings are Bs. Now let's add rules of classification, a universal feature of human societies. One very common classification rule is for ego to refer to his siblings and anyone else in his own generation and descent group

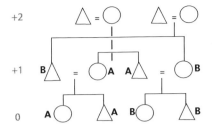

Figure 6.6 A minimal matrilineal society.

(A or B) by terms like 'brother' and 'sister'. In contrast, persons in ego's own generation in the other group are called 'cousins'. From a sociocentric perspective, our hypothetical matrilineal society consists of the following: 1) two descent lines (A and B); 2) two generations ('0' for the zero generation and '+1' for the first ascending generation); and 3) rules that restrict marital relations to those between persons of the same generation but of different descent groups. Since we have only two descent lines, A and B, these are called *moieties*, which are conceived of as opposites. As with clans, moieties are often given names of naturally occurring phenomena.

Let's say Moiety A consists of the clans of furry people and Moiety B consists of the clans of feathered folk. In actuality, moieties may be contrasting colours, as with the Amazonian Munduruku Indians' distinction between red and white moieties, according to ethnographers Yolanda and Robert Murphy. Or moieties can be bird people versus tree people, as among the Tikuna of the upper Amazon River. Any widely perceived division of nature, readily recognised cross-culturally, could be used to distinguish moieties, suggesting that such distinctions reflect an underlying dualism or binary logic in human thinking.

In our hypothetical society, Moiety A includes people from the Bobcat and Groundhog clans. Moiety B includes the Sparrow and Mockingbird clans. Looking at Figure 6.6, let's assume a male ego Bobcat from Moiety A marries a female Sparrow of Moiety B. Because of matrilineal descent, their children will be members of the Sparrow clan in Moiety B. Their son, a Moiety B Sparrow, can marry his mother's brother's daughter, who is, by definition, a member of Moiety A. She could be a Moiety A Bobcat or Groundhog because his mother's brother (her father) is a Sparrow. As a Sparrow, her father must have married a Moiety A woman (the girl's mother), who was either a Bobcat or a Groundhog. Let's say she was a Bobcat. Because of matrilineal descent, the daughter is also a Bobcat from Moiety A. Since there is an exogamous marriage rule, mother's brother's daughter, a Moiety A Bobcat, must marry into the opposite moiety, Moiety B. Her cousin, as a Moiety B Sparrow, is therefore an eligible marriage partner.

The binary division of this society into moieties results in two kinds of cousins: *parallel cousins* and *cross cousins*. Cousins are defined on the basis of opposite-sex linkages, such as from father to sister, or from mother to brother. The children of father's sister and of mother's brother are cross cousins to ego. The identification of cross cousins is important to our hypothetical society for two reasons: 1) they are in the opposite moiety of ego; and 2) they are therefore potential marriage partners and affines. In other words, the children of ego's mother's brother, in the atom of kinship, are marriageable cross cousins. This marriage rule is a simple way to create alliances between small, codependent groups of people. Cross cousins are the people ego could ally with because, by definition, they are members of the opposite moiety and therefore not directly related to ego.

In contrast, parallel cousins are classified as ego's own kin; they are cousins who belong to the same moiety as ego and are therefore unmarriageable. In this society, ego may marry his cross cousin, to whom he is unrelated. But the incest taboo applies to his parallel cousins. Parallel cousins are therefore not potential spouses for ego. The distinction between cross and parallel relations guarantees, for many small-scale societies, the reproduction of the social structure in the next generation. The distinction is expressed linguistically, and it is very important in understanding how people worldwide classify themselves and others.

The Classification of Relatives

Societies—and languages—vary in how kin relationships are encoded in words. In English, we have terms such as *daughter, nephew, brother, mother* and *grandfather*. How people classify those closest to them helps us understand which social relationships are considered important and how society as a whole is organised. Classification terminology also reveals how people think about members of other ethnic groups, societies and nations. There are seven systems of classifying kin, each named after a specific society in which that system was used, with many variations. They are Iroquois, Dravidian, Crow, Omaha, Eskimo, Hawaiian and Sudanese. The study of kin classification systems and their terminologies helps anthropologists understand how terms for relatives and social organisation intersect with political, economic and religious institutions. It is important to understand the underlying reasons for why we classify people the way that we do and why these classifications differ cross-culturally.

For example, in many systems of classification, or kinship terminologies, possible marriage partners are explicitly indicated, with the purpose of setting up exogamous alliances between two or more groups. The simplest terminologies, such as Dravidian (Cultural Snapshot 6.2), are focused on identifying potential mates. Women and men in small-scale societies are themselves a form of wealth because of the labour they provide and because women reproduce society itself. Such societies, seen throughout northern South America, tropical Asia, Oceania, Australia and sub-Saharan Africa, are sometimes said to have an *economy of persons*. In this kind of economy, the labour and reproductive capacity of people are valuable resources, apart from their individual skills or personalities. These societies depend on exogamy.

Sometimes, marriage rules are found in the classification system itself, as in Dravidian terminology (Cultural Snapshot 6.2). Terminologies are also important because they may intersect with complex rules governing how people behave with regard to sex, gender, status, marriage, family and inheritance. Because in some societies people accumulate permanent assets, interest in descent may reflect material concerns. Societies that keep genealogies, tracking where members came from, who their ancestors were and so on, tend to have wealth that can be inherited. Kin terminologies may therefore reflect patterns of inheritance as much as they do restrictions of the pool of sex and marriage partners. Such societies sometimes have specialists who remember or record genealogies. Let's look at two kinship classification systems to see how societies, such as the traditional Hawaiian and Sudanese, name and identify kin and how these terms relate to social organisation.

Hawaiian and Sudanese Kinship Systems

The Hawaiian system, sometimes called a *generational* system, has the fewest terms of the seven systems. The Sudanese, also called *descriptive*, has the most.

Hawaiian has only two terms to refer to members of the first ascending generation: everyone is 'father' or 'mother' depending on sex. In ego's own generation, everyone is either 'brother' or 'sister'. The people that we call 'first cousins' in English would be called 'brother' or 'sister' in the Hawaiian system. Hawaiian terminology recognises two principles: sex and generation. This system is closely associated with ambilineal descent, which enables an individual to select the lineage from which he or she claims descent. Hawaiians and the Northwest Coast Nootka had such descent rules.

The Nuer people, with whom we are already familiar, have Sudanese terminology (Figure 6.7), which uses a different term for each relative. For example, father's sister is *wac*, and father's sister's son is *gat-wac*; mother's brother is *nar*, and his son is *gat-nar*. Affines translate literally; there are individual terms for father's brother's wife, father's sister's husband, mother's sister's husband and mother's brother's wife. In Sudanese terminology, there is no classification or merging at all. In English, for example, cousins, whether male or female, are merged under a single term. The particularistic Sudanese kin terms do not emphasise the nuclear family or any other set of kin relations. This type of terminology

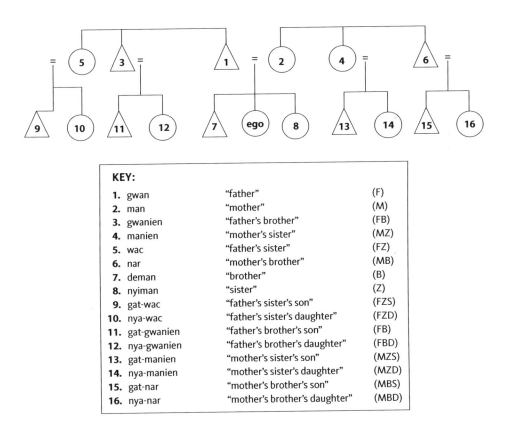

KEY:

1.	gwan	"father"	(F)
2.	man	"mother"	(M)
3.	gwanien	"father's brother"	(FB)
4.	manien	"mother's sister"	(MZ)
5.	wac	"father's sister"	(FZ)
6.	nar	"mother's brother"	(MB)
7.	deman	"brother"	(B)
8.	nyiman	"sister"	(Z)
9.	gat-wac	"father's sister's son"	(FZS)
10.	nya-wac	"father's sister's daughter"	(FZD)
11.	gat-gwanien	"father's brother's son"	(FB)
12.	nya-gwanien	"father's brother's daughter"	(FBD)
13.	gat-manien	"mother's sister's son"	(MZS)
14.	nya-manien	"mother's sister's daughter"	(MZD)
15.	gat-nar	"mother's brother's son"	(MBS)
16.	nya-nar	"mother's brother's daughter"	(MBD)

Figure 6.7 Nuer (Sudanese) kinship terminology (Evans-Pritchard 1990).

is uncommon; it is associated with elaborate rules of inheritance, wherein many different people receive some specific thing (such as a particular kind of cow or the number of bulls or calves) from the person who dies.

CULTURAL SNAPSHOT 6.2

Iroquois versus Dravidian

The terms *Iroquois* and *Dravidian*, in addition to referring to a language and language family, respectively, denote kinship terminologies named for the peoples among whom they were initially identified. In fact, both terminologies are found widely on six continents. Iroquois and Dravidian terminologies appear to be very similar structurally. Both distinguish cross and parallel relatives in the first ascending generation and cross from parallel cousins in ego's generation, as shown in the diagram. The diagram uses a female ego (zero generation), though the logic of the two systems would be the same with a male ego. In both terminologies, the parallel relatives (1, 2) in the first ascending generation and in ego's generation (5,6) are ego's own kin. She calls them *father* and *mother* in the first ascending generation and *brother* and *sister* in her own generation. There is a key difference between the two systems though, which concerns the cross relatives in both generations, numbered 3, 4, 7 and 8 in the diagram. On the first ascending generation, father's sister (3) is called *aunt* in Iroquois terminology; in Dravidian ones, she is called *mother-in-law*. Likewise, mother's brother (4) is called *uncle* in Iroquois; in Dravidian, he is called *father-in-law*. In ego's generation, male cross cousins (7, or father's sister's and mother's brother's sons) and female cross cousins (8, or father's sister's and mother's brother's sons) are called by cousin terms in Iroquois terminologies. In Dravidian, a female ego calls her male cross cousins *husband* and her female cross cousins *sister-in-law*. This difference is important. Societies with Iroquois terminologies tend to prohibit marriage with any first cousins, parallel or cross; societies with Dravidian terminologies generally (but not always) encourage people to marry opposite-sex cross cousins of any degree. For that reason, Dravidian is sometimes said to contain a prescriptive marriage rule, one that prescribes, or recommends, a certain behaviour.

Eskimo Kinship System

A third system of classifying kin is Eskimo. English terminology is a version of the Eskimo classification system, which is associated with bilateral descent. In addition to modern North American society, the Central Eskimo, the Ju/'hoansi, the ancient Aztecs and the ancient Egyptians used this kind of terminology. In the Eskimo system, one set of terms is restricted to members of the nuclear family and not extended to collateral relatives. In other words, only ego's mother is called 'mother'. No other female relative is called by this term. Distinct terms are applied to collateral relatives. In the first ascending generation, the collateral terms are, in English, *uncle*, which applies to father's brother, mother's brother, mother's sister's husband and father's sister's husband; and *aunt*, which applies to mother's sister, father's sister, father's brother's wife and mother's brother's wife.

Figure 6.8 An Inuit (Eskimo) nuclear family, early 1900s. Photo by George R. King; originally published in 1917 in *National Geographic* vol. 31, p. 564.

There is no distinction between cross and parallel cousins. Eskimo terminology is well suited to bilateral descent and its emphasis on ego, with an equivalence in principle of descent and inheritance through both parents. This terminology isolates the nuclear family and applies equivalent terms to the remaining relatives on both sides of the family. In principle, neither the matriline nor the patriline is more important. Nuclear families, or similarly small family units (Figure 6.8), are important in many hunting-and-gathering societies because members spend much if not most of their time together. It therefore makes sense to distinguish them terminologically from other family members.

The Kindred

A bilateral descent rule generates a peculiar, ephemeral group of kinfolk called a *kindred*, or sometimes, *bilateral kindred*. A kindred is the social unit consisting of *all* one's relatives on both sides of the family. Only full siblings have the same kindreds. The kindred is often an active network of mutually supporting relatives. It's ephemeral insofar as it lasts for only one generation, the lifetime of an individual ego, who defines it. Thus, a kindred cannot be corporate.

The kindred in hunting-and-gathering societies such as the Inuit seems to be associated with mobility. Bands move across the landscape according to season and availability of wild food resources. By recognising the largest possible group of family members through bilateral descent (i.e., every relative on both sides of the family), an individual increases the chances of encountering a relative when meeting another band. This enables ego to make claims to resources and assistance, which would be impossible if ego was unrelated.

Bilateral kindreds tend to incorporate new persons who are neither consanguineal nor affinal relatives. This is *fictive kinship*. It often involves the manipulation of kinship terminology to reclassify a stranger as a relative. Among the Ju/'hoansi of the Kalahari Desert, a person may find fictive kin through a culturally established rule of name sharing. If ego is named 'Jack' and ego knows no one in a camp personally, but another man in camp is also named 'Jack', ego may then call Jack's father 'father', Jack's sister 'sister' and so on. Name sharing increases the potential number of kin a person has. Because one's close relatives are often crucial to survival, the more kin one can acquire, even if they're fictive, the better. Once we move beyond the domain of human relatedness as the only important organisational mode of society, more complex factors that transcend kinship and marriage come into play. Societies based on anonymous encounters and allegiances to unseen authorities (such as 'imagined communities', which are nation-states) take us from the edge of kinship and marriage to the archaic state and finally to global networks of individuals and corporate groups that define the societies of most humans today. For that reason, social organisation becomes inseparable from political and economic imperatives, the origins and maintenance of which anthropologists also examine.

Summary

Human social organisation is predicated on one species divided into two sexes. All societies are characterised by a division of labour. Usual marriage forms include monogamy, polygyny and polyandry. Marriage is contracted by means of brideservice, bridewealth or dowry. Postmarital residence determines the nature of living arrangements of social groups. Unilocal patterns result in extended families, whereas neolocal residence leads to nuclear families. All cultures have descent rules. These are either unilineal or cognatic. Human societies are all based on a principle of consanguinity and affinity. Affinity is initially established by recognising and classifying relationships outside the nuclear family. Classification rules have associated kinship terminologies. There are seven types of terminology: Iroquois, Dravidian, Crow, Omaha, Hawaiian, Sudanese and Eskimo.

Further Reading

Anderson 2006; Arensberg 1988; Balikci 1970; Basso 1973; Berdan 2005; Bogoras 1909; Brown 1991; Campagno 2009; Conklin 2001; Eaton and Eaton 1999; Edwards 1991; Evans-Pritchard (1951) 1990; Fox 1967; Goodenough 1955; Goody 1990; Gough 1968; Jankowiak 2001; Lee 2013; Lévi-Strauss (1949) 1969; Lips 2008; Lowie 1928, 1929; Morgan 1870; Murphy and Murphy 2004; Parkin 1997; Radcliffe-Brown 1952; Rivière 1984; Rosman and Rubel 1986; Sahlins 1976a; Stack 1974; Stone 2001; Tonkinson 1991; Weiner 1988; Zeitzen 2008

Cultural Snapshots

6.1   Hart et al. 2001; Ryan and Jethá 2010; Zimmer 2013
6.2   Morgan 1870; Viveiros de Castro 1998

7   Politics and Power

Overview

Complex societies involve the centralisation of power and hierarchy. In Chapter 6, we examined societies in which power and politics are organised principally around notions of relatedness through kinship and marriage. In this chapter, we examine the organisation of societies in which kinship and marriage are less important than power, wealth and a person's position in a social hierarchy. Beyond the family and clan, society becomes increasingly complex and new, nonkin bonds and divisions are formed between individuals and groups. In this chapter, we introduce the elements involved in the transformation of society from small-scale and egalitarian to complex and stratified. First, we look at how political conflicts in a kin-based society can be overcome, then consider why not all groups are complex. Finally, we examine anthropological explanations of hierarchy, centralisation and the state.

The Segmentary Model of Society

The view of society consisting of various levels of inclusiveness defined by kinship is called the *segmentary lineage* model of society. A segmentary lineage system is a good place to begin discussing complexity because complexity involves *segmentation*, or some form of systematic, lawful division of society into groups that have nothing to do with age or sex or gender. A segmentary lineage system can be matrilineal or patrilineal; a segment may be any section of the entire kinship group, such as a clan or lineage. Recall that a clan consists of two or more related lineages.

Kin-based societies with a unilineal descent rule (Chapter 6) can develop a hierarchy through a segmentary lineage system. Even though egalitarian and kin-based, a society like this could mobilise its various segments either for the purpose of warfare, to expand landholdings and defeat other social groups or for insulation from internal conflicts between group members. The Nuer people, with their patrilineal descent rule, bridewealth payments and descriptive Sudanese kinship terminology (Chapter 6) are organised as segmentary lineages.

In the past, closely related lineages in Nuer society joined together for common defence against an enemy for limited periods. Together, these unified segments were able to extend their territory, often at the expense of their non-Nuer neighbours, especially the Dinka people. In some cases, a group of related lineages in Nuer society would unify following a dispute with a Nuer from a different, more distant lineage (Figure 7.1).

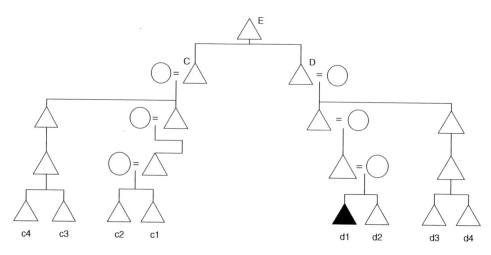

Figure 7.1 A segmentary lineage system with internal strife.

Let's say that a Nuer man got into an argument with another Nuer man over a debt involving cattle, the main type of asset in this pastoral society. In an ensuing brawl, the man killed the debtor. Masculine honour in Nuer society required that a homicide victim's male *agnates*—his male patrilineal relatives—avenge his death by taking the life of the killer. The brothers and male parallel cousins of the deceased, together with their allies, come together to execute the killer. The killer himself is supported by *his* agnates (his brother and his male parallel cousins). Thus, all the men of one lineage segment find themselves aligned against all men of another lineage segment in a blood feud. The social order of Nuer society is now in danger of breaking down in conflict and violence.

But it is at this point that traditional Nuer society displays what Durkheim called *mechanical solidarity* (Chapter 4), which means that different individuals can duplicate the work, activities and social responsibilities of others for various purposes, including kinship, marriage and reproduction. Nuer society depended on large numbers of people who did the same things; for example, all men tended cattle, whereas all women prepared milk and cheese. In addition, all men in a particular kinship unit, at some low level of organisation, could join together by mechanical solidarity as equals in a hostile encounter with other men, so joined together to avenge some injustice, such as a homicide.

In traditional Nuer society, before a destructive blood feud could arise, the killer might take sanctuary with a Leopard Skin Chief, as he was called by British colonial authorities in the 1930s. This chief customarily wore the skin of a leopard tied about his head, which symbolised his special position, though he had no real political power. The chief was believed to be able to predict the future and to curse others through black magic. The abode of the Leopard Skin Chief was sacred, and no violence was permitted there. In the sanctuary of the Leopard Skin Chief, the killer could neither eat nor drink until the chief cut the man's arm with a razor-sharp fishing spear. In this way, he drained out the blood of the dead man, purging the killer of his crime. The chief could then seek justice for the slain man by insisting upon a payment by the killer to the kin of the deceased.

In principle, the relatives of the victim did not want cattle payment; they wanted revenge. According to Evans-Pritchard, 'A Nuer is proud and wants a man's body in vengeance and not his cattle' ([1940] 1969, p. 155). The angry kinspeople would wait near the chief's sanctuary for the first opportunity to avenge their slain agnate by killing his murderer. But if they were unsuccessful, they could request that the Leopard Skin Chief release the offender to them for capital punishment. The chief typically turned down such demands to prevent a blood feud. Rather, he would offer the aggrieved kinspeople a compromise: so many head of cattle for their dead brother. If either side disagreed on the compromise, the chief could threaten them with a curse. Usually, both parties, fearing such a curse, would accept the deal, preventing the blood feud. Instead of collapsing into violence, society—and the complex network of kin and nonkin relationships—continued, although there were likely hard feelings between the two lineages. As in this Nuer example, kinship involves allegiance to one's kin and antagonism towards those who offend them, no matter how distant. It may involve competition, as with the biblical Cain and Abel. Kinship also involves allegiances based on marriage, called *affinal* ties. Affinal ties are not always as stable or reliable as consanguineal ones. The saying 'blood is thicker than water' refers to the fact that blood ties tend to be stronger than ties by marriage.

The segmentary lineage is based on the notion of shared blood and allows for large, unified groups to form in society. In some cases, especially in small-scale societies, a single segment could include everyone, since all members were linked by either blood or marriage. If a dispute arose between a Nuer man and Dinka man, in theory all the segments of Nuer society could link together for common defence.

Social and Political Differentiation

Egalitarianism

The Nuer numbered some 200,000 persons in Evans-Pritchard's day. By the 1990s, there were more than one million Nuer, and their segmentary model of society was breaking down. They were living in a state—Sudan—with a complex bureaucracy, district councils and government parties. A state of any sort exhibits centralised authority, bureaucracy, taxation, territorial boundaries, monopoly on coercion of others (state control of the police, courts and military) and *strata*, which are groups with markedly unequal access to wealth and power. Historian Charles Tilly has a good anthropological grasp of this concept of centralisation, in noting that states are 'coercion-wielding organizations that are distinct from households and kinship groups and exercise clear priority in some respects over all other organizations within substantial territories' (1990, p. 1). States therefore include empires, city-states and theocracies and are distinct from all other kinds of human groups such as lineages, clans, tribes, churches, mosques, temples, synagogues, villages and towns. The strata of states can be rural, urban or both. In more recent times, due to the second Sudanese Civil War and continuing violence, many Nuer were living either in refugee camps in nearby states or even outside Africa altogether. Some 25,000 Nuer live in the United States. Small-scale societies, such as the traditional Nuer of the 1930s, were organised by kinship, not by state bureaucracy and stratification. Regardless of whether they display segmentary lineage organisation, societies like those of the traditional Nuer—the Nuer of the ethnographic present of Evans-Pritchard—rarely number more than 25,000, and often they are smaller than 1,000. The politics of such societies are partly defined by *egalitarianism*.

According to cultural anthropologist Morton Fried (1923–1986), there are three principal types of inequalities in society. Egalitarianism is the first type. In an egalitarian society, age and sex are usually the primary criteria used to distinguish between people. Older people tend to have authority over younger people just as parents have authority over their children. Men tend to take a more prominent role in warfare and in acquiring meat than women. All societies are egalitarian to some extent; for example, most families make distinctions between members on the basis of age and sex. Some individuals in such societies may be held in high esteem and mediate conflicts because of their perceived generosity and wisdom; they may serve as informal, or unrecognised, de facto leaders.

The Ju/'hoansi foragers of southern Africa are notable for their fierce resistance to the development of individual authority. When asked to identify their leader, or 'headman', one Ju/'hoansi man told ethnographer Richard Lee, 'Each one of us is headman over himself'. This ability to make decisions for one's self and one's relatives, rather than appealing to a higher authority, is a feature of egalitarianism. Levelling mechanisms such as arrow sharing maintain egalitarianism. A levelling mechanism keeps all members of a group at about the same status in society. Arrow sharing functions as a levelling mechanism in Ju/'hoansi society by ensuring that certain people—good hunters, for example—do not become more important or have more authority than others who are less fortunate. Some men *are* better hunters than others, depending on some combination of age, fitness, eyesight and skill. But no matter how good a hunter a man is, he is not rewarded with gifts, favours or higher status. In fact, the man who shoots a major game animal, such as an eland or wildebeest, does not own the animal. The owner is the man who made the arrow that killed the prey. Bragging, real or imagined, is frowned upon and met with ridicule or ostracism.

As with the Ju/'hoansi, hunters among the egalitarian Munduruku of the Amazon Basin are required to share game. 'Chiefs' among the Munduruku are really headmen who lead by example, not by giving everyone their marching orders. These headmen cannot coerce others to obey them. Such societies are *acephalous*, which literally means 'headless'. They have no central leadership. During his study of the Araw.eté people, a small indigenous Amazonian society, Brazilian ethnographer Eduardo Viveiros de Castro took several months to uncover who had most influence in the village. He finally discovered not a boisterous chief with designs on other people's time and attention, but a circumspect, almost humble individual. Members of acephalous societies may be very suspicious of someone who refuses to share or tries to accumulate goods. Such a person may be accused of witchcraft, a very serious charge in small-scale societies that can result in capital punishment of the perpetrator.

Egalitarianism and Artificial Scarcities

Different ethnic groups can form a single society and still remain egalitarian among themselves, despite differences of language and custom, when they are economically linked together. Sometimes the bond between them requires the individual groups to specialise in the production of some needed artefact, which all groups could in theory make, but choose not to. Economic differences distinguish the ethnic identity of the Maku of the Northwest Amazon, who speak their own language, from their Tukanoan and Arawakan-speaking neighbours. Speaking unrelated languages and exhibiting differences of costume, ritual and cuisine, these groups interact with one another in a large network of social and economic interdependence.

The Maku people of the Northwest Amazon Basin predominantly hunt and gather; they have only minimal cultivation of crops. The forest itself does not provide much high-energy, carbohydrate-rich foods. To obtain such foods, the Maku exchange meat of game animals with their Tukanoan- and Arawakan-speaking neighbours. The Tukanoans and Arawakans are riverine agriculturalists with complex beliefs regarding Maku sorcery and other dangers that lurk in the rainforest. They believe the Maku are better suited to hunt in the rainforest, whereas they are more apt to make a living by fishing and horticulture. The Maku tend to give the Tukanoans and Arawakans a share of the hunt, while the latter reciprocate with carbohydrate-rich plant foods from their gardens, such as manioc flour, bananas, sweet potatoes and yams.

Societies of the Northwest Amazon combine a postmarital residential practice of virilocality with a marriage rule of linguistic exogamy, which results in many people who are not only bilingual but polyglots. Each group specialises in making certain goods that everyone else needs, known as *artificial scarcities*. Carved stools are made by the Tukano, snuff takers by the Tatuyos, canoes by the Bará, sieves by the Desana and graters by the Içana. These goods are made by each language group and circulate among all. Here, differences of ethnicity seem to be maintained to support economic specialisation and regional exchange within the group, a principle similar to the *kula* ring in the Trobriand Islands (Chapter 4), which Malinowski proposed had an intersocietal peacekeeping function. Specialisation and trade in these items help maintain peaceful intergroup relations. Artificial scarcities are, in a sense, levelling mechanisms that help maintain intergroup egalitarianism.

Ranking

Ranking is the second category of inequality, after egalitarianism, proposed by Morton Fried. It is also the most elusive for the anthropologist. Ranked societies have more distinctions between people than egalitarian ones. They may have cognatic clans, which are ordered by prestige and power in relation to each other, from highest to lowest. The precontact Maori of New Zealand had a system of ranking like this. Ranked or 'semi-complex' societies are centred on an individual sometimes called a 'Big Man' or 'chief'. This person and his or her heirs control the labour of others, starting with extended family members and then expanding out to include distant kin and even nonkin. Local bands or villages are not autonomous in ranked societies. They may instead owe labour and allegiance to a Big Man or a chief.

'Big Men' in Melanesia gain prestige by displaying wealth and feeding people. They may feast multitudes of assembled guests by opening up their storehouses and distributing food. This apparent generosity is intended to repay the loyalty of the guests. The Big Man or Woman receives prestige in exchange. His or—more rarely—her primary function is redistributing wealth that has accumulated through the labour of kin. These kin contribute goods such as clothing, tools, utensils and other gifts so the Big Man can stage a generous communal feast with gargantuan amounts of pork, yams, sweet potatoes and taro. The perceived generosity of the Big Man validates his status. His power is not coercive; instead, it is based on his ability to convince others to work harder and contribute more food to the feast. Economies in Big Man societies are called *redistributive* because of this principle of extravagant feasting.

Redistribution is an important part of societies on the Northwest Coast; in Polynesia, including Hawaii and Tahiti, in parts of Southeast Asia and in parts of Japan. In these societies, ranked cognatic clans existed. The most highly ranked clans had a *paramount chief*—a chief among chiefs—with great personal power. This person held sway over many villages. Some of these groups, to Fried, would have been on the cusp of genuinely unequal, hierarchical access to the resources necessary to sustain life, what he called 'incipiently stratified' society. Cultural anthropologist Robert Carneiro (1927-2020) considered ranked societies to be 'flashpoints'—forms of social organisation with the potential to become more complex and *stratified*."

Stratification

Stratification is the segmentation of society into groups defined by their continual, unequal access to material wealth, power, influence and prestige. Societies that have strata—all states and empires, for example—are thus stratified. Strata are of two types: *caste* and *class*.

The term *caste*, which refers to subgroups of Hindu society in India, comes from the Portuguese term 'casta'. The Portuguese, who set up a trading centre in India in the sixteenth century, noted that Hindus distinguished between members of their society in a way very different from the Portuguese way. Portuguese society was organised into *classes*. A class is a stratum of complex society that has more or less control over resources, technology and land than other classes in the same society. Marriage is not prohibited between members of different classes, though it may not be very common. For example, members of ruling houses or dynasties rarely marry commoners. When they do, they may lose some or all of their privileges.

In contrast to the Portuguese, Hindu society in India was organised into four principal castes to which occupational specialisations were ascribed: priestly caste (Brahmin); military caste (Kshatriya); the rural farm workers (peasants) and shopkeepers (Vaishya); and servants and manual labourers (Sudra). An additional group of people were considered 'untouchable'; contact with them was perceived as polluting by the other castes. These people did tasks that were considered taboo by other castes, such as handling meat, tanning of hides and leather, handling human corpses and disposing of waste of animals and people. The caste system prohibits marriage between people of different castes. In other words, castes are *endogamous*. Caste membership is *ascribed*: one remains in the caste of one's birth for life. In contrast, classes may be either endogamous or exogamous. Families can sometimes be reclassified from one class, such as rich or poor, into another, such as a 'middle' class. In a class society, it is possible to marry up or down on the socioeconomic scale, so marriage can promote mobility between classes. This is not possible in a caste system. Both caste and class are units of social organisation in complex, stratified societies.

Theories of the State

A *state* is a highly complex society with classes or castes and a political hierarchy. In many societies, the rulers inevitably originate in the highest strata, except in cases of adoption. The members of the lowest strata usually support the ruling elite through their work or through taxes paid to the state, its institutions and its personnel. States that have asymmetric relationships with other states and demand tribute are *empires*.

Many archaeologists are interested in pristine state formation. They want to know what makes a chiefdom—a ranked society—become a stratified state. Several pristine states have been identified in the archaeological record. Mesopotamia is one example.

Thousands of years ago, something occurred in what is today modern Iraq to change the way that ancient Mesopotamians organised themselves. Society became stratified, likely for the first time in human history. The process of state formation starts with minimal complexity.

Minimal Complexity

Robert Carneiro defined *minimal complexity* as the temporary union of two or more bands or villages for the purpose of organising labour under a chief. Often, this labour involved warfare and defence using bows and arrows, blowguns and other nonindustrial technology. In ranked societies, the amalgamation of numerous villages that paid tribute to powerful chiefs who commanded them in warfare is called *maximal complexity*. Such societies were found on the Northwest Coast, in coastal Brazil, Hawai'i, northern Japan and elsewhere. Groups within these societies are ranked on the basis of their allegiance to a particular chief. These ranked groups—or cognatic clans—have similar access to goods and services. States differ from many ranked societies in terms of how power and property are distributed throughout the population. In states, there are extreme differences in access to goods and services.

Thomas Hobbes, the seventeenth-century philosopher who imagined life in egalitarian society to be 'nasty' and 'brutish', suggested that pristine states originated as a way to prevent chaos and warfare from destroying society. Current thinking suggests that pristine states developed from complex chiefdoms. Why some, but not all, chiefdoms became states remains unknown, and it is a subject that archaeologists debate. One possibility, also suggested by Robert Carneiro, is *environmental circumscription*. Carneiro argued that states arose in areas where there was limited agricultural land. In such places, chiefs fought to protect their land and, when populations increased, to expand their control. Some chiefs were very successful and were able to increase their territories. Larger territories required more complex forms of social organisation and centralised leadership, enabling some individuals to acquire more resources and dominate others. The acquisition of resources by some led to the formation of different social strata, and the conquest of rival societies generated a slave class. Most ancient states had slavery: the ancient Greek city-states, the Roman Empire and ancient China were dependent on slave labour, used to produce a surplus of wealth to support ruling elites. Southeast Asian, Mesoamerican and Andean states also had slaves, as did some of the societies of the Northwest Coast. In the Aztec empire of Mexico, slaves were of two main types: those captured in battle, who were destined to be sacrificed to the war god Huitzilopochtli; and those forced to work for others or to pay a penalty for a crime they had committed, called *tlacotin*. According to ethnohistorian Frances Berdan, 'People could sell themselves or some member of their family into slavery for subsistence needs' (2005, p. 67).

States cannot coexist with smaller, completely autonomous societies within their borders, and vice versa. Wherever states developed, independent, acephalous (leaderless) groups and ranked societies eventually succumbed to their power. In contrast to egalitarian and ranked societies, states have centralised leadership based not only on kinship but also on stratification. The size of a society—its population and geographic expanse—is associated with the political and economic complexity of the society. Size determines in part how many layers, or strata, there are in a complex society. For example, the United States is often divided into three strata: rich, poor and middle-class. These classes are further subdivided and may be defined in terms of net worth, home ownership, income, investments, real estate, education level and occupation.

Ethnic groups with their own leaders inside state territorial boundaries have the potential to undermine state authority by challenging its ruling strata. Ethnographer James Scott has recently suggested that Southeast Asian highland societies, which are normally much more egalitarian and less sedentary than those situated in fertile bottomlands dependent on irrigation of paddy rice, are frequently seen as threats to the ranked and stratified societies of the fertile valleys. Thus, many states attempt to subsume the populations of other ethnic groups within their borders to prevent conflict over leadership and control of resources.

Complexification

Complexification refers to the increasing heterogeneity of social, political and economic structures in a society. An earlier generation of ethnographers considered this phenomenon to be part of the process of *cultural evolution*. However, not all societies become increasingly complex. Complexification occurs with the fusion of unlike, formerly autonomous groups into a single political entity with centralised authority. These groups could be bands, villages, towns or cities, and they often represent different ethnicities.

An essential anthropological question is whether complexity is inevitable. Does it represent human destiny or the outcome of a series of events at a given time and place? Does complexity come about from chance factors that coincide to propel societies towards greater hierarchy? What roles do diffusion, technology and the environment play? These questions are difficult to answer because there are few examples of pristine states and because the archaeological record is incomplete and difficult to decipher.

Philosophers such as Hobbes and later anthropologists have developed several theories to explain state formation. These theories can be divided into two main types: *voluntary* and *compulsory*. Anthropologists, with some exceptions, tend to subscribe to the compulsory view. The voluntary view was first espoused by Hobbes. He saw human nature as competitive and greedy. To him, humans without government lived in a state of continual war and conflict, wherein human life mattered little. For Hobbes, life without the structure and security of the state was a savage condition he famously described in *The Leviathan* (1651) as 'nasty, brutish, and short'.

Hobbes believed that in order not to be in conflict with each other, people needed to be in 'awe' of some thing or person that they believed to be greater than themselves, such as a monarch. Only by centralisation and the top–down management of society could chaos and the 'war of all against all' be transformed into civil society. For that reason, people were willing to give up part of their personal liberty. They therefore voluntarily submitted to centralised leadership in the form of a king or dictator who ruled over them and who was supposed to protect them from random violence. Hobbes' voluntaristic theory of the state is that the masses of people, not just the elite, actually wanted it. Hobbes' view was first questioned by David Hume, one of the Scottish Enlightenment philosophers of the eighteenth century, who doubted whether the need for law and order and security and government were actually requirements for the wellbeing of all human societies. Hume was familiar with European accounts of indigenous societies of North America. He observed that government is 'not necessary in all circumstances...An *Indian* is but little tempted to dispossess another his hut, or to steal his bow, as being already provided of the same advantages' (Hume [1739] 1955, p. 539; emphasis in original). Hume is most likely correct that any imperative or compulsory model for state organisation was not rooted in biological dispositions of humankind, for anthropologists have studied hundreds of egalitarian societies that do not require top-down hierarchies of class and government power to survive from one generation to the next.

Most of the compulsory models of state origins are materialist. That is the idea that environmental and technological conditions determine social structure and ideology in society. This view holds that people do not choose to submit to a higher authority in the form of a state. Rather, they are forced or compelled. Unilinear evolutionists such as Morgan and Tylor saw the state—and civilisation as a whole—as a natural stage in human intellectual and cultural progress. Complexity for them was destiny. The psychic unity of humankind led to the gradual but inevitable domination of humans over land, resources and technology. These changes in turn led to private property, the nuclear family and literate society.

Hydraulic Theory

Later cultural evolutionists argued the state was destiny for some, but not for all members of our species. Sinologist Karl Wittfogel (1896–1988) hypothesised that the state arose to control water resources and manage irrigation in deserts where food could be produced only through intensive agriculture. This is the *hydraulic theory* of the state. Managing water works and directing the construction of levees, canals, sluice gates and rice paddies required a bureaucracy, in Wittfogel's view. Such a bureaucracy needed a leader, such as a monarch, who could resolve conflicts over how water and other resources were managed and distributed.

Marx called this an autocratic Asiatic mode of production, for this kind of state was based on a massive bureaucracy, as existed in Confucian China (pre-Communist China), and was originally thought to be found only in Asia. Cultural anthropologist Eric Wolf observed that China is the 'oldest living primary civilization', meaning it is a pristine state that has been in existence in some form for about 5,000 years, even if the exact character and ruling dynasties have changed due to conflict, war and conquest. Although often invaded by foreign enemies from the steppe country to the north, the Chinese state never disappeared south of the Great Wall. Nor did it disappear after the Communist Revolution of 1947–1950; it merely changed forms.

We now know that similar states existed in the Andes and along the desert coast of Peru in prehistoric times, though they were destroyed by conquest. New, smaller and more fragmented states arose in the aftermath of their destruction and European colonialism (Chapter 9), states such as Peru, Colombia, Ecuador, Bolivia and Chile. One of the early states that developed on the north coast of Peru was that of the Moche, or Mochica, who ruled several river valleys from AD 200 to 850. The Moche came to prominence 'when large-scale irrigation technology created a new source of wealth', according to archaeologists Luis Jaime Castillo and Santiago Uceda (2008, p. 707). Bigger, better irrigation canals allowed for larger agricultural surpluses that supported a new and wealthier elite. The ruling elites lived in large, well-built structures and were buried in elaborate tombs accompanied by many finely painted ceramic vessels and artefacts made of gold, silver and turquoise; poor people lived in small houses, sometimes far from water sources, and were buried in simple graves with very few artefacts.

Irrigation and the bureaucracy needed to control water were key to state development, according to Wittfogel. He suggested that early primary, or pristine, state-level societies had large, well-trained groups of people who kept track of government expenses and organised work on state-sponsored construction, repair and maintenance of roads, bridges, granaries and irrigation systems. This involved central planning and occupational specialisation in the form of a bureaucracy. The bureaucracy controlled the infrastructure of irrigation—access to reservoirs, dams, dykes—and managed government-owned granaries. Sinologist Owen Lattimore noted, 'The irrigated fields were the best of fields. The conservancy works necessary for establishing and maintaining irrigation were too great for the private enterprise of even the richest landowners. State administration was unavoidable' (1951, p. 39). State-level hydraulic societies relied upon surplus: sufficient food to support not only the people who worked the land but also all the nonagricultural workers and the ruling strata of society itself.

Bureaucracies of early states, such as China, India and those of the Near East, had forms of writing or mnemonic devices not found in nonstate societies (Cultural Snapshot 7.1) and skilled personnel trained in their use. Ancient Chinese bureaucrats, known as *mandarins*, were taught esoterica, which further added to their aura of mystery and power over the working classes. Wittfogel believed that bureaucrats were essential to efficient water distribution and crop production sufficient to feed farmers as well as artisans, ironworkers, miners, bureaucrats, religious specialists and the elite. Bureaucrats also taxed people's labour by drafting them to work on building and maintaining irrigation systems. This kind of forced labour tax is called *corvée labour*, which the Inca state, like China, used for public works projects, including roads, irrigation systems, terracing and food production.

CULTURAL SNAPSHOT 7.1

Ancient Numerary and Literary Devices

Quipu of the Inca (Figure 7.2): colourful knotted cords of string, also spelt *khipu*. The knots and colours had meaning to ancient bookkeepers of the Inca Empire. The knots of some *quipu* represented accounting devices to record taxes and tribute throughout the empire; others were mnemonic devices, or memory aids, to help the holder of the *khipu* accurately relate histories and stories from memory.

Abacus of the ancient Sumerians: a frame into which rods were set that originated in Mesopotamia and spread east across Asia, into Africa and southern Europe. It consisted of beads or balls representing multiples of each other that were moved along the rods, allowing for calculation.

Hieroglyphics of the ancient Maya and ancient Egyptians: these were part-syllabic, part-iconic systems of notation that represented numbers, sounds and words. They were used to record historical events, to identify people in tombs and on sculpture and to write down religious texts.

Alphabetic writing of the ancient Hebrews, Arabs, Greeks and Romans: this was fully alphabetic writing capable of rendering all terms, both abstract and concrete, in sentences that duplicated human speech.

Figure 7.2 Inca *quipu*. Courtesy of Museo Larco Herrera, Lima, Peru.

Inca civilisation depended on intensive agriculture, especially the mass production of maize (corn) in irrigated valleys. Rulers in particular had extensive irrigation systems on their landed estates. Archaeologist R. A. Covey noted that, 'Estate construction involved impressive projects of river canalization and the construction of irrigation canals and terraces' (2008, p. 821). These lands were reserved for the Inca emperor and his cognatic clan, which was the descent group of the ruling hierarchy in Cuzco, the capital of the Inca Empire. The bureaucracies of early societies like those of China and the Andes relied on careful accounting, especially in regard to taxation. Records in almost all states, ancient and modern, were kept by those who specialised in counting and writing, such as scribes, all of whom worked for the state. Record keeping was a respected occupation among the Inca. Record keepers, called *quipucamayoc*, had specialised knowledge of an accounting apparatus called a *quipu* (or *khipu*). *Quipu* were made from colourful, knotted cords of llama wool and cotton fibres (Figure 7.2). According to ethnohistorian Gary Urton, about 700 *quipu* are known to exist.

An average *quipu* had a primary cord about two feet long to which were attached laterally about 60 cords, each measuring about a foot long. Additional shorter cords were knotted to these cords. The type, placement and colour of the knots were used to record tax and tribute payments from each province of the Inca Empire. Some *quipu* also served mnemonic and perhaps even literary purposes, helping *quipucamayoc* recall the Inca past (Cultural Snapshot 7.1).

Wittfogel's hydraulic theory of state origins is based on the premise that people in complex societies require an administrative bureaucracy to redistribute wealth. Support of that bureaucracy required stratification of society, dividing those who laboured in fields and irrigation works from those who did not. Wittfogel's theory showed how rulership and stratification in ancient China functioned in relation to irrigation and agriculture. It did not explain how and why the initial complexity needed to build, repair and maintain the irrigation works came about in the first place. Some twentieth–century anthropologists sought to modify Wittfogel's hydraulic theory to identify the common factor(s) propelling the rise of all early states.

Multilinear Evolution

Julian Steward (Chapter 5) focused on the development of complexity in pristine states or states that were so far apart that they could not have experienced diffusion of political ideas and practices. Pristine states were those that developed first and independently of all others. Steward looked at developments in the Andes, Mesoamerica, the Nile River valley, Mesopotamia and the Near East, India and China. He tried to discern what the different pristine states might have had in common. He called this exercise *multilinear evolution*, referring to the many lines or possible ways in which a society could become increasingly complex and, at the same time, experience changes that paralleled those occurring in other regions of the world. In each case, the lines led to similar results: the stratification of society. To Steward, the differences between the states were superficial. That each had different religious beliefs, artistic styles and ideologies did not change the fact that they all had some fundamental political and economic similarities.

Steward suggested that intensive agriculture, which used irrigation, fertilisers and other labour-demanding inputs (Chapter 8), enabled the production of food *surpluses*. This means the class of people engaged in food production—the peasantry— amassed more food than needed to feed themselves alone. They also produced surpluses of other goods, such as textiles, spices, stimulants, ceramics and stone- and metalwork. Control of such surpluses became key to the development of different tiers of society, separating the haves and the have-nots. Those who controlled the surplus were, in essence, the masters of those who gave up their energy, strength, skill and time to produce it.

Environmental Circumscription

Developed by Robert Carneiro, *environmental circumscription* is one of the most influential anthropological theories of state formation and the origins of complexity. Carneiro identified three factors that were necessary for the development of complexity: 1) *circumscription*, which is the enclosure of narrow, limited areas of arable land by vast tracts of desert or mountains; 2) the existence of ethnically distinct and mutually antagonistic chiefdoms within these limited areas; and 3) population increase within these ethnically distinct societies. Chiefdoms in such circumscribed areas relied upon agriculture and were led by rulers—chiefs—in warfare with their neighbours.

Chiefdoms without agriculture—found on the Pacific Rim, such as societies of the Northwest Coast and the Ainu of far northern Japan, as well as in other groups living in maritime environments with abundant resources, such as salmon and shellfish and numerous plant foods—do not appear to become state-level societies. However, in agricultural chiefdoms in environmentally circumscribed zones, arable land was limited. Therefore, conflicts could not be resolved by the defeated group simply moving away: there was nowhere else to go. In noncircumscribed areas, such as the Amazon River Basin, two societies could war over control of rich riverine land. But the losing side could simply move elsewhere, migrating into the interior of the forest. In contrast, a vanquished chiefdom in a circumscribed area could not survive if its members were forced to abandon their farmland. In order to live, they needed both the irrigation technology to render the desert arable and the nearby rivers that watered their fields. Without access to the rivers and canal systems, a society could not survive in regions such as the coastal desert valleys of western South America.

For Carneiro, circumscription was the key to state formation. His theory described the state at its initiation and suggested that stratification into masters and slaves, or rich and poor, came before everything else. Probably these early societies were organised into castes. This seems to have been the case in ancient South America as well as in Mesopotamia and the Indus River valley in Pakistan and India. After stratification emerges, intensive agriculture follows, with lower castes providing agricultural labour to support higher castes that no longer farm and may not produce anything at all. Those members of state society who do have productive work—that is, they make things others need or want, but do not farm—may be engaged in any number of different occupations. In state-level societies, people *specialise*, becoming, for example, artisans (such as carpenters, masons, weavers, potters, lapidaries, goldsmiths and metallurgists), educators, apothecaries (druggists), surgeons, warriors, priests and priestesses and, as noted previously, people who keep tax records and those who generate official histories of ruling dynasties.

Following initial stratification, state societies tend to increase agricultural production and expand into formerly barren hinterlands, beyond the environmentally circumscribed zones. Irrigation and terracing render unproductive deserts and mountains arable. States transform landscapes profoundly. As the state expands towards empire, and as its population grows and different ethnic groups are incorporated into the emerging polity, neighbouring lands and peoples are conquered and their residents enslaved or forced to pay tribute. Carneiro, like Wittfogel and Steward, was looking at what Fried referred to as pristine states; all other states are the product of diffusion and conquest over time. *Secondary states*, then, ensue from contact with and through the influence of pristine states.

Complexity and Ethnicity

Small-scale societies tend to be built on the belief, real or imagined, that everyone is related. Kinship is one form of relatedness, as we have seen. Another is ethnicity. Ethnic groups may be entire societies, as with the Nuer studied by Evans-Pritchard. Or they may be parts of a larger, more complex whole, such as a state or empire, both of which include multiple ethnic groups. *Ethnicity* is the self-identification of persons as members of a group that defines itself by common customs, a shared language or dialect, and a set of symbols that mark their relatedness, such as ritual, clothing, hairstyle or body ornamentation. These are ethnic boundary markers, as with the differing attitudes to food between the Guajá and the Araweté (Chapter 1). Ethnicity is like culture, except it is more specific. Whereas members of different ethnic groups can share a common culture, they do so only partly and incompletely. African Americans, American Jews and Italian Americans all share part of the culture of the United States, and descendants of Chinese, Indian and Indonesian immigrants share aspects of Malay culture, though each constitutes a separate and distinct ethnicity. This is due to their status as racialised minorities: these groups in Malaysia are defined as 'races', and that categorisation of ethnic groups is a heritage of the British colonial period, which lasted for more than a century.

People with a common ethnicity, or ethnic identity, share a cultural heritage and background that often extends into the very distant past, hundreds or even thousands of years. That does not mean they are biologically more similar to each other than they are to other groups. It simply means they share the same institutions, which have a long history, including those pertaining to supernatural beliefs and practices, namely religion and spirituality. Differences of ethnic identity based on religious criteria as boundary markers often have a sort of branching pattern. For example, many ethnic Arabs profess a belief in Muhammed as a prophet of Allah, though they are divided into two major groups. After Muhammed's death in AD 632, some believers followed the leadership of Ali, Muhammed's relative and son-in-law, and became Shi'ite Muslims. Others recognised a close friend and advisor of the prophet as the new leader of Islam and became Sunni Muslims. Ethnic Arabs therefore may be either Sunni or Shi'ite. Likewise, during the sixteenth-century Reformation, Protestants branched off from Catholics. Buddhism arose out of a Hindu sect. Christianity itself arose from a mixture of Jewish and eastern Mediterranean beliefs and practices 2,000 years ago. Religion, as a feature of ethnicity, and ethnicity itself, crosscut the strata—classes and castes—of state societies.

Whether a society is small-scale and kin-based or complex and composed of strata influences culture, and ultimately individual psychology and enculturation. Kin-based societies, like complex, hierarchical ones, may feature distinctive gender identities, patterns in marriage rules and the sexual division of labour, family structure, postmarital residence patterns, descent rules and kin classification. The state transcends these ordering criteria with differentiation of its population into hierarchical strata and cross-cutting ethnic groups. Such group distinctions become more important for understanding the complex workings of state societies than those based on kinship and similar principles.

Centralisation of Authority

States exert power to exact labour and taxes from the masses and allot responsibility for law and order to a central authority: a government, sometimes represented by an absolute monarch such as a queen, king or emperor; an autocrat such as a dictator; or elected bodies and councils. This is the *centralisation of authority*, unique to states. Centralisation means that a small group of people make crucial decisions for everyone else in society, decisions such as how much they owe in taxes and rent, what kind of work they perform, the kind of punishment meted out for crimes, where they live, what they learn, how they worship, the quality and quantity of food they eat and how much they work.

The highest classes own the means of production (land, other natural resources, labour and the technology used to exploit these) and workers use the means to make products that people can use, such as food, textiles, fibres, fuel and medicine. Peasants in the countryside—the source of farm labour—often have internal strata. Although all are commoners, they may be internally stratified in terms of land ownership in certain Eurasian societies, such as pre-Soviet Russia, where individuals and not just the state could own land. The rich owned the land; the poor rented the land and sold their labour in the fields to the landowning peasants.

Peasants, or a *peasantry*, are agricultural workers who may or may not own land, but who are involved as labourers in modes of production that create a surplus above and beyond the workers' basic needs. Peasant livelihoods depend on the cultivation of the land. The surplus they produce is sometimes extracted by coercive means to support the livelihoods of those who do not work in food production, such as elites. Peasantries have always inhabited rural lands claimed by states, including archaic states, as with the Inca. Taxation of peasantries is found throughout societies based on intensive agriculture, which entails continuous cropping of the land and major changes to the landscape (Chapter 8).

In some cases, peasantries enduring severe exploitation and taxation at the hands of a brutal elite—native or foreign—have taken up arms to overthrow the status quo. Such peasant wars include the Mexican Revolution (1910–1920), the Chinese Communist Revolution (1928–1952) and the Vietnam War (1955–1975). Anthropologist Eric Wolf observed that twentieth-century peasant conflicts shed light on how a class, as opposed to a group defined in ethnic or cultural terms, can work together to take power in state societies. Peasantries, in other words, could form the foundations of new states and state powers.

Ethnic Diversity in States

In all but the smallest of states, ethnic diversity is the rule. The initial, pristine states may have merged chiefdoms representing different ethnicities and languages. States and their strata are normally divided by ethnic groups, which may have their own strata. Ethnic groups may fight over territory and other assets inside states. Some states manage to contain ethnic conflicts by collapsing ethnic differences. Such collapsing is never complete and is the reason for what are called *substrate influences* in language and culture. For example, the Portuguese conquered Malaysia in the early sixteenth century and imposed Catholicism on people who were Hindu, Buddhist and Muslim. In most of Malaysia, the influence of Catholicism has waned. The only place where it survived was among the fisherfolk along the coast. That is because Catholic beliefs permitted people to kill and eat animals, a practice that is significantly restricted in Hinduism, Buddhism and Islam.

Multiethnic states, also called *pluralistic societies*, include modern India, the Inca Empire and Imperial and Communist China. How did these states maintain peace among competing segments of the population? The Incas, for example, incorporated many Andean and coastal societies with diverse languages into the empire, increasing the potential for ethnic conflict. They prevented such conflicts by training the sons of conquered chiefs in Inca administration and the Quechua language. These men were appointed to govern provinces where the local language and customs were quite different from their own, making them unlikely to oppose the Inca emperor and his family because they would not have a power base in the new territories to which they were assigned.

Ethnic conflicts are often managed through state control of the educational system, by emphasising the common nationality of everyone. In Malaysia, ethnic Malays constitute only about half the population; there are large Indian and Chinese ethnic groups, as well as hundreds of others from the Malay Peninsula to eastern Borneo. Since the twentieth century, government schools have sought to promote a common Malay identity, regardless of these differences. At the same time, stratification of society into classes of rural poor and urban elites, who may share common Malay language, custom, dress and religion, can lead to political disputes within the same ethnic group due to differential access to jobs, property and other resources. Social strata within states may have actually originated as distinct societies, ethnic groups distinguished by boundary markers such as language, customs, religion and even land use and management. In archaic states, the lowest strata of society were composed of rural farming people: the peasants. These peasant ethnic groups may have originally been relatively egalitarian among themselves, acephalous and without territorial ambitions. Yet, once incorporated into states, the peasantry became part of a hierarchical system and was internally stratified, distinguishing members by class and differential ownership of land and resources.

Cities and the State

States continually expand or contract their boundaries. Rome, a city-state originally, in a few hundred years became an empire by extending its authority around the Mediterranean Basin and north to Britain and what is today Germany. The Inca Empire likewise started as a city-state in Cuzco, Peru. The empire expanded to include most of the Andes, stretching from Bolivia and Chile north to Ecuador. The Ming and Qing dynasties of China started out in the Forbidden City—today Beijing—but ultimately held sway over vast swaths of Asia. Relatively small states of Western Europe—Portugal, Spain, the Netherlands and Britain—expanded across the globe in the 1500s, and their cultures spread throughout the Americas, Africa, Asia, Australia and the Pacific, destroying or commingling with existing societies. Each state or empire imposed its own language and customs on newly conquered subjects, though at times incompletely. In this way, art, music, science, ideas and language diffused across geographic and ethnic boundaries, over deserts, forests and oceans. States and empires, much more than small-scale societies, have diminished cultural and linguistic differences across the globe. The stratification, centralisation and technologies they employ have made for a less diverse world over the last 5,000 years, with the expansion of concentrated populations in cities.

The city has been defined minimally as a territorial unit of population concentration, with a minimum of 10,000 people per square kilometre (or somewhat more than about 25,000 people/square mile). And traditionally cities were governmental units. In the most recent period of world history, globalisation (Chapter 12), cities are physical, social and economic examples of highly anthropically modified terrain with a multitude of environmental problems such as sustainability and pollution as well as connected social problems of inequality in income, healthcare and housing, sometimes connected to concepts about race and ethnicity. The lowest of the urban underclass will often lack shelter. Homelessness is identified in cities throughout the world (*furosha* in Japan—'floating people'; *os sem teto* 'without a roof' in Brazil; and similarly 'roofless' in India). How to house, count, account for financially and manage homeless populations—in part because they are often mobile—are problems found worldwide. The family form has been affected in racialised populations particularly in the Caribbean but also in the urban Global North, where female-headed households with children are more common than nuclear families; this condition has been called *matrifocality* or matrifocal families, not to be confused with matrilocal, matrilineal or matriarchal terms.

More than one-half the world's population in the twenty-first century now lives in a city, and many anthropologists are focused on a subfield called urban anthropology. The world population today is about 7.8 billion people; it is expected to level off at about ten billion by 2050. Cultural anthropologist Aihwa Ong notes the complex ecology of cities that involves not just terrain and living things but the penetration of giant corporations and world finance. Privatisation in many cities has taken over utilities like water, gas and electricity, as well as telecom services, steel and automobile industries and other industries that in one world city or another were formerly managed by local governments. Some cities are entirely owned by business interests, such as Songdo, just outside Seoul, South Korea, which is a corporate city invented as part of a special economic zone (SEZ) that offers tax and infrastructure incentives to corporations. Some cities have become enormously populated since the middle of the twentieth century. Each megacity is *at least* 1,000 minimal cities. In 1950, there were only three of these: London, New York and Tokyo. Today, there are more than 30, on five continents. These cities and the states they are contained in, together with the global networks of information, migration and capital that penetrate them, have implications for cultural change. Before examining cultural change, which occurred on an enormous scale globally after the onset of colonialism (Chapter 9), we will examine environmental conditions and sustainability issues regarding different kinds of societies before the rise of megacities and international corporations.

Summary

Kin-based societies can be organised into larger polities following a segmentary model of organisation. Societies may be politically organised as egalitarian, ranked or stratified. States are always stratified. Various theories have been proposed to account for the origins of the first states, including voluntarism, the hydraulic hypothesis, multilinear evolution and environmental circumscription. States and stratification are defined by classes, castes, centralisation of authority, ethnic diversity and means for controlling conflict, including ethnic conflict. Cities and megacities are historical and contemporary consequences of states, stratification and international networks of information, migration and finance.

Further Reading

Ambikaipaker 2008; Andaya and Andaya 2001; Blackwood 2006; Boxer 1969; Carneiro 1970, 1998, 2003; Covey 2008; Crossley et al. 2006; Damon 1990 (p. 107); Ellis and Ramankutty 2008; Evans-Pritchard (1940) 1969 (pp. 152, 155); Fausto 2000; Fried 1967; Glaser and Bridgman 1999; Hall 2019; Hobbes (1651) 1985; Hutchinson 1996; Lee 2013 (p. 111); Looser 2019; Low 2019; Michaels 2004; Morgan 1877; Ong 2006; Rosman and Rubel 1986; Schubel and Levi 2000; Scott 1985, 2009 (p. 85); Sinclair 2001; Smith 2003; Stack 1974; Steward 1955; Tylor (1871) 1924; Urton 1997,2008; Viveiros de Castro 1992; Wilkinson 2016; Wittfogel 1957; Wolf 1969

Cultural Snapshot

7.1   Coe 1992; Kroeber 1948; Rogers 2005; Struit 1967; Urton 1997, 2008

8   Ecology, Landscape and Culture

Overview

Nonstates and states have historically affected local environments in dissimilar ways. Nonstate societies sometimes decrease and sometimes increase diversity in their local environments. States have intense impacts on the environment because the food production method—*intensive* or *industrial agriculture*—involves a large energy investment in relation to the land area cultivated. In contrast, *extensive agriculture* has less impact because it uses sunlight and human and animal muscle power.

Environmental Impacts of Humans and Their Ancestors

Humans—more generally, the genus *Homo*—have been transforming nature for thousands of years, affecting the Earth's landscape wherever they have lived. Humans are rather 'untidy' creatures, and they tend to leave behind evidence of their presence. This evidence is more than just fossil bones and teeth; humans can actually influence changes in the genotypes of other organisms and alter their distribution on the landscape. Prehistoric humans have significantly altered regions once thought to be wilderness, such as Amazonia. Modern humans are currently changing how and where organisms live and sometimes determining whether they exist at all. They are also modifying the land itself by building dams, changing the courses of rivers, altering soil composition and cutting down forests. The new landscapes that result, with changed species compositions and distributions, exhibit the consequences of human activities. But these landscapes and the lifeforms they support also constitute *sources* of profound change in human cultures over time. The anthropological approach that examines relationships between humans and the natural world through time is called *historical ecology*. I have found that this approach best explains current and past human behaviour and the effects humans have had on landscapes and species diversity worldwide.

   Historical ecology understands the human species as an agent of environmental change affecting the diversity and distribution of plants and animals. The process of change is called *landscape transformation*, which is directly related to human social and political organisation, including the emergence of complexity and the development of class and caste hierarchies. These transformations can result in what ethnographer Aihwa Ong refers to as 'baroque ecology' insofar as the landscape consists not only of land and people but highly complex flows and counterflows of people, energy, resources, money, information and knowledge (Chapter 7). A good example of baroque ecology is the city-state of Singapore in Southeast Asia. Baroque ecology well describes the landscape of Singapore, which is a highly intricate urban context with transnational impacts. According to Ong, the baroque ecology of Singapore is the 'spatial formation that repositions the city-state as a hub in an ecosystem created from the mobilization of diverse global elements—knowledge, practices, and actors—interacting at a high level of performance' (2006, p. 180). Nonhierarchical or egalitarian peoples also affect their landscapes, but at local and supralocal scales rather than at the scale of a region or continent.

Members of different societies interact with the environment in different, often culturally determined ways. Some societies contribute to local species diversity by creating many small habitats that favour the growth of distinctive organisms. Other societies have turned the landscape into a commodity, something that can be bought and sold, preserved or destroyed. Historical ecology studies these differences and compares the impacts humans have had, over the long term, on the diversity and quality of Earth's environments. Historical ecology takes the position that humans are not naturally destructive, nor are humans of any culture naturally disposed to preserve other species and safeguard the environment. Social and historical factors condition the ways humans behave, not some inborn drive or desire. Modern *Homo sapiens* evolved in Africa about 150,000 years ago yet had very little impact on Earth's environments for most of that time. Major human alterations of the landscape begin with *agriculture*: the cultivation of domesticated crops sometimes accompanied by the rearing of domesticated livestock. There are four major forms of subsistence associated with agriculture: extensive agriculture, intensive agriculture, pastoral nomadism and industrial agriculture. *Extensive agriculture* involves large expanses of land around farming villages. Farmers plant new fields, use them, then select other parts of the land to put to cultivation again, repeatedly relocating their most productive crops over time. Much extensive agriculture is slash-and-burn or shifting cultivation. This technique involves removing tree cover in a patch of forest; burning the felled, dried-out vegetation; and planting crops in and around the charred timber shortly after the beginning of a rainy season. The crops may then grow relatively unhindered by competition, acquire adequate sunlight and even improve soil conditions through the percolation of charred organic matter into the ground. The effects are short-lived, however, and the patch being cultivated is usually not planted with the same crops a second year in a row due to erosion caused by rain and wind, infestation by weeds and insect pests.

What kind of agriculture a society engages in is due in part to the economy of activity. People do not increase, or intensify, their labour effort unless it is required to survive. Intensification can take the form of increasing inputs, such as fertiliser, irrigation, ploughing or through more time, energy and muscle power. In extensive agrarian systems, such intensification is avoided because it is easier to clear more forest land than to replant crops in the same place in consecutive years. In contrast to intensive agriculture, extensive systems tend to have long fallow periods: months or years during which no crops are planted and the soils are renewed.

All forms of agriculture use domesticates. A *domesticate* is a plant or animal whose genotype has been changed by human interference through artificial selection. Domesticates cannot survive and reproduce successfully without continued human assistance. Humans lived without domesticates for at least 140,000 years. At present, some domesticates have been profoundly transformed in terms of their genetic sequences and the phenotypes that result from them, such as the chicken, which ethnographer Steve Striffler refers to as the 'industrial chicken'. When people first domesticated other organisms, landscapes began to change dramatically. But what did the landscape look like before domestication? To get a sense of the effects that humans can have on the environment, let's look at an apparent exception to the idea that preagricultural societies had minimal impacts on the landscape: the sudden disappearance of Pleistocene megafauna in the Americas.

Pleistocene Overkill?

Between about 12,000 and 10,000 years ago—at the very end of the Pleistocene epoch—major changes occurred in the animal populations of North and South America. Most salient was the extinction of Pleistocene *megafauna*, literally 'big animals'. Megafauna that disappeared at the end of the Pleistocene include woolly mammoths, mastodons, sabre-toothed tigers and giant ground sloths, among a host of others. One explanation for these mass extinctions is the *blitzkrieg hypothesis*, also called the Pleistocene overkill hypothesis, formulated by palaeoecologist Paul Martin. This view propounds that human hunting, combined with fire, significantly altered the number and distribution of game animals. Martin argues that the large-scale extinction of Pleistocene megafauna in the Americas occurred after the arrival of humans via the Bering land bridge and their subsequent migration and expansion throughout the hemisphere. This hypothesis is based primarily on computer simulations, rather than on archaeological data. In other words, it's more speculative than empirical.

The Pleistocene overkill hypothesis implicates mobile bands of hunters and gatherers in the extinction of megafauna. These bands arrived from northern Asia and subsisted on resources that they could hunt or collect directly from the environment. According to Martin, they killed whatever animals they could with their fluted Clovis spear points as they moved into North America. Since the animals they hunted had never been exposed to human predators and their formidable hunting weaponry, they were quickly and easily killed in great numbers until they were completely extinguished.

There are some major problems with the blitzkrieg hypothesis, one of which is the timing of human arrival in the Americas. Most of the megafauna went extinct between 12,000 and 10,000 years ago, although a few small, relict populations survived later. However, evidence from South America suggests that humans cohabited with mega-fauna for many thousands of years before the latter went extinct. Giant marsupials in Australia also went extinct in the Late Pleistocene, yet modern humans, the ancestors of today's Aborigines, cohabited with them for as long as 30,000 years. In addition to the human variable, a major climatic change occurred at the end of the Pleistocene. The Earth was warming, glaciers were melting and sea levels were rising. This transitional time period is called the Pleistocene–Holocene transition. Megafauna likely had a very difficult time adapting to the rapidly changing climate and to changes in food availabil-ity. So, while it is possible that human hunting activity contributed to the extinction of megafauna, it was no blitzkrieg. That does not mean native people did not alter the environment by other means. Indigenous North Americans used fire to create patchi-ness in coniferous forests, which were favourable to hunting game such as white–tailed deer. Climate change and the alterations in the availability and distribution of plants and animals were likely much more significant factors than humans in megafaunal extinc-tions. Today, the situation is remarkably similar. Climate is again changing radically, but this time the world is a much more complex place socially, politically and economi-cally (Cultural Snapshot 8.1).

CULTURAL SNAPSHOT 8.1

Is 'Man' Really Causing Global Warming?

Greenhouse gases (GHGs) in the atmosphere have been increasing significantly since the beginning of the Industrial Revolution about AD 1800. GHG production has accelerated over the last 50 years. Most of the increase is due to the combustion of fossil fuels. The increased levels of anthropogenic GHGs in the atmosphere will continue into the future regardless of what steps are taken now to reduce them. However, if steps are not taken and the rate of increase continues, environmental disasters in the mid- to late twenty-first century will be more destructive than anything known on Earth in hundreds of thousands of years and threaten the existence of human civilisation.

The subtitles of two bestselling books on climate change are 'Man, Nature, and Climate Change' (Elizabeth Kolbert's Field Notes from a Catastrophe, 2006) and 'How Man Is Changing the Climate and What It Means for Life on Earth' (Tim Flannery's The Weather Makers, 2005). Yet is 'man', or humanity at large, really responsible for global climate change? Many of the societies we have examined in this book have not yet or only recently experienced the Industrial Revolution. But 75 per cent to 90 per cent of GHGs are from industrial emissions, not from swidden fires or activities related to extensive agriculture or to hunting and gathering. Consider whether the culprit in global warming isn't humanity as a whole, but rather certain kinds of complex sociopolitical and economic organisations, including postindustrial societies and multinational corporations, that depend on fossil fuels to function and profit.

The Impact of Agriculture on Landscapes

The emergence of agriculture about 10,000 years ago allowed for a larger and more predictable food supply and the support and development of more aggregated human populations. In contrast to hunting and gathering, an economy that depends upon collecting food, an agricultural economy produces food through the cultivation of domesticated plants or breeding and rearing of domesticated livestock. Agriculture is the cultivation or breeding of domesticates, whether plant, animal or both. In some societies, such as the pastoral peoples of the Central Asian steppe and East African savanna, plant and animal domestication are found in the same context. In others, as in Amazonia, horticulture—a kind of agriculture that uses domesticated plants only—is central to food production. Agriculture was a momentous occurrence in human history, for without agriculture, state-level society would not exist. Archaeologists and palaeobotanists have unearthed evidence for the independent rise of agriculture at about the same time in Western Asia, China, South America and Mesoamerica. The evidence centres on archaeological evidence, including specialised tools used in processing domesticates, and the remains of domesticated plants themselves, such as ancient pollen, starch grains and phytoliths, all of which are fossil plant parts that can be identified to species.

Semi-domesticates are plant or animal species going in one of two directions: domesticated or wild. These are often weeds. In fact, botanist Edgar Anderson suggested the rise of agriculture was due to weedy 'camp followers' found among human refuse. Through their long association with humans, these plants developed advantageous features, such as faster rates of maturation and bigger, better, more edible parts (seeds, fruit pulp, roots or corms) that were easier to harvest than they had been to collect in their wild forms. The process itself, whereby people derived domesticated organisms from wild ancestors, is called *artificial selection*.

Artificial selection is a sort of natural selection (Chapter 4) driven consciously by cultivators who have a particular endpoint in mind, namely a plant or animal that is better in some way for a particular human purpose. Recall from Chapter 4 that natural selection and evolution of species, and hence artificial selection and the origins of domesticated species, initially depend on phenotypic (outward, obvious) variety among individuals in a population. People who harvested a useful wild plant might favour the reproduction of that variety with superior attributes by nurturing its offspring rather than the offspring of less desirable varieties. For example, most of the wild squash originally cultivated in South America has bitter pulp. The seeds were edible, but the husk was only useful for containers. People began to harvest and then plant the rare, occasional individual varieties of squash with more tasty pulp. In so doing, they gradually developed new varieties, which taste like fleshy, sweet pumpkins. They saved and planted the seeds of the squash with the flavourful pulp, not the seeds of the earlier, wild varieties with a bitter taste.

All important world food crops today, including rice (from the Yangtze River Valley, China), wheat (from Mesopotamia), potato (from the Andes) and maize (from central Mexico), were derived from ancestral plants that are hardly recognisable today (Figure 8.1). Plants were domesticated on six continents not only for food but also for many other uses, such as storage (bottle gourds for containers), clothing (cotton and silk for cloth), stimulants (coffee, betel nut, tea, chocolate), mind-altering substances (coca), medicine (aloe vera, peppermint, turmeric) and scores of seasonings and spices (including black pepper, clove, cinnamon, cardamom and basil), which in some cases became valuable commodities worth trading, defending and fighting for. The first domesticates might not have derived from the most important sources of food. In certain ancient societies, according to archaeologist Christine Hastorf, the original domesticates may have been plants used as spices, such as cayenne pepper in Andean South America. Only later did food crops, such as the potato, become economically and nutritionally important. Some plants that ancient farmers cultivated ultimately lost the ability to reproduce on their own, which is actually evidence of their domestication. Some plants can only be propagated by cuttings of tubers and branches. Manioc, the source of tapioca flour, is one such crop. Other plants produce the female ovules needed to form seeds but were never fertilised. The black dots you can see in a cross-section of a banana are sterile ovules. The wild ancestors of bananas were self-reproducing seed plants with small, not always edible fruits. As domesticates, bananas are propagated by replanting the immature clones (called 'suckers') that grow at the base of the plants. They depend entirely upon human intervention for reproduction.

Like domesticated plants—and unlike their wild ancestors—domesticated animals are dependent on human management. Some species can go feral, or semi-wild, when not cared for, such as pigs, dogs and cats. Feral sheep, goats and cattle are rare in the wild, though all had wild ancestors. For example, the ancestor of cattle was the wild aurochs, an ox-like, aggressive animal that stood almost two meters tall at the shoulder. Humans hunted the aurochs throughout the Pleistocene; the last one died in Europe in the early 1600s.

Figure 8.1 Irrigated field of paddy rice (*Oryza sativa* L.) on the island of Bali. Photo by Author.

Food production, in principle, leads to greater caloric returns per unit of land than foraging simply because more of the area is populated with domesticates—both plants and animals—whereas among foraging societies only a small portion of the landscape is composed of food resources, as with the mongongo nut groves of the Ju/'hoansi foragers of southern Africa and the African oil palm groves of the Mbuti people in central Africa. Babaçu palm fruits and seeds (but not the beetle larvae that sometimes grow in them) were traditional staple foods of the Guajá Indians of eastern Amazonia (Chapter 1). These palms grow well where the ground has been disturbed by extensive agriculture and represent living vegetative residue of an earlier agricultural society. Though until recently all the Guajá were hunter–gatherers, their use of the palm suggests that they, too, have been affected by agriculture. In the tropics, hunter–gatherers and farming people often live in proximity and trade wild and domesticated foods.

The Impact of Hunter-Gatherers on Landscapes

Landscape transformation is not unique to societies that cultivate domesticated plants or herd and breed domesticated livestock. Hunter–gatherers also engage in practices that have nuanced, yet long-lasting impacts on their environments. Cultural anthropologists and archaeologists have identified a number of ways in which hunter–gatherers have affected the landscapes in which they live, both the present and past. One example is broadcast burning, which is the intentional, controlled burning of selected patches of the landscape. Broadcast burning can prevent catastrophic wildfires because it selectively reduces the buildup of fuel in the form of brush and other plant debris. Australian Aborigines, who were historically hunter–gatherers, burned grasslands dominated by sharp, pointy-leaved spinifex grass (*Triodia* spp.). These burns encouraged the growth of other plant species, attracted game animals such as browsing wallabies and kangaroos and made overland travel safer and easier. Likewise, Nukak foragers in the Northwest Amazon discard seeds at their campsites. These seeds, which later grow into trees, grow in concentrated areas such as orchards, making the collection of fruit faster and easier. The central African Mbuti scatter seeds of the African oil palm at their abandoned campsites. The resulting trees form groves or orchards. The palm is not in this environment a true domesticate—it is not wholly dependent upon humans for its survival and reproduction—but its distribution has been significantly influenced by the behaviour of hunting-and-gathering people.

The Paiute of California, hunter–gatherers studied by Julian Steward, neither cultivated domesticated plants nor reared livestock, though they did keep dogs and practised a form of irrigation. Steward found that they diverted rivulets and streams to water groves of pinyon trees, which yielded nuts that were a staple food in their diet. Construction and maintenance of canals and water control features represent major alterations of the landscape, even though these activities are not always associated with agriculture. What is remarkable in these cases is that foraging people with seemingly 'simple' technologies modified the landscape in ways similar to those of people who intensively cultivate domesticates. Acephalous societies without complex forms of social organisation, like agricultural societies with significant class and status differences, also transform landscapes and render them productive for human purposes.

When the Puritans arrived in New England in the 1600s, they found parkland-type landscapes featuring forests alternating with meadows. By the 1700s, many of these landscapes had become completely covered in forest. Warfare and disease greatly reduced the Indian populations, resulting in the elimination of their controlled burning practices, which had created the parklands seen by Europeans, according to historian William Cronon. The parklands increased the variety of habitats on the landscape, prevented wildfires and attracted game, especially white-tailed deer. Ironically, the New England 'wilderness', as it was called in the 1700s, only developed *after* the arrival of Europeans, not before.

Similar parklands were found in western North America. Burning by Indians in these areas reduced the amount of underbrush that could serve as fuel for devastating wildfires, like those seen today. American park managers probably misunderstood indigenous resource management and instead saw any kind of burning as destructive. However, evidence suggests that fire used in a broadcast or controlled sense actually helps to maintain species diversity.

All of these examples show how the cultural practices of foragers can influence plant and animal distributions, as well as the physical form of the landscape itself. Although they do not tend to transform the environment as profoundly as agriculturalists, hunter–gatherers have effects that sometimes enhance productivity and even increase local diversity of the environment over time.

Hunter-Gatherers: Simple and Complex

Simple Hunter-Gatherers

Cultural anthropologists and archaeologists usually divide hunter-gatherers into two groups, simple and complex, on the basis of social organisation. *Simple* foragers do not have political centralisation and socioeconomic hierarchies, like caste and class, yet they, like complex foragers, who are ranked, are just as 'civilised' as people who live in complex, stratified societies in which people are distinguished by caste or class (Chapter 7). Simple hunter-gatherers include the Tiwi of Melville and Bathurst islands, Australia, whose behaviour, according to social anthropologist Kenelm Burridge, can easily resemble Western politics:

> The negotiations of a Tiwi elder attempting to obtain another wife may be contained in the horse trading of a congressman seeking votes. Aboriginal forms of social organization become particular combinations and permutations of at least some of the relations contained in the social organization of an industrialized state.
>
> (Burridge 1973, p. 150)

Simple foraging societies organise their members on the basis of age and sex and are characterised by egalitarianism, individual liberty, mobility, generalised reciprocity and abundant leisure time. Band and family organisation structure camp life such that simple hunter-gatherers have low population densities, high mobility, an emphasis on equality among peers, adequate subsistence and diet and low levels of intergroup violence and warfare, in general. A *complex* foraging society divides people up on the basis of rank, caste or class in addition to age and sex. Neither simple nor complex hunter-gatherers cultivate domesticated plants or breed and raise domesticated livestock. They do not have agriculture. Simple hunter-gatherers are egalitarian peoples with economies based on a principle of sharing, or *generalised reciprocity*. Complex hunter-gatherers are *ranked* peoples who often have economies based on *redistribution*. As discussed earlier, ranked societies tend to have more centralisation of authority than unranked societies. Similarly, complex hunter-gatherers concentrate power to a greater extent than simple hunter-gatherers.

The Ju/'hoansi people, simple foragers of southern Africa studied by Richard Lee in the 1960s, 'eat their way out' of a camp. A band or family group remains in an area long enough to exhaust local food resources and then moves on. These camp areas eventually recover their resources with time. Some simple hunter-gatherers remained in semipermanent camps due to the dependability of certain key food resources. The Paiute Indians are one example: they depended heavily on pinyon nuts, which were predictable resources that the Paiute knew how and where to find. The Shoshone of the Great Basin lived off more dispersed resources and tended to aggregate in large groups in the late fall when pinyon nuts were in season. The Shoshone, like most simple hunter-gatherers, either aggregated in bands or dispersed into nuclear or extended families. When resources were abundant and in season, they aggregated, and when resources were more widely distributed, they broke up into smaller social groups. Simple hunter-gatherers tend to have low population densities—on the order of one person per square kilometre—no identifiable chiefs or leaders, and few cross-cutting groups, such as sodalities. These kin-based societies differentiate between members on the basis of age and sex, not caste or class.

Complex Hunter-Gatherers

Complex hunter-gatherer societies were also kin-based, but people lived in denser permanent or semipermanent settlements and produced surplus food: more than they were able to consume within a few days or a week. Most complex foragers lived by coastal rivers that abounded in maritime resources, including shellfish, sea mammals and fish such as salmon, trout and dogfish. They also used a variety of roots, berries, fruits and other plant products. Because they did not intensify production, the plants and animals they harvested remained plentiful. The technologies used—harpoon, dip net and bow and arrow—did not lead to the extirpation of local resources. In addition, the most recent evidence suggests that the Kwakwaka'wakw, for example, modified the landscape for sustainable use. They removed carnivores from areas they hunted for game; they transplanted edible rhizomes to specific hunting patches, replanted rice-root lily to attract game and built retaining walls and other structures to increase wetlands, which in turn attracted and supported waterfowl. In comparison, simple hunter-gatherers did not significantly change landscapes and their resident biota.

Complex hunter-gatherers were organised, by definition, into hierarchical polities with centralised authority. They defended territories and often had ranked cognatic clans. Complex ranked hunter-gatherer societies have sometimes been called *chiefdoms*. Chiefdoms consist of interrelated families and clans living in multiple settlements that pay homage and tribute to a paramount leader known as a chief. The chief is customarily more influential than anyone else and historically almost always had some connection to leadership in warfare and conquest of land. Chiefdoms tended to be located in areas of abundant and concentrated resources, though they rarely depleted them significantly. Their resource management practices controlled rates of exploitation and sometimes led to local increases in plant and animal diversity.

Complex hunter-gatherers had greater potential to disrupt their environments than simple foragers, even though they often enhanced local environments. For example, they had on average much higher population densities than simple foragers. On the Northwest Coast, the Kwakwaka'wakw studied by Boas had 57 people per square kilometre (57/km2), the Haida, 79/km2 and the Nootka, 72/km2; in contrast, the Mardu of the Western Desert of Australia, who are simple hunter-gatherers, had less than one person for every square kilometre; the Cheyenne of the North American Great Plains had 3/km2; and the Ju/'hoansi of the Kalahari Desert had 13/km2. For comparison, the population density of the United States in 2000 was 206/km2.

Unlike simple foragers, complex hunter-gatherers often used feasts to redistribute resources. *Redistribution* entails the collection of goods from a multitude of families into a central place, then the reapportionment of these goods during a feast. The crowd may be the same people who contributed the goods, as seen with Melanesian 'Big Man' societies, or invited guests from far away, as with the Northwest Coast *potlatch* and the bear sacrifice of the Ainu of Japan. In contrast, the only exchange method available to traditional hunters and gatherers was *reciprocity*.

The Kwakwaka'wakw chief, as with other Northwest Coast groups, gave away large amounts of food, especially salmon, seal meat and shellfish. Feasts were given to commemorate an event, usually the death of a revered elder, a marriage or the recognition of a new heir. Nonedible goods were also given away, including money, blankets, massive sheets of copper, wooden bowls, ladles, house planks, guns and slaves. By throwing a lavish feast—a *potlatch*—the chief gained prestige. The more food and goods that a chief gave away, the higher his status. In many Northwest Coast societies, status and prestige are associated with giving, sharing and redistributing, not with greedily acquiring goods or hoarding them in secret caches. There certainly was one conspicuous twist in Kwakwak'wakw society, and not even the early European visitors failed to notice it for what it was: society was divided into free people and slaves. Slaves were captives taken in war against other Northwest Coast enemies or their progeny. In this sense, Kwakwaka'wakw society more resembled the stratified societies from which the European traders themselves came from than from many Native American societies where egalitarianism seemed to have been the norm in political relationships and authority patterns.

The Ainu of northern Japan were sedentary foragers who depended on seasonal marine resources, especially salmon runs. Ainu chiefs were wealthy in material goods such as boats, sledges and sledge gear and slaves. With such wealth at hand, an Ainu chief could sponsor a bear ceremony, or *iyomante*, which involved a massive giveaway of food to invited guests from near and far. A bear raised by the Ainu as a member of the group was 'sent back' to the spirit world, and its meat distributed. *Iyomante* was the Ainu version of a potlatch.

In Florida, the Calusa chiefs likewise commanded vast maritime resources, including fish, shellfish, birds and mammals. In the 1540s, their chief, known as King Carlos to the Europeans, ruled numerous villages across southwest Florida and had alliances with other native groups. These alliances were probably established through feasts that redistributed goods, services and persons, including King Carlos' sisters, in marriages to other chiefs. There is no evidence of resource depletion in southwest Florida prior to European contact. Rather, there is evidence for increased vegetative diversity. Originally, the Calusa environment was primarily mangrove swamp. The Calusa built shell mounds on top of the swamp, increasing plant diversity by providing habitat for plants that require dry land.

Most of these maritime hunter–gatherer chiefdoms depended on renewable resources, especially, in the North Pacific, on annual runs of spawning salmon and other anadromous fish such as dogfish or sea trout. Anadromous fish spend part of their life cycle in fresh water and part in the ocean. These predictable resources allowed for the production of a surplus in a way that the landscapes of simple foragers did not.

Agrarian Society

Agrarian society is founded on one material principle: the use of nature for the production of domesticated food. Some ranked societies, such as the Calusa, Kwakwak'wakw and others, were technically lacking in agriculture; many others, in Polynesia, Southeast Asia, Africa and South America, had extensive and relatively intensive agricultural production methods. These were not, however, industrial methods such as those seen today, dependent on fossil fuels and genetic engineering. Nonindustrial agriculture without modernisation and globalisation uses sunlight and human and animal labour as the main sources of energy for production. Agrarian societies converted landscapes from their natural forms into profoundly cultural ones. Hunter-gatherers also affected local environments by distributing the seeds of nondomesticated trees and encouraging their growth, a frequent occurrence in South American tropical forests. However, they did not profoundly alter large areas of forest (Cultural Snapshot 8.2). Farmers, however, transform the landscape permanently by changing the distribution of plants and animals, altering the composition of the soil and by cutting down trees and burning brush.

Once food production on formerly wild landscapes began and these landscapes became farmlands, more food per unit area could be produced and harvested. In other words, agriculture allowed for the more intensive use of some plots of land. These changes were accompanied by the growth of human settlements and increased population densities, often in areas where people in the past had camped for short periods of time during the annual round. The emergence of agriculture was a profound event in human history. In Eurasia, this radical change from food collection to food production is called the Neolithic Revolution. It is called the Formative period elsewhere.

CULTURAL SNAPSHOT 8.2

Life after Slash-and-Burn: Management of the *Miir* and the *Milpa*

Slash-and-burn agriculture involves cutting down part of the forest and burning trees and brush to create a field to use for a few years. The Montagnard people of Vietnam considered forest put to slash-and-burn to be something they 'ate' that would come back. The field, called a *miir*, was never completely abandoned. Ethnographer Georges Condominas wrote that a *miir*

> will live on in memory as a guidepost by which the villagers will date events occurring in the course of the year in which it was 'eaten'. After some years... they will return to slash it once again, burn it off, sow in the earth it will have renewed, and harvest the grain its soil will produce.

(1994, p. 352)

Likewise, the Maya of the Yucatán Peninsula, Mexico, do not abandon and forget the fields they have slashed and burned. Ethnographer Eugene Anderson and colleagues note that the field, called a milpa,

> once 'abandoned' is still managed and cropped for game and plants. Farmers can continue to harvest surviving crops, as well as plants that were deliberately left intact or deliberately coppiced instead of being cut to the base. Hunters seek animals in the places they are known to prefer, such as the vicinity of the surrounding crops.

(2005, p. 118)

Many plants in old *milpas* attract specific game animals: bean vines appeal to deer, squash vines lure a large rodent called a paca and various small seeds attract game birds, such as quail. Anderson et al. point out that the result is an 'environment finely packed with diverse species, subspecies, and activities' (2005, p. 118). The Maya do not have a word for 'weed', and virtually all of about 1,000 plant species and 100 animal species have some use, including those in old *milpas*. Such *milpas* are managed landscapes, though they may appear abandoned to outsiders.

Extensive Agriculture

The Tropics

In the tropics, extensive agriculture involves bringing large areas of cropland into production using simple technologies and field rotation. In some cases when forest returns, it's culturally modified by occupation and planting of fruit trees and the like (Figure 8.2). In West Africa, extensive agriculture involves the use of the hoe on savanna landscapes, together with the planting of crops such as peanuts. In much of the tropics where extensive agriculture is practised, the principal form is *swidden agriculture*, which involves cutting shrubs and trees in the forest and burning them. Combustion of that biomass deposits

Figure 8.2 Waorani elder in the Ecuadorian Amazon (in 2019) indicates the forested ridgetop where he and his ancestors used to live, where small-scale extensive agriculture was practised. Photo by Author.

organic material in the soil when rainfall occurs. Perennial crops such as manioc, banana, plantain, sweet potato and domestic yam, and annual crops such as maize and rice, are planted when seasonal rains begin.

Fields, sometimes called swiddens or swidden fields, are not usually cultivated continuously. After three to four years of cultivation, sometimes less, they are left to fallow, or rest. Farmers take seeds and other generative material from their harvests to replant in newly cleared fields. Swidden agriculture is sometimes called *shifting cultivation* because although the farmers are sedentary, they shift or rotate their activities among several fields. Sometimes they return after many years to the old swidden fields, which have become overgrown. If left for 100 or more years, these old fields eventually become a special kind of forest, with biomass and species diversity comparable with that of primary forest, though the species are often different due to the history of human disturbance (Cultural Snapshot 8.3). These are called *cultural* or *anthropogenic forests*.

CULTURAL SNAPSHOT 8.3

Discovery of a Cultural Forest in the Amazon

In 1985, two Ka'apor men whom I considered to be the most knowledgeable about forest types told me that a forest on the site of an old, long-abandoned village looked like a true forest (*ka'a-te*), but that it was in reality very different. They called it *taper* (pronounced ta-pair). This particular forest had been occupied about 60 years earlier until a massacre of Ka'apor people occurred there shortly before the Indians and local Brazilians (called *karaí*) made peace in 1928.

From the village where I was staying, the two men and I walked uphill for a couple of miles. Dense forest crowded both sides of the trail. After about an hour, we arrived at an almost imperceptible opening in the trees on the side of the trail. We had arrived at the *taper* and stepped into it. Machetes were needed to cut our way through the vines and thorns for about 100 feet. It got darker as we went in, since the farther one gets from the main trail, the more the canopy covers and shades the traveller. My two informants led the way, warning me to watch out for thorns (*yu*). We walked until one of the men stopped and kicked a patch of ground. Then, with his machete, he began to scoop out clumps of blackened dirt.

There, covered by only a thin layer of soil, lay a nearly complete ceramic griddle. I had seen similar griddles used to toast manioc flour (called *u'i* in Ka'apor or *farinha* in Portuguese). Nearby was a mirror the size and shape of a silver dollar. A long time ago, someone—perhaps a Ka'apor child—had looked into that mirror. The griddle and the mirror were reminders of a time when people had talked; exchanged glances, gestures and hugs; and breathed in the open air of this village. Ka'apor had been born there. Some had died there, their bones long since dissolved into the soil. The *taper* gave green, living testimony to the lives of those earlier inhabitants and to thousands of years of human society in the Amazon. The *taper* was a cultural forest.

Temperate North America

In temperate zones (areas between the tropics and the poles), extensive agriculture sometimes involves long periods of cultivation and short fallows. For example, the agricultural system of the Iroquois of New York State was extensive. It supplied people with most of their food and raw materials for hundreds of years. By about AD 1350, the Iroquois were cultivating three crops: corn, beans and squash. Women, who were in charge of the fields, planted corn and beans on top of small mounds and squash between the mounds. Corn, or maize, which is one of the most productive cereal grains in the world, provides carbohydrates for energy and some protein; beans have amino acids lacking in corn. Together, corn and beans supply complete proteins to the human diet. Squash has protein and oil in its seeds as well as other vitamins and minerals absent from corn and beans. These three plants functioned as the basis of the food supply not only among the Iroquois but throughout Mesoamerica and North America. They complement each other nutritionally, so it made sense for them to be grown together. They are so important that, in many cultures, the plants are deified in people's belief systems. Among the Iroquois, corn, beans and squash were revered as spiritual sisters. Morgan wrote they were 'supposed to have the forms of beautiful females, to be very fond of each other, and to delight to dwell together' (Morgan [1851] 1995 p. 153).

Iroquois extensive agriculture was like organic agriculture because the soil in the mounds was replenished by the decomposition of the old corn and bean plants from the previous year. This enriched the soil for the next planting and harvest seasons, without chemical or other external inputs. The mounds did not need to be maintained every year. Although the corn yields produced by Iroquois women were lower than modern hybrid corn found in industrial agriculture, the Iroquois were able to produce 25 to 75 bushels of corn per acre without using fertilisers or pesticides, and without the use of extra human labour in ploughing. The mounds also reduced soil erosion. Iroquois extensive farming is an example of sustainable agriculture.

Forest Islands of West Africa

Forests are often thought to be the result of natural factors combined with human avoidance. In other words, forests are still standing only because humans did not cut them down or burn them to the ground. Humans have destroyed forests by overharvesting keystone species, logging and setting fires. However, there are exceptions. In West Africa, the Kuranko, Maninka and Kissia live in a region known as the *forest islands*. These are forested areas in the midst of the West African savannas. Native inhabitants of the region have been accused of reducing the size of the forests and converting them to savanna by means of swidden (extensive) agriculture and by combusting existing biomass.

However, the study of aerial and satellite imagery, together with native accounts of forest history, show that people actually have *expanded* forest islands. In fact, traditional peoples in West African villages have planted or protected trees, such as coffee, African oil palm, rattans, fruit, timber and silk cotton trees, which provide shade and forest cover. The forest islands are an example of how extensive agriculture can enhance local diversity over time.

Some geographers and archaeologists now believe extensive agriculture in Amazonia may have followed a more intensive use of the land upon the introduction of steel axes. Steel enabled indigenous farmers to clear land more rapidly and efficiently than with stone axes, making extensive agriculture practicable. But in large parts of the world, including northern Europe, farmers expanded the frontiers of agriculture by extensive agriculture before they became permanently fixed to the land and switched to more intensive methods of food production.

Intensive Agriculture

Intensive agriculture is the continuous cultivation of domesticated plants and continuous breeding of domesticated livestock in one place over long periods of time, which can only be accomplished by intensive energy inputs, including human manual labour. Peasants in intensive agricultural societies work longer hours than farmers practising extensive agriculture because they must spend more time ploughing, fertilising and building and maintaining terraces (Figure 8.3) and irrigation systems. In areas with insufficient rainfall, irrigation is necessary and requires construction and maintenance of dams, canals, sluice gates and sloped surfaces. The cultivated land in intensive agricultural regimes usually remains arable because it is continuously renewed with nutrients in the form of fertilisers.

Figure 8.3 Rice terraces on hillsides on the island of Luzon, the Philippines, are an example of intensive agriculture. Library of Congress, Prints & Photographs Division, LC-USZ62-98049.

Intensive agriculture requires more energy inputs per unit of land than does extensive agriculture; therefore, farmers usually work harder and longer than those who allow their fields to lie fallow. Intensive agriculture is the type of food production that supported states and empires and is still found today in India, Southeast Asia and parts of tropical Africa and Latin America. Not all these places were particularly favourable for agriculture to begin with. Indeed, some of the earliest farming in the world is now known to have occurred in arid regions of India; ancient crops such as horse gram, mung bean and urd bean were domesticated there by 3500 to 3000 BC. Later civilisations dependent on the *japonica* variety of rice (which came from China), which became important to the Harappan civilisation (2000–1900 BC) of the Indus River Valley. Archaeologists Dorian Fuller and Charlene Murphy argue that

> [i]t is perhaps time we changed our perspective on centers of agricultural origins as naturally occurring only at the rare confluence of favorable environmental conditions into recognizing that potential domesticates were many and their environments were in part determined by traditions of human management traditions of environmental knowledge that developed in many regions around the world, including several in South Asia.
>
> (Fuller and Murphy 2014, p. 7)

South Asian intensive agriculture, as with intensive agriculture elsewhere, is associated with class or caste stratification. It depends on a large, impoverished peasantry engaged full-time in food production. Intensive farming tends to reduce biodiversity. Specifically, traditional, slow-growing or low-yielding varieties of crops grown for purposes of food security tend to get sidelined or go extinct altogether as the centralised state power taxing the peasants demands food revenue from rapidly growing, high-yielding varieties. Archaic states often taxed peasants, demanding certain plants and animals as a form of tribute; for example, llama wool was required by Inca elites, while the Aztecs demanded maize from their subjects. This led historically to the neglect of other plant species that peasants cultivated before they were incorporated into the state.

Peasants planted fewer varieties of crops to meet tax and tribute demands for a handful of preferred crops. In so doing, and given limits on the amount of land under cultivation, varieties that were slow growing, but which had other uses, such as resistance to pests and disease or medicinal value, decreased or disappeared. Biodiversity also tends to decline in state-level economies due to the ecology of fertilisation. Fertilising injects a high quantity of nutrients into the soil. Only a few species developed expressly to take advantage of major nutrient pulses can use all of these nutrients at once. Some aggressive, weedy species rapidly adapt to the availability of nutrients and outcompete other species. As a result, the only plants that might remain after years of intensive fertilisation are the preferred domesticate and a handful of less desirable weedy plants. This is called the *paradox of enrichment*.

Nomadic Pastoralism

Sheep, goats, camels, cattle and horses were domesticated in western Eurasia and chickens and pigs were domesticated in Southeast Asia. Some groups came to depend on rearing livestock alone, especially mobile ungulates such as camels, cattle, sheep and goats, as a form of economic specialisation called *nomadic pastoralism* or *pastoral nomadism*. Pastoral nomads are experts in the production of meat, milk, cheese and wool, which they exchange for agricultural produce of sedentary farming societies, especially in western Eurasia and the steppe country of northern and central China. They moved their herds from pasture to pasture and traded with and sometimes raided the farming peoples. Because traditionally pastoral nomads tended to be mounted on horseback, they had greater mobility than farming peoples, and sometimes conquered them. The farmers conquered by pastoral nomads tended to be peasants engaged in intensive agriculture.

Industrial Agriculture

Industrial agriculture, also known as mechanised agriculture, has only existed since about AD 1850; it uses fossil fuels in internal combustion engines. Instead of burning the landscape, as in extensive agriculture, the combustion of fossil fuels—such as oil and gas—takes place inside machines. This is the means by which most of the plant food on the planet today is produced, though much of it is used to fatten livestock, bred for docility as well as increased meat, egg, milk and wool production. Today, industrial agriculture is associated with genetic engineering and has produced crop varieties—known as GMOs (genetically modified organisms)—through DNA manipulation. GMOs are only found in market-driven, money-based economies because farmers must have money to return to the market every year to buy seeds and sell their produce. GMOs do not reseed, as do crops found in extensive agricultural systems.

In one sense, all domesticates are GMOs, because, by definition, their genotypes have been changed by artificial selection. Modern GMOs, however, involve the direct manipulation of a plant's DNA by costly genetic engineering rather than the collection and replanting of seeds of preferred plants, which is how artificial selection occurred thousands of years ago. Today, poor peasants usually cannot afford to buy GMOs, since these varieties need expensive industrial inputs such as herbicides, pesticides and other fossil-fuel derivatives to grow and flourish. As a result, genetic engineering of crops tends to reinforce existing social inequalities, making it difficult for members of the poorer strata of society to improve their standard of living.

While genetic engineering may allow farmers to produce more food, it does not necessarily go to those who need it most because food is a commodity, an unprocessed good that is bought and sold. Commodities are part of a global market economy, which operates on the principles of supply and demand. That means that food crops are sold on the basis of price rather than need. In 1999, enough grain was produced in the world to feed eight billion people. But these grains were not distributed evenly to the world's populations. Much of the grain was made into animal feed to produce beef and pork for consumption by Europeans and North Americans, rather than sold to poorer countries to feed people directly. Growth of the food supply actually outstrips growth of the human population, even though the world population has reached about 7.8 billion in 2020, an increase of 100 per cent in little more than half a century. Industrial agriculture supports most of the world's population today in one form or another. Yet about a billion people, or one person in seven worldwide, continue to be hungry every day, not because there is insufficient food, but because that food is not distributed equitably.

Today, industrial agriculture, which produces most of the food in the world, is run by a few multibillion-dollar corporations that turn out packaged food products sold in grocery stores but that originate in feedlots and factories. Inside the industrialised societies of the world, agribusiness, which involves the rearing of GMO breeds of livestock and growing of GMO vegetables in a factory or factory-like conditions, has tended to produce vast quantities of food at relatively low prices but with hidden and not-so-hidden health and environmental costs, which have been examined in field studies by cultural anthropologists. Some anthropologists working in a field called science and technology studies (STS) have offered critiques of how contemporary science and technology used in agribusiness and related industries have changed the economy and even the food people eat.

Industrial agriculture produces a surplus of food, yet there are environmental and health costs. Ethnographer Steve Striffler studied one of the poultry processing factories owned by Tyson Foods in the early 2000s. He found that Tyson Foods and a few other giant corporations like Smithfield had in the latter half of the twentieth century produced most of the meat and poultry consumed in the United States by a business model called *vertical integration*. That refers, in the case of what Striffer refers to as the 'industrial chicken' to the corporate control of every level of the production and supply chain, including the hatching, feed mills, processing facilities like poultry plants, food delivery and bringing to market of saleable products like wings, strips and nuggets, which largely replaced the old-fashioned 'chicken-in-a-pot' in terms of how chicken flesh was marketed and sold. By the late twentieth century, chickens gradually replaced pork and beef as the most consumed of American meats. Scientists and technicians changed the chicken itself from the 1950s on; they selected and bred for size and its ability to eat less corn and soy feed tanks to injections of vitamins and antibiotics. According to Striffler, 'A commercial broiler from the 1990s grew to almost twice the weight in less than half the time and in less than half the feed than a broiler from the 1930s' (p. 46). Americans in 2017 were eating 64 pounds of chicken. Since 1970, chicken consumption per capita in the United States has more than doubled.

Meat slaughterhouses and poultry processing plants, which are part of industrial agriculture in Asia and the West, typically employ workers in production lines who are not only at risk of injury on the job because of repetitive, debilitating motions but who are also subjected to a higher risk of contagious diseases due to working very closely together (Figure 8.4). In the 1990s, half a million Latinos moved to the United States;

Figure 8.4 Workers processing chicken on a rail line at a poultry processing plant in Pennsylvania. Note the proximity of one worker to the next. The COVID-19 virus and other avian viruses tend to spread relatively easily in environments like this. Alamy Images.

many of them ended up working in slaughterhouses and poultry plants; into the 2000s, most of the workers in slaughterhouses and poultry plants are immigrants (especially from Latin America but also elsewhere such as Vietnam) and African Americans. All these people were at a greater risk of infection of COVID-19 due to their jobs and in some cases their racialised or ethnic identity. Because these plants are associated with bird and animal products where feedlots and poultry keep many animals close together, compounded by issues of managing waste and controlling disease, dangerous zoonotic viruses (like COVID-19, which can jump from one species to another, say from bats ultimately to people) have been associated with them. In the COVID-19 pandemic of 2020/2021, many production-line workers in slaughterhouses were among the first people to contract and spread the COVID-19 virus in the Midwest. It is only a small group of slaughterhouses in this area that produce by far most of the country's meat supply, because of many years of consolidation and vertical integration, and several of these were forced by the virus to close. At the height of the pandemic during spring 2020, farmers were euthanising 150,000 hogs per day because of the closure of slaughterhouses due to COVID-19, and those that remained open tried to increase the 'line speed', or the amount of meat processed per production line per unit time with fewer employees due to many being out sick with COVID-19. The Department of Agriculture allowed 15 poultry plants to increase line speed to 175 birds (chickens) per minute. Industrial agriculture is connected to the spread and severity of the virus, and in this sense, anthropologists can make a contribution through holistic study that ethnography entails. It's necessary, in other words, to understand the place (slaughterhouses and poultry processing plants), the people (minorities and immigrants), the technology (industrialised production lines), the science (genetically and hormonally altered livestock and poultry), the supply chain and ultimately the consumer to understand the complexity of food production and consumption in modern life. Anthropologists have more recently studied farm-to-table movements and similar food activism that hold promise as a plausible and healthy substitute for the industrialisation of food products.

Summary

For thousands of years, humans have adapted to and managed local landscapes and natural resources. Societies can be differentiated in terms of their impacts on their environments. Simple and complex hunter-gatherers normally have less impact on the landscape than intensive agriculturalists or industrial societies, both of which are associated with higher population densities, aggregation, urbanisation and stratification. These social and economic differences result in varying impacts on the environment, including the environment of disease, such as COVID-19.

Further Reading

Altieri 2004; Anderson 1952; Balée 1994, 2006; Balée and Erickson 2006; Corkery et al. 2020; Cronon 1983; Denevan 2006; Fairhead and Leach 1996; Felt et al. 2017; Fowler and Turner 1999; Fuller and Murphy 2014; Gellner 1988; Hart and Hart 1986; Hastorf 2006; Henke 2008; Huston 1994; J.I. [blog] 2008; Kelly 1995; Kidder 1998; Lee 2013; Martin and Klein 1984; Milanich 1995; Mt. Pleasant 2006; Ohnuki-Tierney 1984; Politis 2007; Pyne 1998; Ribas 2016; Rosenzweig 1995; Rosman and Rubel 1986; Sahlins 1976a; Steward 1938; Striffler 2005; Tonkinson 1991; USDA 2020; Wolverton et al. 2009; Zent and Zent 2004; Zimmerer 1993

Cultural Snapshots

8.1   DeFries et al. 2005; Flannery 2005; Kolbert 2006; Santilli et al. 2005

8.2   Anderson 2006; Condominas 1994 8.3 Balée 2003 (pp. 7–12)

9 Colonialism and the World System

Overview

Up until the late 1400s, sea routes to the Americas, southern Africa, India, Southeast Asia, China and Japan were essentially unknown to Europeans. Although Norse from northern Europe had visited the coast of North America before Columbus, they did not establish permanent settlements there. After 1492, a new global era began as European commercial and imperial interests grew to dominate much of the rest of the world. This is the beginning of the modern world system. European technology led to the conquest of Native peoples; the diseases Europeans brought destroyed millions of lives. Out of this often-violent contact experience, new identities and new cultures emerged. This chapter examines contact, the colonial experience, the modern world system and their combined effects on culture.

What Is Colonialism?

Colonialism lasted for about 600 years, and it is an indelible part of the early modern world, essentially covering the period from the late fifteenth to the late twentieth centuries. Colonialism is the experience of contact and conquest, the product of a military and economic collision of people of distinct cultures speaking different languages. Colonialism is also part of an economic system in which a dominant power siphons resources from the less powerful territories that it controls. Colonialism is associated with the introduction and spread of general purpose money, something essential to the expansion of Europe and the development of a world system.

Cultures of this time period cannot be understood without reference to the formation and development of the world system and colonialism. Colonialism involves *acculturation*, in which groups in contact borrow linguistic and cultural traits from each other. Usually, subaltern groups (the colonised people) are more affected than dominant groups (the colonising people) in contact situations.

Sometimes colonialism leads to *assimilation*, in which subaltern groups are swallowed up by the dominant groups and disappear altogether as intact societies. The process often entails the destruction of the political system of the subaltern group and the collapse of their elite stratum. At the same time, people of a lower stratum in the dominant group may rise to higher positions in the new social order. Colonialism is as old as the oldest empires, but it took on a new meaning with the European expansion beginning in the fifteenth century.

The World System

Early modern colonialism linked the entire world into a new, global framework known as the *world system*. The world system consisted initially of a European core to which raw materials flowed from a *periphery*, the sites of colonial exploitation. Subaltern groups in colonial situations are the people living at the periphery; the dominant groups originate in the core. The European core was a wealth and power centre; the periphery was a source not only of raw materials needed for capitalist production of finished goods but also of cheap labour—especially slave labour—used to extract the raw materials from the periphery. The periphery consisted of thousands of societies in the Americas, Asia, Australia and Oceania. Slavery and other forms of coercion of labour flourished throughout the periphery to lower the costs of raw materials flowing into core economies, which were increasingly based on capitalism, money and markets.

Columbus's Atlantic crossing in the late fifteenth century initiated a period in which indigenous peoples around the world were brought under the control of a small number of European countries. Twentieth-century Italian revolutionary Antonio Gramsci correctly observed that 'America was "discovered" by Christopher Columbus "only" from the point of view of European civilization as a whole' (1975, p. 126). By the 1900s, European countries—especially Great Britain and France—had subjected about 85 per cent of the surface of the Earth to colonialism. European colonial control of parts of Africa and Asia ended only in the 1960s; many of these societies are still suffering from the effects of hundreds of years of control by outside economic and political interests. The effects of colonialism were a major subject of study for twentieth-century ethnographers, especially those from Great Britain, France and the United States. These anthropologists were often employed by their own governments.

Colonialism entered its final phase shortly after World War II and concluded around 1970 when most colonies got their independence from the core powers. The postcolonial period then began. Former colonies still exhibited dependence on the old core for certain finished products such as information technology, as well as services such as education and skilled labour. Attitudes and practices that promote postcolonial conditions are called *neocolonialism*. Postcolonial countries in the Americas, Asia and Africa developed local elites; in some cases, conflicts based on ethnic differences reemerged. Such conflicts had been suppressed by the dominant, core powers under colonialism. Postcolonialism has also involved continuing interest in raw materials by the core, now located in Europe, the United States and Japan. Sometimes the raw materials are information or data, such as DNA. Africa, for example, has greater genetic diversity than any other continent; the genomes of its people are therefore of interest to Western scientists. Yet DNA sampling has been perceived as a modern form of colonialism: extraction of a resource without necessarily benefitting those who produced it.

The Expansion of Europe

In the late 1400s, European economies and societies had begun to recover from the devastating Black Death, or bubonic plague, of the late 1300s and early 1400s. Before the Black Death, which depopulated the continent, wealthy Europeans had developed a taste for certain commodities from the Far East, especially spices and silk. Black pepper, which originated in Southeast Asia, was second only to gold and silver in its monetary value by weight during a 200-year period starting in the mid-1400s.

Before this time, Europeans obtained these goods by overland trade along highways known as the Silk Road. By the late 1400s, however, that route had been shut off by the rise of the Ottoman Turks. That Europeans initiated the modern world system and colonialism since the fifteenth century does not mean that the Chinese or the Arabs could not have accomplished something similar. The real difference is that the European powers sought access to Asia to acquire the wealth of goods exported along the Silk Road but were blocked from that option. During the fifteenth century, shipbuilding and navigation technology improved markedly in Portugal, Italy and Spain. Because the Iberian region was located on a wedge of land between the Mediterranean Sea and the Atlantic Ocean, the Portuguese and Spanish were especially well-positioned for sea exploration and an eventual Atlantic crossing. The Spanish navigators took advantage of the North Atlantic Gyre and associated easterlies—a clockwise pattern of currents and winds—to sail to the Caribbean and North America; the Portuguese used the counterclockwise South Atlantic Gyre and southern westerlies to sail around the southern tip of Africa, eventually into the Indian Ocean and beyond, where they engaged the spice trade (Figure 9.1). (They reached Brazil en route to India by mistake in 1500 by being off course too far to the west.) Demand for goods from East Asia and Southeast Asia coupled with new technology and knowledge of currents and winds made transoceanic voyages a reality. When Europeans realised that the Americas did not have the highly desired spices they were seeking, or at least not the same ones, they went after the gold and silver that they did find there.

When Columbus landed on the island of Hispaniola, which today consists of Haiti and the Dominican Republic, Columbus thought he had reached Japan. He had actually

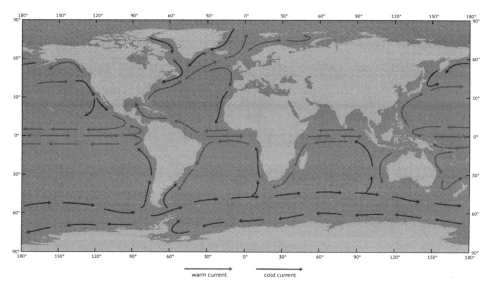

Figure 9.1 Ocean currents. Spanish and Portuguese navigators in the late fifteenth and early sixteenth centuries learned to use prevailing winds (easterlies and westerlies) and the ocean currents of the North and South Atlantic Gyres to cross oceans. Shutterstock Images.

'discovered' the Caribbean Sea, its islands and northern South America. He and his successors eventually realised that the Americas were inhabited by millions of people of different cultures speaking hundreds of languages. Yet Europeans viewed these diverse peoples and societies in monolithic terms. They often lumped these ethnic 'others' into categories such as 'Indians', who were viewed as savages, 'Africans', whose dark skin colour made them suitable for use as slaves, and enigmatic 'Orientals', who included Hindus, Buddhists and Muslims. Contact with other cultures changed the way Europeans saw themselves and the world around them. They began to perceive otherness, or *alterity*, as something demanding explanation; shortly thereafter, they began to study it, leading to the beginnings of anthropology.

Europe and the Americas Encounter Each Other

Expansion of European activities in the Americas and elsewhere occurred rapidly after 1492. The countries most active in exploration, conquest, and settlement were Great Britain, France, the Netherlands, Portugal and Spain. In all cases, indigenous peoples were subjugated to the interests of the Europeans, ultimately through military force. The principal motivation of maritime exploration and colonisation by the European powers was economic. The earliest Europeans to reach Japan were the Portuguese in 1543; they obtained gold from the Japanese to circulate in their trading outposts elsewhere in Asia, including China and India. They used the gold from Japan to buy silver from India, and they used the silver from India to buy Chinese porcelain and silk, which could be traded for spices such as clove, cinnamon and pepper in Southeast Asia. This was initially a circle of lucrative trade controlled by the Portuguese, who dominated the seas; the Japanese would expel them in the early seventeenth century, and their interests elsewhere in Asia would be coveted by other European powers, such as the Dutch and British, in the years to come. Yet the most profound effects of contact with the European world powers would occur elsewhere, thanks to epidemic diseases and the institution of chattel slavery, which were not a predominant feature of the Asian colonial situation.

In the Americas especially, Native Americans succumbed to Old World diseases against which they had no immunity. The British colonists justified their conquest of Indian lands through philosopher John Locke's doctrine of *terra nullius* ('land without an owner'). From the British perspective, because native people did not buy and sell land, they did not own it, and thus others could legally and justifiably take it away from them, by force if necessary. Europeans also believed natives lacked the basis for civilisation. The Portuguese in Brazil considered the Indians there to be *'sem fé, sem rei, sem lei'*, loosely translated as 'lacking religion, government, and law' (Boxer 1969, p. 26). In the European view, native people were therefore fit for slavery and could be expelled from the lands they occupied. Yet the people conquered by Europeans did have a system of land tenure; they simply did not have individual ownership or written documentation the way Europeans did. Rather, natives held land as family groups or through complex social and economic relationships.

The Spanish and Portuguese justified their conquest and occupation of the Americas using a different approach. One of their goals was the conversion of the natives to Catholicism. To that end, they set up missions throughout the Americas and sent missionary priests to civilise and catechise subjugated peoples. Both countries also set up offices of the Inquisition in the colonies to eradicate other religions and non-Catholic varieties of religion, including Protestantism, which was beginning to spread outside Europe by the middle of the sixteenth century. Although the Spanish crown required that its new American subjects be treated as human beings and not as slaves, soldiers and settlers consistently usurped natives' rights and forced them to work on plantations and in silver and gold mines. Wherever contact between Europeans and natives occurred, epidemics of introduced diseases followed, ultimately killing millions of native people.

Because at contact Native Americans had no immunity to Eurasian and African diseases such as smallpox, the common cold, measles and many other viral, parasitic and bacterial infections, an estimated 90 per cent of the aboriginal population of 50,000,000 living in North, Meso- and South America died out within the first 150 years of contact. In the Aztec empire of central Mexico, disease and the effects of slavery reduced an original native population of 12 to 15 million to only one million by 1600. Epidemic diseases from Europe also severely depopulated Australia and Oceania in the colonial period.

In need of more labour and drawn by stories of rich empires to the west, the Spanish arrived in Mexico by 1517. After skirmishes along the coast and into the mountains of central Mexico, the capital city of the Aztec empire, Tenochtitlán, fell to Hernán Cortés in August 1521. Cortés's objective was clear: to amass wealth from precious metals. Under Spanish colonial rule, the city of Tenochtitlán (modern-day Mexico City) became the administrative capital of New Spain and an important economic centre for the Spanish. From Tenochtitlán, the Spanish shipped silver bullion from mines worked by native slave labour back to Spain.

Although defeated by both force of arms and by disease, some native people in Mexico and Central America continued to resist Spanish control during the sixteenth century, but this proved to be futile. By the seventeenth century, some indigenous groups developed into distinct colonial societies, such as the Maya-speaking Cakchiquel of highland Guatemala, according to an ethnohistorical study by cultural anthropologist Robert Hill. The Cakchiquel were able to maintain some autonomy by covertly resisting Spanish rule. Using the concept of 'weapons of the weak' by political scientist and anthropologist James Scott, Hill showed how the Cakchiquel were able to resist some of the more punishing aspects of colonialism by using an arsenal of weapons against their Spanish overlords: 'Included in this arsenal were things like passive non-compliance, false compliance or overcompliance, feigned ignorance, foot dragging, and dissimulation' (1992, p. 123). Hill quotes a colonial-era source that describes how the Cakchiquel resisted missionisation by protecting their own religion without overtly denouncing or denying Christianity:

> They guard secrets of importance to them better than any other race in the world, so much that they would die before revealing what they guard...
>
> They have the custom never to affirm what they see and know, because they always respond 'perhaps it is so', 'perhaps it will be'.

(Hill 1992, p. 124)

Through the sixteenth and seventeenth centuries, local populations in Mesoamerica intermingled biologically and culturally with the conquerors, forming a new category of people who were neither 'European' nor 'Indian'. These *mestizos* were the offspring of Spanish fathers and Indian mothers. Many lived in rural communities and farmed; they became the new peasantry of the colony. Although many indigenous societies had been stratified before the Spanish arrived, after conquest, most Indians became members of one subordinate class, subject to Spanish masters. Like mestizos, *mulattos*—the children of mixed European and African heritage—suffered from the economic and social dominance of the white ruling class of New Spain.

The Trans-Atlantic Slave Trade

On his second voyage to the Americas in 1493, Columbus brought sugar cane from the Canary Islands with him to Hispaniola. By 1516, slaves from Africa were working on sugar cane plantations in the Americas because so many Indians had died from epidemic diseases and reduced the available labour force. Off the coast of Africa, the Portuguese had established sugar mills using the labour of African slaves captured on the coast. Portuguese colonists later exported this technology to Brazil, which became the biggest producer of sugar in the world by the end of the sixteenth century thanks to slave labour imported from Africa. Between about 1500 and 1840, some 12 million Africans were shipped across the Atlantic. An estimated 1.5–2 million died on the voyage. Most went to the Caribbean and to Brazil, but a small percentage came to North America and to British colonies in Asia. Slave uprisings, especially revolts in Haiti, Barbados (1816) and Jamaica (1831–1832), reduced the profitability of the trans-Atlantic slave trade. Most European core countries had abolished the slave trade by the early nineteenth century, though slavery itself continued in periphery countries such as Brazil and Cuba until the late 1800s. Slavery ended in the United States in 1865 as a result of the American Civil War (1861–1865).

The languages, beliefs and cultural practices of millions of Africans affected many indigenous societies throughout the Americas, leading to the formation of hybrid cultures. Indigenous Americans adopted both material and intellectual culture from escaped black slaves and often intermarried with them. Through cultural contact and intermarriage, African and native beliefs melded into new religions. In Bahia, Brazil, an African-derived religion known as Candomblé developed. Candomblé was originally confined to descendants of Afro-Brazilian slaves and Brazilians who had intermarried with them. At one time, practitioners were persecuted, since the official religion of Brazil was Catholicism. The principal gods or saints of Candomblé, called *orixas*, have Catholic counterparts. St. Michael the Archangel is the same as Ogun, the god of war. Oxalá, the high god, is the same as Jesus. This merging of deities from distinct religious traditions is called *syncretism*. Syncretism is found on six continents; one can see it, for example, in the fusion of the deities from Buddhism and Shinto (or animism) in Japan. In Brazil today, some believers in Brazil promote 'pure' Candomblé, a belief system that seeks to discard elements of Catholicism in favour of the worship of 'true' African deities.

Another example of cultural fusion in the Americas is the Garifuna people of Honduras who speak a language derived from multiple ancestral tongues, including indigenous Caribbean languages. The Garifuna employ a kinship terminology native to the Caribbean, and many practice a religion that originated in West Africa among Yoruba-speaking people. Garifuna language and culture initially took shape on the island of St. Vincent in the Caribbean. Some Garifuna believe that their spirits migrate to St. Vincent at death and that the spirits of their African-derived deities are based there.

Millenarianism and New Ethnic Identities

Although Catholicism and Yoruba language and culture have greatly influenced syncretic religions in the Americas, a number of other influences have also affected beliefs and ritual practices. According to ethnographer James Houk, the Orisha religion of Trinidad contains elements of Jewish *cabala*, mystical interpretation of scriptures; *spiritism*, which involves ideas about communication with the dead in *seances*; and Baptist beliefs pertaining to the proper conduct of ceremonies.

Syncretic religious institutions and beliefs emerging in the colonial experience sometimes involved the rejection of the dominant, core culture, and a simultaneous attempt to restore what the periphery groups saw as their ancestors' lifestyles, which they deemed superior to their present, subaltern conditions. People opposed to the core-focused world system and colonial domination who sought revolutionary change in religion and society sometimes organised themselves into *millenarian movements*. Indeed, where most societal upheavals and transformations have occurred in human history, some form of millenarianism can be detected. Some kinds of terrorism seen in today's world are outcomes of millenarianism with an apocalyptic character (Chapter 11). Millenarianism is often associated with the perception that the social and economic conditions of a people have deteriorated; members of millenarian movements attempt to alter these prevailing conditions and improve relations with the supernatural as well as with other societies and cultures. In North America, examples of millenarian movements include the Ghost Dance (Chapter 1) and the Handsome Lake or Old Longhouse Religion of the Iroquois (Cultural Snapshot 9.1; Figure 9.2). The Great Revival movements of the United States in the nineteenth century, which fostered Mormonism and Seventh Day Adventists among many other religious sects, including many that did not survive, were millenarian in character, as were the Anabaptist movements in Europe (Protestant groups opposed to infant baptism) from the sixteenth century onward, which gave rise to the Amish, Hutterites and Mennonites of today. Anthony Wallace, who studied Iroquois ethnohistory, referred to millenarian movements as 'revitalization movements', which he defined as attempts by members of society to renew their culture, often in a context of colonial domination and exploitation.

CULTURAL SNAPSHOT 9.1

Handsome Lake Religion

The Handsome Lake Religion of the Seneca Iroquois is an example of a successful millenarian movement. The Iroquois became impoverished after the American Revolution (1776–1783), in part because they had sided with the British in that war. (Even the indigenous groups who sided with the Americans in the Eastern United States, however, lost lands and sometimes their cultural identities as 'tribes', according to Mashpee ethnographer James Clifford.) By the end of the 1700s, the Iroquois had experienced defeat, loss of hunting grounds, restriction to reservations, depopulation due to disease and warfare, burned-out villages and epidemic alcoholism. The Iroquois traditionally had a strict sexual division of labour in which women cultivated fields (Chapter 8) and men hunted game; reservation life ended that. According to anthropologist Anthony Wallace, the people were living in 'slums in the wilderness'.

In 1797, a shaman named Handsome Lake fell into trance and claimed to have seen four angels, who instructed him to tell his people of the dangers of whiskey, witchcraft and love magic. Handsome Lake had several other visions and started a new religion that emphasised temperance, peace, land retention, acculturation and

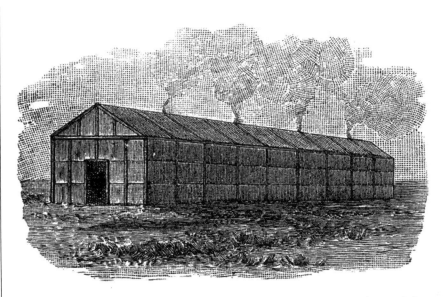

Figure 9.2 Seneca-Iroquois (Tonawanda Band) Council Meeting House, early twentieth century. The Seneca prophet Handsome Lake preached his new religion to all the Iroquois in structures like this one. From the Albert R. Stone Negative Collection, Rochester Museum & Science Center, Rochester, NY.

domestic morality. These values were similar to those of the Quakers and to the Ghost Dance religion led by the Paiute prophet Wovoka in the 1890s (Chapter 1). The Handsome Lake religion (also called the Old Longhouse religion) forbade drinking and required men to work the fields alongside women. In 1802, Handsome Lake travelled to Washington, DC, and met with President Thomas Jefferson. Jefferson promised the Iroquois security and annuities for lands that had been confiscated. The Handsome Lake religion still exists today. Members live and work in mainstream American society while retaining close ties to their indigenous cultural roots.

The Ka'apor of the Brazilian Amazon responded to colonialism by drawing on their religious beliefs. They believe their creator god, called Maíra, mistook the Portuguese and Brazilians for his creation, and gave them highly sought-after Western goods: steel tools, bolts of cloth, glass beads and other forms of wealth. For more than 100 years, from about 1825 to 1928, Ka'apor warriors tried to get the steel and other goods back by raiding white settlers in a frontier war that finally ended when the Ka'apor were offered the desired goods free of charge by the Brazilian government.

The Tupinambá, an extinct society of coastal Brazil, were related linguistically to the Ka'apor. Their colonial experience was marked by enslavement and depopulation by European diseases. The Tupinambá had shamans, people who served as traditional healers, curers or religious specialists. They also had prophets, known as *karaíbas*. Like shamans, prophets are religious figures. Shamans practise divination to cure and to predict the future. Prophets foretell a future that can be accomplished only if people change present-day behaviour, sometimes radically. While divination is based on existing beliefs in the supernatural, prophecy derives from a perceived supernatural gift, a divinely inspired vision of a new life. Shamanism supports the traditional order of society; in contrast, prophetism challenges it by propounding new ways of living and believing. The millenarian movement of the Tupinambá, which developed in the 1500s, was a direct response to colonialism. Tupinambá prophets urged people to abandon their homes, their crops and their allegiances to chiefs and shamans and to make a pilgrimage through the wilderness in search of a 'land without evil'.

The Tupinambá millenarian movement may represent spontaneous grassroots resistance to increasing political complexity. At the time of contact with the Portuguese in 1500, powerful chiefs were emerging among the Tupinambá. Such centralisation is associated with stratification and increasing social inequalities. French social anthropologist Pierre Clastres argued that the Tupinambá people did not wish to submit to centralised authority, the opposite of what Thomas Hobbes predicted. Instead, they rejected complexity using religious means. State formation was impossible when prophets were calling for the abandonment of stable, settled village life to pursue life in a Tupinambá paradise. Millenarian movements like that of the sixteenth-century Tupinambá have been and continue to be powerful forces of social and cultural change. When such movements are successful and become established, new religions may arise.

Cargo Cults. Beginning in the late nineteenth century, missionaries from Britain began to introduce Christianity to the people living in Melanesia, which comprises several islands in the South Pacific. Christianity and the native religion of Melanesia fused to form *cargo cults*, which involve sympathetic magic—simulation of a desired reality—to prosper (Cultural Snapshot 9.2). Cargo cults are a specific kind of millenarian movement. They arose in colonial contexts in which native people were discouraged from practising their own religions. As with Afro-American religions in the Americas, the cults were syncretic. The trappings of Christian belief concealed native elements in the emerging religion, allowing it to thrive. Members of cargo cults preached a new form of liberation. Like Ghost Dance practitioners, cargo cultists looked forward to the return of their ancestors, in all their glory, to earthly existence. They believed that their god had confused his true offspring—native Melanesians—with the Europeans, and had mistakenly given Europeans technology, such as aeroplanes, refrigerators full of food, electric fans and lighting, aluminium roofing and so on. In the pidgin English of Melanesia, these and other Western goods are called *kaga*, or 'cargo', which means wealth or riches.

CULTURAL SNAPSHOT 9.2

'I Can't Get No Satisfaction'

Mick Jagger and The Rolling Stones were on to something real about modern people in their famous 1965 hit *Satisfaction*. Like the Stones, Victorian-era playwright Oscar Wilde captured the paradox of life in Western civilisation in his 1892 comedy *Lady Windermere's Fan*: 'In this world there are only two tragedies. One is not getting what one wants, and the other is getting it'. For anthropologist Marshall Sahlins, the problem is that we want *too* much: 'It was not until culture neared the height of its material achievements that it erected a shrine to the Unattainable: *Infinite Needs*'.

In Melanesia, people sometimes display an insatiable desire for Western goods, which anthropologists have called a *cargo cult*. The list of desired goods includes refrigerators, television sets, cameras, bulldozers, radios, cigarettes and even blonde women for their chiefs. Westerners understand the concept of cargo and its manifestations in Melanesia because our own culture boasts shopping malls, eBay, PayPal and high-tech gadgets of all kinds. Westerners seem to have insatiable appetites not only for material goods and the thrill of acquisition, but also for love and sex. That may be why divorce rates are so high in Western society. Many of us just can't get enough of a good thing. In stark contrast are egalitarian societies with limited needs and ample leisure time. Not surprisingly, traditional egalitarian societies have little conflict, an ethic of sharing and minimal negative or long-lasting impacts on their environments.

At the end of World War II, natives in the Solomon Islands began preparing for the return of their ancestors, who would bring them cargo. Like the Japanese and, later, the Allied soldiers, the ancestors were expected to arrive in large aeroplanes loaded with supplies. Islanders cut a landing strip from the forest, built a large bamboo model of a C–3 transport plane and made wooden walkie-talkies, which they planned to use to guide the planes of their ancestors safely to the ground with their precious cargo. Today, there is an active tourist industry on the island of Vanuatu that appeals to European and North American visitors who want to experience the *alterity*, or otherness, of the 'real' Oceania. Tourists are invited to witness cargo cult ceremonies centred on John Frum, a World War II–era Melanesian prophet. Cargo cults, like millenarian movements more generally, are religious responses to colonialism.

Colonialism in Africa and Australia

As the examples above demonstrate, native groups across the Americas and on several other continents were affected by the expansion of Europe and the implementation of the world economic system. Within this system, Africa was the primary source of slaves for the sugar, tobacco and cotton plantations of the Americas. Yet Europeans conducted most of their trading on the coast of the continent. They were unable to penetrate the interior until the 1830s, partly because they had no immunity to endemic diseases such as malaria, yellow fever and sleeping sickness. European traders used African intermediaries, who raided interior villages for slaves in exchange for iron tools, firearms, textiles, whiskey, tobacco and cash. Only when medical advances had been made, such as the discovery of quinine to treat malaria, did the European powers seize parts of Africa as colonies. The principal core countries at that time were Great Britain and France. One objective was palm oil, which could be used as a lubricant in the engines that drove the Industrial Revolution before petroleum was discovered.

As Europeans colonised Africa, they distinguished themselves from black natives according to racial prejudices of the time. The Dutch East India Company, which settled what is now the Republic of South Africa, instituted a policy of apartheid, or separateness, between whites and native Khoisan-speaking people. Apartheid became legal segregation in 1948. Like the Jim Crow laws in the United States, which lasted from about 1890 to

1965, apartheid forced Africans to live in black 'homelands'; segregated them on public transportation, in schools and in hospitals; and required them to have passes to travel outside their own districts. In 1994, following boycotts, work stoppages and embargos by other countries on their exports, the government of South Africa finally ended apartheid. For the first time ever, people of colour—the majority of South Africans— were able to vote. They elected Nelson Mandela as their new president, a man who had been imprisoned by the South African government for 27 years for his opposition to apartheid.

In contrast to the African continent, which several European powers divided up among themselves, Australia was colonised exclusively by the British. Although Europeans had known the continent for more than 100 years, Captain James Cook claimed it for Great Britain in 1770. To relieve overcrowding in British jails, the government began transporting convicts to Botany Bay, near present-day Sydney, in the 1780s, where a penal colony was established. As in contact situations elsewhere, coastal Aboriginal populations suffered major declines due to diseases introduced by Europeans.

Aborigines living in the desert interior of Australia were less affected by the British until the twentieth century. By the early 1900s, white immigrants began to set up cattle ranches where they traded with the Aborigines. Aboriginal men worked as ranch hands and women did domestic chores, which often included sexual services to the white ranch workers. The Aborigines received goods such as tea, tobacco, flour and sugar for their work. Protestant missionaries began working in the 1930s to convert native Australians to Christianity. In some cases, children were separated from their parents in northern and central Australia to be indoctrinated into Christianity and Euro-Australian culture. This was part of the government's assimilation policy, which compelled children to learn English and discouraged traditional foraging practices.

In Australia and elsewhere, changes occurred not just in language and settlement patterns, but also in social relationships. Money and capitalism, which spread to the periphery with the expansion of the European world system, increasingly defined relationships that had once been based exclusively on kinship and affinity. Like the colonial enterprise more generally, money affected native cultures in powerful, transformative ways.

The Rise of Money and Capital Markets

Money and its association with markets that are controlled by supply and demand are crucial to our understanding of the motivations of Europeans to explore and conquer the rest of the world and the establishment of the modern world system. Money changed the way people related to each other within and between societies, beginning in the early colonial period and continuing to the present. The introduction of money into Europe's colonies—that is, the periphery—changed the ways dominant and subaltern groups interacted and exchanged goods and services.

Anthropologists usually divide money into two forms, special purpose and all-purpose, but this distinction does not hold for the latest forms of money such as cryptocurrency and digital money, which has aspects of both forms, and only partly accounts for money that is transferred via credit and credit cards. All-purpose money, in principle, can purchase anything, at any time or place, as long as the buyer can pay the purchase price. Special purpose money can be used to buy certain things at certain times and places and in given quantities. The Aztecs used special purpose money. Every day, up to 25,000 people exchanged goods in marketplaces, the most famous of which was Tlatelolco in central Mexico. Food, pottery, firewood, clothing, luxury goods such as gold jewellery, gemstones, feathers and services such as hairdressing, carpentry and even prostitution could be obtained there. This kind of money was used in person-to-person relationships and continuing encounters.

Before the conquest of Mexico by the Spanish in 1519, most goods in Aztec markets were bartered. Bartering is a form of negative reciprocity and involves negotiation between buyer and seller. In some instances, special purpose money was used to 'even out' exchanges. Cacao beans, used to make a spicy chocolate drink, and cotton cloaks could be used to pay for merchandise and services. A piece of pine bark for starting a fire was worth five cacao beans; one turkey egg equalled three cacao beans. A possible exchange would have been one piece of pine bark for one turkey egg plus two cacao beans. The cacao would even out the exchange since the bark was considered to be worth more than the egg. In economies using special purpose money, bartering is the primary method of exchange, not money per se.

Cacao beans could be used among the Aztecs in practically any exchange of goods, just as cloth was so used in the Congo River Basin in Africa, pigs and shells in much of New Guinea and cattle among the Nuer people. In ancient Sumer, grain served this purpose, and with the Tiv people of Nigeria, it was brass rods. The armshells and necklaces of the kula ring in the Trobriands have value, but they cannot buy anything or be exchanged for anything other than themselves over a long period of time. The late cultural anthropologist David Graeber referred to shell money, bead money, heads of cattle, feather money, cacao beans and other special purpose monies as 'primitive currencies' that are not used to buy and sell goods and services but rather to organise and 'rearrange' relationships between persons. Cacao beans and these other media of exchange were not the same as all-purpose money, which came into the Americas with the arrival of the European world system and colonialism. In colonial conditions, cacao beans, pigs and cattle were commodities, raw materials that could be transformed into something else. General purpose money, in contrast, does not necessarily have any intrinsic value.

All-purpose money is associated with capitalist markets and the modern world system. Capitalist markets value goods and services by price, which is an abstract number defined in terms of money. General purpose money is: 1) anonymous (that is, anyone who has the right amount of money can buy the goods they desire); 2) convertible (smaller units can be combined to form larger ones and vice-versa); 3) portable; 4) general in the sense that it can be used to buy anything if the price is right; and 5) legal (as in legal tender), that is, issued by a government. All-purpose money can reduce all things, including people and relationships, to an abstract value, or price, though the medium of exchange may not have any value itself. In the past, money was valued in terms of gold. But today, money may be paper, plastic or electronic. As Swedish cultural anthropologist Alf Hornborg put it:

> A unit of money does not relate to a specified commodity in the way that a word relates to a specific concept, nor does it relate to other denominations in any other sense than a purely quantitative one.
>
> (1999, p. 153)

Certain material currencies today do not conform to all-purpose money. The US dollar is used as a currency beyond the borders of the United States (as in Panama and Ecuador), and the euro is obviously used across territorial borders in Europe, though these currencies are anonymous, convertible and in other ways all-purpose. Credit cards and mobile wallets represent all-purpose money to the extent their balances are positive, but they are not anonymous. After the financial crisis of 2008, a new kind of money came into existence that was not legal (that is, not issued by a state or government), though it was anonymous, and was also not material: it was represented only by a series of numbers that were associated with amounts digitally transferred on digital ledgers (blockchain) from one party to another independent of governments and banks—digital currency.

Money can be part of personal relationships of the most intimate sort. Money cannot buy love, but it can buy sex. In classical Greece and Rome, dowry— and sexual access to a wife—was paid in goods, though money could be part of the transaction. In contrast, a prostitute's services were bought with money only. The exchange of goods involves personal relationships, as in the reciprocal economies of the Ju/'hoansi and Guajá. In an exchange mediated by all-purpose money, with exceptions noted, the relationship between the buyer and the seller begins and ends with the exchange itself. Once the transaction occurs, the two parties have no further obligations to each other. That kind of exchange came from the European core to what would become the periphery of the world system.

Money and Empire

A desire for wealth in the form of precious metals, which were easily convertible into money as coinage, motivated men to cross the Atlantic Ocean and explore the Americas and the sea routes to India and beyond. Although money had been in use since about the fifth century BC in Western Europe, it had largely disappeared during the Middle Ages, when exchanges were increasingly made in kind. Peasants produced their own food and clothing and generally paid rent in the form of grain. By the time of Columbus's crossing of the Atlantic Ocean in 1492, however, money in the form of gold and silver coins had largely replaced bartering and in-kind exchanges in European markets. Gold and silver became the basis of the global monetary system and financed Spanish and Portuguese exploration and conquest. The extraction of precious metals at low cost through slave labour helped to sustain European colonialism and the core-periphery relationship.

Alf Hornborg sees a close connection between money and religion: both 'can stand for anything to anybody'. Through missionisation, conversion and expansion of the money-based world economic system, European countries in the colonial period transformed cultures throughout the world. The colonial experience of societies in Asia, Africa, Australia and the Americas also led to the development of new ethnic identities.

Ethnic Identity

Ethnic identity is a social construct, or emic definition, that encompasses cultural and linguistic differences between groups. In most cases, ethnic identity presupposes distrust and dislike of other ethnic entities: it is founded both on a positive expression of difference and a negative, ethnocentric perception of alterity. Ethnicity consists of a multifaceted complex of traits—called *ethnic boundary markers*—that distinguish between two different groups of people. Nuer men in South Sudan receive six deep horizontal scars on their foreheads (called *gaar*) during their rite of initiation into manhood; it is one of many culturally distinguishing features that mark them as Nuer as opposed to men of some other ethnic group (Figure 6.1). Ethnic groups are not like biological species: they may merge with each other, but they may also exist as relatively discrete cultural and economic entities. Allegiances that motivate people to group identification may not be based necessarily on human relatedness or any other concept of genealogical origins. They can be constructed from diverse backgrounds, such as Gypsies. Gypsies have been called tinkers, bohemians, travellers and caravan-dwellers, but they are not easily traceable to only one single ethnic group as is commonly believed (such as Roma and Sinti, which are stereotypical identity constructs). In fact, ethnographer Leo Lucassen and his colleagues found that Gypsies are really best understood instead by the things they traditionally do: they are itinerant travellers, they sell earthenware, they trade horses, they mend kettles, they make music, they fix chair bottoms, they grind knives and they work as copper and tinsmiths. The definition of gypsy occupations is not different from other occupations of those who do not migrate; they are not pastoral nomads (Chapter 8). Their economy traditionally consists of three central facets about the gypsy family, which is a unit of work, mobile and self-employed. That Gypsies are not a genealogically defined ethnic group did not prevent the Nazis from persecuting them as if they were and sending tens of thousands of them to their deaths in World War II concentration camps. In some cases, an ethnic identity is defined by its location, not genealogy. In September 2014, thousands of people took to the streets and set up barricades in the former British protectorate of Hong Kong, a city of seven million people, to protest their subjugation to the Chinese state. Ethnically Chinese—their language is Cantonese, which although it is not the dominant language of China, is spoken outside Hong Kong—Hong Kongers seem to reject that label and embrace their city as a symbol of social identity. One young man inside the protest zone in 2014 claimed, 'I wouldn't say I reject my identity as Chinese, because I've never felt Chinese in the first place…The younger generations [of Hong Kongers] don't think they're Chinese'. After the demonstrations of 2014, there has been a growing sense not only of separate ethnic identity from the mainland Chinese but also a sense of nationalism, even though Hong Kong is not a state, but a city inside a state.

In terms of defining characteristics of ethnicity, barriers of language and outward signals of difference—in dress, music, ritual and occupational specialisations—are erected, according to Norwegian ethnographer Fredrik Barth, upon a groundwork of economic and social interests. Barth found that pastoral nomads of Southwest Asia specialise in rearing and herding livestock, such as camels, horses, goats and sheep. The pastoralists exchange meat, milk and wool for the vegetable produce of settled agricultural peoples, whose lands they traverse every year. The farmers represent a different ethnicity. They wear different clothing, practice a different religion, speak a different language and possess their own folklore. To Barth, ethnicity—recognised differences between culturally defined social groups—defines a division of labour and occupational specialisation that has positive economic ramifications for both groups, which complement each other in exchange for goods and services and contribute to each other's survival. The pastoralists and farmers studied by Barth identify themselves with a certain ethnicity and mark their ethnic membership using cultural and linguistic differences, or *boundary markers*. Such markers may include an imagined past, one that is constructed in light of political realities in the present. In this sense, ethnicity is a political process involving the origin and development of new ethnic groups. Sometimes ethnicity is used to prevent cultural exchange, as a way to resist cultural diffusion, language change, syncretism and acculturation. The desire to maintain ethnic distinctions is frequently seen in colonial situations in which the dominant group has more prestige than the conquered, colonised society.

In states, ethnicity is deeply political and not merely an academic question of understanding cultural similarities and differences; it concerns agents, stakeholders, interest groups and minorities, however defined. The political aspects of ethnicity can affect a group's legal rights to land and resources. The Mashpee Tribe of Cape Cod, Massachusetts, was denied rights to what they considered to be ancestral lands because their identity as a 'tribe' of Indians was not proven satisfactorily in a court case, according to James Clifford. (They were since granted land rights to a reservation in 2015 —which were revoked in 2020). To the court, a 'tribe' must share a common race and territory and have had an established political structure. The Mashpee, however, had intermarried with non-Indians, practised the Christian religion, did not live together in a single place and lacked an indigenous leadership structure. They were not seen as a separate 'Indian' ethnic group; nor, in the court's view, were they different from everyone else on Cape Cod. Despite intermarriage (mostly with other marginalised groups in the American colonial period, especially freed blacks), the lack of a particular line of descent, distinctive religion and other supposed aspects of indigenous culture, the Mashpee were clearly not perceived as white middle-class residents of Cape Cod. In their Christian churches in the past, the liturgy had been given in the Mashpee language. Although they did not have a fixed territory, this was true of many indigenous groups before the arrival of Europeans. Nor did the Mashpee have an indigenous leadership structure; however, many societies prior to contact were acephalous. The Mashpee had in fact adopted some aspects of 'white' culture, but they had modified these in indigenous, Mashpee ways, as Clifford pointed out. The main problem in the Mashpee case was in essentialising—or reducing—the culture of a people to a set formula. Cultures change: they accept and reject outside influences. They are not *essential*, unchanging entities. In fact, cultural identity can be created, contested and remade; as with the Mashpee, identity is hybrid, never 'pure', but rather the product of centuries of diffusion and mixing of ideas and behaviour.

Ethnicity is based on folkloristic or *emic* reconstruction of what the ancestors did: the language they spoke, the clothing and hairstyles they wore, the religion they practised, the houses they built and the professions and occupations at which they worked. Ethnicity within a modern nation-state represents a minority subculture rather than mainstream culture. Ethnicity, like race, is less a scientific, biological concept than a folk construct. It is real, of course, insofar as people live, fight, flee and die because of what it represents.

Ethnic identity generally involves a notion of descent. But unlike kinship, ethnic descent is based on membership in a larger group rather than upon identifiable ancestors. Though members of an ethnic group may not be able to link themselves by kinship or marriage, they do share cultural traditions that often refer to migration from a distant homeland and persecution at the hands of mainstream cultural groups. Ethnic minorities include African Americans and Native Americans in the United States, Kurds in Iraq, Uighurs in China, Aborigines in Australia, Inuit in Canada, Saami in Sweden, Turks in Germany and Senegalese in France.

Early twentieth-century sociologists believed that immigrants to the United States would acculturate and eventually assimilate, losing the linguistic and ethnic features that marked them as foreign. *Assimilation* is the complete disappearance of a culture due to the absorption of its people and cultural traits into another society with a different culture. For example, the pre-Roman Celts of France were defeated by Caesar and ultimately incorporated into Roman society. For the most part, they lost their Celtic language and culture, adopted aspects of Roman culture and the Latin language and, with later generations, became the French people. Assimilation differs from acculturation in that virtually nothing is left of the original culture.

Ethnic Politics and the State

The modern state is, from an anthropological point of view, a human construct. It was defined and refined by living persons (Figure 9.3). The state does not exist independently, or as an inevitable outcome, of human history. Nor is it an abstract entity apart from society itself. The state incorporates society's institutions within it. As institutions administered by the state, public schools inculcate values and employ symbols of nationhood in the educational process. Students recite pledges and anthems; they learn the origin myths of the state's creation and reenact them. They learn to profess adoration and respect for flags; they are taught to revere the sacrifice of fallen soldiers and the moral and intellectual qualities of various founding fathers and mothers long dead.

Ethnicity becomes more complicated, nuanced and contingent within states when compared with ranked or egalitarian societies. The dominant group in the state may see an ethnic group as problematic when its values or practices differ from theirs. Territorial claims by ethnic groups may threaten a state's declared boundaries. Economic concerns may motivate members of a group to establish a nationalist identity with objectives that are perceived to undermine the integrity of the state. Nationalist minorities, which are especially common in southeastern Europe and western Asia, have become increasingly prominent since World War II. Cultural anthropologist Clifford Geertz observed that practically all the postcolonial states, those arising from the ashes of contact, conquest and colonialism, were 'bundles of competing traditions gathered accidentally into concocted political frameworks rather than organically evolving civilizations' (1973, p. 244).

In some cases, ethnic factionalism and minority conflicts in postcolonial states led to the dissolution of entire nations. The European country of Yugoslavia, which was formed

Figure 9.3 Street scene from the West Side of New York City. States or civilisations always consist of more than one ethnic group. Alamy Pictures.

after World War II, contained large, conflictive ethnic groups, or minorities, that claimed territories that crossed newly established borders. Upon the death of the Yugoslavian dictator Josip Tito (1892–1980), the competing minorities in the country began to fight among themselves. In the mid-1990s, the country broke apart along ethnic lines, with Serbs, Croats and Herzegovinians claiming territorial rights as nations. Members of the groups spoke different dialects of Serbo-Croatian and used different alphabets. Religious differences—between Christian and Muslim Serbs, for example—further divided groups with competing land claims. These ethnic differences—in language, religion and cultural heritage—developed into stereotypes and eventually became the basis for genocide. In the Bosnian War of 1992–1995, people's lives depended on their ethnicity, according to ethnographer Eugene Hammel. Some of the worst atrocities since the Nazi death camps occurred during the three-year war, including the execution of 8,000 unarmed Muslim men and boys at Srebrenica in 1995 by Bosnian Serbs. Tens of thousands of people, including women, children and other innocent civilians, died before Bosnia and Herzegovina emerged. The breakup of Yugoslavia was an extremely lethal case of nationalist groups competing over territory and using ethnic differences to justify the wholesale slaughter of those who did not share the same language, religion and cultural history.

Summary

Colonialism, a process that accompanied the global expansion of European commercial interests in the late 1400s, affected millions of people worldwide. It was responsible for the Atlantic slave trade, and the deaths of millions of Native Americans due to the spread of Old World diseases against which they had no immunity. Colonialism brought people from different backgrounds, languages, cultures and continents together in new situations, resulting in new religions and ethnic identities. In many cases, these new religions and identities were responses to the experience of colonialism and expressed deep dissatisfaction with the status quo by native peoples subject to colonial powers.

Further Reading

Barth 1969; Bayliss-Smith et al. 2003; Berdan 2005; Bilefsy and Simons 2008; Burns 2011; H. Clastres 1995; P. Clastres 1989; Clement 1999a, 1999b; Clifford 1988; Crehan 2002; Crump 1981; Dannenmaier 2008; Denevan 1992; Du 2002; Fisher 2019; Graeber 2011 (p. 112); Graves 2001; Gregor 1977; Hammel 1995; Hart et al. 2001; Harvey 1989; Headland 1987; Holler 2007; Holtzman 2008; Hostetler and Huntington 1980; Houk 1995; Impey 2000; Ingold 1999;Johnson 2007; Kaplan 2011; Kehoe 2006; Lindstrom 2004; Lucassen et al. 1998; MacLeod 2007; Marx (1844) 1977a (p. 109); McGrane 1989 (pp. 33–34); Meriwether 2007; Mintz 1985; Moore 1994; Paquette 2007; Pels and Salemink 1999; Peterson 1999; Pietz 1999; Said 2003; Sansi 2007; Scott 1985, 2009; Shukla 2003; Simmel (1900) 1978; Spencer and Gillen (1899) 1938; Thornberry 2002; Tonkinson 1991; Trigger 1999; Truitt 2020; Voices 2011; Wallace 1966; Walvin 2007; Weatherford 1998; Wolf 1997; Wong and Wong 2014; Worsley 1968

Cultural Snapshots

9.1   Clifford 1988; Kehoe 2006; Wallace 1969
9.2   Lindstrom 2004 (pp. 20, 31, 32); Sahlins 1976b (p. 39)

10 Collapse and Change

Overview

What can anthropology contribute, if anything, to the understanding and amelioration of crises of our globalised world? Do anthropologists have the answers needed to solve the problems of poverty, hunger, pandemic disease, environmental degradation, warfare, genocide and terrorism? I believe they have a lot to contribute to every one of these questions. We will address them in Chapter 11, but first, we need to know a little more about where the human species has been, where it came from and where it's going. What forces make society more complex and stratified? What causes society to simplify or, in some cases, cease to exist altogether? This chapter will take a look at the loss of complexity—the loss of technology, skill and knowledge—and explore some possible explanations for why simplification occurs.

What is the future not just of civilisation, but of cultural and sociopolitical diversity in an increasingly pluralistic, globalised human reality? Thanks to globalisation and the spread of Western ideology, culture and values to the rest of the world, human societies are more similar than ever before. This homogenisation is facilitated in part by technology and the speed of communication across national frontiers never before seen in human history. The world has become smaller due to time–space compression. Yet it is also more technologically complex and data oriented.

The emergence of complexity among human groups has been explained from several archaeological perspectives. The theories are of two principal types: voluntary or compulsory (Chapter 7). Societies become more complex and make greater distinctions in rank, caste or class because their members can no longer sustain an egalitarian lifeway due to ecological, political or economic factors. Alternatively, people enter into a contract of rule by the state because they wish to avoid what they perceive as the chaos and violence that is part of human nature. The latter is the Hobbesian view, which we examined earlier. Many archaeologists and cultural anthropologists have taken a relativistic approach to egalitarian society, perhaps somewhat romantically deeming it to be superior to complex civilisation.

While there are several ways to explain the collapse of ancient societies, each of which I discuss in the forthcoming sections, it is more difficult to explain the emergence of complexity, or exactly how 'much from little' comes about in societies (Chapter 2; Cultural Snapshot 2.4). It can also be problematic in predicting what kinds of social and ecological systems have sustainability, which contrasts with collapse. It can be the case that people do not even realise when their society is collapsing, rather than merely being transformed, since many cases of collapse take place over a long stretch of historical time, and the end result is not necessarily a society that is better or worse, but one that is simply changed. Archaeologists John Haldon and colleagues have pointed out:

> When we speak of 'collapse'. . . . we should be aware that those who experienced the historical event in question may not have been aware (and indeed might not agree) that anything was collapsing at all, even if they did perceive rapid change.
>
> (Haldon et al. 2020, p. 12)

The hallmark features of complex civilisation include hierarchy, social strata, centralisation of authority, taxation or tribute, ecclesiasticism, record-keeping devices, writing or numeracy, craft and professional specialisation and public works projects such as irrigation dams and reservoirs, roads, bridges and monumental architecture. Among the theories explaining how this set of phenomena surfaces are multilinear evolution, the hydraulic hypothesis, environmental circumscription and agricultural intensification (Chapter 7). The availability of a food surplus and conflict over resources, probably rooted in ethnic allegiances, are often major factors influencing when and how complexity develops. But why do societies fall apart or collapse, whether people in the society see it that way or not? By exploring the historical and ecological context of collapse, anthropologists have produced four major explanations: overshoot, revolt and rebellion, climate change and conquest and colonisation.

Explanations for Collapse

Overshoot

One explanation for the collapse of complex preindustrial societies such as the lowland Maya or the ancient Anasazi of the North American Southwest is the overuse and depletion of natural resources through activities such as deforestation, which is what archaeologists call *overshoot*. Overshoot means that a human population exceeds the carrying capacity of its habitat. *Carrying capacity* is the maximum number of people that a habitat can support. When the demands placed on the land and its resources are too great—that is, when demand exceeds the land's carrying capacity—collapse can occur. This involves the loss of political complexity, a major shift in settlement patterns and population distribution and decentralisation of leadership. This seems to have happened in the first millennium AD in Mesopotamia. The people who lived in the early state of Ur overirrigated the land, leading to saline pollution of canals needed for food production and the destruction of the tax base of peasants. The population dispersed, the hierarchical organisation of society caved in and the dynasty ended. Incidentally, this area of the world is probably where the very first civilisation arose.

Revolt and Rebellion

In addition to overshoot, collapse can result from poorly organised power structures, political infighting, weak leadership, overtaxation of peasantries upon which elites rely and other kinds of human social errors. The labour of peasants, which was almost always taxed as *corvée* in states of the ancient and colonial worlds (Chapter 7), is needed for intensive agriculture and the production of a food surplus. In pre-Communist China, *mandarins*, the bureaucrats of the ruling class (Chapter 7), often grew extremely long fingernails as symbolic proof that they did not perform manual labour. In contrast, peasants who wore rags and lived in hovels were described as 'draught animals' (Lattimore 1951, p. 49). They were required by the state to toil in fields of wheat or rice to generate a surplus to feed the mandarins and the rest of the ruling elite. Indeed, in many societies of the ancient world, ruling dynasties overtaxed peasants, who fled or revolted and ultimately overthrew the state.

Climate Change

This explanation suggests that some ancient complex societies, such as the Classic Maya, the Easter Islanders and the Anasazi, 'collapsed' due to deteriorating environmental conditions and climate change, in part engendered by humans. As Thomas Malthus (1766–1834) pointed out in the early 1800s, when human population growth exceeds the growth of the food supply, collapse is inevitable. This view is consistent with Hobbes's belief that people are not very good at managing themselves or their resources, and hence need government to control their impulses. Government takes shape in class stratification, economic and political centralisation and monumental public works, such as irrigation systems, royal highways and large buildings (Figure 10.1). In other words, to Hobbes, without institutions, rules and regulations provided by government, humans will destroy the very environments that sustain them: they will foul their own nests regardless of the consequences to future generations. Yet it is clear from the archaeological and historical

Figure 10.1 Ruins of the Mayan city of Palenque. Featured here is the Temple of the Circle and another structure in the urban core. Courtesy Middle American Research Institute, Tulane University.

records that governments collapse, sometimes due to internal problems; sometimes, as in the case of climate change, the causes are external.

Conquest and Colonisation

Entire societies have been destroyed by conquest and colonisation (Chapter 9). The disappearance of the Native American empires of the Aztecs and Inca, the crushing of African states such as Dahomey and the destruction of kingdoms of western India and Southeast Asia by the Portuguese, Dutch and English are all examples of societies that succumbed to the fifteenth- and sixteenth-century expansion of European protocapitalism—the early modern world system—together with its pathological handmaidens, smallpox, measles and the common cold, which killed millions of the indigenous inhabitants of the Americas and Oceania.

A Multivariate View of Collapse

Research in archaeology, ethnography and ethnohistory suggests that the end of society as we know it has occurred many times in the past and can occur in many different ways, some of which are interrelated. A notion of multiple causes—or a multivariate view—is usually the best way to unravel the reasons for collapse, which environmental historian Jared Diamond has defined as 'a drastic decrease in human population size and/or political/economic/social complexity over a considerable area, for an extended time'. Collapse doesn't just occur to complex, stratified groups and elites. Egalitarian societies have also given up technologies and environmental knowhow that may have seemed indispensable in the past.

A single model of collapse cannot explain every case in which a society abandons agriculture. Some Amazonian societies have actually enhanced the biodiversity of their local landscapes by creating more heterogeneous environments, as with cultural forests in the Amazon (Cultural Snapshot 8.3). People also modified soils in the Amazon, increasing microbial diversity and improving soil fertility. Archaeologist J. G. Frazier recently observed that vast areas of land modified by humans have 'recovered' from those activities and 'many human-modified landscapes have greater biological diversity than nonmodified' (2010, p. 354–355). The tendency worldwide has been for rural people to migrate to urban centres for reasons of employment, healthcare and education, and that is reflected in the fact that since 2015 more than half the world's population lives in cities, and by 2050, cities are expected to account for about 68 per cent of the world's population, which will be close to ten billion. The notion that humans have invariably altered environments in an inherently negative way is a reflection of what archaeologist Rebecca Dean calls the 'dark view of the environment popular in the 1990s and 2000s' (2010, p. 10). To understand collapse, anthropologists must take into consideration all the relevant factors. Environmental destruction, or 'ecocide', natural disasters and climate change may all contribute to collapse or loss of social complexity. However, social and political instabilities, which lessen the efficiency of government and limit the services they render, may be critical factors, as was the case with some of the Maya city-states and the Roman Empire.

Collapses of Civilisation

Sudden collapse, with the complete loss of complex social organisation and advanced technology, rarely occurred in the past, and then only when major natural disasters occurred,

such as volcanic eruptions or massive earthquakes. Most cases of collapse involve simplification, which took place among the Maya between AD 750 and 1000 and the Roman
Empire between AD 250 and 600. In both cases, new, less centralised societies emerged
from previous, more complex ones. The societies of the Maya and Romans experienced long periods of decline, not sudden environmental disasters. Many other societies
ended in similar ways. Archaeological research from Mesoamerica has demonstrated how
Maya society changed over hundreds of years, long before the Spanish conquest, which
began in 1519. Agricultural intensification occurred during the Classic period (ca. AD
300–750). It involved increasing the amount of energy, including human muscle power,
expended per unit of land to increase production of food and fibre; impressive city centres
with temples, stelae and pyramids were built (Figure 10.1). Intensification led to more
concentrated land-use practices, more land under production, stratification, centralisation and increasing population size. Surplus production and sociopolitical complexity
climaxed around AD 750 and was followed by collapse, a period that archaeologists have
termed the Terminal
   Classic (AD 750–1000).
   Maya life underwent major transitions during the Terminal Classic: loss of population
in certain centres, simplified design in ceramic decoration and termination of record-
keeping. The notion that kings descended from gods also came to an end as political
organisation became less centralised. These are key features of the Maya collapse, though
archaeologists disagree about the causes. Some suggest that severe drought caused declines
in food production, which undermined the Maya sociopolitical system. Others argue
that agricultural intensification caused environmental degradation and a loss of ecological
diversity.
   The Maya collapse is sometimes popularly thought to have been the result of over-
exploitation of land and resources, or a case of overshoot. According to archaeologist Cameron McNeil and her colleagues, the Mayans who lived in the city of Copan,
Honduras, which collapsed around AD 810, were 'skillful managers of their landscape'.
Anthropologist and biologist Jared Diamond had earlier argued that the collapse of Copan
and other Maya cities was due to leaders' failure to stop environmental degradation, but
McNeil's study of pollen from the Copan site indicates that about two-thirds of the area
was tree-covered at the very moment of urban collapse. This was not a society destroying
its landscape and the surrounding biodiversity, according to McNeil. In fact, as Copan's
urban centre (the acropolis) reached the apex of its development around AD 400, and the
Mayan language and culture were becoming widespread in the area surrounding the city
itself, the forest was actually expanding until society's collapse more than 400 years later.
Environmental mismanagement and overshoot do not explain every case of collapse.
   Agricultural intensification by the Maya did lead to radical alterations of the landscape.
They built mounds, cleared forests and raised fields. In some areas, they built specialised ditches to increase crop production. Still, some of the latest evidence suggests that
the Maya decline was due to social and political factors affecting the ruling class, not so
much environmental degradation, if that even occurred. The ruling classes were bloated
with an excess of patronage: too many people owed favours to the rulers. Ruling classes
were swelling in relation to the rest of the population, meaning that increasing numbers of people did not perform agricultural or other productive labour. Those who did
farm were being taxed to the limit of their ability to provide their own muscle power
to feed both themselves and a bloated ruling class. Thus, the end of the Classic Maya is
most likely not, therefore, an archaeological example of the neo-Malthusian concept

of overshoot, featuring overpopulation and concomitant wreckage of the environment. Rather, it seems to have involved the swelling of a single class of people who did not work, not the entire population, which compounded tensions between rich and poor people or between elites and peasants.

In fact, the Maya 'collapse' may not have been a collapse at all, but rather a transition to a simpler, more rural society. Yet explaining the event has occupied hundreds of researchers for many years. Archaeologist James Aimers counts more than 400 books, chapters and articles on the Maya collapse published between 1997 and 2007 alone, and notes that 'interest in the lowland Maya collapse is stronger than ever' (2007, p. 329). Likewise, the collapse of the Roman Empire has drawn huge scholarly interest dating back to the Enlightenment. Both the Maya and Roman cases are problematic in the sense that no single answer explains their collapses.

On the surface, the ancient Maya and the Romans appear to have little in common. Their peoples spoke different languages, occupied different continents with different climates and had different technologies. The Romans had a patriarchal kinship system, the Maya a system of double descent. Maya civilisation consisted of several independent city-states in Guatemala, Belize, El Salvador, Honduras and Mexico; the Romans had an empire straddling the Mediterranean and extending from Britain in the northwest to Egypt in the southeast. Roman engineers erected extensive bridge, road and aqueduct systems along with monumental public architecture (Figure 10.2). At the beginning of the twentieth century, many of their constructions were still in use, such as the 2,000-year-old aqueduct at Segovia, Spain. While the Maya built temples, pyramids and

Figure 10.2 The Roman Coliseum. Some scholars believe the Roman Empire collapsed due to misguided internal policies and excesses of patronage not merely to invasion by outsiders. Shutterstock Images.

causeways, they are most notable for developing sophisticated astronomical, calendrical and mathematical systems. They had a zero concept, for example, which enabled them to count and calculate with much greater ease than the Romans, who represented numbers with the unwieldy system known to us today as Roman numerals. The ancient Hindus also knew the zero and transmitted it to the Arabs. Our system of numerical notation is called Arabic because Europeans got the zero concept from Arab scholars. It made writing and calculating large numbers much easier; in the Roman system, the number 1888 (which relies on the zero concept through the decimal system) is MDCCCLXXXVIII, which Alfred Kroeber (1948, p. 468) pointed out consists of 'thirteen figures of seven different kinds'. Presumably, Mayan mathematicians were more sophisticated than their Roman counterparts.

Yet there are certain common features between the two societies: Maya cities and the Roman Empire were both centralised and territorial. Both were stratified, with classes of elites and commoners. Their leaders attained their positions and power either from inheritance or by military conquest, not by elections or consensus of the governed. Both civilisations relied on a peasantry to produce essential goods. The Maya grew corn, squash and beans; the Romans grew wheat, olives and grapes. Both practised agricultural intensification, building irrigation systems to produce surpluses to support elite and artisan classes. And, finally, both societies changed radically over the courses of their collapses.

Evidence of a loss of complexity in the Roman Empire includes a decline in the quality of the pottery, reduction of imported goods and the cessation of inscriptions and monumental public works. Basic services of government became more limited, yet by the end of the Roman Empire, there were more civil servants than ever, swelling from 1,000 in the first two centuries AD to more than 30,000 by AD 300. By AD 367, emperor Valentinian lowered the standards and expanded the number of people who could have *clarissimus* ('most distinguished status'), which essentially vastly increased the size of the aristocracy by adding an increasingly large layer of bureaucrats to the highest echelon of Roman society. By AD 400, the highest-ranked 6,000 imperial Roman bureaucrats had positions on a par with that of senators. There were more governors, tax collectors and even emperors than ever before and an expansion of the numbers of individuals at the highest ranks of Roman society in the fourth and fifth centuries AD. This lack of efficiency was compounded by economic problems, such as inflation. Governmental top-heaviness made Rome vulnerable to invasion by Germanic tribes from the north. It was not that Roman armies were so easily defeated; rather, the government was inefficient in paying and supplying troops and in providing services to everyone, including the commoners whose labour provided the empire's infrastructure. This weakening of the state began a few hundred years before Rome actually fell, slowly but surely.

Likewise, in several Maya city-states, there was a breakdown in the notion of the divine right of kings and conflicts between ruling dynasties, which weakened centralised government. The Maya masses began to resist the increasing demands of the elite to serve as warriors. Commoner classes no longer saw the kings as divine; instead, ruling classes were considered despotic and problematic, a perspective the Maya shared with commoners of fifth-century Rome.

Neither the Maya nor the Romans went extinct. Millions of descendants of the Classic Maya still live in Belize, Guatemala, Honduras and Mexico. Their languages continue to be spoken, though these are fast changing and in some cases in danger of being lost. Descendants of the Romans live on throughout Europe, and the Latin language survives in altered form in the Romance languages, several of which (Spanish, Portuguese, French) are spoken as first languages by hundreds of millions of people on six continents.

After the Terminal Classic, about 1,200 years ago, Maya societies became less complex: less stratified, less centralised and less aggregated. The Roman Empire ceased to rule most of the Mediterranean world in the fifth century AD. By AD 600, the Middle Ages—a period of general decline in education, science and technology—had begun. Losses of complexity like those of the Maya and Romans have occurred repeatedly in world history. Such collapses may be sudden, as when a natural catastrophe occurs, or gradual, as economic and political conditions deteriorate.

Chiefdoms, in particular, tend to be unstable sociopolitical forms, which may be why no chiefdoms exist in the world today. For every chiefdom that became a state, hundreds of others vanished in prehistory or were crushed at European contact by disease and colonisation. The Calusa people of southwest Florida were organised into a chiefdom when the Spanish arrived in the sixteenth century. Two thousand people could stand inside the house of the Calusa chief 'without being very crowded' according to an early Spanish visitor. According to Darcie MacMahon and William Marquardt, the 'Calusa leader's house would have been about half the width of a football field and would have reached from the goal line almost to the 30-yard line' (2004, p. 91). The Calusa chief had 'vassal chiefs' and received tribute from numerous villages. Tribute payments included feathers, food and war captives. The Calusa also salvaged gold and silver from Spanish shipwrecks off the Florida coast and used these and other goods to establish alliances with other Florida chiefs. While the Calusa chiefdom was wealthy and powerful, it was doomed by European contact. Disease and conflicts with the Spanish depopulated the Calusa until by 1711 only a few hundred were left. By the end of the eighteenth century, the Calusa chiefdom had all but vanished, leaving only archaeological remains. The same is true of every other chiefdom documented from the colonial period.

Collapse of society can occur within the territorial boundaries of a nation-state, especially when the central authority is diffuse or absent, in peripheries far from the urban core. That is the case with indigenous societies that were completely destroyed by the introduction of new viruses from the Old World, from the beginnings of colonialism in the late fifteenth and early sixteenth centuries, in the Americas. Epidemic diseases are fairly recent in human history, and they are associated with urbanisation, crowding, poor sanitation and lack of hygiene. Measles and smallpox are only around 1,900 years old. Except for the sporadic pandemic ('Spanish' flu of 1918 and the COVID-19 virus of 2020/2021, for example), epidemics have been less frequent because of acquired, or herd immunity. On the other hand, because of deforestation in the Democratic Republic of the Congo in Africa, new zoonotic diseases that involve severe haemorrhaging similar to Ebola (Cultural Snapshot 11.1) are expected to emerge since the habitats of wildlife are destroyed and the usual vectors of zoonotic viruses are found in areas disturbed by humans, such as mosquitoes, ticks, rats and bats. Wet markets—where live animals, including exotic animals like pangolins, snakes and primates, are butchered and sold—are suspected to be the origins of H5N1 influenza, SARS and possibly COVID-19, though research on that remains incomplete. The COVID-19 virus (SARS-CoV-2), which had killed more than three million people by mid-2021, as well as SARS and MERS, are all thought to be related to close-contact between humans and animals, such as by butchering. HIV, yellow fever, rabies and Lyme disease are also zoonotic. There have been epidemics and pandemics of these diseases before, and they have killed many millions, though they do not usually lead to the complete collapse of states.

On the other hand, such viral syndromes have the capacity to destroy indigenous groups living in small, dispersed settlements and camps. Early humans up to 10,000 years ago mostly lived in small groups; if a deadly zoonotic virus were to break out, it could kill off a small group, or a few small groups that are in proximity, but it wouldn't become a pandemic because there would be no reservoir of susceptibles for the virus in order to keep reproducing itself, once it went through a localised population. Small communities—as in Amazonia after the conquest of the Spanish and Portuguese—had been depopulated by introduced diseases. Once small surviving groups dispersed after the disease outbreaks were over, the disease usually became a 'fade-out'. Renewed contact with nonindigenous explorers, missionaries, soldiers, settlers—often after several centuries—could reintroduce the original disease, this time with high mortality, because of a loss of acquired or herd immunity. This is how small groups—and many tribal groups in Amazonia and in some other parts of the world that are very small in population, often not numbering more than 100 people in total—with their cultures, languages and social organisations completely died out since the onset of the modern world system, the colonial world.

Even if not wiped out by disease, egalitarian societies with agricultural technology have also vanished from the planet, or else become so transformed in terms of technology and culture that they are barely recognisable as the societies they once were. Such changes are particularly notable in a comparison of foraging and farming societies in the present. Several foraging groups were not always foragers, and numerous farming groups depend on resources harvested by hunters and gatherers, such that the line between them blurs.

Foragers and Farmers

In the late modern period of American anthropology, researchers have studied contemporary simple foraging societies—such as the Ju/'hoansi, Mardu and Aché—to know more about our common heritage, rooted deep in the Palaeolithic past. Some 150,000 years ago, the first anatomically modern humans were hunter-gatherers. Foraging continued to be the only economic system that humans pursued for at least 140,000 years until agriculture and animal domestication began to emerge in Mesopotamia and elsewhere about 10,000 years ago. Practitioners of the comparative method of the nineteenth century believed that one way to learn about the past was through the study of simpler societies in the present (Chapter 4). In the late twentieth century, the comparative method has been used with more ethnographic sophistication and is referred to as *ethnographic analogy*, which involves the comparison of a past society to a modern one known ethnographically. Yet in some cases, the legitimacy of the method has been questioned because 1) many modern foragers do not rely entirely on foodstuffs they hunt and gather from the wild; 2) some foragers hunt and gather species associated with people who are agricultural; 3) foragers are not 'true' foragers, because they cultivate some domesticates; or 4) the foragers are descended from farmers—they have a history of plant and animal domestication and thus are not appropriate analogues for nonagricultural societies. These critiques of forager studies suggest that 'true' foragers may not exist and some, perhaps most, foragers were not always foragers.

Do Foragers Exist?

A recent anthropological theory called the 'wild yam question' presents a challenge to the use of foragers as ethnographic models for past human populations. The yam question is also known as the 'exclusion hypothesis'. Wild yams are tubers that grow underground and comprise an essential food resource for many hunter–gatherers in temperate and tropical deserts, like those found in southern Africa and western Australia. In such environments, wild foods rich in carbohydrates that grow underground are easily found when guided by traditional knowledge.

The wild yam question, or foraging exclusion hypothesis, is the notion that high-energy, carbohydrate–rich foods, such as wild yams, are too scarce in tropical forest environments to permit foragers to survive by foraging alone. Some foraging groups in tropical forests, such as the Batek of the Malay Peninsula, certainly gather wild yams (*Dioscorea* spp.), but they also gather and trade forest products such as rattan, fragrant wood and *Parkia* (a leguminous tree genus of tropical forests) seed pods for rice, flour, sugar and other cultivated items. The practices of foragers like the Batek have led anthropologists to wonder whether exclusive hunting and gathering in the rainforest—without any cultivated foods in the diet—is actually possible. In the Malaysian case, it probably was possible. The speakers of an Austronesian language, Proto-Austronesian, took off in boats from the island of Taiwan about 2,000 years ago, and spread with their highly advanced maritime technology together with rice agriculture across the Pacific and Indian oceans, from Rapa Nui (Easter Island) in the east to Madagascar in the west. In the middle of this vast expansion, which is truly one of the most remarkable diasporas in human prehistory, the early Austronesians (who are ancestors of many of the Hawaiians, Maori, Malagasy, Malay and Indonesian peoples today) settled along coastlines in Southeast Asia, including peninsular Malaysia. They would have exchanged products of the coast there, such as fish, shellfish, trade goods and rice, for items gathered by the hunting-and-gathering peoples of the interior, such as honey, resins, bamboo, rattan, fine timber and hornbill beaks. These original hunting-and-gathering peoples have come to be known as *Orang Asli* in the Malay language, which means 'aboriginal people'. The Batek are one such group. All the Orang Asli originally spoke Austro-Asiatic languages, which are mostly found in mainland Southeast Asia. Some of them, however, speak Austronesian languages today because they 'lost' their original language due to contact and subjugation by the dominant coastal cultures. In that way, they are similar to the Pygmies, though the likelihood that prehistoric foraging was the first lifestyle practised by modern humans in the tropical forest continues to be a matter of debate.

The wild yam question is called the exclusion hypothesis because it suggests that full-time foraging in tropical forests is excluded, or impossible, due to limitations on the production of food energy in pristine rainforests. The hypothesis derives from the observation that there are no tropical forest foraging societies today that survive exclusively by hunting and gathering. Instead, all existing tropical foragers are dependent on agriculture to some extent, either directly or indirectly.

Many, if not most, tropical forest foragers—in Amazonia, Africa and Asia—have long-established links to nearby agricultural peoples with whom they trade game meat, hides, wild honey and other foraged products for starchy plant foods, such as bananas, plantains and manioc grown by the agriculturalists. One example of a foraging group that trades with farmers is the Maku people of Amazonia. *Maku* is actually a catch-all term for the people of six or seven different ethnic groups who speak similar languages, according to ethnoarchaeologist Gustavo Politis. For the most part, the Maku exist by hunting game and gathering honey and fruit. They trade with the Tukanoan people, riverine farmers who grow manioc and other important carbohydrate sources. The Maku exchange meat for manioc because starchy plant foods are neither easily found nor abundant in tropical forests, according to biological anthropologist Katharine Milton. This finding is consistent with the observation of social anthropologist Pierre Clastres that in tropical forests of the Americas, it is the *absence*, not the presence, of agriculture that needs explanation since carbohydrates are so essential to the human diet.

Agriculturalists worldwide tend to give pejorative names to hunters and gatherers living in tropical forests nearby, and their trade relationships are tinged with ethnocentric assumptions of superiority. In the Tukanoan language, *Maku* actually means 'servant' or 'slave', reflecting perceived ethnic and status differences. Such attitudes are also found in the relationship between farmers and the Pygmies of equatorial Africa, who depend on them for carbohydrates, in this case, bananas, plantains and manioc. Unlike the Maku, who speak a language different from the Tukanoans, the three main Pygmy groups—Aka, Efe and Mbuti—speak languages that are the same or similar to those spoken by their agricultural neighbours. Certain cognate, or related, words are shared by the three Pygmy languages, suggesting a long-term Pygmy heritage of hunting and gathering within the rainforests of Africa. The cognates refer to traditional technology, such as a specialised borer for yams, a certain kind of axe, a bark container and a cooking method. The languages also share words for animals and plants that are economically important. Their vocabularies include terms for various nut and bee species, mushrooms, caterpillars and anthills, according to ethnobiologist Serge Bahuchet.

The Pygmies have a subordinate or subaltern class relationship to the Bantu and Sudanic-speaking farmers with whom they interact. Pygmy women 'marry up' when they wed male farmers, a marriage form called *hypergamy;* however, farmer women do not marry Pygmy men, as this would constitute *hypogamy*, or 'marriage down'. Farmers tend to fear the forest and have constructed elaborate mythologies about its dangerous spirits. Living in their riparian settlements, the Tukanoans of the Northwest Amazon are similarly fearful of the surrounding forest. Both the African farmers and the Tukanoans depend upon foragers for hunted game. Although the Pygmies tend to work in the fields for the farmers, farmers rarely work at Pygmy tasks. The Pygmies derive more food energy from agricultural produce than the farmers do from the game provided by Pygmies, though wild honey appears to have been especially prized as a Pygmy trade item. On the small island nation of Sri Lanka, off the southeast coast of India, Vedda foragers, who call themselves by the *autonym* (a person's name for themselves) *Wanniyala-aetto*, trade with neighbouring farmers who speak Tamil and Sinhala languages. *Vedda* is actually a Sanskrit word that means 'hunter', a term that indicates the nature of the relationship between the Wanniyala–aetto and the farmers with whom they engaged in silent trade, according to British social anthropologists Charles and Brenda Seligman. The Vedda/Wanniyala–aetto are among the hunter-gatherer groups that Richard Fox has called 'professional primitives' (1969, p. 139).

In the past, when the Wanniyala-aetto people gathered sufficient game meat, honey, beeswax and other forest products such as wild tubers and medicinal herbs, they piled them up in the centre of a large trading field near a Tamil or Sinhala agricultural village. The Wanniyala-aetto then called out or drummed loudly before retreating to the edge of the clearing. The village people would come to inspect the goods in the field and place agricultural foods such as bananas or rice flour next to the forest goods. The farmers would then retire to the opposite side of the field. Once the Wanniyala-aetto visitors had examined the products of the villagers and found them acceptable, they would take the agricultural goods and depart, signalling the end of the transaction. If the produce was unsatisfactory, the Wanniyala-aetto would return to their side of the field and await a better offering. These four ethnographic examples show how dependent tropical forest foragers have been on some kind of agriculture.

Loss of Agriculture

The Guajá Indians of eastern Amazonia (Figure 10.3), whose demographically induced polyandry we briefly examined in Chapter 1, are hunter-gatherers who traditionally hunted and fished, but derived much of their food energy from the starchy central layer, or mesocarp, of the fruit of the babaçu palm (*Attalea speciosa*) (Chapters 1 and 8). The palm is preadapted to conditions where fire is used to reduce forest cover to charred organic material for improving soil and opening up space for crops. Babaçu germinates far underground and remains there for as long as seven years. When the surface vegetation is burned off, babaçu seedlings can survive the surface combustion. Later, they may grow to dominate the landscape. Babaçu palm forests are found in the remains of old village sites of agricultural neighbours of the Guajá, such as the Ka'apor. The Guajá traditionally use these old village sites and camp near them during the year. Guajá foraging therefore was indirectly dependent on the carbohydrate-rich babaçu palm grown by the Ka'apor. The Guajá also availed themselves of other living artefacts left behind by the agriculturalists who preceded them. The cultural forests (Cultural Snapshot 8.3) they lived in, many of which were tropical fruit orchards, including babaçu palm, were the products of hundreds of years of human modification of the landscape and its biota.

Figure 10.3 Guajá youth at leisure, 1989. Photo by Author.

Although the Guajá are considered hunters and gatherers, they have several words for domesticated plants, including maize, yams, beans, calabash and guava. These words have cognates in other Tupí-Guaraní languages spoken by agriculturalists. This linguistic evidence suggests that the Guajá themselves may have been agriculturalists in the past. Even though the Guajá have evidently lost a cognate term for manioc, they refer to a mythic underground people as the 'little manioc people' (*manio-'i*, literally 'manioc-little'). This suggests that manioc has its most important economic part—the tuber—underground, which is true, and therefore implies that the Guajá had some familiarity with agriculture in the past. They know something about the cultivated plant, even though they didn't cultivate it themselves for many generations.

More striking evidence that the Guajá were once farmers and later became foragers is that they do not traditionally possess fire-making technology. Women are responsible, in fact, for keeping the fire going and for carrying a torch from a small tree, *Sagotia racemosa* (called *miriko'y*, 'the woman tree'), burning with resin on the end of it when they move from camp to camp. This lack of fire-making ability is also true for a few other hunter-gatherers in Amazonia, such as the Tupí-Guaraní-speaking Yuquí and the Carib-speaking Akuriyo. Fire-making technology has been an indispensable part of human biocultural evolution since the evolution of the genus *Homo*. The only explanation for the lack of fire-making technology among the Guajá is that their ancestors—along with those of the Yuquí of Bolivia and the Akuriyo of Suriname—lost the technology. They are not the only ones in the world to have done so. The Mbuti Pygmies of the Ituri Forest in Congo likely also lost the ability to make fire. Like the Guajá, women are in charge of keeping it going. According to ethnographer Colin Turnbull, 'Every woman, when moving camp, carries with her a burning ember wrapped heavily in fire-resistant leaves' (1968, p. 58). The Mbuti case makes the Amazonian cases more plausible: the counterintuitive proposition that fire making is not universal, as was once thought, is a fact.

The evidence suggests that the Amazonian groups at least underwent *agricultural regression*: they abandoned those crops and technologies, such as manioc and fire, which are essential for cooking and processing agricultural foods. This regression was accompanied by social simplification of society more generally. Population densities fell and people became more mobile and less centralised. These are key characteristics of simple foraging societies—pristine or not—when compared with agrarian ones.

Some anthropologists believe people who give up agriculture, or who give up intensive agriculture to grow crops that require less work and attention than paddy rice and irrigated wheat fields, are not undergoing social collapse, but rather choosing to become more mobile to avoid being subjugated, or turned into subaltern peasants, by more powerful agricultural societies. James Scott, for example, argues that highland societies of Southeast Asia—people who occupy a moderate- to high-altitude region across eastern India, Burma, Thailand, southwestern China and Indochina—are descendants of lowland peasant peoples. At some point in the past, the people of this region decided to escape working in fields for others by taking to the hill country, where there was no government, no state, no mandarins, no sultans. It was a land without centralised authority, without leaders. There in the high country, they did not practice intensive agriculture, but rather became more mobile, practising some extensive agriculture, such as slash-and-burn, and in recent centuries cultivating fast-growing crops, such as introduced maize (*Zea mays*) from the Americas. They freed themselves from the demands of paddy-rice civilisation found in riparian, irrigated bottomlands, all of which were state controlled. Scott further posits that these highland people *chose* to be more mobile to perpetuate an egalitarian lifeway and to avoid control by the state. This behaviour is the opposite of Hobbes's assertion that people require states to enjoy harmonious, productive lives.

In contrast to the Southeast Asian example, however, the Amazonian groups who lost agriculture probably did not choose foraging lifestyles initially, even though today they savour their differences from farming peoples. I have heard Guajá people say proudly *nɔ tum awa /nuh toom awá/* ('real people don't plant crops'). In every case known of agricultural regression in South America, the group gave up not only agriculture but fire-making technology as well. Survival as foragers was therefore tenuous, at least in the beginning. Amazonian farmers of the past probably did not give up important technologies such as fire, extensive agriculture and cultural forests (Cultural Snapshot 8.2) because they thought it would be a good idea to try out a new and better way of life. Rather, they did it because they were forced to by circumstances such as contact, conquest, depopulation, colonialism and hostile neighbours. Those circumstances are no longer extant, yet historical contingencies—springing mostly from the legacy of contact—may lead people to sacrifice technology associated with sedentary lifestyles and to adopt, eventually with pride and a sense of ethnic distinctiveness, a much more mobile, nomadic existence.

The causes of agricultural regression in Amazonia—an orderly, comprehensive breakdown in the cultivation of domesticated plants—are rooted in historical contingencies that involved the displacement of peoples during the European conquest, as well as the epidemics, depopulation, slavery and warfare that followed colonisation (Chapter 9). In other words, societies that abandoned agricultural crops and technologies were operating within a very specific context, a time when multiple factors converged that led to radical changes in how people made a living. Because the regression from agriculture to foraging in the Amazon is the product of historical events, one must exercise caution when using ethnographic analogies and interpreting past human societies using contemporary foragers as models.

Historical, ethnographic and linguistic data suggest that there are few roads to complexity, but many possible paths to cultural, societal and political simplification. The proposition that human societies follow a trajectory of technological advancement and greater sociopolitical complexity is simply untrue. Once agrarian society and stratification have emerged, contingent factors of history and environment lead to either further development of complexity (Chapter 7) or collapse. Globalisation (Chapter 12) is an instance of increasing complexity in the modern world. Agricultural regression is an example of the collapse of traditional technology, which breaks down old social structures as new trends and opportunities emerge, including more foraging, higher mobility and lower population densities.

Summary

Many societies have collapsed or become more simplified in the wake of sociopolitical and environmental challenges. Two examples are the Classic Maya and the fifth-century Roman Empire. Today, many hunter-gatherers are dependent on agriculturalists. The foraging exclusion hypothesis proposes that for tropical forests, agriculture actually preceded foraging, so that the foragers we see today are secondary, not primary, foragers. Some hunter-gatherers may have actually been farmers in the past who abandoned agriculture and somehow lost agricultural knowledge and technology. Such hunters and gatherers are not appropriate ethnographic analogies for Palaeolithic human society. Cultures are influenced by historical and contingent events, which need to be taken into account in understanding both the processes that lead to increasing cultural complexity as well as those that lead to simplification and eventual collapse.

Further Reading

Aimers 2007; Anderson et al. 1991; Bahuchet 1993; Bailey et al. 1989; Balée 1999, 2010; Bulbeck 2004; Catton 1980; P. Clastres 1989 (p. 85); Cormier 2003; Dean 2010; Diamond 2005; Earle 2002; Ellis and Ramankutty 2008; Endicott and Endicott 2008; Fox 1969; Frazier 2010; Fried 1967; Goldsworthy 2009; Grinker 1994; Grove and Rackham 2001; Haldon et al. 2020; Harvey 1989; Headland 1987; Heather 2007 (p. 31); Hecht et al. 2014; Holland 1998; Kiley 2020; McNeil et al. 2010; Mercader 2003; Milanich 1995 (p. 49); Milton 1984; Newson 1998; Politis 2007; Sahlins 1976b; Scott 2009; Seligman and Seligman 1911; Sharer 1994; Stegeborn 1999; Tainter 1988, 2006; United Nations 2018; Wolverton et al. 2009; Woods and McCann 1999

11 Applications of Cultural Anthropology

Overview

In this chapter, we address whether research and knowledge generated by cultural anthropology can change people's lifestyles for the better. Following a discussion of ethics in anthropology, we examine the current debate over the role of anthropology in military conflicts. The chapter concludes with a discussion of some of the areas where applied anthropologists are currently working: health and disease, food security, ethnotourism and economic cooperatives.

Applied Anthropology

Applied anthropology is anthropology 'put to use'. It is sometimes called the *fifth field* of anthropology and involves anthropologists putting their skills and knowledge into practice to aid the people they study, inform public policy or contribute to some other real-world purpose. There are many jobs for anthropologists outside of museums or universities, often with federal or state agencies. Sometimes these applications generate controversy. Applied anthropologists study subjects as diverse as agriculture, alcohol and drug abuse, development policies and practices, the effects of disasters, employment and labour, education and land use and land claims. They work in the areas of cultural resource management, urban development and healthcare. In 1968, only about one-fourth of new PhDs in anthropology were in nonacademic, applied positions. By the 1990s, about two-thirds of some 400 anthropologists who received PhDs each year in the United States were being hired outside the university. Today, most applied anthropologists are involved in some kind of research or administration and management. Applied anthropology is a major growth industry and is likely to keep growing, as the skills derived from participant observation and other anthropological methods (Chapter 5) are increasingly recognised for their scientific validity. Only a few universities actually consider applied anthropology to be a true fifth field and separate subdiscipline. One, the University of South Florida, actually grants a doctorate in the field. Many anthropologists are ambivalent about applied anthropology because it is not always clear who will benefit when applying anthropological knowledge to a real-world problem. In some situations, the application of anthropological knowledge even has the potential to harm people.

Of course, all ethnography involves social interaction and hence has effects on people. No matter how much the ethnographer tries to minimise the impact that he or she has in a community where fieldwork is done, some kind of disruption to daily life occurs due to the very nature of participant observation. The American Anthropological Association

(AAA), which is the main professional organisation of anthropology in the United States, revised its Statement on Ethics in November 2012. The statement reflects the complex relationships that develop between the ethnographer and the people and communities where he or she works. The preamble of the statement observes:

> Anthropology—that most humanistic of sciences and scientific of humanities—is an irreducibly social enterprise. Among our goals are the dissemination of anthropological knowledge and its use to solve human problems. Anthropologists work in the widest variety of contexts studying all aspects of the human experience, and face myriad ethical quandaries inflected in different ways by the contexts in which they work and the kinds of issues they address.
>
> (AAA 2012a)

This Statement on Ethics further observes that anthropologists have responsibilities to many entities: to those studied, the public, the discipline of anthropology, students, sponsors, one's own government and that of one's host country. Above all, the AAA ethics statement holds that the most important of these obligations is the requirement that the ethnographer avoids any behaviours or writings that would imperil the people with whom he or she works. That is summed up neatly in the first principle of anthropological ethics, in three words: *Do No Harm*.

It is not always possible to foresee what might harm the people an ethnographer chooses to study. In an extreme example, after American ethnographer Cora DuBois had finished fieldwork on Alor Island, the Japanese conquered it in World War II. The new commanders of the island discovered that certain Alorese believed—based on their interactions with DuBois—that the Americans were likely to win the war because Americans were 'good people'. The Japanese commanders had those Alorese rounded up and beheaded. Of course, most ethnography does not entail such chilling risks to the human subjects one studies, but all ethnographers are trained to be aware of the kinds of psychological or physical risks their research might pose. Usually, ethnographers are required to present their research plans to institutional review boards (IRBs) at their universities to ensure that their work does not pose an unacceptable risk to human subjects. They are also required to get informed consent from informants. Such documents or verbal explanations are intended to let informants know the scope of the research and its potential risks or benefits. It may also be necessary for ethnographers to get the approval of the governments of the countries where they do fieldwork.

For the past 50 years, applied anthropologists have mostly worked in the aid industry, which transfers capital and technology from Europe and North America to poor countries in Asia, Africa and Latin America. In the Cornell University Vicos Project (1953–1962), American anthropologist Allan Holmberg, together with his students and collaborators, funded by the Carnegie Corporation, purchased a *hacienda* (estate) in the Peruvian Andes named Vicos. This hacienda had a resident population of several hundred Quechua-speaking peasants who lived as serfs. They were required to work for the estate three days a week in exchange for being allowed to use small plots of land for their own agricultural production. They were sometimes beaten if they did not perform services required of them. Their health and living conditions were poor. It was Holmberg's aim to improve the lives of these people through an applied anthropological methodology he called *participant intervention*.

By purchasing the estate, the Vicos project freed the serfs from the labour requirements of the hacienda and helped them form a cooperative, democratic organisation with their own leadership to replace the former ranch managers. The ownership of the ranch was eventually passed from Holmberg and his associates to the local people. By 1962, health and wellbeing, according to some measures, had improved. However, there was some evidence that an elite had emerged. By 1996, the local cooperative ceased to exist and the estate returned to private ownership. Overall health and economic conditions of the Quechua population in the 1990s were evidently much better than they had been when the Vicos project began.

The concept of participant intervention usually refers specifically to Vicos, and it has largely been replaced by a host of different terms, such as *participatory development* and *activist anthropology*. Nevertheless, its basic tenets and aims continue to motivate many applied anthropologists who want to improve the living conditions of others, especially indigenous and ethnic minorities. As culture brokers, applied anthropologists represent the needs and interests of indigenous societies to government policymakers, aid organisations and nongovernmental organisations (NGOs). Many, if not most, anthropologists believe, myself included, that all ethnographic work should be applied to some extent. In other words, anthropologists need to be engaged with the people they study, not simply standing by as observers, but endeavouring to support and advocate for the communities in which they work.

New Methods, New Research

Applied anthropologists today tend to engage in rapid fieldwork rather than long-term participant observation. Rapid fieldwork involves ethnographic glimpses of a particular problem, usually accompanied by a report to the sponsor of the research, for the purpose of implementing a policy. Such ethnography may occur at multiple sites, where data are quickly gathered via questionnaires, key informant interviews, focus groups and via the internet. The traditional hallmark of fieldwork in cultural anthropology—one to two years living and observing a host community—is no longer the norm. This is because clients who hire applied anthropologists demand prompt research results. Rapid fieldwork may work well in situations in which the anthropologist has already done long-term participant observation in the traditional sense, as he or she has already established relationships in a community, speaks the language and is familiar with local beliefs and practices.

Some kinds of research may not involve fieldwork at all, but takes place exclusively via email, blogs, online surveys and social networking. For example, email can be used to administer questionnaires and surveys or conduct life history interviews, provided informed consent has been given. Applied anthropologists can help design urban mediascapes, such as the electronic display environment of Times Square in New York City. They can enhance the physical and virtual social spaces in which people work, facilitating information exchange within businesses and governments. This kind of organisational research identifies and makes explicit the cultural rules that operate in such organisations to create more durable bonds between participants, or build 'social capital', a term coined by French sociologist Pierre Bourdieu.

Applied anthropologists increasingly collect data using multimedia, especially video. For example, in the 1990s, Terence Turner helped the Kayapó Indians of central Brazil acquire and use video technology to make films about their own culture. The Kayapó documented indigenous concerns about land boundaries that they presented to the

Brazilian government to get assistance in protecting their territory. Turner's work represents engaged anthropology; that is, anthropology that is responsive to issues and problems as they are perceived by local communities and indigenous groups such as the Kayapó.

Who Benefits?

Who benefits? is a key question in applied anthropology because it has sometimes been unclear for whom an anthropologist is working: For the sake of research? For the benefit of informants and the native society? Or to benefit a government or other institution? One form of applied anthropology, sometimes called *development anthropology*, has been criticised as contributing to a colonial mentality in which rich nations help poor nations 'develop' economically. Often this development aid involves industrial agriculture, networks of highways and the use of capital-intensive technologies. In many cases, development did not help poor nations to eliminate poverty or gender and minority discrimination; instead, it sometimes exacerbated existing inequalities and made the lives of many poor people—women, especially—worse.

International development aid can also cause environmental destruction. In the 1970s, the World Bank funded a highway project that was supposed to alleviate poverty in northeastern Brazil. The highway into the Amazon was intended to make it easier for poor peasants to move into new regions where farmland and agricultural credit and financing were available. However, the highway was built directly through the lands of the Ka'apor Indians, who were never consulted. The development project deforested about 4,000 square miles and displaced about 200 people from their ancestral lands. Today, the area is densely populated with settlers and the forest that once existed there is gone, replaced by small farms, open fields, towns and cities. Many Ka'apor were pushed into a forest enclave about the size of the state of Delaware (about 2,000 square miles). The remaining forest is continuously decreasing due to incursions by loggers, farmers and ranchers since external aid supports economic development in the area. Anthropological research can also benefit national governments. Applied anthropology in Britain began as part of a government strategy to effectively manage the empire's colonies in Africa and Asia. Radcliffe-Brown (Chapter 4) actually taught a course in applied anthropology in the early 1920s at the University of Cape Town to improve cultural understanding between whites and blacks in South Africa. Conflict between native inhabitants and European colonists was very costly in both military and economic terms, and anthropology was viewed as a way to ease tensions.

On the other hand, Radcliffe-Brown sought to distinguish between those anthropologists who worked to implement British imperial policies and those field-oriented anthropologists who conducted ethnographic research to generate knowledge. The same is true of Malinowski, who differentiated anthropologists from those he snidely referred to as 'practical men': administrators and missionaries in the service of colonial powers. Like Radcliffe-Brown, French anthropologists were employed in the early twentieth century to reduce racial tensions in French colonies in Africa.

In at least one case, anthropological research was undertaken in part to benefit the fieldworkers themselves. During the Great Depression in the 1930s, the US government created jobs through New Deal programmes that employed anthropologists. Most of this work was centred on projects with American Indians living on reservations and focused on education, nutrition, culture contact and land issues.

Today, applied anthropologists work for clients, which makes the question of who benefits much clearer. Clients can be tribes, native corporations, state or federal agencies or an NGO, such as an international aid organisation. One recent study in applied anthropology focused on farmer experiments with rice, an introduced crop, in Ghana, Africa. The anthropologists consulted for a governmental policy group to help farmers manage water, use fertilisers, select new rice varieties and participate in research on how to increase rice production. In another study, supported by the National Institute on Drug Abuse, applied anthropologists studied ecstasy (or MDMA) and the rave and club participants and suburban teenagers who use it. They also studied its production and distribution. Unlike the heroin and cocaine drug epidemics, which can be studied at particular sites, ecstasy does not have a single or principal manufacturing region or centre. Applied anthropological research showed that ecstasy production was spread across several countries of Eurasia, leading the anthropologists to suggest that new methodological tools were needed to study some 'post-ethnographic' social problems. Applied research like this seeks rapid solutions to current problems. Few problems are more urgent than intergroup violence and national survival. Because conflict often involves people of different cultures, religions and ethnicities, applied anthropologists have been involved in warfare since at least the 1940s.

Anthropology and the Military

Anthropological knowledge can be used in warfare and in counterinsurgency operations to describe and evaluate the political and military capabilities of opposing forces. In the past, the US government sought to predict the actions of enemies through national character studies. Since World War II, anthropological research has been used to understand and manipulate the attitudes of ethnic and linguistic groups to further American military objectives.

Cultural Anthropology in World War II

Applied anthropology was especially important during World War II. In fact, the Society for Applied Anthropology was founded in 1941, the same year that the United States entered World War II. More than 90 per cent of American anthropologists joined the Allied war effort in some capacity. Many were part of the War Relocation Authority, the office responsible for the camps where Japanese Americans were interned during the war. Anthropologists acted as liaisons between the camp authorities and the inmates. Cultural anthropologist Robert Redfield, a specialist on Mexico (Chapter 5), proposed that camp inmates govern themselves democratically, but that only Japanese Americans born in the United States be allowed to hold elected office. He wrote, 'These communities must be democracies…but they may not be pro-Japanese democracies' (quoted in Price 2008, p. 152). Other cultural anthropologists, such as Ruth Benedict and Margaret Mead (Chapter 4), worked for the Office of Strategic Services (OSS) during the war. In that capacity, they carried out culture and personality studies of national character, targeting countries that were either friends or foes of Allied forces in World War II. Some of the data on the Japanese national character that Ruth Benedict used in her book *Chrysanthemum and the Sword* (1946) came from data gathered by applied anthropologists working in US internment camps.

Counterinsurgency Efforts during the Cold War

American citizens widely supported the Allied effort in World War II, and rarely questioned the appropriate use of information gathered by applied anthropologists. However, applied anthropologists are not always on the 'right' side in military matters. In 1964, the US Army created Project Camelot to prevent the spread of Soviet communism in Latin America during the Cold War (1945–1991). The intention was to create a counterinsurgency programme that used anthropological insights to thwart peasant revolts and other subaltern political movements in developing countries. Another Cold War example is Project AGILE, a CIA-sponsored programme to help the governments of Thailand and Vietnam develop methods to combat insurgencies within their own countries in the 1960s and 1970s. This programme used anthropological knowhow to determine which villages seemed to be most susceptible to Viet Cong political pressure.

Both Camelot and AGILE met with widespread disapproval in the anthropological community because they endangered the people studied and brought the objectivity of the entire discipline into question. If anthropologists serve in espionage and military capacities, they may become suspect, exposing themselves and other anthropologists to potential violence and preventing future research by undermining the relationships of trust that develop in the course of field research.

Embedding Anthropologists and the Human Terrain System

An unknown number of applied anthropologists served as part of the US military's Human Terrain System (HTS) from 2006 to 2014. HTS 'embedded' anthropologists and other social scientists in Human Terrain Teams (HTTs) were attached to combat units so their expertise could be used on the ground, mainly in determining the difference between friend and foe in places where US military forces were operating, known as the 'operational environment'. HTS was active in Iraq and Afghanistan, where two different wars were fought for control of those territories. The Iraq War (2003–2017) and the Afghanistan War (2001–_) have a limited though continued US military presence. In 2007, the AAA condemned the employment of anthropologists in the military because such employment could violate the then AAA code of ethics and put both anthropologists and their informants in physical danger. The HTS embedding procedure can be in conflict with at least two of the principles of the current (as of November 2012) AAA statement on ethics: to 'do no harm' and to 'be open and honest regarding your work' (AAA 2012b). On the one hand, proponents of HTS argue that embedding trained social scientists in HTTs could help save innocent lives by directing combat units' military power away from friends, or harmless targets, in what was called the Global War on Terror (2001–2013). On the other hand, the possibility of endangering not only local people who are the subjects of anthropological study but also the anthropologists themselves by explicitly using tools of the profession to conduct espionage is real. Ethnographer Marcus Griffin, who was an embed for the 101st Airborne Division, indicated HTS could bring the expertise of applied anthropology to local situations by identifying the causes of slow economic growth, poverty and undernourishment. On the other hand, the military strategy behind such studies was principally to identify what makes community members vulnerable to recruitment by terrorists.

I believe anthropological participation in military projects like HTS is questionable because it is unlikely whether professional ethics can be used to guide such research, if that is what it really is. Espionage and combat techniques are not the same as the pursuit of knowledge based on participant observation and other methods in the toolkit of cultural anthropology. Anthropologists can do nothing to prevent military officials from reading their ethnographies; in fact, such knowledge may help to increase the respect for and understanding of how other societies function. Direct engagement or embedding of anthropologists in military operations, however, is a different matter, and arguably at odds with the ethics of the profession.

Ethnography at a Distance (Again) and the Study of Terrorism

Terrorism, warfare and genocide can still be studied ethnographically and in accordance with the ethical principles of the AAA. Such research necessarily involves ethnography at a distance. Ruth Benedict's study of Japan during World War II was carried out from afar; she could only carry out ethnography at a distance (Chapter 4) because she was a foreign enemy and embedding at the time was out of the question. Any onsite research was simply impossible. Cultural anthropologist George Marcus more recently called for *multisited ethnography* to study 'global linkages' affecting place-based societies, given that no particular area is free of impacts from the outside world. Some parts of the world are more or less dangerous for fieldwork because of ongoing warfare, such as South Sudan (home of the Nuer, many of whom are refugees in the United States due to long-standing civil wars there), Iraq, Afghanistan, Somalia, Sudan, Syria and Yemen. It is difficult to carry out ethnography in such places because of the 'intensity of the violence, the unpredictability of the combatants, and the suspicion of working under-cover for foreign intelligence services', according to cultural anthropologist Antonius Robben (2010b, p. 3). Cultural anthropologists studying terrorism and other forms of extreme group violence, such as genocide, have been able to do research either after the fact or by using the tools intrinsic to ethnography at a distance, including multisited ethnography.

Genocide involves use of the state military, police and paramilitary forces to annihi-late a target population based on their perceived race, ethnicity or political allegiances. Such forces have crushed civilian populations since antiquity. Julius Caesar's army killed one million and enslaved another million Gauls (the Celtic people of France) during the first century BC. The Romans further engaged in *ethnic cleansing*, a term coined during the Bosnian War of the early 1990s, of the Iceni people in southeastern Britain in AD 60, killing thousands of them and only losing about 400 Roman soldiers in the pro-cess. The objective was to eliminate Iceni opposition to Roman rule. In World War I, the Ottoman Turks executed more than one million Armenian civilians and sent their orphans into exile. In a mere 100 days in 1994, ethnic Hutu militias killed about 800,000 minority Tutsi people in Rwanda.

In terms of the numbers of civilians killed by a state because of their ethnic or racial category, the German Nazi effort to exterminate the Jews of Europe during World War II is the most salient historical case known. The Nazis killed about 5,721,000 Jews, or a little more than two-thirds of the entire Jewish population of Europe from 1939 to 1945. Although the Nazi state was completely defeated, states do not necessarily learn history lessons very well. A few states since 1945 have also resorted to genocidal prac-tices. In Cambodia, after the Vietnam War (1954–1975), the Khmer Rouge—the party in power—killed 600,000 civilians in an attempt to bring about a peasant utopia in that country; in total, a quarter of Cambodia's population of eight million died during the Khmer Rouge's hold on power. Ethnographers have studied mass executions by state military forces in ways similar to the salvage ethnographers of the early twentieth century by seeking to meet with and speak to survivors of such events and territorial displace-ments. Ethnographers by and large cannot get any closer to view genocide first-hand and still report on it.

Genocide is done by states; terrorism, on the other hand, originates with violent, non-state insurgencies possessing one principal, immediate objective; namely, the provocation of generalised fear. The term *terrorism* in its modern usage comes from a phase of the French Revolution known as *la terreur* (1794–1795), in which the radical faction known as the Jacobins temporarily took control of military and police forces to impose a 'reign of terror' in French society, mainly in an effort to exterminate by guillotining the pre-revolutionary nobility of the country. The French republic was still an inchoate political organisation, and the Jacobin party collapsed with the executions of its own leaders after a short period of time. Terrorism denotes the ability of a nonstate, insurgent, paramilitary group to bring about a widespread state of fear in the general population. The victims of terrorists are those who fear them and their penchant for maiming and murdering non-combatants. More often than not, terrorists ultimately seek the destruction of state power to either replace it with themselves or to legitimise their own right to political existence. Terrorism can occur anywhere on any continent in any society, though it tends to be focused on urban targets, the most spectacular having been the 9/11 attacks against New York City and Washington, DC, in 2001. From 1990 to 1995, the Japanese millenarian cult Aun Shinrikyo tried to infect millions of Japanese city dwellers with botulin neuro-toxin (the most poisonous substance on Earth) but lacked sufficient equipment and skill to aerosolise it, producing few known casualties. In 1995, however, the same group released sarin nerve gas in the Tokyo subway, killing 13 people and injuring thousands.

The ideology of apocalyptic terrorists tends to be comparable with that of other mil-lenarian movements, such as cargo cults, in that they tend to hold a belief that a better world will follow upon their religiously prescribed—and in this case violent—rituals. Islamist terrorists tend to have a belief that ancient, original Islam will come to prevail on the globe thanks to their terroristic acts. Al Qaeda and ISIS (or ISIL), based in the Middle East, have objectives that involve religious apocalypticism (belief in the end of the world) and suggest that a more satisfying spiritual future will follow once their immediate goals of strict, Sunni-type Islamisation, enabled by mass violence and the use of fear as a currency, have been implemented. These groups subscribe to religious and calendrical symbolism to underscore their metaphysical beliefs about reality. Al Qaeda's detonation of ten bombs inside the Atocha train station in Madrid, Spain, killed 191 people and injured about 1,500 others. The attack occurred on March 11, 2004, exactly 911 days after the 9/11 attacks in the United States; this timing was deliberate and symbolic. Several other attacks involving individuals inspired by Islamist millenarianism have occurred since that time (Figure 11.1). The issue for ethnography becomes how to study terrorism without con-tributing to or strengthening ethnocentric biases, such as Islamophobia, that ultimately lead to dead ends in solving the crisis. Islamophobia is itself a form of state persecution in Myanmar, where one million Rohingya (minority Muslims probably originating in east-ern India) along the coast of the country are required to prove their families have lived in Myanmar for more than 60 years to be considered second-class citizens only, or be sent to detention camps and deported to neighbouring Bangladesh; on both sides of the Myanmar/Bangladesh border, Rohingya live in wretched refugee camps.

Ethnographers are uniquely positioned to study the beliefs of terrorists because, how-ever alien these might seem to Western perspectives, they are deemed to be palatable or even reasonable to their adherents. To do so, one has to examine the people who are allied to terrorist groups as scientifically as possible and try to envision the object of study using one's cultural relativism; otherwise, the object's cause and motive cannot ever be understood, and therefore cannot be disabled. Ethnographer Scott Atran has actually

Figure 11.1 The slogan '*Je suis Charlie*' ('I am Charlie') was widely seen and heard in France and numerous other Western countries by millions of people shocked by the brazen murder on 7 January 2015 of 12 people at the Paris weekly *Charlie Hebdo* by Islamist terrorists, purportedly because the magazine published satirical portraits of the Prophet Muhammad.

studied suicide terrorists (after the fact, or at a distance, in multisited venues). He has interviewed members of their families in diverse Middle Eastern locales and has found that several of them believe in noninstrumental value: that is, instead of valuing pragmatic things like health, money and love, the stuff that is important to them is not material, but spiritual and otherwordly. Several of them, according to Atran, have been well educated, were well off financially and came from traditionally well-respected families before they committed suicide. They were not 'lone wolves' or otherwise insane, but rather deliberate and calculating in their self-destruction (and in their murder of others). They see themselves as weapons of sacred power rather than as sacrificial victims of mindless terrorism. Atran's work proves that it takes cultural anthropology with its ethnographic toolkit to fully understand campaigns of fear, genocide and terrorism and what motivates their followers and activists.

On the other hand, embedding ethnographers on military assignments is a specific example of what a few anthropologists have called *security anthropology*, and it does not tend to promise growth of knowledge in the field. I question whether it's anthropology at all. Some ethnographers focus on issues related to immigration, policing, border control and counterterrorism; that does not mean they are engaged in servicing an interested client who is paying for information on these matters. In light of policing that has resulted in extrajudicial deaths of minority citizens, applied anthropologist Nolan Kline argues that applied anthropology can recommend the end of programmes that supply military armaments to municipal police forces; refrain from bringing tanks to suppress peaceful demonstrators (what he calls 'asymmetrical warfare on activists'); take note that police activities that affect minorities have implications on the entire population; and promote activism of all groups that have been subjected to undue police violence, including LGBTQ (lesbian, gay, bisexual, trans, queer) persons as well as African Americans and Latinos. These are positive suggestions based on real ethnography.

What Is More Anthropological, *Occupy* or *Business*?

Anthropologists have been involved in leading the global justice movement (concerned with levelling vast disparities of income between the Global South and the rest of the world as well as closing the gap between the vastly wealthy and the miserably poor). Some of them subscribe to the political philosophy known as *anarchy*. Meaning 'no government', anarchy is a movement designed to level socioeconomic differences worldwide by elimination of the state, and all states. Some have become prominent in the media, including David Graeber, now an anthropology professor at the London School of Economics, who in 2006 was interviewed by Charlie Rose on PBS.

Anthropologists have participated in or even led the protest of several international economic events, such as the World Trade Organization meetings in 1999 in Seattle, the 3rd Summit of the Americas in Quebec in 2001, the 2002 World Economic Forum in New York and in the Occupy Wall Street movement of 2011 also in New York and several other US cities (Figure 11.2). On the other side of the coin, cultural anthropologists have been employed in organisations—this work is sometimes called *organisational anthropology*—both in the nonprofit sector and others of the business world. The conflicts of interest between professional ethics (from the AAA statement on ethics) and delivery of

Figure 11.2 Occupy Wall Street, an anarchy movement, in New York City, 12 November 2011. Shutterstock Images.

a product ordered by a business client can and do occur in business anthropology, according to business anthropologists Rita Denny and Patricia Sunderland. At the same time, as they note, there is increasing interest in global financial communities to have 'Chief Culture Officers' also located in the C-suite (that is, top corporate management offices, such as those of Chief Executive Officer, Chief Financial Officer, Chief of Intelligence Technology). That is because the biggest firms typically have principal offices in diverse urban locales, such as New York, Hong Kong, Tokyo, Frankfurt and London, and smaller offices elsewhere such as Rio de Janeiro, Moscow, Beijing and New Delhi. The employees are drawn from diverse languages and cultures; business anthropologists are trained to deal with cultural similarities and differences (most of them are trained primarily in cultural anthropology). Business anthropologist Patricia Ensworth points out that anthropological skills can be used in the business workplace where people speak 'native languages' of corporate culture, which anthropologists are uniquely prepared to decode and differentiate. In the study of business anthropology, Patricia Ensworth notes that Trobriand economics as described by Malinowski serves as a model for 'cultural analysis of high-tech' kinds of enterprise concerned with investment banking; equity, commodity and currency trading; and traffic in mortgages, interest rates and bonds.

Prospects for Applied Anthropology in a Globalised World

Cultural anthropologists are well placed to evaluate corporate and state policies and programmes that affect peoples and landscapes around the world. Contemporary issues such as food security, ecological restoration, transnationalism and refugee studies are all topics to which applied anthropology can contribute. Because anthropological data are drawn from participant observation on a local level, ethnographers can evaluate and explain how events, policies and decisions made on a state or global level will influence the lives of peoples as diverse as the Maya, the Nuer and the Nayar. Once studied as communities or tribes in remote locations, members of these societies now live transnational lives that connect traditional landscapes to a technologically linked globalised world where they are often minorities (Chapter 12). Here we examine some of the fields in which applied anthropologists are most active: medical anthropology, especially HIV/AIDS education and prevention programmes; food policy; ethnotourism; and the formation of indigenous cooperatives.

Medical Applications

Medical anthropologists have been key in addressing relationships of biological syndromes and diseases with political and socioeconomic conditions. Medical anthropologists have pointed to inequality in access to healthcare by minorities with limited access to healthcare as responsible for high mortality rates from COVID-19 in 2020, such as people of the Navajo Nation in the Four Corners area of the United States. Low-income people in high-density cities have also been susceptible (Figure 11.3) Ethnographer Lisa Hardy noted a connection between the anti-racism demonstrations and protests in the United States and elsewhere and COVID-19 during 2020, in terms of inequality and racialisation of minorities:

> Those living with racisms of multi-generational and present oppression, ongoing settler colonialism, and the violence of immigration policing are most at risk for serious

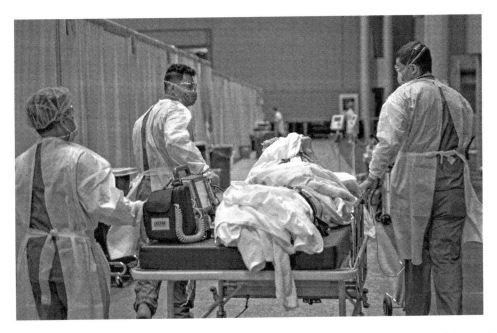

Figure 11.3 US Army members transport COVID-19 patient to the ICU at Javits New York Medical Station in New York City in 2020. Alamy.

impacts including death [from COVID-19]. It is therefore not surprising that people rose up after police killed Breonna Taylor and George Floyd, with and in support of the Black Lives Matter (BLM) movement against the violence of policing—another symptom of extreme and growing inequality.

(Hardy 2020, p. 3)

Hardy led a team of researchers that conducted structured interviews with 50 adult respondents concerning the COVID-19 pandemic. They concluded that:

Understandings of the biology of a virus are woven into perceptions of politics, inequality, and the fractures of a divided nation. To understand social and political responses to the global pandemic it is essential that we continue to investigate xenophobia, inequality and racism alongside the biological impact of SARS-CoV-2.

(Hardy 2020, p. 1)

To some extent, medical anthropologists have noted vulnerability to the pandemic is compounded by the fact that some people who do not have time off from their jobs (sanitation workers, domestic workers, gardeners, grocery store clerks, nannies) or who are otherwise more exposed to infection in their daily life are often identified by poverty, racialisation and gender status. Medical anthropologists have also studied the relationship of COVID-19 (and other diseases) to ordinary cultural behaviours. Quarantine behaviour, border control and ways of adhering to handwashing and mask-using vary culturally, even as the disease spreads exponentially with millions already dead on the planet, and for many, these behaviours are different if not new. Classroom and conference meetings have become virtual; virtual reality is different from in-person contact and can be understood with tools of an emerging field of study called digital ethnography. South African ethnographers Lenore Manderson and Susan Levine pointed out in the middle of the pandemic that

> People are bumping elbows instead of hugging, kissing or shaking hands...University systems, museums, and theaters everywhere are shutting down; increasingly, it seems, *entire cities* are doing so.
>
> (Manderson and Levine 2020, p. 358)

With cities closing and people losing jobs, insurance and even their living quarters because they cannot pay the rent or mortgage, those who cannot quarantine remain at risk of infection and often severe consequences caused by COVID-19 until acquired (or herd) immunity via vaccination is achieved. Understanding the relationship between society, culture and disease is the principal aim of medical anthropology and its applications.

Anthropologists have long had a contribution to make to improving health conditions in developing countries, most of which for historical reasons are in the tropical regions of the world—often today called the Global South—where they navigate between medical science and native concepts of illness. Anthropologist and physician Paul Farmer, for example, has connected poverty and HIV/AIDS in Haiti to political inequalities and economic development that make it difficult for subsistence farmers and their families to survive without moving to cities or engaging in behaviours that put them at risk of infection. He has shown how individual health is linked to international economic policy.

Applied anthropologists have been widely involved in HIV/AIDS education and prevention projects throughout Africa that have great potential to improve the health of poor people (Cultural Snapshot 11.2). In 2007, sub-Saharan Africa accounted for 67 per cent of all people with HIV and 72 per cent of all deaths from AIDS in the world. A recent issue of the journal *Practicing Anthropology*, for example, featured accounts by applied anthropologists on the AIDS epidemic in Africa. Among the projects discussed were attempts to educate at-risk women in monogamous relationships, recruitment and retention of local health workers, evaluation of the abstinence model in Zimbabwe and ways to improve peer-education programmes and strengthen existing healthcare systems.

Another important direction in medical anthropology of the HIV/AIDS epidemic involves the ethnographic concept of *biological citizenship*. In Africa, medical anthropologists Nadine Beckmann and Janet Bujra have shown that nongovernmental support groups called People Living with HIV and AIDS (PLHA) take the cause of people and their families affected by HIV/AIDS in several countries, such as Tanzania, to the centre stage of politics in the world arena. Their research shows that traditional family and social support networks break down under the weight of HIV/AIDS because of the high cost of caring for the sick individual or several sick individuals—which is often the case—in the same family. Biological citizenship is an attempt to form coherent support groups in light of the ravages of the HIV/ AIDS epidemic that can petition global networks of medical and pharmaceutical concerns for better access by Africans to antiretroviral therapies as the epidemic continues to exhibit global health and economic implications. Biological citizenship in a sense links together people as if they were members of the same ethnic group, sharing a point of origin, common ancestry and mutual interests:

what they share, of course, is not necessarily language and culture, but a similar stratum in the world system of today, one defined by chronic and costly epidemic disease. Much of the mortality in the recent Ebola epidemic can be attributed to poverty and lack of health infrastructure, according to medical anthropologist and physician Paul Farmer (see Cultural Snapshot 11.1).

While many applied medical anthropologists work on HIV/AIDS, there is work to be done on many other diseases, on patient–provider interactions, on health education and on the structure of healthcare systems. One emerging issue in many countries with high rates of immigration is how to resolve potential conflicts between Western biomedicine and traditional beliefs about healthcare and illness. Negotiating this divide presents anthropologists with fieldwork opportunities in their own towns and cities.

Applied anthropology can also contribute to health education for people who, because of cultural and economic barriers, do not have adequate information on disease causes and incidence. Such populations are usually disadvantaged minorities. For example, cervical cancer rates and mortality are much higher in Latina women than in non-Latina white women in the United States. The primary cause of cervical cancer is human papillomavirus (HPV) infection, which can be prevented through vaccination. Applied anthropologist John Luque and his colleagues have demonstrated recently that Latinas, in comparison with non-Latina white women, are much less likely to know that HPV causes cervical cancer and of the available vaccine. They are less likely to get screened for cervical cancer and, when diagnosed, they are more likely to be in the advanced stages of the disease. Related to the increased rates of cancer and mortality is the fact that Latinas are less likely to have health insurance and more likely to lack a primary healthcare provider. The goal of Luque and colleagues is to design a health education module to inform vulnerable Latina women about HPV and the available vaccine.

Applied anthropology has also helped supply information to women in abusive domestic situations. For example, domestic violence around the world is associated with higher rates of sexually transmitted infections. Anthropologists have contributed to the effort to educate disadvantaged women—and their partners—on this topic. They have also developed programmes to educate people on sex, gender and sexuality and promoted gender equality.

CULTURAL SNAPSHOT 11.1

Ethnography of VHFs and Hotspots

Ebola is one of several viral haemorrhagic fevers (VHFs); others are Marburg and Lassa fevers. The cause of Ebola is a filovirus; it consists of a short strand of RNA with seven genes coding for eight proteins. First described in 1976 in equatorial Africa, its symptoms involve the acute onset of fatigue, fever and diarrhoea. Late symptoms include pain or inability to swallow food or fluids, lack of appetite, hiccoughs, shock and intense bleeding (haemorrhaging) from the nose, vagina, mouth and eyes. The disease occurs when the virus enters the mouth, open wounds and the mucous membranes (*conjunctiva*) around the surface of the eye (an early indicator is conjunctivitis); the virus then spreads into the lymphatic and vascular systems, ultimately targeting the inner surfaces of blood vessels. Late-stage patients and recently deceased patients are still shedding the virus and are very contagious; many people get the disease from preparing corpses for burial. A sharp outbreak occurred in Liberia and quickly spread to Guinea and Sierra Leone in early 2014; several cases were reported elsewhere in the world around that time, including a few in the United States, of individuals who had travelled to West Africa. According to medical anthropologist and physician Paul Farmer, a third of all Ebola cases ever known had been registered in the month of September 2014 alone. Between 1 March 2014 and 1 October 2014, more than 3,500 people had died from Ebola; mortality was about 50 per cent. Farmer argues that the reason mortality was so high, especially in Africa, is because of poverty and lack of adequate healthcare infrastructure. The epidemic was contained in the United States because, according to Farmer, the United States 'has the staff, stuff, space and systems' to deal with it, whereas Africa does not. In July 2015, The World Health Organization announced a vaccine for Ebola that appears to be 100 per cent effective. It is still important to understand the local context of epidemic disease whether vaccines exist or not, and this understanding is partly based on anthropological work. Ethnographers are trying to pinpoint the complex interplay of social and biological factors involved in the transmission not only of Ebola but also of other VHFs. Medical anthropologists Hanna Brown and Ann Kelly suggest the need to identify what they call hotspots:

> The hotspot speaks to the temporary convergence of rainfall, political designs, cat populations, armed conflict, economic strategies, agricultural techniques, built environments, and practices of care that create the conditions for disease. The hotspot…remains anchored by an ethnographic preoccupation with the intimate textures of transmission.
>
> (2014, pp. 281–282)

Ethnographers are uniquely equipped to study temporary field convergences of diverse factors associated with disease because of their long-term familiarity with the field.

Food Security and Overnutrition

Anthropologists have long been interested in issues of subsistence and food production. Today, they are contributing to national and international policies on food security, a question of critical concern worldwide (Figure 11.4). Applied anthropologists have evaluated the effects of the Green Revolution, which sought to increase food production in poor countries by providing high-yield crops and new technologies, often at a high price. Today, applied anthropologists study the potential of genetically modified organisms (GMOs) to solve world hunger and food insecurity. With a billion people going hungry every day, these are hugely important questions. Anthropologists also investigate how government policies and practices related to the distribution of food aid can help resolve social problems linked to hunger and poverty (Cultural Snapshot 11.2).

Figure 11.4 Woman processing rice in Madagascar, a poor country with food insecurity. Alamy.

CULTURAL SNAPSHOT 11.2

'Food Insecurity Is a Disaster in Its Own Right'

Applied anthropologists have contributed to a better understanding of the food security issues that confront the poorest people in the world. About one billion people (out of a world population of almost eight billion) go hungry every day (Chapter 8); most live in very poor countries. Applied anthropologists Pauline Gwatirisa and Lenore Manderson did research among Shona–speaking people in urban Zimbabwe, Africa, one of the poorest countries in the world. Their ethnographic research identified a relationship between poverty, the prevalence of HIV/AIDS and food insecurity.

Food security means 'access by all peoples at all times to sufficient food for an active, healthy life' (World Bank 1986 in Gwatirisa and Manderson 2009, p. 105). In food security terms, Zimbabwe is a disaster, since at least half of the population requires food aid. Organisations such as the Food Security Network and the World Food Program supply some of this aid, which the government distributes. But it is not enough, given the combined effects of droughts and crop failures, political and economic instability, land degradation, farmers' deaths from HIV/AIDS, outmigration, urban unemployment and hyperinflation.

HIV/AIDS is called *mukondombera* ('wipes out') in Shona. Tragically, 21 per cent of Zimbabweans are infected with HIV; 3,000 of them die of AIDS every week. Gwatirisa and Manderson found that families caring for relatives with HIV/AIDS face the most difficult challenges. Ironically, some of the neediest people are those who have family members earning a government salary, which disqualifies them from receiving aid. Due to inflation, many Zimbabweans cannot afford antiretroviral drugs (ARVs). When they can, they have less money for food. Yet sufficient food is as critical as ARV therapy to health and wellbeing. Lack of food exacerbates the condition of HIV/AIDS patients and increases their susceptibility—and that of other family members—to other diseases and increases mortality rates of everyone. As Gwatirisa and Manderson point out, 'Food insecurity is a disaster in its own right'.

Overnutrition, a phenomenon related to the global obesity epidemic, is a different, yet related subject of study. More than 300 million people are obese, of which more than one-third are in the developing world. The human body essentially is programmed to store food energy, a trait that was selected for in hominin evolution because food supply was less predictable in the past than it is in countries using agricultural technology today. For most of modern human history, the production and consumption of food were about equal. But today, food is abundant in fully industrialised, capitalistic societies and in some rapidly developing ones; people in many of these contexts have access to much more food than they need to survive. At the same time, physical activity levels have dropped. Global obesity is further complicated by the fact that many societies and the poorest classes in modern states are adopting low-quality, high-energy foods as they abandon higher-quality traditional subsistence foods. Many people in that category of obesity, substandard nutrition, and poverty have been among the more susceptible persons to exhibit symptoms resulting in hospitalization, ventilation (if it's even available) and death from the COVID-19 virus during the pandemic of 2020/21. Applied anthropologists have examined cultural differences in food and physical activity to better understand the local causes and consequences of the global obesity epidemic.

Demystifying Ethnicity and Ethnotourism

Applied anthropologists have critiqued *ethnotourism*, in which tourists visit natives in their own villages or communities, as a venue that puts primitivism on display and exhibits native people as exotic others. This has occurred since the 1990s in the Kalahari Desert of southern Africa among many Ju/'hoansi groups, some of whom have marketed themselves to tourists as primordial, simple, unacculturated foraging people. Cultural anthropologist Eric Wolf points out that 'pristine primitives' simply do not exist. Applied anthropologists have sought to demonstrate the value in culture as it actually is, not through misrepresentation to generate fast, though not necessarily reliable, income. Despite some temporary economic benefits, ethnotourism may actually exacerbate inequalities among native people by favouring those who market themselves to outsiders most effectively. Actually, ethnotourism itself is not problematic from the perspective of most applied anthropologists; it is, rather, the idea of appealing to Euro-American concepts of primitiveness, alterity and exoticness that can sometimes harm rather than help local communities.

Ethnotourism may form a significant proportion of the gross domestic product in some less developed countries (Figure 11.5). The industry is associated with the global expansion of the anthropological concept of culture and of the economic benefits that

Figure 11.5 Tourist with a backpack follows Ju'/hoan people walking along a trail in Namibia, Africa. Ethnotourism, like ecotourism, is a phenomenon of the most recent version of the world system. Shutterstock Images.

can accrue to those who market that concept. Primitiveness, however imaginary, is very marketable: it sells. In the Peruvian Amazon, environmental service-sector professionals have asked native peoples such as the Ese Eja Indians to 'reinvent' their past and appear to be more 'connected' to nature and tradition than they actually are. The idea is that tourists want to see 'authentic' natives and experience what they believe to be traditional life. In fact, such cultural performances deny who the Ese Eja really are, presenting them as 'living fossils' when in reality they live in a 'posttraditional' community as part of a globalised socioeconomic system. Most people in Amazonia today live in and around cities; they are not forest-dwelling foragers or horticulturalists any longer, but people who wear jeans and t-shirts, speak Portuguese or Spanish and go to school and work for wages. Anthropologists are in a unique position to describe this reality rather than mystify it.

Aiding Cooperatives

The twenty-first-century anthropologist can no longer engage in long-term participant observation as Malinowski did a century ago. Today, anthropologists must return something valuable to the community or society studied. Often, they provide advocacy of some sort of assistance in bringing the needs of local peoples to the attention of government officials. Although not their full-time occupation, this is a critically important aspect of applied anthropology. Major issues of concern to many indigenous and peasant people today include environmental degradation, crop failures and loss of forest resources and biodiversity in general. Anthropologists can contribute to the description and critical analysis of such problems and provide recommendations on how to mitigate the impact of activities such as mining, logging, oil development and dam construction. They can also be active both inside and outside of NGOs working on indigenous rights and conservation of lands inhabited by indigenous people. Many anthropologists are employed today by leading environmental organisations such as the World Wildlife Fund (WWF), The Nature Conservancy (TNC) and Conservation International (CI) that seek to protect biodiversity and maintain healthy ecosystems.

The potential for conflict of interest often exists in such situations, as with anthropological research more generally, as noted in the AAA Statement on Ethics. TNC was recently criticised for obtaining revenue from oil and gas drilling on lands that are supposed to have been protected from exploitation and degradation. According to applied anthropologist Mac Chapin, the largest environmental NGOs have from time to time received funds from corporations and governments that did not always favour the rights of indigenous peoples. Ethnographers inside such organisations could be in a position to help mitigate such conflicts of interest and to promote indigenous rights, especially when these potentially have the additional effect of expediting the conservation of plants, animals and species-rich landscapes.

Beginning in the 1960s, several indigenous groups in Latin America began to form cooperatives—small nonprofit corporations and associations with legal recognition—for the purpose of defending their rights to their land, language and indigenous culture. The Shuar Federation of eastern Ecuador in the Amazon lowlands was the first such cooperative, and it serves as a prototype for the others. It was formed to defend land rights and preserve cultural heritage. Similarly, several indigenous groups of Amazonia, such as the Ka'apor of Brazil and the Sirionó of Bolivia, have recently formed nonprofit corporations for the express purpose of protecting their cultural heritage and the biodiversity of their landscapes. In 2003, I was involved in helping the Ka'apor form their organisation, which was designed to protect their lands from outside intrusions and to preserve culture and language. These nonprofit organisations, much like cooperatives of many rural farming societies in the world today, seek to apply the advantages of corporate organisation, such as revenues in a common fund, to the protection of ancient forms of social and political organisation.

Rural cooperatives have members who increasingly are affected by the same kinds of economic, political and social forces that affect people in cities. Many people formerly classified as peasants move back and forth from farms to the city and find employment in different kinds of jobs, including commercial agriculture or manufacturing. They have been called *peasantworkers* or *worker-peasants*.

Despite the many similarities between peasant and indigenous cooperatives, a major difference exists in their internal social organisation. Lowland Amazonian societies have traditionally been egalitarian and concerned with local environmental issues; their nonprofits are communal, and participants identify themselves with an indigenous ethnic group. In contrast, rural cooperatives associated with peasantries often speak a national language, such as Spanish, Portuguese, Chinese, Malay or English, and are partially or fully invested in the global capitalist system. They need to sell the products of their labour to meet subsistence requirements. In addition, rural cooperatives are often divided into classes of rich and poor. Some of them own land, resources and technology, whereas others do not. As peasants, many rent the land of others richer than themselves.

Cooperatives are a remarkable phenomenon, for as their members change—opening bank accounts, learning to navigate complex financial systems, engaging with people who speak other languages and live other lives—they become better able to protect their traditional lands and heritage. Sometimes, individual indigenous and peasant peoples are involved in multiple cooperatives. For example, the Kaxinawa Indians of western Brazil formed a partnership with conservation biologists to monitor and protect wildlife diversity in their forested habitat. In the course of this collaboration, they trained their own indigenous agroforestry agents, who joined a cooperative linking all indigenous agroforestry agents in the region.

Indigenous cooperatives are important in protecting species diversity because traditional ecological knowledge, or TEK, often contains information unknown to conservationists, ecologists and environmental managers. The Huna Tlingit people of southeastern Alaska know how to manage glaucous-winged gull nests and eggs sustainably. The eggs form part of their traditional diet. According to ethnobiologist and applied anthropologist Eugene Hunn and his colleagues, Huna Tlingit traditionally harvested eggs without causing a depletion of the gull population because they have a traditional rule to not collect eggs from any nests with three or more eggs. Three eggs are needed for embryo formation; three eggs are also the modal clutch size. Instead, they harvest nests with only one or two eggs. This knowledge, and many other TEK systems like it worldwide, shows that the ecological knowledge of traditional people (i.e., rural peasantries or indigenous societies) can support biodiversity. The key to preserving that knowledge is in strengthening the cooperatives. The short-term future of biodiversity on much of the planet, in fact, is likely tied to the resilience and continuity of indigenous and traditional cooperatives.

Many cooperatives stress improved access to education for the people they represent. As a result of efforts by cooperatives, governments and other NGOs, indigenous intellectuals are emerging in various parts of the world. These university-educated native people may work as journalists, lawyers and social activists, promoting the interests of their local communities. For example, in Malaysia, several cooperatives for indigenous people, known as Orang Asli, exist. Many Orang Asli people live in poverty, though a few Orang Asli groups now have a few of their own professionals, including businesspeople, physicians, engineers, economists and even anthropologists, whose numbers are expected to increase in the coming years, according to Malaysian anthropologist Razha Rashid. Cooperatives and their members challenge traditional state-level control and organisation. Their structure, development and effects are an area of ethnographic study surfacing now in an increasingly globalised world.

Summary

Applied anthropology—the fifth field—developed in the context of cultural anthropology after World War II. Applied anthropology involves practical use of anthropological data and often facilitates change to local cultures. Applied military anthropology, in particular, has been the subject of controversy. More anthropologists today work in applied fields than in any other. Subjects of particular interest to applied anthropologists are health and disease, food security, ethnotourism and indigenous economic cooperatives.

Further Reading

Agar and Reisinger 2003; Atran 2003; Balée 1979, 2003; BBC 2019; Beckmann and Bujra 2010; Bentley et al. 2010; Bourdieu 1985; Brondizio 2008; Chapin 2004; Churchill and Nelson 2009; Constantino et al. 2008; Crewe and Harrison 1998; Doughty 2002; Denny and Sunderland 2014; Ensworth 2014;

Feldman 2009; 'False Start' 2019; Field and Fox 2007; Foley 2007; Frank 2007; Freidenberg 2011; Fuentes 2011; Gardner and Lewis 1996 (pp. 30, 32); Gillis 2014; González 2009; González et al. 2009; Graves 2001; Hardy 2020; Henig 2014; Henley 2006; Himmelgreen and Crooks 2005; Hinsley 1999 (pp. 183–184); Hinton 2010; Hunn et al. 2003; Kearney 1996; Kidder 2004; Kline 2015; Low and Smart 2020 ; Luque et al. 2010; Maguire et al. 2014; Manderson and Levine 2020 ; Low 2020 ; Manganas 2010; Marcus 1995; Maynard-Tucker 2008; Mead 2008; Millen 2008; Nolan 2003; Pels and Salemink 1999; Peluso and Alexiades 2005; Perlez 2014; Petryna 2002; Pink 2006 (pp. 6–7); Rafail 2014; Rappaport 2007; Rashid 1995; Robben 2010a; Rödlach 2006; Rohde 2007; Rose 2006; Ruby 2000; Stavenhagen 1997; Sylvain 2005; Tomas 1991 (pp. 97–100); Touissaint 2007; Tusan 2014; Van Willigen 1993; Weinberger 2008; Wolf 1997; Wolf and Jorgenson 1970; Zubay et al. 2005

Cultural Snapshots

11.1   Brown and Kelly 2014; Farmer 2014; Puskoor and Zubay 2005
11.2   Gwatirisa and Manderson 2009

12 Globalisation and Indigeneity

Overview

In the past, cultural anthropologists tended to focus on small communities in foreign countries, gather the ethnographic facts and then extrapolate from these to write about humanity in general. Such writing often took the form of debunking false doctrines of human nature (Cultural Snapshot 4.3) based on one or more supposed universals. Cultural anthropologists were the first scholars who actually took the time to learn indigenous languages, study traditional cultures in the field and carry out participant observation with empathy for their subjects. In other words, they were the first outsiders to try to understand culture, in a professional way, from the natives' point of view. They were the first to get inside cultures authentically.

Today, much ethnography has to be *multisited* because the people studied by cultural anthropologists are on the move, thanks to globalisation. In this chapter, we look at globalisation and its effects on non-state societies, local traditions and associated languages. We will examine the emerging concept of *indigeneity*, which refers to a special kind of ethnicity, one that includes a belief in aboriginality or a primordial association with a place or region. Finally, we assess the prospects for understanding the processes of global change and indigeneity in the twenty-first century.

Globalisation

Throughout this book, we have talked about cultures in terms of the spaces they occupy: the Nuer herding cattle in the pastures of southern Sudan, the Ka'apor and Guajá hunting amid the tropical forests of eastern Amazonia. The Mardu of the Western Desert of Australia and the Ju/'hoansi of the Kalahari are conceptualised in terms of their desert camps, rock art and sophisticated ecological knowledge. Even though cultures such as these have been affected by hundreds of years of colonialism, they have still been traditionally viewed in terms of *place*.

Cultural anthropologists went off to study them, coming back to the Western world to write ethnographies. That time is now past. Natives can no longer simply be 'objects' of study in some exotic land-, sea- or snowscape. *Globalisation* is the twenty-first-century reality that anthropologists must engage with. Globalisation is the postmodern world economic system that collapses cultural barriers through rapid, long-distance migrations of peoples; instantaneous cross-cultural and cross-linguistic communication via the internet and other digital technologies; and erasure of cultural differences and ethnic boundaries thanks to accelerated rates of diffusion. Globalisation involves the expansion of international trade, transfers of capital across national boundaries, the migration of millions of people, the spread of invasive species and the near-instantaneous transmission of language and ideas through electronic media. Globalisation is not entirely new—it is part of a process initiated in the 1500s with European expansion—but its twenty-first-century form is unprecedented, in part because of new transportation and information technologies. Globalisation is part of the reason that cultural traditions of small-scale egalitarian societies around the world have disappeared at a speed never before seen in history. It is also partly the reason that citizens of wealthy Western nations are seeing many of the people who carry these same cultural traits and traditions up close, in their midst, for the first time.

Earlier Kinds of Globalisation?

Hohn and Sorensen originally defined globalisation as 'the intensification of economic, political, social and cultural relations across borders' (1995, p. 1). In that sense, globalisation has been occurring ever since people from different societies have been in contact with each other. But *globalisation* as I use the term here is much more than an intensification of relations at any time in history: it denotes a qualitatively distinctive kind of world system that has come into being early in the twenty-first century. Globalisation involves international connections on a diminished scale of time and space never before known. In that sense, I agree with Hohn and Sorensen's definition of globalisation but would limit the term to referring to the world system of the current century.

Certainly, earlier kinds of global connections involving humans existed, starting with the Pleistocene migration of hominins out of Africa to Europe and Asia (Chapter 1) more than one million years ago. Much later in the Near East, around 11,000 years ago, hunters and gatherers who had been harvesting wild wheat began *planting* domesticated wheat. This transformation in subsistence was the beginning of agriculture: the cultivation of domesticated plants. Agriculture expanded rapidly to the rest of western Asia, Africa and Europe. It also arose and spread quickly in South America, Mesoamerica and East Asia. For agriculture to advance across the globe, people had to not only adopt the idea of domestication but also become adept with working in new technologies for cultivating, weeding, harvesting, processing and storing foods.

With agricultural surpluses, populations increased between 11,000 and 9,000 years ago. By about 10,000 years ago, people began domesticating animals such as cattle, goats and sheep in Eurasia. *Domestication* is the process whereby a wild species loses its ability to reproduce autonomously due to changes in its genome induced by humans through artificial selection. Agriculture and animal domestication allowed people to settle down and establish villages. This *sedentary*, or settled, agricultural lifestyle soon spread westwards into Europe and eastwards into Asia. The expanding farming populations brought new languages with them and came into contact with existing hunters and gatherers in what may have been the first world system on the planet. Societies separated by thousands of miles became linked through a shared economic and trade system despite their diverse languages and cultural practices. The initial European world system was made possible by agriculture, which supported much larger populations than hunting and gathering.

Another kind of world system occurred after states and empires arose. The Roman Empire (Chapter 10)—the core of such a world system—had control over the Mediterranean and Europe and connections far south into Africa and far east to India. Before the end of the Roman Empire in the fifth century AD (Chapter 10), people as far away as the Rufiji River Basin in Tanzania, East Africa, had trade contact with the Mediterranean. A Roman garrison had been located since about AD 290 near present-day Aswan, Egypt, somewhat downstream from the Nuer people of today. Roman contacts, established through commercial exchanges of exotic and valuable commodities such as gold, pottery and livestock, extended south into present-day Mozambique, perhaps to gain access to elephant ivory. The Romans also maintained long-distance trade with India between 200 BC and AD 400, exchanging iron goods and textiles for spices, exotic wood, ivory, precious stones, pearls, silk and pottery.

After AD 1400, a new or modern world system arose on the European continent. Its overseas connections were more durable and intense than those of the Roman Empire. As we saw in Chapter 9, at the conclusion of the Middle Ages, the colonial world system, which consisted of a European core and a series of European colonies in Africa, Australasia and the Americas, called the *periphery*, developed and lasted up until the mid-twentieth century. The basic idea of the modern world system is that the European core extracted raw materials from the periphery. These raw materials included gold and silver to mint coinage, pay workers and finance capital projects; furs for winter clothing; spices and sweets, such as sugar, coffee and chocolate, for the elite; and slaves, initially from the Americas but later from Africa, for work on sugar, coffee, and cotton plantations. This was the era of colonialism.

Some would argue that what is called globalisation today is just another version of the European-dominated world system, a continuation of the colonial period into the twenty-first century. Others, myself included, would argue that the colonial world system was followed by a transitional postcolonial or neocolonial world system. This system developed after World War II and pitted the rich countries of Europe, North America and Japan against the poor developing countries of South America, Africa and Southeast Asia. It also included the period of the Cold War of the West and Soviet communism with proxy wars mostly in the Global South. Globalisation—the development of a twenty-first-century world system—soon followed.

With each change in the world system, one can detect the increased importance of communication in reducing the conceptual and communicative distance among cultures, languages and peoples. This condensation of cultural and linguistic differences is expressed in the concept of the 'global village', built around the notion of the expansion of television in the 1960s. None of the mid-twentieth-century innovations in communication, however, came close to the revolutionary development of the internet and electronic media such as texting, Zoom, Skype and instant messaging. The velocity of global communications has been enhanced by the development of the microchip industry. Today, the chips powering microprocessors are a mere 7.5 nanometres wide, which is just three times the width of a strand of DNA. Before microchip technology, no one could imagine just how far the internet and information highway would take the planet and its population into instantaneous communication (Figure 12.1) and discourse on a global scale.

The Twenty-First Century

The colonial and postcolonial world systems that developed after the Middle Ages involved the transfer of commodities from the periphery to the *core*, or colonial centres of power. However, in a globalised economy, commodities, capital and people move rapidly back and forth across national boundaries. They are linked by all-purpose money and new kinds of money (Chapter 9) under the control of international financial corporations,

Figure 12.1 Cell phone towers help accelerate the transmission of information across great distances in real time. Shutterstock Images.

giant investment banks, mortgage holding companies, equity trading operations and other institutional features of the capitalism of our time. These corporations do not have roots in any one country, and most of the money they deal with is totally electronic. The people moving back and forth speak different languages, participate in different cultures and exhibit *cosmopolitanism*, or familiarity with multiple cultures and languages. Cosmopolitanism is a distinctive feature of globalisation: more and more people around the globe are bilingual or even multilingual to navigate the various economic and cultural conditions of contemporary life. That cosmopolitanism exists among people of many different social strata and ethnicities and reaches across formerly distinct societies and states.

Follow the Money

Money has now fully penetrated most of the even nonindustrial, acephalous, egalitarian societies. On the one hand, its form has changed from exclusively portable coinage or paper currency to partly electronic, with payments accomplished through data transferred via credit cards or completely contactless mobile payments that can be made with cell phones or other smart devices. According to the US Federal Reserve (the equivalent of a national bank), Americans owned around 511 million cards in 2020 for the purchase of diverse goods and services. A certain portion of purchases was used exclusively in e-commerce, where one does not make contact with another person and only handles one's credit card or mobile device to supply the number, the security code and the expiration date to complete a purchase. The mobile wallet, an app on one's smartphone or smartwatch (Figure 12.2) that features credit information permits one to make contactless purchases in many venues worldwide; money can be sent directly from one's bank

Figure 12.2 A man pays for an item with his smartwatch. Shutterstock Images.

account to others via apps that have mobile payments (as with Venmo or PayPal). To make purchases with the mobile wallet, you merely wave your phone before an appropriately prepared online terminal; the barcode on the phone will be read and if your credit is good, the purchase will be made. Cash is still used, but physical money is often not needed for purchases anymore, and in many cases will play no part in a transaction. The globalised world is increasingly using money in cashless form in part because of the COVID-19 pandemic; people are avoiding touching anything that might increase their chances of infection—real or perceived—and have been using contactless cards to make payments online or over readers more frequently in 2020—before there were any vaccines available-- than ever before. It is unclear how much the behaviors changed by the COVID-19 pandemic, including contactless exchanges of all kinds, will persist after the pandemic ends. These are changes regardless that make the modern world system different from globalisation.

In the era of globalisation, money's anonymity—its impersonal quality—can be increasingly disguised, as in the blockchain (or distributed ledger) of cryptocurrency like bitcoin (though not with credit cards). Often in the past, the use of money has been masked for reasons related to shame, taste and magic. The Japanese traditionally envelop gift money inside paper because it is considered poor taste to quantify—express as a numerical value—a gift. Americans often do the same. The custom of wrapping gifts in the United States did not start until the 1930s with the onset of the Great Depression. Wrapping gifts is a way of concealing one's poverty, covering up the shame of the giver for offering something perceived to be of little value.

The Nuer traditionally did not have money. They were a pastoral people dependent on cattle herds and sorghum crops. In the 1930s, Nuer bridewealth, which is the payment the groom's family makes to the bride's, normally consisted of 40 head of cattle (Chapter 6), according to pioneering ethnographer Evans-Pritchard. Recall that the proper marriage gift ideally involved the groom's family paying 20 head of cattle to the family of the father of the bride and 20 head to the family of the mother of the bride. More than 50 years later, ethnographer Sharon Hutchinson found that the Nuer, who had endured two civil wars as well as loss of tribal autonomy, still used cattle in bridewealth payments, but not exclusively. Under certain circumstances, cattle and money were mutually convertible, depending on whether the bride's father would accept money in lieu of cattle. Hutchinson discovered that money was not always considered an appropriate method of exchange because blood (from cattle) was thought to bind people together; money, lacking blood, could not. As noted in Chapter 9, money is not productive; it doesn't refer to anything other than itself. With the Nuer, money was not totally general or anonymous, as all-purpose money is supposed to be. In fact, for traditionally egalitarian societies, like the Ju/'hoansi, all-purpose money isn't convertible either—it took ethnographer Richard Lee 15 minutes to explain to a disappointed Ju/huan confidant who was expecting for services rendered a payment of £10—on a banknote that showed the insignia of '£10'— that the two £5 notes with which Lee was paying him amounted to the same *value* as £10. From the perspective of the Nuer groom, the value of his money depended on his prospective father-in-law, not on whether the monetary amount was correct or not.

Many idioms in Nuer culture create oppositions between livestock and people on the one hand and money on the other. Cattle and people have blood, unlike money. Cattle are warm; money is cold. Cattle are alive; money is lifeless. Money has no blood, milk, breath, awareness, name, temperament or history of exchange, in contrast to every cow or bull. An entire series of contrasts flows from this dualism of values between cattle and money in Nuer culture. Of course, all-purpose currency is supposed to be anonymous and impersonal. But that's part of the problem: people can't quite accept the coldness of the money in all exchanges, which is why the origins of coinage and currency are of interest to Nuer people. Regardless of the anonymity of all-purpose money, Nuer people are concerned about where it came from. In *following the money*, the Nuer ensure that it is no longer anonymous.

This aura of something being personal is especially true with regard to Nuer *shit money*. Shit money is money derived from sales of homebrew to local bars. People who worked in the bars handled bucket latrines to dispose of patrons' excrement. The Nuer considered the money received from bar owners to be contaminated and were wary of its use. According to Hutchinson, 'a cow bought with "shit money" cannot survive' (1996, p. 84); such cattle were prohibited from being used in bridewealth payments. On the island of Bali, money itself—the paper or the coinage—is considered sacred if it was controlled by a religious group involved in sharing water for rice irrigation, known as *subak*. Ethnographer Stephen Lansing observed that if one of the administrators used any cash from the subak's money to pay for a service, or if they lost money no matter how small the amount due, such as to a fine for not keeping irrigation canals clean, the funds must be restituted by the original bills themselves. It is not the amount that matters as much as the fact that the cash, however minimal, was considered sacred and could not be replaced by merely secular bills. Genuine all-purpose money—as well as digital money—lacks such an aura of spirituality, even if some mystery pertains to the nonmateriality of some money forms.

All-purpose money, along with political and economic developments and new technologies, facilitated the expansion of a widespread network of trade, culture, language and personal encounters. That network can be grasped in a visit to a shopping mall on any of the six continents. It is readily seen in the worldwide spread of high fashion in clothing and women's handbags, for instance, which begins on runways in New York, Paris, Milan and London, and is soon seen worldwide in designer boutiques like Louis Vuitton,

Michael Kors and Gucci (Figure 12.3). And it can be seen in more mundane settings such as fast-food chains, bottled soft drinks, packaged foods and many other items that are bought and sold daily around the world. Another aspect of globalisation is the movement of people themselves to new cultural situations where they live and work in close association with people who may not share their language, culture or sense of belonging to a particular place. Anthropologists Zuzana Búriková and Daniel Miller did participant observation with 50 *au pairs* (foreign babysitters and caregivers who reside in the homes of host families) in London in 2004. Slovaks from relatively disadvantaged backgrounds who became *au pairs* in London found that the white, inexpensive IKEA furniture from Scandinavia that decorates their rooms is more impersonal—cold—than the furniture in the host families' private rooms. Furniture, and other aspects of the material world to which the *au pair* is exposed in the new setting, reflects the distance to be maintained between the host family and the *au pair*. That is at least partly because the *au pair* is contracted for only a short time. The 'pseudo-family' relationship between the hosts and the *au pair* is designed to end in a set time period. The Slovaks and other Eastern Europeans who travel to the United Kingdom, Australia and the United States to provide childcare are an example of how culturally and linguistically cosmopolitan people are becoming due to globalisation.

The ease and lowered cost of air transportation, the breakdown of international restrictions on travel (the pandemic of 2020/2021 being an exception), the expansion of China's gargantuan economy to meet Western consumer demands and the massive refugee populations created by civil wars in Africa, Southeast Asia and the Americas

Figure 12.3 A young woman elegantly dressed in the latest high fashion, originating on runways and sold in shopping malls on six continents. Shutterstock Images.

have all contributed to new social and economic links that traverse national boundaries. Anthropological studies of border crossings and migrations fit under the rubric of multi-sited ethnography. Because of new technologies, instant electronic transmission of funds through global financial corporations is now possible, bypassing borders and expediting economic change in every corner of the world. Together, these factors have created a single global economy. It can be studied ethnographically in one place—a Ka'apor village, a Pashtun encampment in Afghanistan, or in Trafalgar Square—but often it involves research in more than one place, connected in intricate ways to other places, sometimes at great physical distances away.

Globalisation, however, did not appear overnight; it was facilitated by the post–World War II establishment of international organisations, such as the United Nations and its various agencies, including UNESCO (United Nations Educational, Scientific and Cultural Organization) and the United Nations Development Program (UNDP). After the end of the Cold War (1945–1991) and the demise of the Soviet bloc, international organisations that already existed served as an infrastructure for the early stages of globalisation. Institutions critical to the development of twenty-first-century globalisation include the World Bank, the International Monetary Fund (IMF), the World Trade Organization (WTO) and regional organisations, such as the European Union and the Association of Southeast Asian Nations (ASEAN). Multinational corporations lubricate world trade and the international division of labour, for example, by outsourcing textile manufacturing to China, Vietnam, Honduras and other countries. Due to labour demands, people are increasingly mobile and migratory, more so than ever before in human history. Their movements are enabled by email, the internet and mobile phones, which make our world smaller, more compact and significantly different from what it was only a generation ago.

As the latest world system, globalisation brings with it the highest degree of time/space compression yet known (Chapter 10). The globalised, cosmopolitan people who use these technologies, experience time and space in new ways and exist *between* states promise to be at the *centre* of ethnographic inquiry.

Globalisation and Cultural Anthropology

Globalisation requires cultural anthropology to adjust dramatically to new realities. Now more than ever, cultural anthropologists need to be prepared not only to examine traditional societies on the ground and in the field but also to study how they engage with the corporate structures that are part of the global economy (Cultural Snapshot 12.1). This kind of work has been called 'ethnography of the commodity chain', which involves looking for knowledge of a resource at its source, in the field, and tracing the export and manipulation of the resource across middlemen (economic agents between core and periphery) to final sale and consumption in world markets. To some extent, work of this sort is already carried out in applied anthropology. As discussed in Chapter 11, traditional foods and traditional ecological knowledge (TEK) are becoming commodities on the world market, according to cultural anthropologist Miguel Alexiades.

Cultural anthropology can no longer study a single site, village or camp to capture an entire culture in today's globalised world. Cultures now stretch across both virtual and physical spaces, crossing continents, oceans and national boundaries in ways unimaginable before. Today, there are 25,000 Nuer people living in the United States, refugees from the civil war in Sudan of the early 2000s, the third civil war in that country since the end of World War II. They are in the middle of a Nuer *diaspora*, which is the outward spread of a culture via migration. Like West African slaves caught in an earlier diaspora, the Nuer were expelled from their homeland by violent forces beyond their control.

Nuer society must be studied on more than one continent, and this is what ethnographer Dianna Shandy did. She conducted research in Nuer refugee camps in Africa and with urban Nuer in the United States. But can the Nuer still be Nuer without their cattle, living in New York City instead of East Africa? Evans-Pritchard was clear on the importance of cattle in Nuer culture:

> It has been remarked that the Nuer might be called parasites of the cow, but it might be said with equal force that the cow is a parasite of the Nuer, whose lives are spent in ensuring its welfare. They build byres, kindle fires, and clean kraals for its comfort; move from villages to camps, from camp to camp, from camps back to villages for its health; defy wild beasts for its protection; and fashion ornaments for its adornment... In truth the relationship is symbiotic: cattle and men sustain life by their reciprocal services to one another.
>
> ([1940] 1969, p. 36)

CULTURAL SNAPSHOT 12.1

A Case Study in Globalisation: Açaí and 'Ethnography of the Commodity Chain'

Have you ever wondered what 'Amazing Amazonian açaí juice' is? You may have seen it in a plastic container in the health food section of your grocery store. Or you may have seen it advertised on Oprah Winfrey or the internet. Its advocates say it improves metabolism, helps burn calories, promotes healthy heart function, boosts energy, fights cancer, lowers cholesterol and so on. A miracle food?

The açaí products available in the United States are generally made from the exocarp, or outermost layer, of a palm fruit from the Amazon. The fruits have been collected and the palms managed in dense stands in swamps for centuries, first by Indians, and later by peasants, known as *caboclos*, who today live along the river margins of the Amazon. Until the mid-1990s, açaí was considered poor people's food. Then it began to draw attention as an international 'fashion food'. The history of açaí is the reverse of sugar's history in Europe. Sugar started as rich people's food and later became poor people's food, according to ethnographer Eduardo Brondizio.

Although managed, cultivated and produced exclusively by poor peasant farmers in the Amazon, demand for açaí began to increase during the 1980s and 1990s, in part due to flights between Belém and southern Brazil. Today, açaí is found in smoothies, cough syrup, shampoo, soap, candy and liqueurs. Although the *caboclos* are directly responsible for the expansion of the açaí swamp forests in the Lower Amazon, their traditional knowledge tends to be ignored by the local elite, and hence by the outsiders who come to the region to purchase the product. Brondizio's 'ethnography of the commodity chain', includes the people who are making the most financial profit from açaí production and the various middlemen who market, store, ship and advertise the product abroad, as well as those small farmers and rural peasants whose roles in the global economy may be otherwise hidden or overlooked.

Perhaps, surprisingly, the answer to whether the Nuer can maintain their culture in the United States during the early 2000s without their cattle is *yes*. Nuer refugees living in the United States still reckon kinship patrilineally, and they still arrange for bridewealth to be paid in cattle to the family of the bride through contacts they have maintained, thanks to digital communication technologies, in Ethiopia, where the refugee camps are located. Nuer based in the United States, who are considered 'rich', pay 20 to 25 cows per bride (equivalent to $1,500–$2,000), whereas Nuer in camps only pay 10 to 25 cows ($700–$1,000). Even more recently, some US-based Nuer are beginning to substitute novel things of value in their new surroundings for cows, which few of them can own because they live in multiplex units in urban locales. Ethnographer John Holtzman, who studies Nuer refugees in Minnesota, notes that for several men the family car is replacing cattle as what constitutes value; Americans seem to value cars in ways parallel to how the Nuer in South Sudan esteem their cows, so there is perhaps some cultural continuity in this idea. Clearly, globalisation by itself does not erase indigeneity and the sense of belonging to a particular place and culture: it may even facilitate it in certain circumstances.

Indigeneity

Indigeneity is the sense of belonging to some specific place and being someone who is native or aboriginal, a descendant of the first people to live in the place considered to be a homeland. Indigenous people have a distinctive ethnicity; they are culturally unlike the dominant, mainstream society in which they live and often exist in subaltern (that is, not dominant) enclaves, either in the place of origin or where they have ended up in diasporas. A sense of indigeneity may involve the use of an identifying term to establish a distinct identity relative to the rest of society. But who are indigenous people? And what does it mean to be indigenous in a globalised world?

The term *indigeneity* has gained considerable currency in the twenty-first century. A great deal is at stake in how it is used and understood by cultural anthropologists. There are two principal ways to define it. One is relational and refers to how people who are not traditional in their customs interact with a nation–state that surrounds them. The other is definitional and refers to how people define themselves, for example, as 'tribal', and as members of societies with age-old institutions that existed before contact, invasion and colonialism. In the Mashpee example from Chapter 9, a critical legal question was whether the Mashpee could demonstrate that they had their own cultural institutions. The answer was that they could, though their language was gone. They could not, however, demonstrate that they had an identity that distinguished them from mainstream society or a common relationship to the land. As a result, they were initially denied recognition as a legitimate indigenous unit of American society. Cultural anthropologists are ultimately in the best position to interpret the cultures and languages of the people described by the term *indigenous*. Indigenous people have *bona fide* legal status in the UN and its various agencies and international tribunals, and in nation-states and NGOs. The problem seems to be, however, that indigeneity has many meanings and uses depending on where one happens to be. If indigeneity only involves being native to a place, then all of us are 'indigenous'. Cultural anthropologist Alan Barnard points out that the human species itself is indigenous to Africa. But 'indigenous' can take on special meaning in legal, governmental and international contexts and is often meant to include only *some* people. Indigenous people only comprise 200 to 300 million individuals among a world population of almost eight billion. Yet the number appears to be growing, and not just because of population increases. People are increasingly self-identifying as indigenous, declaring themselves to be part of an indigenous society.

The UN Declaration on the Rights of Indigenous Peoples, adopted in 2007, was meant to refer to the human rights of a select group of people around the globe. Yet the document does not exactly say *who* indigenous people are; it does not use ethnonyms or identify any specific culture areas or regions. But the document is clear that indigenous peoples are those who are not part of the dominant, upper strata of the world's states. That is because one of the key features of indigenous peoples is that they have 'suffered from historic injustices…[including] colonization and dispossession of their lands, territories and resources' (UN 2008, p. 2). The document refers to subaltern groups that exist in the midst of dominant, mainstream ones.

Indigenous has replaced words such as *tribal, aboriginal* and *native* in many anthropological and other social science contexts. Indigenous people have preceded societies of historic times in most of the world's nation-states and population centres. For example, in the United States, indigenous groups were forced to surrender their lands and many cultural institutions in the face of 'manifest destiny': the expansion of Euro-Americans across the North American continent in the nineteenth century. Similarly, during the 1500s and 1600s, the Japanese continually pushed the indigenous Ainu people, who were hunters and gatherers, first into northern Honshu and eventually into a much smaller region on the island of Hokkaido. The ancient Austronesian-speaking Malays displaced the Austro-Asiatic–speaking Orang Asli from coastal Malaysia. The Romans displaced the Celtic peoples of Gaul, now called France, when Julius Caesar defeated them in war. Early Swedes and Norwegians displaced the hunting, fishing and reindeer-herding Saami as they expanded, pushing them into the mountains and the northernmost regions of Scandinavia. In all cases, the displaced peoples spoke different languages—the indigenous languages of the country—before their conquest, subordination and, in some cases, assimilation, by the conquering society.

Resurgence

In some cases, indigenous identities have reemerged after years of colonialism. The American Indian Movement (AIM), founded in 1968, sought to improve the lives of Native Americans in the United States. Elsewhere, indigenous groups are experiencing a resurgence of interest in preserving their native languages and ethnic identities. Linguistic anthropologists facilitate efforts in language preservation in North America and elsewhere. The Ainu, who number about 25,000 people, were once officially declared assimilated to Japanese culture and society. The official view of the Japanese government in the 1980s, for example, was that Japan was a culturally homogeneous state without minorities and ethnic differences. This view is changing, partly because of Ainu activism. Ainu have established an organisation that supports their distinct identity with a homeland known as Ainu Moshiri.

In some cases, indigeneity was not completely erased by colonialism, though official government discourse, as well as the interests of the upper economic strata, tended to mask it. In Brazil, since the 1990s, there has been a resurgence both of Native American and Afro-Brazilian identities that have been recovered and reestablished through ethnohistoric records and life histories. This is the case with the Xocó Indians and Afro-Brazilians of a village called Mocambo (which means 'refugee slave settlement') in northeastern

Brazil. Before their resurgence, lands of the two groups overlapped and they acknowledged bonds of kinship and marriage. Some eventually chose to identify as Indians, others as descendants of escaped slaves. Both groups eventually obtained title to their land.

In the United States, Native Americans need to supply evidence of descent to qualify as indigenous. In Brazil, proving genealogy is not necessary to establish ethnicity. Rather, descendants must show that they reside upon land that had been earlier occupied by people considered either indigenous or escaped slaves. It is therefore a matter of documenting land tenure to prove ethnicity and establish rights under new laws that allow indigenous people to live on reservations protected by federal agents and permit descendants of slaves to occupy lands with similar protections. Neither the Xocó nor the Mocambo people of northeastern Brazil are ethnically distinct or pristine primitives. Rather, they are people who have succeeded in legalising their ethnic identities, according to ethnographer Jan Hoffman French. The resurgence of indigeneity in Western countries and in Japan is associated with globalisation. It represents a new trend in how minority people worldwide perceive their own cultures and their relationships to economically dominant strata of societies within modern states.

Challenges to the Concept of Indigeneity

The 2007 UN Declaration on the Rights of Indigenous Peoples was supported by 143 member nations. Eleven nations abstained, and four voted against it: the United States, New Zealand, Australia and Canada. These nations have since signed the declaration. One of the reasons given for their initially negative votes was that the declaration seemed to allow for political independence of indigenous groups. Such independence could lead to the secession of indigenous societies and the establishment of states within states. That is the geopolitical fear of acknowledging the reality of indigeneity in many national contexts worldwide. The definition of indigeneity has been very broad, and misperceptions have arisen over the political and economic aims of those promoting it. *Indigenous* originally referred to small-scale, local groups with direct connections to certain places. Today, it has become what Frances Merlan describes as a 'geocultural category' that not only transcends ethnic divisions but crosses oceans and international boundaries.

In Sweden, the indigenous Saami are divided among themselves, and by the Swedish government, over what makes a person Saami. According to the Swedish Saami parliament, it is necessary to be a full-time reindeer herder to have legal status as a Saami. Despite the fact that Saami have distinctive clothing, music and handicrafts and speak languages unrelated to Swedish, reindeer herding—not language or any other cultural characteristic—is key to legal identification as Saami. 'It is the herder who is a Saami *par excellence*, without question', according to ethnographer Hugh Beach (2007, p. 5). In the Saami case, herding has become the key marker of indigeneity, despite the many other cultural characteristics that are distinctively Saami. What people do helps define them.

The Saami identification with reindeer is similar to the Nuer and their cattle. Nuer living as refugees in the United States continue to identify with cattle in their homeland and to employ them, even if only symbolically, in bridewealth and other financial transactions. How long can that association last, given that the Nuer may never return to their land of origin, or if that landscape is so altered they can no longer make a traditional living there? The Nuer people are in a diaspora, forced off their lands into either refugee camps or global migrations. What happens to Nuer identity if they continue to be separated from their cattle and their homeland amid emergent, transnational, globalising forces?

They still possess their concepts about patrilineal descent and bridewealth, but their cattle may be located thousands of miles away, and the groom and bride may never even see them.

As these examples demonstrate, indigenous identity is not a given. It is not some primordial identity handed down unchanged from one generation to the next. The land claim of the Mashpee of Cape Cod (Chapter 9) is a case in point, showing how genealogy is virtually irrelevant to indigeneity as a principle of identity. Adding to the confusion in the Mashpee case was the conflict between the mainstream American image of Native Americans and the reality, which included a Mashpee shaman who earned a living in real estate. To many Americans, a shaman might be indigenous, but a realtor couldn't be a 'real' Indian. Mashpee culture had changed, and because of that, the very identity of the Mashpee people was challenged in court. One of the legal criteria for *being* indigenous in certain international courts is simply *claiming* to be indigenous. This criterion reinforces the idea that part of being an indigenous person is a sense of belonging to a certain culture.

A challenge to the maintenance of an indigenous identity across the world is the gradual encroachment of political and economic interests upon lands claimed by indigenous peoples. This is part of the notion of 'injustices' addressed in the UN Declaration. Such encroachment with dispossession is occurring in tropical rainforests of Amazonia, Southeast Asia and Oceania, as well as in the Arctic, where exploration and development of mineral and oil resources are leading to the construction of roads, quarries, drilling platforms and open-pit mines. Across the Arctic, these projects encroach upon lands traditionally used for hunting, fishing and reindeer herding and alter the socioeconomic structure of nearby towns and villages. In some cases, reparations may be sought in the form of cash awards or land restitution.

CULTURAL SNAPSHOT 12.2

The Concept of Hybridity

Many cultural anthropologists today use the term hybridity, which refers to a new kind of cultural mixing that differs from acculturation (Chapter 10). Acculturation refers to two societies that are in physical proximity, such as daily contact between Spanish colonists and Amazonian indigenous people in the 1500s. Hybridity involves cultural mixing that derives from the instantaneous communication and worldwide networks of transportation associated with globalisation. New ethnicities are emerging when people who are widely separated in space come into contact via the internet or television and when people from rural homesteads migrate to cities and across national boundaries. In the 'deruralization of the world', from 1950 to 2000, according to Immanuel Wallerstein, between 30 per cent to 60 per cent of the world's population went from living in the countryside to living in cities. In many cases, people carry rural traditions into urban contexts, while at the same time adopting bits and pieces of global culture from electronic media and the hybridised people around them. Hip-hop music, which originated in the 1980s in urban black America, has spread to the entire world, becoming a musical emblem of globalisation (Figure 12.4). It was heard in protests against racial hatred and injustice around the world in 2020 alongside organisations like Black Lives Matter. American pop music

Figure 12.4 Hip-hop group Public Enemy in concert in Benicacsin, Spain, July 2015. The spread of hip-hop is a fact of globalisation. Christian Bertrand/Shutterstock.com.

is said to be 'blacker' because of it. Hip–hop is a form of transnational 'blackness', a black identity that extends globally from Brazil to Cuba to South Africa. In this sense, 'blackness' is much more than skin colour. In the airport of the indigenous city of El Alto, Bolivia, one of the leaders of the local rap movement sings, 'estamos con la raza, yo!' ('we are with the people, yo!'). He is alerting his listeners to his shared identity with other *hybrid* indigenous people, including urban blacks in the United States, North African immigrants to Paris and the Maori of Auckland, New Zealand.

Land dispossession threatens the 'ancestral roots' that people have with the landscape and its resources. Indigenous people across the world, including the Nuer, the Ka'apor and the Canadian Inuit, tend to have strong connections to particular places. They often have a sense of being the first inhabitants of a place, and they tend to distinguish themselves from societies and ethnic groups that engulf or surround them through these land-based identifications. That connection—spiritual, historical and ecological—persists through time, even when the people whose indigenous identity is in question find themselves spread across the globe.

Indigeneity, Globalisation and Language Loss

Globalisation has brought with it a vast mixing of peoples and languages, both face to face and electronically via the internet, instant messaging and mobile phones. English is the prestige language that governs these communications: it is the language spoken by those who dominate socially, politically and economically. It is the de facto language of international finance and trade and the official language of the European Union. Following contact in the 1500s, European languages became the *prestige* languages in the colonies. Spanish subsumed indigenous languages in the Caribbean and Central and South America. Portuguese dominated in Brazil and parts of Africa; English in North America, parts of Africa and Australia; Dutch in Indonesia; and French on various islands in the Caribbean and Oceania as well as equatorial Africa and Indochina. These languages tended to supplant local languages. The colonisers spoke the prestige languages, which ruled in the workplace, at church, in school and in government affairs. Despite the challenge represented by prestige languages, some local indigenous languages persisted.

Today there are about 6,000 languages left on Earth. Twenty-two countries today have 100 or more languages spoken in them: Papua New Guinea, Indonesia, Nigeria, India, Cameroon, Australia, Mexico, Democratic Republic of Congo, Brazil, Philippines, Russia, the United States, Malaysia, China, Sudan, Tanzania, Ethiopia, Chad, New Hebrides, Central African Republic, Burma and Nepal. Together, these countries account for 85 per cent of the 6,000 languages, though some conservative estimates put the total number of remaining languages at only 4,000. About half of indigenous languages are *moribund*; that is, they are near extinction because there are few speakers and because children are learning a prestige language rather than an indigenous one. At least 3,000 languages will likely go extinct in the twenty-first century. This language loss is directly related to globalisation and to the worldwide reach of electronic media, such as email, mobile phones and the internet. Dominant languages are like 'cultural nerve gas', extinguishing cultural and linguistic differences around the world (Figure 12.5).

Figure 12.5 Sirionó elder, one of the last fluent speakers of that indigenous language, Bolivian Amazon, 2007. Photo by author.

Languages and cultures are becoming fewer and more homogeneous because people are all communicating within the context of a single globalising culture and language, namely English in its many dialects. In a few hundred years, this language may be the only language spoken on the globe unless things change relatively soon. The languages today that are dying off at a rate of several dozen per year are not prestige languages: they are not the languages spoken by the colonisers or dominant groups from the early modern world system. Once one of these languages goes extinct—when the last speaker dies—there is little chance that it will be revived. The same may be said for cultures, though there may be attempts to bring them back, often for economic reasons related to tourism, or to resurrect them in a form that is thought to be primordial. Indigeneity is highly marketable, as we saw in the discussion of ethnotourism (Chapter 11).

Indigeneity and Landscapes

The first European explorers tended to consider the indigenous people they encountered to be worthless savages who lacked intrinsic rights to the lands they occupied; they were to be either enslaved or expelled, as we saw in Chapter 9. But these indigenous people often farmed and settled the land quite effectively, and in the process, they transformed it beyond any sort of 'natural' state. In many cases, the landscapes that the first explorers considered to be savage wilderness were in fact gardens, orchards, green enclaves and cultural forests. This was the case even in the most remote and supposedly 'primitive' places where the explorers dared venture. Apart from Antarctica, which had no original population at the onset of colonisation, the last lands to be populated by humanity on a permanent basis were the islands of Oceania. Late prehistoric societies of Micronesia altered the surrounding landscapes and seascapes, though the first Europeans in the area, such as Ferdinand Magellan and Captain Cook, saw them as pristine. There is such extensive terracing and transformation of island summits on the northern islands of the Palau Archipelago, for example, that they are referred to as 'sculpted landscapes'. These landscapes are and were indigenous.

Around 1800, the Marovo Lagoon on New Georgia in the Solomon Islands had irrigated, terraced taro fields; young slash–and–burn swiddens of taro and yams; and old fallow, or anthropogenic, forest with groves of *Canarium* trees, which produced edible nuts high in fats. According to ethnographers James Fairhead and Melissa Leach, these old fallows, like the Ka'apor *taper* forest in Amazonia (Cultural Snapshot 8.3), were orchard-like and attracted not only people but also game animals.

In West Africa, the vast forest islands of Guinea contain evidence of human occupation and transformation. These forests were formed where there were no forests before as a result of indigenous human activity. People deliberately planted, transplanted and cultivated fruit trees and established firebreaks around plantings to protect them. Savanna soils actually improved with human occupation and cultivation, and shady orchards developed.

In the Amazon Basin of South America, we find extensive mounds, ditches, raised fields and other manipulations of the earth itself, such as the recently discovered and spectacular geoglyphs of Acre, western Amazonia. In an area only about 155 miles wide, there are more than 450 of these geoglyphs of varying sizes and shapes but mostly perfect or near-perfect rectangles and circles. They are often about 13 acres in size with ditches 10–15 feet deep and up to 36 feet wide all along the edges. These were mostly built by indigenous people between 2,500 years ago and 1,000 years ago (Figure 12.6). Ironically,

Figure 12.6 Ancient circular geoglyph in eastern Acre, Brazil. Geoglyphs like this were only noticed after forest cover was removed for cattle ranching. Photo by Edson Caetano. Courtesy Denise Schaan.

researchers only discovered the geoglyphs after large-scale deforestation for cattle pastures occurred in the 1980s.

On the opposite side of the continent, in the Amazon estuary, are anthropogenic mounds built to provide perennial water sources for fish, thus creating a reliable food source for humans. Extensive causeways in the Bolivian Amazon appear to have had a similar function: to control water on a massive scale and raise fish and snails for food, according to archaeologist Clark Erickson. Around a time before AD 1500 at Ibibate Mound Complex in the Llanos de Mojos, people intentionally dug dirt out of the ground to raise a vast 60-foot-high platform mound, on top of which a powerful chief probably resided. In so doing, they created a borrow pit at the base of the mound that has functioned as a perennial source of drinking water to this day. The area is otherwise nearly devoid of potable water in the dry season. Many of the trees on the mound are fruit trees, while there are few such trees in the savanna itself. People actually contributed to species diversity by building the mounds, where plants could grow without being flooded in the rainy season. The mounds built by humans, in other words, are richer in plant species than the surrounding natural savanna.

Ibibate is a case of *primary landscape transformation*: changes caused by human activity in which species turnover is nearly complete. Such turnover did not involve a decline in species diversity, but rather a local increase, because the high ground people built favoured more species of trees than could grow in the swamp bottomland that was the original habitat. Like the organic-rich Amazon Dark Earth sites, found scattered throughout the

Figure 12.7 An Orang Asli man and the author, in Pahang, central peninsular Malaysia, 2012. Indigenous identities are often closely tied to knowledge of the landscape and its resources. Photo by Hood Salleh.

Amazon Basin where settlement was dense and long-lasting before the Europeans arrived, the soil of Ibibate is the product of ancient human activity. In fact, 13 per cent of the material is likely broken pottery.

All the landscapes discussed above are inseparable from the members of the societies— the indigenes—that begot them (Figure 12.7). These are built, living environments that are ultimately anthropogenic in terms of biotic diversity, yet anthropogenic of a distinctive sort. These landscapes are not industrial or postindustrial artefacts of Western civilisation. They are indigenous and deserve the full protection of the UN Declaration on the Rights of Indigenous Peoples and any other national and international rulings that favour indigeneity and the fundamental human rights of indigenes. Land rights are inseparable from human rights.

Cultural Anthropology as Transduction

The role of anthropology is now, and will continue to be, that of *transduction*; of being like part of an electronic circuit, the transducer, that gets the energy from one place to another, minimising its loss along the way. In this case, anthropology's role is getting native knowledge and native aspirations into a framework that outsiders can comprehend. In some cases, cultural anthropologists become activists and advocates, practising a kind of applied anthropology (Chapter 11). To some extent, anthropology has always been applied because its findings are used to address real world problems. Boas' cultural relativism and antiracist and anti-Semitic positions were scientifically sound, but controversial in his day. Boas confronted common, intolerant attitudes of his time and paved the way for a more objective, engaged anthropology. In a globalised world, anthropologists cannot be mere observers sitting on the sidelines, watching and recording information about cultures and the people who live them. They need to engage indigenous agendas, rights and claims in field, academic and public settings.

Increasingly, indigenous groups are organising themselves into small corporations and cooperatives. Tribal egalitarianism is no more. One no longer needs the chief or headman to gain access to a village and its inhabitants. Now one needs to find the head of the local indigenous cooperative. Indigenous agendas are often environmental conservation plans or projects that advance a group's land and conservation interests. The most important attitude required of the ethnographer is sincerity and sensitivity to these local agendas, which have often been formed through consensus and elections. It may be one of the great benefits and ironies of globalisation that the worldwide dissemination of the corporate model, involving election to office of a cadre of trustees or officers, may actually enable indigeneity to survive. Future ethnographers will document and advocate for that survival. Cultural anthropology is not just a textbook discipline with little application to the needs and concerns of modern people. There is indeed a place for it in the globalised world of the twenty-first century: the field, where ethnographers will continue to participate, observe and explain what it means to be human.

Summary

Globalisation involves new challenges to the field of cultural anthropology because fieldwork is less likely to be carried out in a single site, or community, the way it was for much of the twentieth century. That is because many of the people in the lens of cultural anthropology are spread across the globe thanks to changes in transportation and electronic media.

Globalisation is having an impact on indigenous societies in terms of language, identity and land rights, and how these are managed for posterity. Cultural anthropology can contribute to a better understanding of the relationships between globalisation and cultural change in situations of indigeneity in the twenty-first century thanks to the special expertise and knowledge that ethnographers bring to the table.

Further Reading

Alderman 2020; Alexiades 2009; Arrow 2005; Associated Press 2015; Balée 1994, 2006; Barnard 2006; Bayliss-Smith et al. 2003; Beach 2007; Bellwood 2001; Blench 2008; Broadbent 2010; Búriková and Miller 2010; Chami 2001a, 2001b; Clifford 1988; Consumer Credit-G.19; Dannenmaier 2008; Dark 2007; De Langhe and de Maret 1999; Dixon 1997; Dominguez 1994; Erickson 2008; Erickson and Balée 2006; Evans-Pritchard (1940) 1969, (1951) 1990; Fairhead and Leach 1996; Flannery 2005 (pp. 286–287); French 2009; Giddens 2000; Goodale 2006; Harvey 1989 (pp. 240–241); Holtzman 2008; Isaac 2014; Johnston and Slyomovics 2008; Kearney 1996; Krauss 1992; Kroskrity and Field 2009; Kwok-bun 2005; Langstroth 1996; Lansing 2006; Lee 2013 (pp. 165–166); Mauer 2006; McLuhan 1962; Merlan 2009 (p. 303); Mintz 1985; Nicholls 2011; Pärssinen et al. 2020; Phalan et al. 2011; Pink 2006; Rainbird 2004 ; Sahlins 1976a; Schaan 2006, 2012; Senders and Truitt 2007; Shandy 2007; Siddle

1997; Spindler and Stockard 2007; Sutton 2008; Talboys 2005; Thornberry 2002; Truitt 2020; World Archaeological Conference (WAC) 2008; Wallerstein 1974 (p. 80), 2005; Whitaker 2010; Williams 1985; Wolf 1997

Cultural Snapshots

12.1   Brondizio 2008; Wallerstein 2005
12.2   Goodale 2006; Kowk-bun 2005; Lazar 2008; Perry 2008; Wallerstein 2005

Concluding Remarks

Cultural anthropologists in the twenty-first century could be dealing with the possibility of a homogeneous set of behaviours and ideas shared across the globe. That trend towards homogeneity of culture seems to be the way the world is headed right now, in part because of the internet and the internationalisation of finance, trade, migration, ideas, art, music and behaviour, all of which are becoming globalised. Whether this trend will continue, however, is debatable.

Cultural anthropology, along with every other human science, makes no claim to prediction or experimentation, though we can demonstrate the reality of extant phenomena, such as shared beliefs and behaviours that can and do change with time: *culture*. And we can document the contested aspects of culture. But we cannot predict future patterns, lifestyles or events, which is why the future contributions of cultural anthropology are essentially unlimited. No other discipline is poised to compare and contrast cultural information holistically and systematically, using data acquired from participant observation and the methodologies developed over more than a century of ethnographic and ethnological research. In sum, cultural anthropology has the tools needed to understand long-term trends and both the past and future prospects of humanity and culture. Even so, debate continues over a few issues.

In this book, I've shown both the scientific and the humanist dimensions of this extraordinary field. Indeed, humans cannot be understood by separating the two, given their cultural and linguistic diversity and their evolutionary heritage over the last few million years. To study humans, we need science and humanism. For that pragmatic reason, I disagreed with the October 2011 comments of then Governor Rick Scott (now Senator) of Florida, namely, that anthropology is

> a great degree if people want to get it. But we don't need [anthropologists] here…I want to spend our money getting people science, technology, engineering and math degrees…so when they get out of school, they can get a job.

He later apologised. Scott was not alone in his initial assessment. Other conservative current and former governors such as Scott Walker of Wisconsin and Rick Perry of Texas sought to cut spending in human sciences. Actually, the BA or BS in anthropology is a very good degree for many different fields, and business leaders have called for more, not fewer, people with BAs in anthropology and other liberal arts fields instead of MBAs. Employment of master's degree anthropologists is very good; anthropology is ranked as the sixth-best science job by US News and World Report, with a predicted increase of

5 per cent in jobs between 2019 and 2029. These jobs are mainly in archaeology, as in cultural resource management and in biological anthropology, as in forensics.

They have proven to be wrong about the inability of graduates in anthropology to get a job upon graduation compared with those with science and mathematics degrees. Few disciplines in higher education provide workplace skills during a four-year course of study. Nor is a degree in most of the STEM (science, technology, engineering, maths) or business fields an automatic ticket to employment. Those degrees, while certainly valuable, are not necessarily better than an undergraduate degree in anthropology.

US News and World Report in May 2020 observed:

> Anthropology majors study humanity, and they examine how linguistics, culture, biology and history shape human diversity. The degree arms students with critical thinking and problem-solving skills. Students in this major learn to pick up new ideas quickly and communicate those ideas effectively. Because of this, majoring in anthropology equips graduates for a variety of jobs in the private and public sectors.

Anthropologists can be effective in jobs usually thought to be reserved for STEM graduates or MBAs, such as Gillian Tett, an anthropology PhD from Cambridge. Tett predicted the economic crisis of 2008 before others based on her analysis of credit-default swaps and debt obligations based on collateral:

> I happen to think anthropology is a brilliant background for looking at finance… Firstly you're trained to look at how societies or cultures operate holistically, so you look at how all the bits move together…Bankers like to imagine that money and the profit motive [are] as universal as gravity. They think it's basically a given and they think it's completely apersonal. And it's not. What they do in finance is all about culture and interaction.
>
> (*The Economist* 2011)

The anthropology department at the University of Central Florida (UCF), which is the second-largest university in the United States with 60,000 students enrolled, is seeking to counter 'recent swipes at the profession' by assigning tenure-track and senior faculty to teaching courses like the one you are likely taking now, and by having them advise freshmen and sophomore students directly. Professors Beatriz Reyes-Foster and Ty Matejowsky (2014, p. 3) at UCF stated that in

> dispelling misconceptions that portray anthropology as an impractical degree, we aim to offer realistic advice for undergraduates considering anthropology as a college major. Students can pursue their intellectual interests, study what they enjoy, and still find viable employment after graduation provided they create strong resumes and cultivate good connections early on in their collegiate journeys.

Anthropology is and always has been at the conceptual centre of a liberal arts education precisely because it straddles the ideascape of biological science, social science and the humanities. Indeed, these boundaries of academic knowledge can seem rather meaningless within the context of anthropology because of the scope of its subject matter. Anthropology is above all about sound scholarship on humanity, in all its variations, at all times and places. That is where its holism comes from.

Cultural anthropology is the key to the entire field because of the concept of culture, which has been emerging in various milieus outside the university. I visited the United Buddy Bears travelling exhibit in Kuala Lumpur, Malaysia, in December 2011 (it's in Berlin as of 2020), sponsored by the United Nations (Figure 13.1). United Buddy Bears is composed of 147 life-sized fibreglass bears, arranged paw-to-paw, with their bodies painted by artists commissioned from each of the countries they represent. One of the principal aims of the exhibit is to 'promote art, unity and peace', emphasising appreciation of diverse cultures found in all nations. The subtitle of the exhibit is *The Art of Tolerance*. When I saw those words, I recalled that cultural anthropologists have been stressing tolerance longer and more persuasively than scholars in virtually any other field. The Buddy

Figure 13.1 The United Buddy Bears in Kuala Lumpur, Malaysia, 2011. According to the brochure, 'each bear stands for the people of the different countries and their culture, yet not for political systems'. Photo by author.

Bears exhibit represents twenty-first-century cultural relativism, and it speaks to broader impacts that are made possible with anthropological training in the context of a liberal arts education.

Anthropology as a discipline, however, is in flux. Cultural anthropologist Ryan Jobson recently wrote that the origins of the discipline—rooted in colonialism, which often depended on disappropriation of indigenous peoples' lands and chattel slavery of African captives—are what financially enabled the Enlightenment and evolutionism of the nineteenth century, the foundations of the field and the notion of objectifying the other (or different societies from the anthropologist, especially subordinated ones). It can be seen as a sort of 'racial capitalism'. For many years, the field was a 'white public space' that subscribed to the eventual assimilation of societies that were the subalterns of the world system. On the other hand, most anthropologists by far today and since Boas subscribe philosophically to some form of cultural (though not ethical) relativism, and most favour equity, diversity and inclusion in institutions that have historically marginalised underrepresented minorities and LGBTQ individuals. That is certainly the case in most universities that seek more rather than less diversity in faculty and students. Another problem ironically lies in the objective strength of the discipline: the four-field model is disputed in some universities (though not most), because of the divergence in specialisation in each of the four fields, growing and deepening in jargon and analysis apart from the central concept of anthropological holism.

In my mind, holism is how the field can be fully decolonised and where a new humanism, which Jobson calls for, could take root. The search for a meaningful role to play in university and society at large, both local and global, is not limited to anthropology, or any of its subdisciplines, today. While modernity and the modern world system that existed throughout the colonial and neocolonial periods may be over, globalisation represents an intellectual as well as an economic challenge.

Even in a rapidly changing and globalised world, some fundamental structures of the discipline of anthropology remain, including the four-field approach. Most undergraduate degrees in anthropology still require courses in all four fields. Virtually all programmes in the United States have anthropology professors with qualifications in at least one and often more than one of the fields. An education in general anthropology—all four fields—provides a broad liberal arts foundation with a focus on the human species. Cultural anthropology is the ideal place to start building that foundation for understanding humans in all their diversity.

Grounding in anthropology is also needed to understand and influence current trends in language and culture. Languages are disappearing from the globe, whether through linguistic hybridisation and assimilation or outright extinction, at the rate of several dozen per year. Cultures are more amorphous than languages, but they are likewise being transformed on a daily basis by globalisation and its attendant processes of mechanisation and engineering of agriculture, capital accumulation, landscape transformation and habitat destruction, civil war and diaspora. Globalisation is not good or bad in moral terms; it is simply a phase of human history. Cultural anthropology is well situated to study, describe and explain the effects of globalisation both locally and globally. And cultural anthropologists are well-positioned to advocate responsibly and intelligently for the rights of those who, due to political and economic inequalities, are unable to safeguard their own rights to language and culture.

Cultural anthropologists have an essential role to play in advancing knowledge and promoting peace and equity. They can convey the needs and wants of members of non-Western, small-scale societies to world leaders and policymakers so that everyone can participate fully and equitably in a global world. Knowledge gained from participant observation plays a fundamental part in that role, which is likely to expand in the current century as the need for getting inside cultures—and understanding better how they vary in time and space—grows ever greater worldwide.

Further Reading

American Anthropological Association 2010; Bureau of Labor Statistics, US Department of Labor 2020; Dixon 1997; *The Economist* 2011; Jobson 2020; *Miami Herald* 2011; Nicholson 2007; Reyes-Foster and Matejowsky 2014; Stoller 2013; United Buddy Bears 2011; US News and World Report 2020; Wallerstein 2005

Glossary

acculturation horizontal transmission of culture through contact between societies

acephalous characteristic of a society without a formal leader; literally 'headless'

achieved status status acquired independently of one's birth; contrast with *ascribed status*

activists group, often affinal, that takes a central role in rites of passage, especially rites of initiation and mortuary rites; contrast with *mourners*, who are consanguineal kin of the novices

affine in-laws; contrast with *consanguines*

affinity the relationship of in-laws to one another

age grade an age-based life cycle category, such as infancy or young adulthood

age set a sodality found in many South American and African societies wherein youths of roughly the same age are recruited into a specially named group that often has secret lore and ceremonies

agnates relatives in one's patrilineal group

agriculture cultivation or breeding of domesticates

alterity otherness or difference, often of ethnic minorities

ambilineal descent kin group membership determined either through one's father or through one's mother, but not both; basis for cognatic clans

animatism belief in impersonal supernatural forces

animism belief in souls or spirits

anthropoid primates a primate group that includes monkeys, apes and hominins, but not prosimians

anthropology scientific study of human beings and their closest primate relatives, both living and extinct

apical ancestor real or imagined founder of a cognatic clan

applied anthropology sometimes called the fifth field of anthropology; involves putting into practice skills and knowledge acquired via participant observation and ethnographic findings

arbitrary feature of language in which no meaningful link exists between a word and the thing signified

archaeology also called anthropological archaeology; the systematic study of past human societies, both historic and prehistoric

artificial selection phenotypic selection by humans

ascribed status status assigned at birth; contrast with achieved status

avunculocality residence pattern in which a married couple resides with the family of the bride or groom's mother's brother

band   largest cooperative social unit of simple hunter-gatherers

bilateral descent   kin group membership traced through both the mother's and father's lines

biological citizenship   sense of common membership in a group experienced by those who share the affliction of an epidemic disease such as HIV/AIDS, Ebola and others, and the stigmatisation that sometimes attends it

bipedalism   habitually walking on two legs; a form of locomotion associated with humans and early hominins

blade tool   a cutting edge made by people that is at least twice as long as it is wide; a profusion of blade tools in the archaeological record is one of the indicators of the emergence of behaviourally modern humans in the last 100,000 years

blitzkrieg hypothesis   Paul Martin's idea that Late Pleistocene human hunters caused the extinctions of large game animals in the Americas

brideservice   practice found in many egalitarian societies in which a prospective groom works for the bride's relatives

bridewealth   goods paid by the groom's family to the bride's family; also called bride-price

caste   endogamous (in-marrying) social group defined by occupation

circumcision   removal of the foreskin of the penis, a rite of passage for males in many societies

clan   unilineal descent group usually associated with a plant or animal founder represented by an emblem, or totem; several lineages comprise a clan

class   stratum of complex society that has more or less control over resources, technology and land than other classes in the same society

cognatic descent   kin group membership traced either ambilineally or bilaterally

collective conscience   Durkheim's concept of culture; idea that the members of a society share a similar set of values and attitudes

community   arbitrary reference sample in cultural anthropology, such as a town or county, taken to be representative of an entire society

community studies   research programme of twentieth-century anthropology focusing on the community as a basic unit of society within states

consanguines   relatives to whom one is biologically related; contrast with *affines*

contingency   unpredictable chance or historical events deriving from material, ecological or ideological causes

corporate group   kin group that holds goods or land in common

couvade   practices and taboos surrounding a belief that an infant's father is in a ritually dangerous situation immediately after an infant's birth

cross cousins   children of siblings of the opposite sex, e.g., the children of father's sister or the children of mother's brother

cultural anthropology   the systematic study of similarities and differences of learned and shared human behaviours and ideas

cultural ecology   theory developed by Julian Steward that assumes a causal relationship between the environment and social organisation of egalitarian societies

cultural evolution   idea that culture becomes more complex through time

cultural materialism   research programme associated with Marvin Harris in which infrastructure (modes of production and reproduction) determines key aspects of the structure (society), which in turn influences superstructure (science, art, religion, ideas)

cultural relativism principle that learned and shared behaviours and concepts should be understood as if they were intellectually and morally equivalent to all others; basic premise of the Boasian research programme and modern anthropology

culture learned, shared human behaviour and ideas that change with time

DNA acronym for the molecule deoxyribonucleic acid, which stores genetic information

demand sharing kind of generalised reciprocity when one asks another for food or some other good or service and is never refused

descriptive system kinship classification system in which each relative is known by a different term; syn. Sudanese

diaspora large-scale dispersal or outmigration of people from their homelands

diffusion the horizontal transmission of culture and language from one society to another

displacement attribute of language that allows for symbolic representation of other times and places than the here and now

domesticate an organism or population of organisms with a distinctive genome that has been produced by artificial selection and is dependent upon humans for reproduction

dowry a woman's inheritance usually received while her parents are still living; contrast with *bridewealth*

ecological anthropology twentieth-century research programme founded by Roy Rappaport focusing on analysis of humans as populations within ecosystems

economic rationality the idea that people seek to maximise benefits and minimise costs of goods and services

egalitarianism form of social organisation in which power differences are based on age and sex or gender

ego the individual who is the point of reference in a kinship diagram

egocentric an individual person's (ego's) perspective on kinship; contrast with *sociocentric*

emic perspective interpreting culture from the viewpoint of the insider

enculturation vertical transmission of culture from one generation to the next; usually refers to infants and children learning the rules and language of the culture into which they were born

endogamy the practice of marrying within one's group

environmental circumscription Carneiro's theory of state formation in which complex societies develop out of chiefdoms in areas where limited arable land is surrounded by desert or mountains

epigraphy decipherment of ancient writing, such as hieroglyphs

epistemological relativism the idea that any way of understanding the nature of reality, whether through science, religion, art, etc., is as good as any other; principle of postmodernism

ethnic boundary markers visual and auditory cues that together mark off one group's sense of common origins and identity from others

ethnic group a subunit of society; members are considered distinct due to specific cultural and linguistic differences they exhibit when compared with the majority

ethnicity self-identification of a person with a group that defines itself through common customs, a shared language or dialect and a shared memory of origins, persecution and migration

ethnobiology the study of relationships between human beings and other life forms

ethnocentrism the attitude that one's own culture is morally superior to others

ethnographic analogy   comparison of a past society with one known from recent ethnographic study

ethnographic present   the time period in which ethnographic fieldwork is conducted

ethnography   the study of a particular society through field research using the methods of cultural anthropology; the written product of such research

ethnohistory   the study of historical documents composed by outsiders that provide information about a given society

ethnology   also known as cross-cultural comparison; the comparative analysis of cultures

ethnonym   designation for a cultural group, such as Araweté or Guajá

etic perspective   interpreting culture from the perspective of an outsider using data collected from observations of behaviour

exogamy   the practice of marrying out of a defined group

field notes   writings of observations and dialogue recorded during ethnographic work, usually involving discussions between an ethnographer and one or more informants

fieldwork   the practice of ethnography and its principal methodology, participant observation

free listing   method used to elicit the most important items in a shared cultural domain

functionalism   theoretical perspective of Malinowski that the purpose of social institutions is to meet the needs of its members and to maintain and perpetuate society

generational system   kinship classification system that distinguishes individuals by sex and generation only; syn. Hawaiian

genome   the entire genetic sequence of a species

genotype   the genetic code of an individual

globalisation   postmodern economic system that links peoples and societies worldwide through rapid communication, transportation and diffusion

historical particularism   school of thought associated with Franz Boas in which societies are viewed as unique products of their history and environment

hominids   the human family, which include modern humans, the African great apes and early hominins

hominins   members of the taxonomic tribe Hominini that includes humans, early hominins, chimpanzees and bonobos

Homo   genus that includes modern humans and fossil hominins, such as *Homo erectus, H. Neandertalensis* and others

Homo erectus   Pleistocene ancestor to modern humans living from about 1.9 million years ago to about 400,000 years ago

Homo Neanderthalensis   Early European hominins existing about 350,000 to 25,000 years ago; a small part of the *H. sapiens* genome derives from Neandertal DNA

Homo sapiens   anatomically modern humans, originating about 150,000 years ago in Africa

hypergamy   marriage to someone of higher social, political or economic status

hypogamy   marriage to someone of lower social, political or economic status

indigeneity   ethnicity that includes a belief that one's ancestors were the first inhabitants of a region; aboriginality

informant   a person chosen by an ethnographer to answer research questions about that person's culture

kindred   social unit that includes all relatives on both sides of the family

levirate   marriage rule in which a man marries the wife of his deceased brother

lineage   unilineal kin group tracing descent from a known human ancestor

linguistic anthropology the systematic study of languages, their diversity across human societies and the relationship of language to culture

materialism theoretical perspective in which technology, resources and the environment are the primary determinants of social structure

matrilineal descent tracing kin relationships and inheritance through the female line

method research procedure employed to evaluate a hypothesis

millenarian movement large-scale effort to revitalise society; often occurs in colonial contexts

moiety one of a pair of unilineal descent groups in a society

money all-purpose, anonymous unit of exchange used in setting prices of goods in market economies

morpheme unit of meaning in language

mourners consanguineal kin of a novice undergoing a rite of passage

multilinear evolution idea that societies adapt to their environments in a number of different ways rather than by progressing along a single evolutionary path

multisited ethnography the study of societies that are dispersed on the globe due to some of their members remaining in locales of origin, while others inhabit new destinations via migrations away from the locales of origin

neolocality residence pattern in which married couple establish a home separate from that of their families

noninstrumental value qualitative social value rather than quantitative monetary value

palaeoanthropology a subfield of physical anthropology concerned with the biology, culture and technology of fossil hominins

parallel cousins children of same-sex siblings, e.g., the children of mother's sister or of father's brother

participant observation definitive field method of cultural anthropology, involving anthropological fieldwork by an ethnographer on site for a year or more

patrilineal descent tracing kin relationships and inheritance through the male line

patronym father's name

peasants, peasantry a class of persons engaged full time in food production in state societies; taxes and tribute produced by peasants support classes that do not work in food production

phoneme unit of sound in language

physical anthropology also known as biological anthropology; the study of humans as part of nature, including the study of human evolution and the anatomy and behaviour of humans' closest living and extinct primate relatives

plural marriage marriage involving multiple partners. See also *polygyny*; *polyandry*

polyandry marriage of one woman to more than one man at the same time

polygyny marriage of one man to more than one woman at the same time

positivism nineteenth-century research programme stressing the infallibility of science in the search for objective knowledge; associated with philosopher Auguste Comte

potlatch redistributive feast of the Pacific Northwest Coast

primatology study of nonhuman primate anatomy and behaviour

primogeniture inheritance rule favouring the oldest son

productivity feature of language in which a limited number of phonemes and syntactic rules can be used to generate an infinite number of meaningful sentences

reciprocity exchange of goods and services common to all societies

redistribution   a method of exchange in which many producers contribute goods that are then reallocated by a person specifically designated to fulfil that task, such as a Big Man

salvage ethnography   part of the Boasian research programme; involved collection of as much information as possible from elderly Native informants before traditional cultures disappeared

sexual division of labour   division of economic activities on the basis of sex

spear thrower   a device enabling a hunter to propel a spear farther and faster through the air than if thrown by hand alone; emerges as a common feature of modern human toolkits

sociality   human propensity to live in groups, a trait shared with many primates

society   a population sharing a common culture

sociocentric   group perspective on kinship; contrast with *egocentric*

sodality   group organised for a specific purpose

sororate   marriage rule in which a woman marries the husband of her deceased sister

stereotypes   simplified, usually pejorative, ideas about other groups that are believed to differ in fundamental ways from one's own group

stratification   segmentation of society on the basis of differential access to resources

stratum   a non-kin group in a stratified society with differential access to resources; pl. strata

structural-functionalism   theoretical perspective of Radcliffe-Brown that social institutions function as part of an interrelated and interdependent whole; society is analogous to an organism

structuralism   theoretical perspective that human society is organised around sets of binary oppositions, such as moieties

superorganic   Alfred Kroeber's concept of culture as a configuration of learned and shared thoughts, values and attitudes that exist beyond any single individual

syncretism   merging the elements of multiple religions; Candomblé is a syncretic religion

syntax   the set of unconscious linguistic rules for making grammatical sentences

taboo   a rule prohibiting a behaviour

teknonymy   practice of referring to a parent using his or her child's name

terrorism   violent non-state insurgencies against perceived, established national and world powers; some terroristic groups are apocalyptic and display features of millenarianism or revitalisation movements

time allocation   a quantitative method for determining how much time people spend doing various activities

totemism   belief in descent from plants, animals or natural phenomena; found in societies with unilineal descent groups such as clans and associated with emblems representing the totem plant or animal

trope   a literary device, style or genre

uxorilocality   residence pattern in which a married couple resides with the family of the wife; also called *matrilocality*

virilocality   residence pattern in which a married couple resides with the family of the husband; also called *patrilocality*

References

AAA. 2012a. "Principles of Professional Responsibility." *AAA Ethics Blog*, November 1. Available at http://ethics.americananthro.org/category/statement/.

———. 2012b. "Be Open and Honest Regarding Your Work." *AAA Ethics Blog*, November 1. Available at http://ethics.americananthro.org/ethics-statement-2-be-open- and-honest-regarding-your-work/.

Abe, H.N. 1995. "From Stereotype to Context: The Study of Japanese Women's Speech." *Feminist Studies* 21(3):647–671.

Adams, W.Y. 1998. *The Philosophical Roots of Anthropology*. Stanford, CA: Center for the Study of Language and Information.

Agar, M., and H.S. Reisinger. 2003. "Going for the Global: The Case of Ecstasy." *Human Organization* 62(1):1–11.

Aimers, J.J. 2007. "What Maya Collapse? Terminal Classic Variation in the Maya Lowlands." *Journal of Archaeological Research* 15:329–377.

Albach, B. 2007. "Stanford Anthropology Merger Riles Some." *Palo Alto Daily News*, February 18.

Alderman, L. 2020. "Our Cash-Free Future is Getting Closer." *New York Times*, July 6.

Alexiades, M.N. 2009. "The Cultural and Economic Globalisation of Traditional Environmental Knowledge Systems." In *Landscape, Process and Power: Re-evaluating Traditional Environmental Knowledge*, edited by S. Heckler, pp. 68–98. Oxford: Berghahn.

Altieri, M. 2004. *Genetic Engineering in Agriculture: The Myths, Environmental Risks, and Alternatives* (2nd ed). Oakland, CA: Food First Books.

Ambikaipaker, M. 2008. "Globalization and Bangsa Malaysia Discourse in Racial Crisis." In *Overcoming Passion for Race in Malaysian Cultural Studies*, edited by D.C.L. Lim, pp. 127–152. Boston, MA: Brill.

American Anthropological Association (AAA). 2010. *AnthroGuide 2010–2011*. Washington, DC: American Anthropological Association.

Ames, K.M., and Herbert, D.G. Maschner. 1999. *Peoples of the Northwest Coast: Their Archaeology and Prehistory*. London: Thames and Hudson.

Andaya, B.W., and L.Y. Andaya. 2001. *A History of Malaysia*. Honolulu: University of Hawai'i Press.

Anderson, A.B., P.H. May, and M.J. Balick. 1991. *The Subsidy from Nature: Palm Forests, Peasantry, and Development on an Amazon Frontier*. New York: Columbia University Press.

Anderson, B. 2006. *Imagined Communities*. Rev. ed. New York: Verso.

Anderson, E.A. 1952. *Plants, Man, and Life*. Berkeley: University of California Press.

Anderson, E.N., A.D.X. de Cen, F.M. Tzuc, and P.V. Chale 2005. *Political Ecology in a Yucatec Maya Community*. Tucson: University of Arizona Press.

Arensberg, C.M. 1988. *The Irish Countryman*. Prospect Heights, IL: Waveland.

Arrow, K.J. 2005. "Foreword." In *Economics of Globalisation*, edited by P. Gangopadhyay and M. Chatterji, pp. xi–xiv. Burlington, VT: Ashgate.

Associated Press. 2015. "IBM Claims Smaller Chip Breakthrough." *New York Times*, July 10, p. 7A.

Atran, S. 1993. *Cognitive Foundations of Natural History*. Cambridge, UK: Cambridge University Press.

Atran, S. 2003. "Genesis of Suicide Terrorism." *Science* 299(5612):1534–1539.

Aveni, A. 1995. *Empires of Time: Calendars, Clocks, and Cultures*. New York: Kodansha International.

Awaya, T. 1999. "Organ Transplantation and the Human Revolution." *Transplantation Proceedings* 31(1–2):1317–1319.

Bahuchet, S. 1993. "History of the Inhabitants of the Central African Rain Forest." In *Tropical Forests, People and Food*, edited by C.M. Hladik, A. Hladik, O.F. Linares, H. Pagezy, A. Semple, and M. Hadley, pp. 37–54. Paris: UNESCO.

Bailey, R.C., G. Head, M. Jenike, B. Own, R. Rechtman, and E. Zechenter. 1989. "Hunting and Gathering in the Tropical Rain Forest: Is It Possible?" *American Anthropologist* 91:59–82.

Balée, W. 1979. "Environmental Destruction in Northern Maranhão." *Anthropology Resource Center Newsletter* 3(4):7.

———. 1994. *Footprints of the Forest*. New York: Columbia University Press.

———. 1997. "Classification." In *The Dictionary of Anthropology*, edited by T. Barfield, pp. 64–66. Oxford: Blackwell.

———. 1999. "Mode of Production and Ethnobotanical Vocabulary." In *Ethnoecology*, edited by T.L. Gragson and B. Blount, pp. 24–40. Athens: University of Georgia Press.

———. 2003. "Review of *Participating in Development: Approaches to Indigenous Knowledge*, P. Sillitoe, A. Bicker, and J. Pottier, eds." *Journal of Anthropological Research* 59:557–559.

———. 2006. "The Research Program of Historical Ecology." *Annual Review of Anthropology* 35:75–98.

———. 2009. "The Four-Field Model of Anthropology in the United States." *Amazônica* 1(1):28–53.

———. 2010. "Contingent Diversity on Anthropic Landscapes." *Diversity* 2(2):163–181.

———. 2013. *Cultural Forests of the Amazon: A Historical Ecology of People and Their Landscapes*. Tuscaloosa: University of Alabama Press.

Balée, W., and C.L. Erickson, eds. 2006. *Time and Complexity in Historical Ecology*. New York: Columbia University Press.

Balikci, A. 1970. *The Netsilik Eskimo*. Garden City, NJ: Natural History Press.

Barnard, A. 2006. "Kalahari Revisionism, Vienna and the 'Indigenous Peoples' Debate." *Social Anthropology* 14(1):1–16.

Barry, H. 1996. "Initiation Rites." In *Encyclopedia of Cultural Anthropology*, Vol. 2, edited by D. Levinson and M. Ember, pp. 652–656. New York: Henry Holt.

Barth, F. 1969. *Ethnic Groups and Boundaries*. Boston: Little, Brown.

Bar-Yosef, O. 1998. "The Chronology of the Middle Paleolithic of the Levant." In *Neandertals and Modern Humans in Western Asia*, edited by I.T. Akazaw, K. Aochi, and O. Bar-Yosef, pp. 39–56. New York: Plenum Press.

Basso, E.B. 1973. *The Kalapalo Indians of Central Brazil*. New York: Holt, Rinehart and Winston.

Bayliss-Smith, T., E. Hviding, and T. Whitmore. 2003. "Rainforest Composition and Histories of Human Disturbance in Solomon Islands." *Ambio* 32(5):346–252.

BBC. 2019. "Rwanda Genocide." Available at: https://www.bbc.com/news/world-africa-26875506

Beach, H. 2007. "Self-Determining the Self: Aspects of Saami Identity Management in Sweden." *Acta Borealia* 24(1):1–25.

Beard, C. 2004. *The Hunt for the Dawn Monkey*. Berkeley: University of California Press.

Becker, E. 1973. *The Denial of Death*. New York: Free Press.

Beckerman, S., and P. Valentine, eds. 2002. *Cultures of Multiple Fathers*. Gainesville: University Press of Florida.

Beckmann, N., and J. Bujra. 2010. "The 'Politics of the Queue': The Politicization of People Living with HIV/AIDS in Tanzania." *Development and Change* 41(6):1041–1064.

Befu, H. 1963. "Gift-Giving in a Modernizing Japan." *Monumenta Nipponica* 23(3–4):445–456.

Bellwood, P. 2001. "Archaeology and the Historical Determinants of Punctuation in Language-Family Origins." In *Areal Diffusion and Genetic Inheritance*, edited by A.Y. Aikhenvald and R.M.W. Dixon, pp. 27–43. New York: Oxford University Press.

———. 2005. *First Farmers: The Origins of Agricultural Societies*. Oxford: Blackwell.

Benedict, R. 1946. *The Chrysanthemum and the Sword*. Boston: Houghton Mifflin.

Bentley, J.W., P. Van Mele, and G.K. Acheampong. 2010. "Experimental by Nature: Rice Farmers in Ghana." *Human Organization* 69(2):129–137.

Berdan, F.F. 2005. *The Aztecs of Central Mexico* (2nd ed.). Belmont, CA: Thomson-Wadsworth.

Berlin, B. 1992. *Ethnobiological Classification: Principles of Categorization of Plants and Animals in Traditional Societies.* Princeton, NJ: Princeton University Press.

Berlin, B., and P. Kay. 1969. *Basic Color Terms.* Berkeley: University of California Press.

Bernard, H.R. 1994. *Research Methods in Anthropology* (2nd ed.). Thousand Oaks, CA: Sage.

Besnier, N. 1990. "Language and Affect." *Annual Review of Anthropology* 19:419–451.

Bestor, T.C. 2004. *Tsukiji: The Fish Market at the Center of the World.* Los Angeles: University of California Press.

Bidney, D. 1954. "The Idea of the Savage in North American Ethnohistory." *Journal of the History of Ideas* 15:322–327.

Bilefsky, D. 2014. "France Moves to Clarify the Rules on Full Veil." *New York Times*, October 21, p. A9.

Bilefsy, D., and M. Simons. 2008. "Serbian Officials Provide Details on Arrest of Karadzic." *New York Times*, July 22.

Blacking, J. 1973. *How Musical is Man?* Seattle: University of Washington Press.

Blackwood, E. 2006. "Marriage, Matrifocality, and 'missing' men." In *Feminist Anthropology*, edited by P.L. Geller and M.K. Stockett, pp. 73–88. Philadelphia: University of Pennsylvania Press.

Blench, R. 2008. "Bananas and Plantains in Africa." Paper presented at the Sixth World Archaeological Congress, Dublin, June 29–July 5.

Boas, F. (1911) 1991. "Introduction." In *Handbook of American Indian Languages*, edited by F. Boas, pp. 1–83. Lincoln: University of Nebraska Press.

———. 1938. *The Mind of Primitive Man.* New York: Macmillan.

———. 1943. "Recent Anthropology." *Science* 98:311–314, 334–337.

———. 1948. *Race, Language and Culture.* New York: Macmillan.

Bogoras, W. 1909. *The Chukchee*, Vol. 3. New York: G. E. Stechert.

Borgatti, S.P. 1992. *ANTHROPAC 4.983/X.* Columbia, SC: Analytic Technologies.

———. 1999. "Enhanced Elicitation Techniques for Cultural Domain Analysis." In *Enhanced Ethnographic Methods: Audiovisual Techniques, Focused Group Interviews, and Elicitation Techniques*, edited by J.J. Schensul, M.D. LeCompte, B.K. Nastasi, and S.P. Borgatti, pp. 115–151. Walnut Creek, CA: AltaMira Press.

Bourdieu, P. 1985. "The Forms of Capital." In *Handbook of Theory and Research for the Sociology of Education*, edited by J.G. Richardson, pp. 241–258. New York: Greenwood.

Boxer, C.R. 1969. *The Portuguese Seaborne Empire, 1415–1825.* London: Hutchinson.

Bricker, V.R. 1999. "Color and Texture in the Maya Language of Yucatan." *Anthropological Linguistics* 41(3):283–307.

Broadbent, N.D. 2010. *Lapps and Labyrinths: Saami Prehistory, Colonization and Cultural Resilience.* Washington, DC: Smithsonian Institution Scholarly Press and Arctic Studies Center.

Brondizio, E.S. 2008. *The Amazonian Caboclo and the Acai Palm: Forest Farmers in the Global Market.* New York: New York Botanical Garden.

Brooker, R.J. 2009. *Genetics: Analysis and Principles.* Third edition. New York: McGraw-Hill International Edition.

Brown, C.H. 1984. *Language and Living Things.* New Brunswick, NJ: Rutgers University Press.

Brown, D.E. 1991. *Human Universals.* Philadelphia: Temple University Press.

Brown, H., and A.H. Kelly. 2014. "Material Proximities and Hotspots: Toward an Anthropology of Viral Hemorrhagic Fevers. *Medical Anthropology Quarterly* 28(2):280–303.

Brown, M.F. 2014. *Upriver: The Turbulent Life and Times of an Amazonian People.* Cambridge, MA: Harvard University Press.

Buchanan, L., Q. Bui, and J.K. Patel. 2020. "Black Lives Matter may be the Largest Movement in U.S. History." *New York Times*, July 8th, A15.

Bulbeck, D. 2004. "Indigenous Traditions and Exogenous Influences in the Early History of Peninsular Malaysia." In *Southeast Asia: From Prehistory to History*, edited by I. Glover and P. Bellwood, pp. 314–336. New York: Routledge Curzon.

Bureau of Labor Statistics, US Department of Labor. 2020. Occupational Outlook Handbook, Anthropologists and Archeologists, Available at: https://www.bls.gov/ooh/life-physical-and-social -science/anthropologists-and-archeologists.html.

Búriková, Z., and D. Miller. 2010. *Au Pair*. Cambridge: Polity Press.

Burke, P. 2015. "I'm an Ethnomusicologist." *Humanities* 26(1):25–27.

Burling, R. 2005. *The Talking Ape*. New York: Oxford University Press.

Burns, J.F. 2011. "Basque Separatists Halt Campaign of Violence." *New York Times*, October 21.

Burridge, K. 1973. *Encountering Aborigines: Australia and the Australian Aboriginal—A Case Study*. New York: Oxford University Press.

Burton, R. 1985. *Bird Behavior*. New York: Alfred A. Knopf.

Campagno, M. 2009. "Kinship and Family Relations." In *UCLA Encyclopedia of Egyptology*, edited by W. Wendrich, J. Dieleman, E. Frood, and J. Baines. Los Angeles: UCLA. Available at http://digital2 .library.ucla.edu/viewItem.do?ark=21198/ zz001nf68f.

Cannon, G. 1990. *The Life and Mind of Oriental Jones: Sir William Jones, the Father of Modern Linguistics*. Cambridge: Cambridge University Press.

Carneiro, R.L. 1970. "A Theory of the Origin of the State." *Science* 169:733–738.

———. 1998. "What Happened at the Flashpoint? Conjectures on Chiefdom Formation at the Very Moment of Conception." In *Chiefdoms and Chieftaincy in the Americas*, edited by E.M. Redmond, pp. 18–42. Gainesville: University Press of Florida.

———. 2003. *Evolutionism in Cultural Anthropology*. Boulder, CO: Westview.

Carsten, J. 1997. *The Heat of the Hearth: The Process of Kinship in a Malay Fishing Community*. New York: Oxford University Press.

Castillo, L.J., and S. Uceda. 2008. "The Mochicas." In *Handbook of South American Archaeology*, edited by H. Silverman and W.H. Isbell, pp. 707–729. New York: Springer.

Catton, W.R., Jr. 1980. *Overshoot: The Ecological Basis of Revolutionary Change*. Urbana: University of Illinois Press.

Chami, F. 2001a. "The Archaeology of the Rufiji Region since 1987 to 2000." In *People, Contacts and the Environment in the African Past*, edited by F. Chami, G. Pwiti, and C. Radimilahy, pp. 7–20. Dar es Salaam: University of Dar es Salaam.

———. 2001b. "Chicken Bones from Neolithic Limestone Cave Site, Zanzibar." In *People, Contacts and the Environment in the African Past*, edited by F. Chami, G. Pwiti, and C. Radimilahy, pp. 84–97. Dar es Salaam: University of Dar es Salaam.

Chapin, M. 2004. "A Challenge to Conservationists." *World Watch Magazine* 17(6):17–31.

Chomsky, N. 1957. *Syntactic Structures*. The Hague: Mouton.

———. 1965. *Aspects of the Theory of Syntax*. Cambridge, MA: MIT Press.

Churchill, E.F., and L. Nelson. 2009. "Information Flows in a Gallery-Work-Entertainment Space." *Human Organization* 68(2):206–217.

Clastres, H. 1995. *The Land-Without-Evil*. Translated by J.G. Brovender. Urbana: University of Illinois Press.

Clastres, P. 1989. *Society Against the State*. Translated by R. Hurley and A. Stein. New York: Zone Books.

Clement, C.R. 1999a. "1492 and the Loss of Amazonian Crop Genetic Resources I: The Relation between Domestication and Human Population Decline." *Economic Botany* 53:188–202.

———. 1999b. "1492 and the Loss of Amazonian Crop Genetic Resources II: Crop Biogeography at Contact." *Economic Botany* 53:203–216.

Clifford, J. 1988. *The Predicament of Culture: Twentieth-Century Ethnography, Literature, and Art*. Cambridge, MA: Harvard University Press.

Clifford, J., and G. Marcus, eds. 1986. *Writing Culture*. Berkeley: University of California Press.

Codere, H. 1950. *Fighting with Property: A Study of Kwakiutl Potlatching and Warfare, 1792–1930*. Monographs of the American Ethnological Society No. 18. New York: J. J. Augustin.

Coe, K. 2003. *The Ancestress Hypothesis*. New Brunswick, NJ: Rutgers University Press.

Coe, M.D. 1992. *Breaking the Maya Code*. New York: Thames and Hudson.

Comte, A. 1975. *Auguste Comte and Positivism: The Essential Writings*. Edited by G. Lenzer. New York: Harper and Row.

Condominas, G. 1994. *We Have Eaten the Forest*. Translated by A. Foulke. New York: Kodansha International.

Conklin, B.A. 2001. *Consuming Grief*. Austin: University of Texas Press.

Constantino, P.de.A.L., L.B. Fortini, F.R.S. Kaxinawa, A.M. Kaxinawa, A.P. Kaxinawa, L.S. Kaxinawa, J.M. Kaxinawa, and J.P. Kaxinawa. 2008. "Indigenous Collaborative Research for Wildlife Management in Amazonia." *Biological Conservation* 141(11):2718–2729.

Consumer Credit-G.19. 2020. *US Federal Reserve*. Available at: https://www.federalreserve.gov/rele ases/g19/current/

Corkery, M., D. Yaffe-Bellamy, and A. Swanson. 2020. "Powerful Meat Industry Holds More Sway After Trump's Order." *New York Times*, April 29.

Cormier, L.A. 2003. *Kinship with Monkeys*. New York: Columbia University Press.

Covey, R.A. 2008. "The Inca Empire." In *Handbook of South American Archaeology*, edited by H. Silverman and W. Isbell, pp. 809–830. New York: Springer.

Crehan, K. 2002. *Gramsci, Culture and Anthropology*. Berkeley: University of California Press.

Crewe, E., and E. Harrison. 1998. *Whose Development? An Ethnography of Aid*. New York: Zed Books.

Crocker, W.H., and J.G. Crocker. 2004. *The Canela: Kinship, Ritual, and Sex in an Amazonian Tribe* (2nd ed.). Belmont, CA: Thomson/Wadsworth.

Cronon, W. 1983. *Changes in the Land*. New York: Hill and Wang.

Crossley, P.K., H.F. Siu, and D.S. Sutton, eds. 2006. *Empire at the Margins: Culture, Ethnicity, and Frontier in Early Modern China*. Berkeley: University of California Press.

Crump, T. 1981. *The Phenomenon of Money*. London: Routledge and Kegan Paul.

Damon, F.H. 1990. *From Muyuw to the Trobriands*. Tucson, AZ: University of Arizona Press.

Dannenmaier, E. 2008. "Beyond Indigenous Property Rights: Exploring the Emergence of a Distinctive Connection Doctrine." *Washington University Law Review* 86:53–110.

Dark, K.R. 2007. "Globalizing Late Antiquity." In *Incipient Globalization? Long-Distance Contacts in the Sixth Century*, edited by A. Harris, pp. 3–14. BAR International Series No. 1644. Oxford: Archaeopress.

Darnell, R. 1977. "History of Anthropology in Historical Perspective." *Annual Review of Anthropology* 6:399–417.

Darwin, C. (1859) 1998. *The Origin of Species* (1st ed.). Ware: Wordsworth.

Davies, S.G. 2007. *Challenging Gender Norms: Five Genders among Bugis in Indonesia*. Belmont, CA: Thomson Wadsworth.

Dean, R.M. 2010. "The Importance of Anthropogenic Environments." In *The Archaeology of Anthropogenic Environments*, edited by R.M. Dean, pp. 3–14. Carbondale, IL: Center for Archaeological Investigations, Southern Illinois University at Carbondale.

de Condorcet, MarieJeanAntoineNicolas. (1795) 1955. *Sketch for a Historical Picture of the Progress of the Human Mind*. Translated by J. Barraclough. London: Weidenfeld and Nicolson.

DeFries, R., F. Achard, C. Justice, N. Laporte, K. Price, C. Small, and J. Townshend. 2005. "Monitoring Tropical Deforestation for Emerging Carbon Markets." In *Tropical Deforestation and Climate Change*, edited by P. Moutinho and S. Schwartzman, pp. 35–44. Belém: Instituto de Pesquisa da Amazônia, Environmental Defense Fund.

De Langhe, E., and P. de Maret. 1999. "Tracking the Banana: Its Significance in Early Agriculture." In *The Prehistory of Food*, edited by C. Gosden and J. Hather, pp. 277–296. London: Routledge.

Denevan, W.M. 1992. "Native American Populations in 1492: Recent Research and a Revised Hemispheric Estimate." In *The Native Population of the Americas in 1492* (2nd ed.), edited by W.M. Denevan, pp. xvii–xxxviii. Madison: University of Wisconsin Press.

———. 2006. "Pre-European Forest Cultivation in Amazonia." In *Time and Complexity in Historical Ecology*, edited by W. Balée and C.L. Erickson, pp. 153–163. New York: Columbia University Press.

Denny, R., and P. Sunderland, eds. 2014. *Handboook of Anthropology in Business*. Walnut Creek, CA: Left Coast Press, Inc.

de Saussure, F. (1916) 1959. *Course in General Linguistics*. New York: Philosophical Library.

Descola, P. 1996. *The Spears of Twilight*. New York: New Press.

Diamond, J. 2005. *Collapse: How Societies Choose to Fail or Succeed*. New York: Viking.

di Leonardo, M. 2001. "Margaret Mead vs. Tony Soprano." *The Nation* 272(20):29–35.

Dixon, R.M.W. 1997. *The Rise and Fall of Languages*. Cambridge: Cambridge University Press.

Dominguez, V.R. 1994. *White by Definition*. New Brunswick, NJ: Rutgers University Press.

Doughty, P.L. 2002. "Ending Serfdom in Peru: The Struggle for Land and Freedom in Vicos." In *Contemporary Cultures and Societies of Latin America: A Reader in the Social Anthropology of Middle and South America*, edited by D.B. Heath, pp. 225–243. Prospect Heights, IL: Waveland Press.

Douglas, M. 1966. *Purity and Danger*. New York: Ark.

Du, S. 2002. *Chopsticks Only Work in Pairs*. New York: Columbia University Press.

Dumont, L. 1970. *Homo Hierarchicus: An Essay on the Caste System*. Translated by M. Sainsbury. London: University of Chicago Press.

Dunbar, R.I.M. 2003. "The Social Brain: Mind, Language, and Society in Evolutionary Perspective." *Annual Review of Anthropology* 32:163–181.

Duranti, A. 2001. "Linguistic Anthropology: History, Ideas, and Issues." In *Linguistic Anthropology: A Reader*, edited by A. Duranti, pp. 1–38. Oxford: Blackwell.

Durkheim, E. (1893) 1933. *The Division of Labor in Society*. Translated by G. Simpson. Glencoe, IL: Free Press.

———. (1895) 1964. *The Rules of the Sociological Method*. New York: Free Press.

———. (1912) 1995. *The Elementary Forms of Religious Life*. Translated by K.E. Fields. New York: Free Press.

Earle, T. 2002. *Bronze Age Economics*. Boulder, CO: Westview.

Early, J.D., and J.F. Peters. 1990. *The Population Dynamics of the Mucajai Yanomama*. San Diego, CA: Academic Press.

Eaton, S.B., and S. Boyd Eaton. 1999. "Hunter-Gatherers and Human Health." In *Cambridge Encyclopedia of Hunters and Gatherers*, edited by R.B. Lee and R. Daly, pp. 449–456. Cambridge: Cambridge University Press.

The Economist. 2011. "More Anthropologists on Wall Street Please: Education Policy." October 24. Available at: http://www.economist.com/blogs/democracyinamerica/2011/10/education-policy.

Edmonson, M.S. 1971. *Lore: An Introduction to the Science of Folklore and Literature*. Dallas: Holt, Rinehart and Winston.

Edwards, J.N. 1991. "New Conceptions: Biosocial Innovations and the Family." *Journal of Marriage and the Family* 53(2):349–360.

Eggan, F. 1963. "The Graduate Program." In *The Teaching of Anthropology*, edited by D.G. Mandelbaum, G.W. Lasker, and E.M. Albert, pp. 409–420. Washington, DC: American Anthropological Association.

Ehrenreich, J.D. 2013. "Mardi Gras Indians." In *Encyclopedia of Race and Racism*, Second Edition, vol. 3, edited by P.L. Mason, pp. 105–110. New York: Macmillan Reference USA.

Ellis, E.C., and N. Ramankutty. 2008. "Putting People in the Map: Anthropogenic Biomes of the World." *Frontiers in Ecology and the Environment* 6:439–447.

Ember, C. 1996. "Gender Differences and Roles." In *Encyclopedia of Cultural Anthropology*, Vol. 2, edited by D. Levinson and M. Ember, pp. 519–514. New York: Henry Holt.

Endicott, K.L. 1999. "Gender Relations in Hunter-Gatherer Societies." In *The Cambridge Encyclopedia of Hunters and Gatherers*, edited by R.B. Lee and R. Daly, pp. 411–418. Cambridge: Cambridge University Press.

Endicott, K.M., and K.L. Endicott. 2008. *The Headman Was a Woman: The Gender Egalitarian Batek of Malaysia*. Long Grove, IL: Waveland Press.

Ensworth, P. 2014. "The Anthropologist as IT Troubleshooter on Wall Street." In *Handboook of Anthropology in Business*, edited by R. Denny and P. Sunderland, pp. 202–222. Walnut Creek, CA: Left Coast Press, Inc.

Erickson, C.L. 2008. "Amazonia: The Historical Ecology of a Domesticated Landscape." In *Handbook of South American Archaeology*, edited by H. Silverman and W.H. Isbell, pp. 157–183. New York: Springer.

Erickson, C.L., and W. Balée. 2006. "The Historical Ecology of a Complex Landscape in Bolivia." In *Time and Complexity in Historical Ecology: Studies in the Neotropical Lowlands*, edited by W. Balée and C.L. Erickson, pp. 187–233. New York: Columbia University Press.

Evans-Pritchard, E.E. (1940) 1969. *The Nuer*. New York: Oxford University Press.

———. (1951) 1990. *Kinship and Marriage among the Nuer*. New York: Oxford University Press.

Fagan, B. 2010. *Cro-Magnon*. New York: Bloomsbury.

Fairhead, J., and M. Leach. 1996. *Misreading the African Landscape*. Cambridge: Cambridge University Press.

"False Start." 2020. *The Economist* 437 (9219): 33–35.

Farmer, P. 2014. "Diary: Ebola." *London Review of Books* 36(20):38–39.

Fausto, C. 2000. *Os índios antes do Brasil*. Rio de Janeiro, Brazil: Jorge Zahar.

Feldman, G. 2009. "Radical or Revolutionary?" In *The Counter-Counterinsurgency Manual*, edited by C. Besteman et al., pp. 77–99. Chicago, IL: Prickly Paradigm Press.

Felt, U., R. Fouché, C.A. Miller, and L. Smith-Doerr, eds. 2017. *The Handbook of Science and Technology Studies*. 4th ed. Cambridge, MA: MIT Press.

Ferguson, Adam. (1767) 1995. *An Essay on the History of Civil Society*. Edited by F. Oz-Salzberg. Cambridge: Cambridge University Press.

Field, L., and R.G. Fox, eds. 2007. *Anthropology Put to Work*. New York: Berg.

Finlayson, L. 2004. *Neandertals and Modern Humans*. Cambridge: Cambridge University Press.

Firth, R. 1989. "Second Introduction (1988)." In *A Diary in the Strict Sense of the Term*, Malinowski, pp. xxi–xxxi. Stanford, CA: Stanford University Press.

Fisher, M. 2019. "'One Country', Two Nationalisms." *New York Times*, September 27.

Flannery, T. 2005. *The Weather Makers*. New York: Grove Press.

Fleisher, M.F. 1995. *Beggars and Thieves: Lives of Urban Street Criminals*. Madison: University of Wisconsin Press.

Foley, D.E. 2007. "Reflections on the Symposium." In *Anthropology Put to Work*, edited by L. Field and R.G. Fox, pp. 217–223. New York: Berg.

Fowler, C.S., and N.J. Turner. 1999. "Ecological/Cosmological Knowledge and Land Management among Hunter-Gatherers." In *Cambridge Encyclopedia of Hunters and Gatherers*, edited by R.B. Lee and R. Daly, pp. 419–425. Cambridge: Cambridge University Press.

Fox, R. 1967. *Kinship and Marriage*. New York: Penguin.

———. 1969. "'Professional Primitives': Hunters and Gatherers of Nuclear South Asia." *Man in India* 49:139–160.

Frank, G. 2007. "Collaborating to Meet the Goals of a Native Sovereign Nation: The Tule River Tribal History Project." In *Anthropology Put to Work*, edited by L. Field and R.G. Fox, pp. 65–83. New York: Berg.

Frazier, J.G. 2010. "The Call of the Wild." In *The Archaeology of Anthropogenic Environments*, edited by R.M. Dean, pp. 341–369. Carbondale, IL: Center for Archaeological Investigations, Southern Illinois University at Carbondale.

Freidenberg, J. 2011. "Researching Global Spaces Ethnographically." *Human Organization* 70(3):265–278.

French, J.H. 2009. *Legalizing Identities: Becoming Black or Indian in Brazil's Northeast*. Chapel Hill: University of North Carolina Press.

Freud, S. 1938. *The Basic Writings of Sigmund Freud*. Translated by and Edited by A.A. Brill. New York: Modern Library.

Fried, M. 1967. *The Evolution of Political Society*. New York: Random House.

Fuentes, C.M.M. 2011. "Breaking the Pathways between Domestic Violence and Sexually Transmitted Infections." *Human Organization* 70(2):128–138.

Fuller, D.Q., and C. Murphy. 2014. "Overlooked but Not Forgotten: India as a Center for Agricultural Domestication." *General Anthropology* 21(2):1, 5–8.

Fuller, T. 2014. "Want to Touch a Dog? In Malaysia, It's a Delicate Subject." *New York Times*, October 27, p. A4.

Funderburg, L. 2013. "The Changing Face of America." *National Geographic* 224(4):80–91.

Galvin, K.-L. 2001. "Schneider Revisited: Sharing and Ratification in the Construction of Kinship." In *New Directions in Anthropological Kinship*, edited by L. Stone, pp. 109–124. Lanham, MD: Rowman and Littlefield.

Gardner, K., and D. Lewis. 1996. *Anthropology, Development, and the Post-Modern Challenge*. Chicago, IL: Pluto Press.

Gates, H. 2004. "Refining the Incest Taboo." In *Inbreeding, Incest, and the Incest Taboo*, edited by A.P. Wolf and W.H. Durham, pp. 139–160. Palo Alto, CA: Stanford University Press.

Geertz, C. 1973. *The Interpretation of Cultures*. New York: Basic Books.

Gellner, E. 1988. *Plough, Sword and Book*. London: Collins Harvill.

George, A. 2011. "Interview with Svante Pääbo." *New Scientist* 211(2828):30–31.

Gibbon, A. 2011. "Skeletons Present an Exquisite Paleo-Puzzle." *Science* 333:1370–1372.

———. 2013. "Ardi's a Hominin—But How Did She Move?" *Science* 340:427.

Giddens, A. 2000. *Runaway World: How Globalization Is Reshaping Our Lives*. New York: Routledge.

Gillis, J. 2014. "Group Earns Oil Income Despite Pledge on Drilling." *New York Times*, August 4, p. A12.

Glasser, I., and R. Bridgman. 1999. *Braving the Street: The Anthropology of Homelessness*. New York: Berghahn.

Gmelch, G. 1992. "Superstition and Ritual in American Baseball." *Elysian Fields Quarterly*, 11(3):25–36.

Goggin, J.M., and W.H. Sturtevant. 1964. "The Calusa: A Stratified Nonagricultural Society (with Notes on Sibling Marriage)." In *Explorations in Cultural Anthropology: Essays in Honor of George Peter Murdock*, edited by W.H. Goodenough, pp. 179–219. New York: McGraw-Hill.

Goldsworthy, A. 2009. *How Rome Fell: Death of a Superpower*. New Haven, CT: Yale University Press.

González, R. 2009. "Embedded." In *The Counter-Counterinsurgency Manual*, edited by Besteman et al., pp. 197–113. Chicago, IL: Prickly Paradigm Press.

González, R., H. Gusterson, and D. Price. 2009. "Introduction." In *The Counter-Counterinsurgency Manual*, edited by C. Besteman et al., pp. 1–22. Chicago, IL: Prickly Paradigm Press.

Goodale, J.C. 1994. *Tiwi Wives*. Prospect Heights, IL: Waveland Press.

Goodale, M. 2006. "Reclaiming Modernity: Indigenous Cosmopolitanism and the Coming of the Second Revolution in Bolivia." *American Ethnologist* 33(4):634–649.

Goodall, J. 1986. *The Chimpanzees of Gombe*. Cambridge, MA: Harvard University Press.

Goodenough, W. 1955. "A Problem in Malayo-Polynesian Social Organization." *American Anthropologist* 57:71–83.

Goody, J. 1990. *The Oriental, the Ancient, and the Primitive*. Cambridge: Cambridge University Press.

Gough, K. 1968. "The Nayars and the Definition of Marriage." In *Marriage, Family and Residence*, edited by P. Bohannan and J. Middleton, pp. 49–71. Garden City, NJ: Natural History Press.

Graeber, D. 2011. *Debt: The First 5,000 Years*. Brooklyn, NY: Melville House.

Gramsci, A. 1975. *Prison Notebooks*, Vol. II. Translated by and Edited by J.A. Buttigieg. New York: Columbia University Press.

Graves, J.L., Jr. 2001. *The Emperor's New Clothes: Biological Theories of Race at the Millennium*. New Brunswick, NJ: Rutgers University Press.

Gray, R.E., and F.M. Jordan. 2000. "Language Trees Support the Express-Train Sequence of Austronesian Expansion." *Nature* 405:1052–1055.

Green, R.E., et al. 2010. "A Draft Sequence of the Neandertal Genome." *Science* 328:710–722.

Gregor, T. 1977. *Mehinaku: The Drama of Daily Life in a Brazilian Indian Village*. Chicago, IL: University of Chicago Press.

Grinker, R.R. 1994. *Houses in the Rainforest*. Berkeley: University of California Press.

Grove, A.T., and O. Rackham. 2001. *The Nature of Mediterranean Europe*. New Haven, CT: Yale University Press.

Guynup, S., and N. Ruggia. 2004. "For Most People, Eating Bugs Is Only Natural." *National Geographic News*, July 15. Available at http://news.nationalgeographic.com/ news/2004/07/0715_040715_tvinsectfood.html.

Gwatirisa, P., and L. Manderson. 2009. "Food Insecurity and HIV/AIDS in Low-Income Households in Urban Zimbabwe." *Human Organization* 68(1):103–112.

Haldon, J. et al. 2020. "Demystifying Collapse." *Millennium* 17(1). doi:10.1515/mill-2020-0002.

Hall, E.T. 1990. *The Silent Language*. New York: Anchor Books.

Hall, T. 2019. "Homelessness and the City." In *The Routledge Handbook of Anthropology and the City*, edited by S. Low, pp. 55–68. New York: Routledge.

Hallowell, A.I. 1960. "The Beginnings of Anthropology in America." In *Selected Papers from the American Anthropologist*, edited by F. de Laguna, pp. 1–90. Evanston, IL: Row, Peterson.

Hammel, E. 1995. "Science and Humanism in Anthropology: A View from the Balkan Pit." *Anthropology Newsletter* 36(7):52.

Hardy, L. 2020. "Connection, Contagion, and COVID-19." *Medical Anthropology*. doi:10.1080/01459 740.2020.1814773

Harris, M. 1974. *Cows, Pigs, Wars, and Witches*. New York: Random House.

———. 1976. "History and Significance of the Emic/Etic Distinction." *Annual Review of Anthropology* 5:329–350.

———. 1979. *Cultural Materialism*. New York: Random House.

Harris, M., and C. Kottak. 1963. "The Structural Significance of Brazilian Racial Categories." *Sociologica* 25: 203–209.

Harris, M., J.G. Consork, and B. Byrne. 1993. "Who Are the Whites?" *Social Forces* 72(2):451–462.

Harrison, K.D., and E. Raimy. 2007. "Language as an Emergent System." *Soundings* 90(1–2):77–90.

Hart, C.W.M., A.R. Pilling, and J.C. Goodale. 2001. *The Tiwi of North Australia* (3rd ed.). Belmont, CA: Wadsworth.

Hart, T.B., and J.A. Hart. 1986. "The Ecological Basis of Hunter-Gatherer Subsistence in African Rain Forests." *Human Ecology* 14:29–55.

Harvey, D. 1989. *The Condition of Postmodernity: An Enquiry into the Origins of Cultural Change*. Oxford: Basil Blackwell.

Hastorf, C.A. 2006. "Domesticated Food and Society in Early Coastal Peru." In *Time and Complexity in Historical Ecology*, edited by W. Balée and C.L Erickson, pp. 87–126. New York: Columbia University Press.

Haudricourt, A.-G. 2010. *Des gestes aux techniques: Essai sur les techniques dans les sociétés pré-machinistes*. Edited by A.-G. Haudricourt. Paris: Éditions de la Maison des Sciences de l'Homme.

Headland, T.N. 1987. "The Wild Yam Question: How Well Can Independent HunterGatherers Live in a Tropical Rain Forest Ecosystem?" *Human Ecology* 15:463–491.

Heather, P. 2007. *The Fall of the Roman Empire: A New History of Rome and the Barbarians*. New York: Oxford University Press.

Hecht, S., K.D. Morrison, and C. Padoch. 2014. *The Social Lives of Forests: Past, Present, and Future of Woodland Resurgence*. Chicago, IL: University of Chicago Press.

Henig, D. 2014. "Scott Atran on War, Fight, Conflicts in the Middle East and the US Foreign Policy." *Anthropology News*, November/December, p. 45.

Henke, C.R. 2008. *Cultivating Science, Harvesting Power*. Cambridge, MA: MIT Press.

Henley, P. 2006. "Anthropologists in Television: A Disappearing World?" In *Applications of Anthropology: Professional Anthropology in the Twenty-First Century*, edited by S. Pink, pp. 170–189. New York: Berghahn.

Henshilwood, C.S., and C.W. Marean. 2003. "The Origin of Modern Human Behavior." *Current Anthropology* 44:627–651.

Henton, C. 1995. "Pitch Dynamics in Female and Male Speech." *Language and Communication* 15(1):43–61.

Hertz, R. 1973. *Right and Left*. Translated by R. Needham and C. Needham. Chicago, IL: University of Chicago Press.

Hewlett, B.S. 1991. *Intimate Fathers*. Ann Arbor: University of Michigan Press.

Hewlett, B.S., and L.L. Cavalli-Sforza. 1986. "Cultural Transmission among Aka Pygmies." *American Anthropologist* 88(4):922–934.

Hill, R.M. 1992. *Colonial Cakchiquels: Highland Maya Adaptation to Spanish Rule, 1600–1700*. Fort Worth, TX: Harcourt Brace Jovanovich.

Himmelgreen, D.A., and D.L. Crooks. 2005. "Nutritional Anthropology and Its Application to Nutritional Issues and Problems." In *Applied Anthropology: Domains of Application*, edited by S. Kedia and J. van Willigen, pp. 149–188. Westport, CT: Praeger Publishers.

Hinsley, C.M., Jr. 1981. *Savages and Scientists: The Smithsonian Institution and the Development of American Anthropology 1846–1910*. Washington, DC: Smithsonian Institution Press.

———. 1999. "Hopi Snakes, Zuñi Corn: Early Ethnography in the American Southwest." In *Colonial Subjects: Essays in the Practical History of Anthropology*, edited by P. Pels and O. Salemink, pp. 180–195. Ann Arbor: University of Michigan Press.

Hinton, A.L. 2010. "'Night Fell on a Different World': Dangerous Visions and the War on Terror, a Lesson from Cambodia." In *Iraq at a Distance: What Anthropologists Can Teach Us about the War*, edited by A.C.G.M. Robben, pp. 24–56. Philadelphia: University of Pennsylvania Press.

Hobbes, T. (1651) 1985. *Leviathan*. London: Penguin Books.

Hoebel, E.A. 1988. *The Cheyennes* (2nd ed). Fort Worth, TX: Harcourt Brace.

Hogbin, I. 1996. *The Island of Menstruating Men*. Prospect Heights, IL: Waveland Press.

Hohn, H.H., and G. Sorensen. 1995. *Whose World Order? Uneven Globalization and the End of the Cold War*. Boulder, CO: Westview.

Holland, J.H. 1998. *Emergence*. Reading, MA: Addison-Wesley.

Holler, J. 2007. "Mexico City." In *Encyclopedia of Western Colonialism since 1450*, Vol. 2, edited by T. Benjamin, pp. 775–776. Detroit, MI: MacMillan References USA.

Holtzman, J.D. 2008. *Nuer Journeys, Nuer Lives: Sudanese Refugees in Minnesota* (2nd ed.). New York: Pearson.

Hornborg, A. 1999. "Money and the Semiotics of Ecosystem Dissolution." *Journal of Material Culture* 4(2):143–162.

Hostetler, J.A., and G.E. Huntington. 1980. *The Hutterites in North America*. Fort Worth, TX: Harcourt Brace.

Houk, J.T. 1995. *Spirit, Blood, and Drums*. Philadelphia: Temple University Press.

Hume, D. (1739) 1955. *A Treatise of Human Nature, Being an Attempt to Introduce the Experimental Method of Reasoning into Moral Subjects*. Edited by L.A. Selby-Bigge. Oxford: Clarendon Press.

Humphrey, C. 2006. "On Being Named and Not Named: Authority, Persons, and Their Names in Mongolia." In *The Anthropology of Names and Naming*, edited by B. Bodenhorn and G. Vom Bruck, pp. 157–176. Cambridge: Cambridge University Press.

Hunn, E., D.R. Johnson, P.N. Russell, and T.F. Thornton. 2003. "Huna Tlingit Traditional Environmental Knowledge of Conservation and the Management of a 'Wilderness' Park." *Current Anthropology* 44:S79–S103.

Hunt, G.R., and Gray, R.D. 2004. "Direct Observations of Pandanus-Tool Manufacture and Use by a New Caledonian Crow (*Corvus moneduloides*)." *Animal Cognition* 7(2):114–120.

Hunter, J.P. 2008. "Anthropologist Helps Soldiers Understand Iraqis' Needs." *U.S. Department of Defense DoD News*, January 25. Available at http://archive.defense.gov/ news/newsarticle.aspx?id=48766.

Hurston, Z.N. 1969. *Dust Tracks on a Road*. New York: Arno Press.

Huston, M.A. 1994. *Biological Diversity*. Cambridge: Cambridge University Press.

Hutchinson, S.E. 1996. *Nuer Dilemmas: Coping with Money, War, and the State*. Berkeley: University of California Press.

Impey, O. 2000. "Urushiware of the Orient." In *Japanese and European Lacquerware*, edited by M. Kühlenthal, pp. 15–30. Munich: Areitshefete des Bayerischen Landesamtes für Denkmalpflege.

Ingold, T. 1999. "On the Social Relations of the Hunter-Gatherer Band." In *The Cambridge Encyclopedia of Hunters and Gatherers*, edited by R.B. Lee and R. Daly, pp. 399–410. Cambridge: Cambridge University Press.

Isaac, M. 2014. "The Next Step in Money. Maybe." *New York Times*, October 21, p. B1.

Isbell, W.H. 1997. *Mummies and Mortuary Monuments*. Austin: University of Texas Press.

Itakura, H., and A.B.M. Tsui. 2004. "Gender and Conversational Dominance in Japanese Conversation." *Language in Society* 33(2):223–248.

J.I. 2008. "Sea Lice, Aquaculture and 'Namgis Resistance.'" *Kwakwaka'wakw*, December 9. Available at http://kwakwakawakw.blogspot.com/2008/12/sea-lice-aquaculture-and-namgis.html.

Jackson, A.T. 2011. "Shattering Slave Life Portrayals: Uncovering Subjugated Knowledge in U.S. Plantation Sites in South Carolina and Florida." *American Anthropologist* 113(3):448–462.

Jackson, J. 1990. "'I Am a Fieldnote': Fieldnotes as a Symbol of Professional Identity." In *Fieldnotes: The Makings of Anthropology*, edited by R. Sanjek, pp. 3–33. Ithaca, NY: Cornell University Press.

Jankowiak, W. 2001. "In the Name of the Father." In *New Directions in Anthropological Kinship*, edited by L. Stone, pp. 264–284. Lanham, MD: Rowman and Littlefield.

Jefferson, T. (1785) 1999. *Notes on the State of Virginia*. Edited by F.C. Shuffelton. New York: Penguin.

Jobson, R.C. 2020. The Case for Letting Anthropology Burn: Sociocultural Anthropology in 2019. *American Anthropologist* 122(2): 259–271.

Johnson, A. 1975. "Time Allocation in a Machiguenga Community." *Ethnology* 14:301–310.

———. 2003. *Families of the Forest*. Berkeley: University of California Press.

Johnson, P.C. 2007. "On Leaving and Joining Africanness through Religion: The 'Black Caribs' across Multiple Diasporic Horizons." *Journal of Religion in Africa* 37(2):174–211.

Johnston, B.R., and S. Slyomovics, eds. 2008. *Waging War, Making Peace*. Walnut Creek, CA: Left Coast Press, Inc.

Jones, J.L. 2009. "Speaking of Race." *Anthropology News*, September, p. 23.

Kahn, M. 1994. *Always Hungry, Never Greedy: Food and the Expression of Gender in a Melanesian Society*. Prospect Heights, IL: Waveland Press.

Kaplan, M. 2011. "Genomics in Africa." *Cell* 147(1):11–13.

Karim, W-J.B. 1981. *Ma' Betisek Concepts of Living Things*. London: Athlone Press.

Kearney, M. 1996. "Peasants." In *Encyclopedia of Cultural Anthropology*, Vol. 3, edited by D. Levinson and M. Ember, pp. 913–917. New York: Henry Holt.

Kehoe, A.B. 2006. *The Ghost Dance: Ethnohistory and Revitalization* (2nd ed.). Long Grove, IL: Waveland Press.

Kelly, C. 2006. *The Roman Empire*. New York: Oxford University Press.

Kelly, R.C. 2000. *Warless Societies and the Origin of War*. Ann Arbor: University of Michigan Press.

Kelly, R.L. 1995. *The Foraging Spectrum*. Washington, DC: Smithsonian Institution Press.

Keyes, C. 1997. "Ethnic Groups, Ethnicity." In *The Dictionary of Anthropology*, edited by T. Barfield, pp. 152–154. Oxford: Blackwell.

Kidder, T. 2004. *Mountains beyond Mountains*. New York: Random House.

Kidder, T.R. 1998. "The Rat That Ate Louisiana." In *Advances in Historical Ecology*, edited by W. Balée, pp. 141–168. New York: Columbia University Press.

Kiley, S. 2020. "Hunting for 'Disease X'." Available at: https://www.cnn.com/2020/12/22/africa/drc-forest-new-virus-intl/index.html.

Kline, N. 2015. "Militarizing Life." *Anthropology News* 56(5–6):5.

Kluckhohn, C. 1961. *Anthropology and the Classics*. Providence, RI: Brown University Press.

Knight, C. 1991. *Blood Relations*. New Haven, CT: Yale University Press.

Kobayashi, H., and S. Kahshima. 1997. "Unique Morphology of the Human Eye." *Nature* 387:767–768.

Kolbert, E. 2006. *Field Notes from a Catastrophe*. New York: Bloomsbury.

Krauss, M.E. 1992. "The World's Languages in Crisis." *Language* 68(1):4–10.

Kroeber, A.L. 1948. *Anthropology*. New York: Harcourt, Brace and World.

Kroeber, A.L., and C. Kluckhohn. 1952. *Culture: A Critical Review of Concepts and Definitions*. Papers of the Peabody Museum of American Archaeology and Ethnology, Harvard University Press 47(1):1–223.

Kroeber, T. 2004. *Ishi in Two Worlds*. Berkeley: University of California Press.

Kroskrity, P.V., and M.C. Field, eds. 2009. *Native American Language Ideologies: Beliefs, Practices, and Struggles in Indian Country*. Tucson: University of Arizona Press.

Kwok-bun, C. 2005. "Introduction: Globalization, Localization, and Hybridization." In *East-West Identities: Globalization, Localization, and Hybridization*, edited by C. Kwokbun, J.W. Walls, and D. Hayward, pp. 1–19. Boston, MA: Brill.

Lai, C.S.L., S.E. Fisher, J.A. Hurst, et al. 2001. "A Forkhead-Domain Gene Is Mutated in a Severe Speech and Language Disorder." *Nature* 413:519–523.

Langstroth, R.P. 1996. "Forest Islands in an Amazonian Savanna of Northeastern Bolivia." Unpublished PhD dissertation, University of Wisconsin, Madison.

Lansing, J.S. 2006. *Perfect Order: Recognizing Complexity in Bali*. Princeton, NJ: Princeton University Press.

Larsen, C.S. 2011. *Our Origins* (2nd ed.). New York: W. W. Norton.

Latham, R. (Trans. educ.). 1958. *The Travels of Marco Polo*. London: Penguin Books.

Lattimore, O. 1951. *Inner Asian Frontiers of China* (2nd ed.). Boston, MA: Beacon Press.

Lazar, S. 2008. *El Alto, Rebel City*. Durham, NC: Duke University Press.

Lee, R.B. 2013. *The Dobe Ju/'hoansi* (4th ed.). Belmont, CA: Wadsworth.

———. 2007. "The Ju/'hoansi at the Crossroads: Continuity and Change in the Time of AIDS." In *Globalization and Change in Fifteen Cultures*, edited by G. Spindler and J. E. Stockard, pp. 144–171. Belmont, CA: Thomson Higher Education.

Lee, R.B., and R. Daly. 1999. *The Cambridge Encyclopedia of Hunters and Gatherers*. Cambridge: Cambridge University Press.

Leslie, C. 1963. "Teaching Anthropology and the Humanities." In *The Teaching of Anthropology*, edited by D.G. Mandelbaum, G.W. Lasker, and E.M. Albert, pp. 485–491. Washington, DC: American Anthropological Association.

Lévi-Strauss, C. (1949) 1969. *The Elementary Structures of Kinship*. Boston, MA: Beacon Press.

———. (1955). 2012. *Tristes Tropiques*. Translated by J. Weightman and D. Weightman. New York: Penguin Classics.

———. 1963. *Structural Anthropology*. New York: Basic Books.

———. 1976. *Structural Anthropology*, Vol. II. Translated by Med. Layton. New York: Basic Books.

Lewis-Williams, D. 2002. *The Mind in the Cave*. London: Thames and Hudson.

———. 2010. *Conceiving God*. London: Thames and Hudson.

Lindstrom, L. 2004. "Cargo Cult at the Third Millennium." In *Cargo, Cult and Culture Critique*, edited by H. Jebens, pp. 15–35. Honolulu: University of Hawai'i Press.

Linton, R. 1937. "One Hundred Percent American." *The American Mercury* 40: 427–429.

Lips, H. 2008. *Sex and Gender* (6th ed.). New York: McGraw-Hill.

Livingston, F.B. 1958. "Anthropological Implications of Sickle Cell Gene Distribution in West Africa." *American Anthropologist* 60:533–562.

Looser, T. 2019. "21st Century City Form in Asia." In *The Routledge Handbook of Anthropology and the City*, edited by S. Low, pp. 421–433. New York: Routledge.

Low, S. 2019. "Introduction: Engaging the City and the Future." In *The Routledge Handbook of Anthropology and the City*, edited by S. Low, pp. 3–24. New York: Routledge.

Low, S., and A. Smart. 2020. "Thoughts about Public Space during Covid-19 Pandemic." *City and Society* 32. doi:10.1111/ciso.12260.

Lowie, R.H. 1928. "A Note on Relationship Terminologies." *American Anthropologist* 30:263–268.

———. 1929. "Relationships Terms." *Encyclopedia Britannica* (14th ed.) 19:84–86.

Lucassen, L., W. Willems, and A. Cuttaar, eds. 1998. *Gypsies and Other Itinerant Groups: A Socio-Historical Approach*. New York: St. Martin's Press.

Lucy, J.A. 1992. *Language Diversity and Thought*. New York: Cambridge University Press.

Luque, J.S., H. Castañeda, D.M. Tyson, N. Vargas, S. Proctor, and C.D. Meade. 2010. "HPV Awareness among Latina Immigrants and Anglo-American Women in the Southern United States: Cultural Models of Cervical Cancer Risk Factors and Beliefs." *NAPA Bulletin* 34:84–104.

MacCabe, C., and H. Yanacek, eds. 2018. *Keywords for Today: A 21st Century Vocabulary*. New York: Oxford University Press.

Mackin, J.A, Jr. 1997. *Community over Chaos*. Tuscaloosa: University of Alabama Press.

MacMahon, D.A., and W.H. Marquardt. 2004. *The Calusa and Their Legacy*. Gainesville: University Press of Florida.

MacLeod, M. 2007. "Export Commodities." In *Encyclopedia of Western Colonialism since 1450*, Vol. 1, edited by T. Benjamin, pp. 474–479. Detroit, MI: MacMillan References USA.

Maguire, M., C. Frois, and N. Zurawski, eds. 2014. *The Anthropology of Security: Perspectives from the Frontline of Policing, Counter-Terrorism and Border Control*. London: Pluto Press.

Malinowski, B. (1922) 1984. *Argonauts of the Western Pacific*. Prospect Heights, IL: Waveland Press.

———. 1944. *A Scientific Theory of Culture*. Chapel Hill: University of North Carolina Press.

———. (1967) 1989. *A Diary in the Strict Sense of the Term*. Stanford, CA: Stanford University Press.

Manderson, L., and S. Levine. 2020. "COVID-19, Risk, Fear, and Fall-out." *Medical Anthropology* 39(5):367–370.

Manganas, N. 2010. "Mass-Mediated Social Terror in Spain." In *Representing Humanity in an Age of Terror*, edited by S. McClenne and H.J. Morello, pp. 187–205. West Lafayette, IN: Purdue University Press.

Marcus, G.E. 1995. "Ethnography in/of the World System: The Emergence of Multi-Sited Ethnography." *Annual Review of Anthropology* 24:95–112.

Martin, P.S., and R.G. Klein, eds. 1984. *Quaternary Extinctions*. Tucson: University of Arizona Press.

Martin, T.R. 1996. *Ancient Greece, from Prehistoric to Hellenistic Times*. New Haven, CT: Yale University Press.

Marx, K. (1844) 1977a. "Economic and Philosophical Manuscripts." In *Karl Marx: Selected Writings*, edited by D. McLellan, pp. 75–112. Oxford: Oxford University Press.

———. (1867) 1977b. *Capital*, Vol. 1. Translated by S. Moore and E. Aveling. New York: International Publishers.

Mauer, B. 2006. "The Anthropology of Money." *Annual Review of Anthropology* 35:15–36.

Mauss, M. 1990. *The Gift*. Translated by W.D. Halls. London: Routledge.

Maynard-Tucker, G. 2008. "Insecurities Confronting HIV/AIDS Programs in Africa." *Practicing Anthropology* 30(4):21–25.

McGrane, B. 1989. *Beyond Anthropology*. New York: Columbia University Press.

McLuhan, M. 1962. *The Gutenberg Galaxy: The Making of Typographic Man*. London: Routledge and Kegan Paul.

McNeil, C., D.A. Burney, and L.P. Burney. 2010. "Evidence Disputing Deforestation as the Cause for the Collapse of the Ancient Maya Polity of Copan, Honduras." *Proceedings of the National Academy of Sciences of the United States of America* 107(3):1017–1022.

Mead, S.F. 2008. "Crossing the Border: Poverty, HIV, and the Women of the Ghana-Togo Corridor." *Practicing Anthropology* 30(4):4–7.

Meek, R.L. 1973. *Turgot on Progress, Sociology and Economics*. Cambridge: Cambridge University Press.

Meggitt, M.J. 1965. *The Lineage System of the Mae Enga of New Guinea*. New York: Barnes and Noble.

Meltzer, D.J. 1985. "North American Archaeology and Archaeologists, 1879–1934." *American Antiquity* 50(2):249–260.

Mercader, J., ed. 2003. *Under the Canopy*. New Brunswick, NJ: Rutgers University Press.

Meriwether, J. 2007. "Apartheid." In *Encyclopedia of Western Colonialism since 1450*, Vol. 1, edited by T. Benjamin, pp. 81–85. Detroit, MI: MacMillan References USA.

Merlan, F. 2009. "Indigeneity, Global and Local." *Current Anthropology* 50(3):303–333.

Miami Herald. 2011. "Scott: Florida Doesn't Need More Anthropology Majors." *Miami Herald*, October 10. Available at http://miamiherald.typepad.com/nakedpolitics/2011/10/ scott-florida-doesnt-need -more-anthropology-majors.html.

Michaels, A. 2004. *Hinduism*. Trans. B. Harshar. Princeton, NJ: Princeton University Press.

Milanich, J.T. 1995. *Florida Indians and the Invasion from Europe*. Gainesville: University Press of Florida.

Millen, J.V. 2008. "Health Worker Shortages and HIV/AIDS: Responses and Linkages." *Practicing Anthropology* 30(4):8–16.

Milton, K. 1984. "Protein and Carbohydrate Resources of the Maku Indians of Northwestern Amazonia." *American Anthropologist* 86:7–27.

————. 1991. "Comparative Aspects of Diet in Amazonian Forest-Dwellers." *Philosophical Transactions of the Royal Society of London B* 334:253–263.

Miner, H. 1956. "Body Ritual among the Nacirema". *American Anthropologist* 58: 503–507.

Mintz, S.W. 1985. *Sweetness and Power*. New York: Viking.

Mithen, S. 1996. *The Prehistory of the Mind*. London: Thames and Hudson.

Mitra, P. 1933. *A History of American Anthropology*. Calcutta: University of Calcutta.

Moffitt, J.C. (Dir.) 2008. *Dana Carvey: Squatting Monkeys Tell No Lies* [video]. Santa Rosa, CA: Dana Carvey Enterprises; Home Box Office.

Moore, J.H. 1994. "Putting Anthropology Back Together Again." *American Anthropologist* 96(4):925–948.

Morcote-Ríos, G., Gaspar Morcote-Ríos, F.J. Aceituno, J. Iriarte, M. Robinson, and J.L.Chaparro-Cárdenas. 2021. "Colonisation and Early Peopling of the Colombian Amazon during the Late Pleistocene and the Early Holocene: New evidence from La Serranía La Lindosa." *Quaternary International* 578:5–19.

More, T. (1516) 1949. *Utopia*. Translated by and Edited by H.V.S. Ogden. Northbrook, IL: AHM Publishing.

Morgan, L.H. (1851) 1995. *League of the Ho-De'-No-Sau-Nee or Iroquois*. North Dighton, MA: J. G. Press.

————. 1870. *Systems of Consanguinity and Affinity of the Human Family*. Washington, DC: Smithsonian Institution.

————. 1877. *Ancient Society*. New York: Henry Holt.

Morwood, M.J., P. Brown, S.T. Jatmiko, E. Wahyu Saptomo, K.E. Westaway, A.D. Rokus, R.G. Roberts, T. Maeda, S. Wasisto, and T. Djubiantono. 2005. "Further Evidence for Small-Bodied Hominins from the Late Pleistocene of Flores, Indonesia." *Nature* 437:1012–1017.

Moseley, M.E. 1992. *The Incas and Their Ancestors*. London: Thames and Hudson.

Mt. Pleasant, J. 2006. "The Science Behind the Three Sisters Mound System: An Agronomic Assessment of an Indigenous Agricultural System in the Northeast." In *Histories of Maize*, edited by J. Staller, R. Tykot, and B. Benz, pp. 529–537. Burlington, VT: Academic Press.

Murphy, R.F. 1971. *The Dialectics of Social Life*. New York: Basic Books.

Murphy, Y., and R.F. Murphy. 2004. *Women of the Forest* (3rd ed.). New York: Columbia University Press.

Nanda, S. 1999. *Neither Man nor Woman: The Hijras of India* (2nd ed.). Boston, MA: Wadsworth.

Newson, L.A. 1998. "A Historical-Ecological Perspective on Epidemic Disease." In *Advances in Historical Ecology*, edited by W. Balée, pp. 42–63. New York: Columbia University Press.

Nicholls, H. 2011. "Swarm Troopers." *New Scientist* 211(2829):34–37.

New York Times. 2008. "Selected Poems by Kay Ryan." Available at http://www.nytimes.com/2008/07/17/books/17poet-extra.html.

Nicholson, P.J.M. 2007. "The Intellectual in the Infosphere." *Chronicle of Higher Education* 53(27):B6.

Nimuendaju, C. 1948. "The Tucuna." In *Handbook of South American Indians*, Vol. III: *The Tropical Forest Tribes*, edited by J.H. Steward, pp. 713–715. Washington, DC: Government Printing Office.

Nolan, R.W. 2003. *Anthropology in Practice: Building a Career Outside the Academy*. Boulder, CO: Lynne Rienner.

Nuckolls, J.B. 2010. "The Sound-Symbolic Expression of Animacy in Amazonian Ecuador." *Diversity* 2:353–369.

Nuwer, H. 1999. *Wrongs of Passage: Fraternities, Sororities, Hazing, and Binge Drinking*. Bloomington: Indiana University Press.

Ohnuki-Tierney, E. 1984. *The Ainu of the Northwest Coast of Southern Sakhalin*. Prospect Heights, IL: Waveland Press.

Ong, A. 2006. *Neoliberalism as Exception: Mutations in Citizenship and Sovereignty*. Durham, NC: Duke University Press.

Pääbo, S. 2014. *Neanderthal Man: In Search of Lost Genomes*. New York: Basic Books.

Pandya, V. 2007. "Observed Nature and Organized Culture: Indigenous Knowledge Systems among the Ongees of Little Andaman Island." Paper presented at the International Experts Meeting: Indigenous Knowledge and Changing Environments, UNESCO, LINKS Programme, Cairns, August 19–23.

Paquette, G. 2007. "Justification for Empire, European Concepts." In *Encyclopedia of Western Colonialism since 1450*, Vol. 2, edited by T. Benjamin, pp. 673–681. Detroit, MI: MacMillan References USA.

Parkin, R. 1997. *Kinship: An Introduction to the Basic Concepts*. Oxford: Blackwell.

Pels, P., and O. Salemink. 1999. "Introduction: Locating the Colonial Subjects of Anthropology." In *Colonial Subjects: Essays on the Practical History of Anthropology*, edited by P. Pels and O. Salemink, pp. 1–52. Ann Arbor: University of Michigan Press.

Pärssinen, M. et al. 2020. "The Geoglyph Sites of Acre, Brazil." *Antiquity* 94(3780):1538–1556.

Pelto, P.J., and G.H. Pelto. 1993. *Anthropological Research: The Structure of Inquiry*. Cambridge: Cambridge University Press.

Peluso, D.M., and M.N. Alexiades. 2005. "Indigenous Urbanization and Amazonia's Post-Traditional Environmental Economy." *Traditional Dwellings and Settlements Review* 16(2):7–16.

Perlez, J. 2014. "Myanmar Policy's Message to Muslims: Get Out." *New York Times*, November 7, pp. A1, A8.

Perry, M.D. 2008. "Global Black Self-Fashionings: Hip Hop as Diasporic Space." *Identities: Global Studies in Culture and Power* 15:635–664.

Peterson, N. 1999. "Introduction: Australia." In *The Cambridge Encyclopedia of Hunters and Gatherers*, edited by R.B. Lee and R. Daly, pp. 317–323. Cambridge: Cambridge University Press.

Petryna, A. 2002. *Life Exposed: Biological Citizens after Chernobyl*. Princeton, NJ: Princeton University Press.

Phalan, B., M. Orial, A. Balmford, and R.E. Corlen. 2011. "Reconciling Food Production and Biodiversity Conservation: Land Sharing and Land Spacing Compared." *Science* 333:1289–1291.

Pickering, R., R.H.G.M. Dirks, Z. Jinnah, D.J. de Ruiter, et al. 2011. "*Australopithecus sediba* at 1.977 Ma and Implication for the Origins of the Genus *Homo*." *Science* 333:1421–1423.

Pietz, W. 1999. "The Fetish of Civilization: Sacrificial Blood and Monetary Debt." In *Colonial Subjects: Essays in the Practical History of Anthropology*, edited by P. Pels and O. Salemink, pp. 53–81. Ann Arbor: University of Michigan Press.

Pink, S. 2006. "Introduction." In *Applications of Anthropology: Professional Anthropology in the Twenty-First Century*, edited by S. Pink, pp. 3–26. New York: Berghahn.

Pinker, S. 1999. *Words and Rules*. New York: HarperCollins.

Pitulko, V.V., P.A. Nikolsky, E.Y. Girya, A.E. Basily, et al. 2004. "The Yana RHS Site: Humans in the Arctic before the Last Glacial Maximum." *Science* 303(5654):52–56.

Plato. 1999. *Great Dialogues of Plato*. Translated by W.H.D. Rouse. New York: Penguin.

Polanyi, K. 1957. "The Economy as Instituted Process." In *Trade and Market in Early Empires*, edited by K. Polanyi, C.M. Arensberg, and H.W. Pearson, pp. 243–270. Glencoe, IL: Free Press and Falcon Wing's Press.

Politis, G. 2007. *Nukak*. Walnut Creek, CA: Left Coast Press, Inc.

Pollard, S. 1968. *The Idea of Progress*. London: C. A. Watts, and Co.

Pratt, M.L. 1986. "Fieldwork in Common Places." In *Writing Culture: The Poetics and Politics of Ethnography*, edited by J. Clifford and G. Marcus, pp. 27–50. Los Angeles: University of California Press.

Price, D.H. 2008. *Anthropological Intelligence*. Durham, NC: Duke University Press.

Puskoor, R., and G. Zubay. 2005. "Ebola Viruses." In *Agents of Bioterrorism: Pathogens and Their Weaponization*, edited by G. Zubay et al., pp. 59–78. New York: Columbia University Press.

Pyne, S. 1998. "Forged in Fire." In *Advances in Historical Ecology*, edited by W. Balée, pp. 64–103. New York: Columbia University Press.

Quinlan, M. 2005. "Considerations for Collecting Freelists in the Field: Examples from Ethnobotany." *Field Methods* 17:219–234.

Rabinow, P. 1977. *Reflections on Fieldwork in Morocco*. Berkeley: University of California Press.

Radcliffe-Brown, A.R. 1929. "Age Organization-Terminology." *Man* 12–14:21.

———. 1952. *Structure and Function in Primitive Society*. London: Cohen and West.

Rafail, P. 2014. "What Makes Protest Dangerous? Ideology, Contentious Tactics, and Covert Surveillance." *Research in Social Movements, Conflicts and Change* 37:237–265.

Rainbird, P. 2004. *The Archaeology of Micronesia*. Cambridge: Cambridge University Press.

Rappaport, J. 2007. "Anthropological Collaboration in Colombia." In *Anthropology Put to Work*, edited by L. Field and R.G. Fox, pp. 21–44. New York: Berg.

Rappaport, R. 2000. *Pigs for the Ancestors: Ritual in the Ecology of a New Guinea People* (2nd ed.). Prospect Heights, IL: Waveland Press.

Rashid, R. 1995. "Introduction." In *Indigenous Minorities of Peninsular Malaysia: Selected Issues and Ethnographies*, pp. 1–17. Kuala Lumpur: Intersocietal and Scientific.

Read, D.W. 2001. "What Is Kinship?" In *The Cultural Analysis of Kinship*, edited by R. Feinberg and M. Ottenheimer, pp. 78–117. Urbana: University of Illinois Press.

Renfrew, C., and P. Bahn. 1996. *Archaeology* (2nd ed.). London: Thames and Hudson.

Reyes-Foster, B., and T. Matejowsky. 2014. "Why Undergraduates, Why Now?" *Anthropology News* 55(5–6):3.

Ribas, V. 2016. *On the Line*. Berkeley: University of California Press.

Rice, P. 2014. "Paleoanthropology, Part I." *General Anthropology* 21(1):10–13.

———. 2015. "Paleoanthropology, Part I." *General Anthropology* 22(1):9–12.

Rivière, P. 1984. *Individual and Society in Guiana*. New York: Oxford University Press.

Robben, A.C.G.M., ed. 2010a. *Iraq at a Distance: What Anthropologists Can Teach Us about the War*. Philadelphia: University of Pennsylvania Press.

———. 2010b. "Ethnographic Imagination at a Distance: An Introduction to the Anthropological Study of the Iraq War." In *Iraq at a Distance: What Anthropologists Can Teach Us about the War*, edited by A.C.G.M. Robben, pp. 1–23. Philadelphia: University of Pennsylvania Press.

Rödlach, A. 2006. *Witches, Westerners, and HIV*. Walnut Creek, CA: Left Coast Press, Inc.

Rogers, E.M. 1983. *Diffusion of Innovations* (3rd ed.). New York: Free Press.

Rogers, H. 2005. *Writing Systems: A Linguistic Approach*. Malden, MA: Blackwell.

Rohde, D. 2007. "Army Enlists Anthropology in War Zones." *New York Times*, July 13.

Romney, A.K., and R. D'Andrade. 1964. "Cognitive Aspects of English Kin Terms in Transcultural Studies in Cognition." *American Anthropologist* 66:146–170.

Rony, F.T. 1996. *The Third Eye: Race, Cinema, and Ethnographic Spectacle*. Durham, NC: Duke University Press.

Rose, C. (host and executive producer). 2006. *A Conversation with Anarchist David Graeber* [video]. Charlie Rose. New York: Public Broadcasting Service (PBS).

Rosenzweig, M.L. 1995. *Species Diversity in Space and Time*. Cambridge: Cambridge University Press.

Rosman, A., and P.G. Rubel. 1986. *Feasting with Mine Enemy*. Prospect Heights, IL: Waveland Press.

Roughgarden, J. 2004. *Evolution's Rainbow*. Berkeley: University of California Press.

Ruby, J. 2000. *Picturing Culture: Explorations of Film and Anthropology*. Chicago, IL: University of Chicago Press.

Rupp, K. 2003. *Gift-Giving in Japan*. Stanford, CA: Stanford University Press.

Ryan, C., and C. Jethá. 2010. *Sex at Dawn: The Prehistoric Origins of Modern Sexuality*. New York: Harper Collins.

Sahlins, M. 1972. *Stone Age Economics*. Chicago, IL: Aldine.

———. 1976a. *Culture and Practical Reason*. Chicago, IL: University of Chicago Press.

———. 1976b. *The Use and Abuse of Biology: An Anthropological Critique of Sociobiology*. Ann Arbor: University of Michigan Press.

Said, E.W. 2003. *Orientalism*. New York: Penguin.

Sanjek, R. 1990. "A Vocabulary for Fieldnotes." In *Fieldnotes: The Making of Anthropology*, edited by R. Sanjek, pp. 92–121. Ithaca, NY: Cornell University Press.

Sansi, R. 2007. *Fetishes and Monuments: Afro-Brazilian Art and Culture in the 20th Century*. New York: Berghahn.

Santilli, M., P. Moutinho, S. Schwartzman, D. Nepstad, L. Curran, and C. Nobre. 2005. "Tropical Deforestation and the Kyoto Protocol." *Climatic Change* 71(3):267–276.

Savage-Rumbaugh, S., S.G. Shanker, and T.J. Taylor. 1998. *Apes, Language, and the Human Mind*. New York: Oxford University Press.

Schaan, D.P. 2006. "São tartarugas até lá embaixo! Cultura, simbolismo e espacialidade na Amazônia pré-Colombiana." *Revista de Arqueologia Americana* 24:99–124.

——— 2012. *Sacred Geographies of Ancient Amazonia: Historical Ecology of Social Complexity*. Walnut Creek, CA: Left Coast Press.

Schaffer, R., and D.G. Skinner. 2009. "Performing Race in Four Culturally Diverse Fourth Grade Classrooms: Silence, Race Talk, and Negotiation of Social Boundaries." *Anthropology and Education Quarterly* 40(3):277–296.

Schneider, D.M. 1984. *A Critique of the Study of Kinship*. Ann Arbor: University of Michigan Press.

Schniedewind, W.M. 2004. *How the Bible Became a Book*. Cambridge: Cambridge University Press.

Schubel, J.R., and Carolyn Levi. 2000. "The Emergence of Megacities." *Medicine and Global Survival* 6(2): 107–110.

Scott, J.C. 1985. *Weapons of the Weak*. New Haven, CT: Yale University Press.

———. 1998. *Seeing Like a State: How Certain Schemes to Improve the Human Condition Have Failed*. New Haven, CT: Yale University Press.

———. 2009. *The Art of Not Being Governed: An Anarchist History of Upland Southeast Asia*. New Haven, CT: Yale University Press.

Seeger, A. 2004. *Why Suyá Sing: A Musical Anthropology of an Amazonian People*. Urbana: University of Illinois Press.

Seligman, C.G., and B.Z. Seligman. 1911. *The Veddas*. Cambridge: Cambridge University Press.

Senders, S., and A. Truitt. 2007. *Money: Ethnographic Encounters*. New York: Berg.

Service, E. 1963. *Profiles in Ethnology*. New York: Harper and Row.

Shandy, D.J. 2007. *Nuer American Passages: Globalizing Sudanese Migration*. Gainesville: University Press of Florida.

Sharer, R.J. 1994. *The Ancient Maya* (5th ed.). Stanford, CA: Stanford University Press.

Shenk, M.K. 2006. "Models for the Future of Anthropology." *Anthropology News* 47(1):6–7.

Shostak, M. 2000. *Nisa: The Life and Words of a !Kung Woman*. Cambridge, MA: Harvard University Press.

Shukla, S. 2003. *India Abroad*. Princeton, NJ: Princeton University Press.

Siddle, R. 1997. "Ainu: Japan's Indigenous People." In *Japan's Minorities: The Illusion of Homogeneity*, edited by M. Weiner, pp. 17–49. London: Routledge.

Simmel, G. (1900) 1978. *The Philosophy of Money*. Translated by T. Bottomore and D. Frisby. London: Routledge and Kegan Paul.

Sinclair, K. 2001. "Mischief on the Margins: Gender, Primogeniture, and Cognatic Descent among the Maori." In *New Directions in Anthropological Kinship*, edited by L. Stone, pp. 156–174. Lanham, MD: Rowman and Littlefield.

Sloane, P. 1999. *Islam, Modernity and Entrepreneurship among the Malays*. New York: St. Martin's Press.

Smedley, A. 1993. *Race in North America*. Boulder, CO: Westview.

Smith, J.J. 1993. "Using ANTHROPAC 3.5 and a Spreadsheet to Compute a Freelist Salience Index." *Cultural Anthropology Methodology Newsletter* 5(3):1–3.

Smith, M.E. 2003. *The Aztecs* (2nd ed.). Malden, MA: Blackwell.

Spencer, B., and F.J. Gillen. (1899) 1938. *The Native Tribes of Central Australia*. London: Macmillan.

Spencer, H. 1870. "The Origin of Animal Worship, etc." *Fortnightly Review* 13:535–550.

Spindler, G., and J.E. Stockard, eds. 2007. *Globalization and Change in Fifteen Cultures*. Belmont, CA: Thomson Higher Education.

Spradley, J.P. 1979. *The Ethnographic Interview*. Orlando, FL: Holt, Rinehart and Winston.

Stack, C. 1974. *All Our Kin*. New York: Harper and Row.

Stavenhagen, R. 1997. "Indigenous Organizations: Rising Actors in Latin America." *CEPAL Review* 62:63–75.

Stegeborn, W. 1999. "Wanniyala-aetto." In *The Cambridge Encyclopedia of Hunters and Gatherers*, edited by R.B. Lee and R. Daly, pp. 269–273. Cambridge: Cambridge University Press.

Steward, J.H. 1938. *Basin-Plateau Aboriginal Sociopolitical Groups*. Washington, DC: Government Printing Office.

———. 1951. "Levels of Sociocultural Integration: An Operational Concept." *Southwestern Journal of Anthropology* 7(4): 374–390.

———. 1955. *Theory of Culture Change*. Urbana: University of Illinois Press.

Stocking, G.W., Jr., ed. 1974. *The Shaping of American Anthropology, 1883–1911*. New York: Basic Books.

Stoller, P. 2013. "The Real News of Anthropology." *Huffington Post*, February 26. Available at http://www.huffingtonpost.com/paul-stoller/the-real-news-of-an-thropo_b_2744551.html.

Stone, L., ed. 2001. *New Directions in Anthropological Kinship*. Lanham, MD: Rowman and Littlefield.

Strathern, M. 1992. *After Nature*. Cambridge: Cambridge University Press.

Striffler, S. 2005. *Chicken: The Dangerous Transformation of America's Favorite Food*. New Haven, CT: Yale University Press.

Stringer, C. 2012. *Lone Survivors*. New York: St. Martin's Griffin.

Struit, D.J. 1967. *A Concise History of Mathematics*. New York: Dover.

Sutton, M.Q. 2008. *An Introduction to Native North America* (3rd ed.). Boston, MA: Pearson Education.

Sylvain, R. 2005. "Disorderly Development: Globalization and the Idea of 'Culture' in the Kalahari." *American Ethnologist* 32(3):354–370.

Tainter, J.A. 1988. *The Collapse of Complex Societies*. Cambridge: Cambridge University Press.

———. 2006. "Archaeology of Overshoot and Collapse." *Annual Review of Anthropology* 35:59–74.

Talboys, G.K. 2005. *Way of the Druid: The Renaissance of a Celtic Religion and Its Relevance for Today*. New York: Maple-Vail.

Tatum, B.D. 1997. *"Why Are All the Black Kids Sitting Together in the Cafeteria?" and Other Conversations about Race*. New York: Basic Books.

Thornberry, P. 2002. *Indigenous Peoples and Human Rights*. Manchester: Manchester University Press.

Tierney, J. 2008. "Tips from the Potlatch: Where Giving Knows No Slump." *New York Times*, December 16, 2008. Available at http://www.nytimes.com/2008/12/16/sci-ence/16tierney.html?_r=.

Tilly, C. 1990. *Coercion, Capital, and European States, AD 990–1990*. Cambridge, MA: Basil Blackwell.

Tomas, D. 1991. "Tools of the Trade: The Production of Ethnographic Observations on the Andaman Islands, 1858–1922." In *Colonial Situations: Essays in the Contextualization of Ethnographic Knowledge*, edited by G.W. Stocking, Jr., pp. 75–108. Madison: University of Wisconsin Press.

Tomasello, M. 1999. "The Human Adaptation for Culture." *Annual Review of Anthropology* 28:509–529.

———. 2003. *Constructing a Language: A Usage-Based Theory of Language Acquisition*. Cambridge, MA: Harvard University Press.

Tonkinson, R. 1991. *The Mardu Aborigines* (2nd ed.). Fort Worth, TX: Holt, Rinehart and Winston.

———. 2007. "The Mardu Aborigines: On the Road to Somewhere." In *Globalization and Change in Fifteen Cultures*, edited by G. Spindler and J.E. Stockard, pp. 225–255. Belmont, CA: Thomson Higher Education.

Toussaint, S. 2007. "Potential Collaborations and Disjunctures in Australian Work Sites: An Experiential Rendering." In *Anthropology Put to Work*, edited by L. Field and R. Fox, pp. 161–180. New York: Berg.

Trautmann, T.R. 2011. *India: Brief History of a Civilization*. New York: Oxford University Press.

Trigger, D.S. 1999. "Hunter-Gatherer Peoples and Nation-States." In *The Cambridge Encyclopedia of Hunters and Gatherers*, edited by R.B. Lee and R. Daly, pp. 473–479. Cambridge: Cambridge University Press.

Truitt, A. 2020. "Money." In *The Cambridge Encyclopedia of Anthropology*, edited by F. Stein et al. doi:10.29164/20money.

Turnbull, C.M. 1968. *The Forest People*. New York: Simon and Schuster.

Tusan, M. 2014. "The Armenian Genocide and Foreign Policy." *Phi Kappa Phi Forum* 94(2): 13–15.

Tylor, E.B. (1871) 1924. *Primitive Culture* (2 vols.). New York: Brentano's.

———. 1889. "On a Method of Investigating the Development of Institutions Applied to Laws of Marriage and Descent." *Journal of the Royal Anthropological Institute of Great Britain and Ireland* 18:267.

United Buddy Bears. 2011. *United Buddy Bears 08 Dec. 2011–15 Feb. 2012 @ Pavilion Kuala Lumpur: The Art of Tolerance*. Kuala Lumpur: Exhibit Brochure.

United Nations. 2008. *United Nations Declaration on the Rights of Indigenous Peoples.* Available at http://www.un.org/esa/socdev/unpfii/documents/DRIPS_en.pdf.

United Nations. 2018. "68% of the World Population Projected to Live in Urban Areas by 2050, Says UN." Available at https://www.un.org/development/desa/en/news/population/2018-revision-of-world-urbanization-prospects.html.

Urton, G. 1997. *The Social Life of Numbers.* Austin: University of Texas Press.

———. 2008. "The Inca Khipu: Knotted-Cord Record Keeping in the Andes." In *Handbook of South American Archaeology,* edited by H. Silverman and W.H. Isbell, pp. 831–843. New York: Springer.

USDA. 2020. "Food Availability and Consumption." Available at https://www.ers.usda.gov/data-products

US News and World Report. 2020. "Best Science Jobs." Available at https://money.usnews.com/careers/best-jobs/rankings/best-science-jobs.

van Gennep, A. (1909) 1960. *The Rites of Passage.* London: Routledge and Kegan Paul.

Van Willigen, J. 1993. *Applied Anthropology: An Introduction* (revised ed.). Westport, CT: Bergin and Garvey.

Vilaça, A. 2010. *Strange Enemies: Indigenous Agency and Scenes of Encounters in Amazonia.* Translated by D. Rodgers. Durham, NC: Duke University Press.

Viveiros de Castro, E. 1992. *From the Enemy's Point of View.* Translated by C. Howard. Chicago, IL: University of Chicago Press.

———. 1998. "Dravidian and Related Kinship Systems." In *Transformations of Kinship,* edited by M. Godelier, T. Trautmann, and F.E. Tjon de Sat, pp. 332–385. Washington, DC: Smithsonian Institution Press.

Voices. 2011. "Human Genome: What's Been Most Surprising." *Cell* 147(1):9–10.

Wade, B.C. 2004. *Thinking Musically: Experiencing Music, Expressing Culture.* New York: Oxford University Press.

Wade, N. 2006. *Before the Dawn.* New York: Penguin Books.

Wallace, A.F.C. 1966. *Religion.* New York: Random House.

———. 1969. *The Death and Rebirth of the Seneca.* New York: Random House.

Wallerstein, I. 1974–1980. *The Modern World System* (3 vols.). New York: Academic Press.

———. 2005. "After Development and Globalization, What?" *Social Forces* 83(3):1263–1278.

Walvin, J. 2007. "Abolition of Colonial Slavery." In *Encyclopedia of Western Colonialism since 1450,* Vol. 1, edited by T. Benjamin, pp. 2–6. Detroit, MI: MacMillan Reference USA.

Weatherford, J. 1998. *The History of Money.* New York: Three Rivers Press.

Weinberger, S. 2008. "The Pentagon's Culture Wars." *Nature* 455:583–585.

Weiner, A.B. 1988. *The Trobrianders of Papua New Guinea.* Fort Worth, TX: Harcourt Brace College Publishers.

Weir, A.A.S., J. Chappell, and A. Kacelnik. 2002. "Shaping of Hooks in New Caledonia Crows." *Science* 297:981.

Welch, J.R. 2021. "Camaraderie, Mentorship, and Manhood." ms.

Weller, S.C., and A.K. Romney. 1988. *Systematic Data Collection.* Newbury Park, CA: Sage.

Wen-Hsiung, L., and M.A. Saunders. 2005. "The Chimpanzee and Us." *Nature* 437:50–51.

Westermarck, E. 1891. *The History of Human Marriage.* London: MacMillan.

Whitaker, J.A. 2010. "Review of Au Pair." *Journal of the Anthropological Society of Oxford* 2(1–2):85–86.

Wierzbicka, A. 1997. *Understanding Cultures through Their Key Words.* New York: Oxford University Press.

White, C. 2009. *An Uncertain Cure: Living with Leprosy in Brazil.* New Brunswick, NJ: Rutgers University Press.

White, L.A. 1959 (2007). *The Evolution of Culture.* Walnut Creek, CA: Leftcoast Press.

White, T.D., B. Asfaw, Y. Beyene, Y. Halie-Selassie, C.O. Lovejoy, and G. Suwa. 2009. "*Ardipithecus Ramidus* and the Paleobiology of Early Hominids." *Science* 326(5949):75–86.

Whitley, D.S. 2005. *Introduction to Rock Art Research.* Walnut Creek, CA: Left Coast Press, Inc.

———. 2009. *Cave Paintings and the Human Spirit.* Amherst, MA: Prometheus Books.

Wilford, J.N. 2013. "Michael J. Norwood, 62; Helped Find 'New Human.'" *New York Times*, August 6, p. B12.

———. 2014. "Paintings in Indonesia May Predate Oldest Known Cave Art." *New York Times*, October 9, p. A17.

Wilkinson, David. 2016. "Amazonian Civilization?" *Comparative Civilizations Review* 74: 81–100.

Williams, S. 1985. *Diocletian and the Roman Recovery*. London: B. T. Batsford.

Wittfogel, K.A. 1957. *Oriental Despotism: A Comparative Study of Total Power*. New Haven, CT: Yale University Press.

Wittgenstein, L. (1922) 1996. *Tractatus Logico-Philosophicus*. London: Routledge.

Wolf, A.P. 2004. "Explaining the Westermarck Effect or, What Did Natural Selection Select For?" In *Inbreeding, Incest, and the Incest Taboo*, edited by A.P. Wolf and W. Durham, pp. 76–92. Stanford, CA: Stanford University Press.

Wolf, A.P., and W.H. Durham, eds. 2004. *Inbreeding, Incest, and the Incest Taboo*. Stanford, CA: Stanford University Press.

Wolf, E.R. 1964. *Anthropology*. New York: W. W. Norton.

———. 1969. *Peasant Wars of the Twentieth Century*. New York: Harper and Row.

———. 1997. *Europe and the People without History*. Berkeley: University of California Press.

Wolf, E.R., and J.G. Jorgensen. 1970. "Anthropology on the Warpath in Thailand." *New York Review of Books* 15(November 19):26–30.

Wolverton, S., R.L. Lyman, J.H. Kennedy, and T.W. La Point. 2009. "The Terminal Pleistocene Extinctions in North America, Hypermorphic Evolution, and the Dynamic Equilibrium Model." *Journal of Ethnobiology* 29(1):28–63.

Wong, E., and A. Wong. 2014. "Seeking Identity, 'Hong Kong People' Look to City, Not State." *New York Times*, October 8, pp. A4, A8.

Wong, K. 2014. "The 1 Percent Difference." *Scientific American* 311(3): 100.

Woods, W., and J.M. McCann. 1999. "The Anthropogenic Origin and Persistence of Amazonian Dark Earths." *Yearbook of the Conference of Latin Americanist Geographers* 25:7–14.

World Archaeological Congress (WAC). 2008. "Business Plenary." *Sixth World Archaeological Congress*, July 4, Dublin.

Worsley, P.M. 1968. *The Trumpet Shall Sound* (2nd ed.). New York: Schocken Books.

Worster, D. 2001. *A River Running West: The Life of John Wesley Powell*. Oxford: Oxford University Press.

Yanagisako, S., and D. Segal. 2006. "Welcoming Debate: Exploring Links and Disconnects among the Quadrants." *Anthropology News* 47(1):8–11.

Zeitzen, M.K. 2008. *Polygamy: A Cross-Cultural Analysis*. New York: Berg.

Zent, E.L., and S. Zent. 2004. "Amazonian Indians as Ecological Disturbance Agents." In *Ethnobotany and Conservation of Biocultural Diversity*, edited by L. Maffi and T.J.S. Carlson, pp. 79–111. New York: New York Botanical Garden.

Zimmer, C. 2013. "Monogamy and Human Evolution." *New York Times*, August 6, p. D6.

Zimmerer, K.S. 1993. "Agricultural Biodiversity and Peasant Rights to Subsistence in the Central Andes during Inca Rule." *Journal of Historical Geography* 19:15–32.

Zubay, G., ed. 2005. *Agents of Bioterrorism: Pathogens and Their Weaponization*. New York: Columbia University Press.

Index

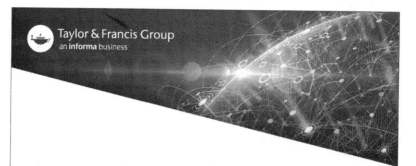